HOOSIER
PHILANTHROPY

PHILANTHROPIC AND NONPROFIT STUDIES
Dwight F. Burlingame and David C. Hammack, editors

HOOSIER
PHILANTHROPY

A State History of Giving

—⦙—

EDITED BY
Gregory R. Witkowski

INDIANA UNIVERSITY PRESS

This book is a publication of

Indiana University Press
Office of Scholarly Publishing
Herman B Wells Library 350
1320 East 10th Street
Bloomington, Indiana 47405 USA

iupress.org

Manufactured in the United States of America

First printing 2022

Cataloging information is available from the Library of Congress.

ISBN 978-0-253-06413-4 (hdbk.)
ISBN 978-0-253-06414-1 (pbk.)
ISBN 978-0-253-06415-8 (web PDF)

For my mother, Mary Witkowski

CONTENTS

ACKNOWLEDGMENTS

THIS VOLUME STARTED OFF AS an idea to create a text that engaged with the local community where I taught. At the Lilly Family School of Philanthropy, many students either were born in Indiana or planned to work there. Most giving is done locally, and I felt it important to give students a sense of the long history of philanthropic engagement in the state. I wanted to indicate that the many "new trends" they were engaging with in their coursework had, in fact, long roots in their hometowns and that many of the questions we ask about philanthropy today were already discussed a century or more ago. My desire to create a text that would help students understand their own philanthropic traditions came at a propitious time because the state of Indiana was planning to celebrate its bicentennial.

Indiana University and the Indiana Historical Society worked with many partners to hold a conference to mark this bicentennial. My colleague Dwight Burlingame provided the first support for the idea, followed quickly by Kyle McKoy at the Indiana Historical Society and Jason Kelly, director of the IUPUI Arts and Humanities Institute. My thanks to all three of them for supporting the concept early and persistently. Bill Enright, who was a board member of Lilly Endowment, likewise found the project interesting and set up a meeting with Clay Robbins, chairman and CEO of Lilly Endowment Inc. Clay's support was incredibly important in terms of increasing the impact of the conference and growth of this project. He was kind in sharing contacts and open in his support. I most appreciated his ability to provide consistent feedback when asked and his recognition that this should be an independent project. In addition, he graciously delivered the keynote speech, which has been included as a foreword. It was a tour de force in person, and hopefully you will agree that its power remains in script.

When it came to both institutional and financial support, Daniel Smith, president of the Indiana University Foundation (IUF), provided generous and essential backing. The foundation provided a large grant and institutional support, including the time of a number of employees. Paula Jenkins, vice president at IUF, spent a tremendous amount of time and energy working through ideas and helping to engage practitioners who could participate in the conference. I owe her a special thanks. Additional funding was provided by the IUPUI chancellor's office with support from Dean Amir Pasic. The conference itself could not have happened in the way it did without the contributions of Mary Morgan and Chelsie Roberts, who were event planners extraordinaire. Their work made it happen. Nancy Bell, Carrie Birge, James Connolly, Karen Garinger, Haley Girard, Adriene Kalugyer, Marilyn Kuhn, Bethan Roberts, Eric Sandweis, Phil Scarpino, and Julie Scholl all made valuable contributions to the conference as well.

This book emerged from the conference presentations. I could not include all of the papers in the book I would have liked to have included. I am appreciative of all of the participants, including those whose contributions did not fit with the themes of the book. My thanks to the panel commentators who provided feedback to the authors: Bob Barrows, Lehn Benjamin, David Bodenhammer, David Craig, Kevin Cramer, Phil Goff, Nancy Robertson, Phil Scarpino, and Richard Turner. In addition to the academic papers presented, the conference included discussions with practitioners from throughout Indiana. Speakers included twenty-seven executive directors, directors, CEOs, and presidents of nonprofit organizations. These discussions cannot be cited but informed my interpretation of contemporary trends.

As the book itself developed, input from two blind reviewers proved important. Their comments were invaluable in helping to shape the work. Dana Doan, a PhD student at the Lilly Family School of Philanthropy, put in many hours editing the work to bring each individual contribution into line with Indiana University Press standards. As a PhD student and longtime nonprofit practitioner, Dana represented one of the audiences for the book, so I asked her to make substantive comments when she found material unclear. Her comments likewise greatly strengthened the text. Thomas Cox, Ruth Hansen, Merrill Sovner, Peter Weber, and Robert Wright read versions of the introduction and contributed important feedback that helped to shape it into what it is. I am grateful I was able to draw on such a network of colleagues and friends for feedback as I grappled with making sense of two hundred years of philanthropic development.

My move to Columbia University slowed down the publication. I appreciate the patience of the contributors and especially of Gary Dunham at IU Press in working through some of the complication that resulted from this transition. My thanks go to all the contributors who worked hard to research and write these essays that now constitute a contribution both to Indiana's history and to the field of nonprofit studies.

Finally, this book was completed during a challenging period for me personally. My father's health declined, and my mother, who for years had been a wonderful caregiver, was faced with her own health issues. I am glad I had some time together with them before my father passed. A number of colleagues went above and beyond during this period, and I wish to thank them for their support: Beth Gazley, Tyrone Freeman, Mark Roseman, Andre

DeTienne, Kevin Cramer, Phil Goff, and Marianne Wokeck. I appreciate the support of so many friends and family members as well, especially Paul Anderson, Rachel Cohen, Tom Cox, Will Gray, Steve Hall, Andrew Hedges, Greg Judge, Poyan Lofti, Lorraine and Bob Neger, Kevin Smyth, Fumie Sunahori, Mary Witkowski, and Patricia and Ron Witkowski. Their encouraging words during a difficult time made completion of this work possible. I dedicate this book to my mother, who in caring for my father gave as much as her health allowed—and yet still tried to give more.

FOREWORD

Philanthropic Variety: Perspectives of an Indiana Practitioner

N. CLAY ROBBINS

Editor's Note: The following presentation was delivered on February 18, 2016, as the keynote address at the conference "Hoosier Philanthropy: Understanding the Past, Planning the Future" held at the Indiana Historical Society. It has been slightly modified for print. The presentation began with thanks for the organizers and hosts and concluded by reading William Miller Herschel's poem "Ain't God Good to Indiana." Because he is a born and bred Hoosier who is now chairman and CEO of Lilly Endowment, the most influential philanthropic organization in Indiana, I am grateful that Clay Robbins has agreed to allow us to publish his speech.

I APPROACH THIS PRESENTATION WITH a bit of trepidation because of a speech I gave many years ago about philanthropy to what turned out to be a very uninterested crowd. I am hoping and am fairly confident that you all are at least interested in this topic. The Speech from Hell, as I call it now, was to several hundred twentysomethings who were active in the IT community. I had been asked to make some comments about philanthropy by their conference organizers to give them a framework on how they might think about their own philanthropy and what causes in Indiana they might consider supporting.

The event was held in the evening during a dinner at one of the big hotels in downtown Indianapolis. The program ran way over, and so, by the time I got up to speak, it was forty-five minutes after I was supposed to speak. Then I discovered that because they had put my speech on a teleprompter, I could not easily cut it or advance through it to get it done quicker. By the time I began, many of the young IT leaders had imbibed for a couple hours, and let's just say they were not thinking philanthropically. They were not interested in how the tax laws organized the philanthropic sector or in the statute of uses or in whether faith animates giving. Several of them were laughing—not with me—and walking around the room. The crowning blow came when the balloons that were hanging in the ceiling ready to be released at a certain time when a special announcement was to be made by someone else were accidentally released, and all of them fell and started popping when they landed on candles on the tables. As you can imagine, it took some time for me to speak again publicly about philanthropy.

The title of my presentation is "Philanthropic Variety: Perspectives of an Indiana Practitioner." Because this conference celebrates our state's bicentennial, I want to spend a few minutes highlighting the adjective *Indiana* in my speech's title, developing my credibility as a Hoosier. I am a born and bred Hoosier and proud of it. I was born early in the morning on Race Day, which was always May 30 at that time. The OB who delivered me expedited my mom's labor so that he could go to the race. By the way, Sam Hanks won the race (Indianapolis 500) that year. Until I was in high school, my birthday cake always had candles that were stuck in little race cars, and there were checkered flags all over the house.

I know that we pronounce Versailles (VerSALES), Vincennes (Vinsens), DuBois (DuBOYZ). I know that it is worth the drive

to the Nashville House to get the fried biscuits and apple but-
ter. I know what catawampus means, and I know that mangoes
are actually green peppers. I have been to the New Ross Steak
House and the Covington Beef House, and the Iron Skillet, Copper Kettle, and Hollyhock Hill, and I know there is a division of
opinion about whether the Bluebird or Copper Kettle in Morris-
town has the best fried chicken. By the way, either place would be
hard-pressed to beat Gray Brothers' fried chicken in Mooresville.
I know that Kathy's restaurant in Morgantown has the best pie
around. I know that you should watch for the peaches sign the
first of July every year at Adrian's Orchard and the cinnamon
rolls at Boyden's Bakery and the yeast donuts at Long's are unrivaled. I have been several times to the Myers Dinner Theatre in
Hillsboro, and I began playing euchre in the first grade. I know
to expect snow at basketball sectional time. And for those of you
who have been to French Lick, I know that "when nature won't,
Pluto will."

Both sides of my family have been Hoosiers for many, many
years. In fact, my great-great-great-great-great-grandfather immigrated from County Wexford, Ireland, in middle of the 1700s,
fought in South Carolina in the Revolutionary War, and then
moved to Shelby County, Indiana, right about the time that the
state was formed. I still have family in Shelby County. When I
grew up, my favorite book was *The Bears of Blue River* by Charles
Major. I remember being scared of the Fire Bear. I thought about
this when I attended Flat Rock Y camp in fourth grade on the
Shelby County / Decatur County border.

I grew up on the south side of Indianapolis and went to Perry
Township schools, as did both my parents. I went to Southport
High School as a freshman and sophomore until my class was
split when Perry Meridian High School was founded. I am proud
to be a member of the first graduating class from Perry Meridian. To show you how far I have come in life, my after-graduation
party in 1975 was held at German Park. Last summer, we had our

fortieth class reunion—guess where?—at German Park. It actually was a perfect location, and we had a blast.

My dad was a basketball star at Southport High School in the
early '40s and then played for the legendary coach Tony Hinkle
at Butler. From the time I was potty-trained, I attended most
Southport High School basketball games. My dad died when I
was six, so my aunt—his sister—and her husband, picked me
and my brother up nearly every Friday night during my childhood to take us to a Southport game somewhere in the state.
Those were simpler days; there was such a spirit of community
connected to those basketball games. Everybody went to them.
While I understand the rationale for class basketball, much was
lost when it ended.

When I grew up, my family never talked about philanthropy,
as it is typically thought of today. We did not have the money
to make charitable contributions other than to our church. I do
not remember my friends' families talking about it either. What
I did see, though, was a generosity of spirit. I suppose we could
call it neighborliness. When someone in the community needed
help, we helped. When someone had an illness or death in the
family, others swooped in with food and other types of support.
Certainly there were bake sales and candy and cookie sales, chili
suppers, and fish fries. A lot of the giving was in-kind. My grand-
mother was a charter member of the White Cross Guild connected to Methodist Hospital through which she made bandages
for wounded soldiers and other injured people. My grandfather
was a foreman at General Motors, and he always had a lot of gad-
gets and mechanical equipment. He loved it when we would have
deep snows because he would take his car out with all kinds of
equipment to help dig people out of snow drifts.

My brother and I were the beneficiaries of this kind of generosity in a significant way. As I mentioned earlier, our father died
when I was six and my brother was two. My dad had lived in the
community his whole life and had many friends. I cannot begin

to tell you how those friends embraced our family and supported us. I always knew that if I ever got in trouble or needed something, they would be there. My four aunts and my grandparents rallied around us as well. A couple of years ago on the fiftieth anniversary of my dad's death, I sent a letter to eight different families on the south side who were among those who watched over us to express our family's appreciation and gratitude.

My brother and I also were the beneficiaries of a more typical form of philanthropy that actually changed the course of our lives. And this philanthropy related to Eli Lilly and began my connection to the magnificent generosity of the Lilly family and the founders of Lilly Endowment. In the fall of my senior year at Perry Meridian, my guidance counselor came to me and told me about a brand-new scholarship competition Wabash College was offering through which the Lilly Scholarship would be awarded. It was created by the college in honor of Eli Lilly, who then was a member of Wabash's board of trustees and a significant donor to the college. It was a full-ride scholarship, and it also offered funding for a summer abroad. I never dreamed that I could go to a college like Wabash, because we did not have the necessary resources. To make a long story short, I received one of the scholarships and that fall enrolled at Wabash College. Four years later, my brother, Lee, received one as well. Moreover, the year that I was graduated from Wabash, my mom, who was a secretary at Ayres, received a job offer from Eli Lilly and Company, from which she retired several years later. We are deeply grateful for the secure retirement she has enjoyed from the company.

My educational experiences at Wabash broadened my worldview and that expanded view was enhanced by the seven-some weeks I spent between my junior and senior year in Europe. The next summer I traveled throughout Europe on a Wabash choir tour. I mention this international travel because after all my comments about my Indiana connections, I want you to know I have been out of the state. In fact, while I was a young attorney at Baker and Daniels, my wife, Amy, and I lived in Brussels, Belgium, for a year. I worked as an exchange associate in a Belgian law firm. While there I met other young attorneys, a few of whom I still interact with regularly.

As an aside, I want to tell you a story that I think is relevant to the comments I will make later about philanthropy. One of the attorneys I met was a French attorney named Jean Michel. My wife and I really hit it off with him, and he has become a lifelong friend. He married Valerie, a brilliant young French woman who also now is a respected attorney in Paris. Valerie's dad was in the French diplomatic corps. He was the ambassador to Pakistan, Iran, and Denmark, and he also was stationed in Moscow and in Washington, DC, at times throughout his career. Consequently, she lived as a child in many different countries and speaks many languages fluently. They have two children the ages of our sons, who now all are in their twenties.

About fifteen years ago, she called me one day and said she wanted me to help find a summer camp that her kids could attend in Indiana. Now bear in mind that her kids lived in a prestigious arrondissement in Paris. She said she wanted them to come to learn English and American culture. She did not want them to go to some sailing camp on the East Coast, where they would be with a lot of other French kids who come to elite American camps. I immediately thought of Culver and suggested that, but she thought it was too upscale for what she wanted, so I told her that I had gone to Flat Rock Y camp in fourth grade (near Shelbyville) and described it. She loved that idea. So for five or six years, every summer, Julie and Philippe would come to our house, and we would take them to Flat Rock for three weeks. Valerie would come to work and visit friends in other cities in the States during these periods, but on the weekends between the camp weeks, she would come to get the children, and they would stay in a Holiday Inn in what they called Ville de Shelby from Saturday morning until they had to go back to Flat Rock Sunday afternoon.

One weekend their dad, Jean Michel, came, and he wanted to eat at the Compton Cow Palace in Ville de Shelby. So I took him there wondering how it would compare with the Michelin-starred restaurants around their home in Paris. He ordered one of their skillet breakfasts that had sausage gravy poured all over it. He asked me what it was, and I said it was the Hoosier version of béarnaise sauce. He ate the whole plate and loved it. The whole family loved the generous hospitality they received in Indiana. Both parents had studied Tocqueville and knew what he thought about the civic strength and spirit of volunteerism in American communities. They certainly found that in Ville de Shelby and through all those they encountered at the Y, and we often discussed the differences and similarities in civic life in France and in the United States.

I have described my background and my Hoosier roots to set up how my perspectives on philanthropy have been formed. I suspect because of how deeply I was embedded in community growing up, I developed a belief in the value of moderation and achieving a proper balance in most everything. I learned to try to withhold judgment until I had the facts. In a tightly knit community, one knows that someone who displays a negative or disagreeable behavior in one context may well act very honorably in another context. I also learned that you can get things done or changed better and in a sustained way if you do it in an evocative manner rather than in a heavy-handed, forced way. I also learned to value humility. Arrogance and excessive pride can get one in trouble in a community where people are well-known to each other and know each other's faults and strengths.

I think these values I learned growing up in a typical Hoosier community have influenced my approach to and views about philanthropy. I think they explain why I have found the values of the founders of Lilly Endowment to be so compelling. Susan Wisely, who for years was Lilly Endowment's director of evaluation and resident scholar on philanthropy, taught me a great deal during the time we worked together before her retirement. She wrote an excellent article in 1997 entitled "Pursuit of a Virtuous People." It is about Lilly Endowment, its history, the values of its founders and her way of thinking about philanthropy. It was published in the Winter 1997–1998 edition of the journal *Advancing Philanthropy*. In the article, she elaborates on the importance the Endowment's founders placed on their religious faith and how it inspired their philanthropy. She noted that Eli Lilly had a mission for the Endowment. He said, "I would hope we could help improve the character of the American people." For him, character was developed purposefully through education and faith, and the development of character led to virtue. Virtuous people live lives connected to one another and in so doing build strong communities. These values and insights undergirded the founders' selection of education, community development, and religion as the three main areas of endeavor for the Endowment. They saw the potential in the intersections among them. Since the Endowment's founding in 1937 by J. K. Lilly Sr. and his sons, Eli and J. K. Jr., its leaders have steadfastly sought to align its grant making with the founders' intentions. The Endowment has continued to place a special emphasis on grant making in Indiana and on religion.

J. K. Lilly Sr. encouraged his sons, J. K. Jr. and Eli, to be conservatively progressive, and that philosophy was evident in their leadership of their company and the establishment and administration of Lilly Endowment. Susan notes in her article that the Endowment acts from two contrasting convictions: that tradition is an important resource and that fundamental rethinking is often necessary to respond fully to new challenges and circumstances. The article called for a balance between prudence and creativity. These sentiments align with my thoughts about balance and moderation. It is important to note that moderation and balance do not mean inaction. To me they mean being thoughtful and deliberate.

As you all have heard today in many presentations and panels and will hear tomorrow, there is a multitude of causes supported by philanthropy today in Indiana, the country, and throughout the world. Furthermore, there is an expanding variety of philanthropic approaches, styles, forms, opinions, and policies. From my perspective, the positives far outweigh the negatives of all this variety. Some are attempting to make the case that only certain causes are worth philanthropic support. Some would say that support should be provided only for poverty reduction or only to combat global warming or to alleviate hunger and disease in Third World countries. While I agree that these causes are very compelling, and I support those who advocate for others to support them, I would not favor any proposal to coerce or regulate philanthropy in this respect.

From my experience and observation, it seems to me that many, many people give to causes and organizations for which they have a passion or some other form of emotional attachment. For some people, their passion is for the arts in general or some particular art form. They believe that the arts contribute greatly to our quality of life. They believe the arts make us human and distinguish us from other life forms. I am not sure they would be as philanthropic if they were told they had to give only to the eradication of global warming. Some people are grateful to a children's hospital because their grandchild's life was saved there. One might argue that a million dollars that grandparents give a children's hospital in Illinois could save more children who are starving in a Third World country if it were given there instead. The grandparents, however, are emotionally connected to what happened to their grandchild. The hospital is where they are motivated to give.

With the challenges American society faces with the numbers of people who are not participating in the prosperity of our country and the lack of consensus on the role government should play in addressing societal issues, there will be pressure from some for philanthropy to be coerced to address certain needs that they would prioritize over others. This is where moderation and a balance between prudence and creativity—and careful deliberation—will be needed. For centuries the law has recognized an expansive view of what is considered properly supported by philanthropy. For decades this has been supported by incentives in federal tax law through broad definitions of charitable, educational, and scientific.

One of the rationales underlying these expansive definitions, I believe, is that more philanthropy will be generated if people can give to causes they personally care about. I think we should be very careful about moving away from this sort of policy. While, as I have said, I do not think favoring one charitable cause over another should be embedded in regulation, I do want to reiterate that I do think it is quite appropriate for people to attempt to advocate for certain causes that they think are more important than others. If they persuade others to donate to them rather than some other cause, more power to them. This notion that what donors care about is tied to their philanthropic giving is evident in the current donor choice dynamics for organizations such as United Ways. Fellow Hoosier, Brian Gallagher, the president and CEO of United Way Worldwide, stopped by my office for a brief visit this morning. Lilly Endowment has supported collaborative efforts of United Way Worldwide and the Indiana University Lilly Family School of Philanthropy to understand better these donor trends. Brian knows that increasingly individual donors to United Way campaigns want to shape how their contributions are used.

Personally, I believe that a well-run United Way is in a better position than many donors to know what the most strategic needs are in a community and what organizations are best able to meet those needs. But many donors do not feel that way. More and more businesses are giving to projects and programs that enhance their brand or profile with their customers or align with their business interests or the interests of their employees or other stakeholders. Frequently consultants advise businesses to do just this. While I would support their right to give as they please, in my view the causes they support are too often not the most important or strategic causes for the communities in which the grants are given. For those in the community who are dedicated to a particular compelling cause, it is incumbent on them to make the case for the businesses to support them. This can be hard to do. United Ways more and more have to work to find ways to meet both the highest priority needs of their communities and the needs and desires of donors. Telling the donors that a United Way only accepts unrestricted gifts will likely reduce contributions to the United Way.

We have noticed a similar challenge for Indiana community foundations. As I suspect many of you know, Lilly Endowment began an initiative in 1990 to help build the community-foundation field in Indiana. It is called the GIFT initiative, which is shorthand for Giving Indiana Funds for Tomorrow. Because of the magnificent generosity of Indiana residents in communities large and small, it has resulted in philanthropy far beyond our initial expectations. When the GIFT initiative began, there were fewer than a dozen community foundations in Indiana, and their aggregate asset value was $70 million. At the end of 2014, there were ninety-four community foundations, and each of Indiana's ninety-two counties is served by at least one of them. Their total assets were nearly $3 billion at the end of 2014. Of that amount, Lilly Endowment has provided $323 million, so you see most of the giving has come from local communities. Since the beginning of the initiative, more than $915 million in total grants have been approved by the community foundations and that does not include the substantial grant making of the Central Indiana Community Foundation.

I note this information about the GIFT initiative to acknowledge the philanthropic spirit of Hoosiers and also to make a point about the challenge of attracting unrestricted gifts. Much of the giving to the community foundations has been restricted in the form of donor-advised funds or field-of-interest funds or funds for a particular organization or cause. While these restricted gifts are valuable and laudatory, Indiana community foundations—like United Ways—need unrestricted gifts to respond strategically to the issues they determine are the most compelling in their communities. The Endowment has attempted to help with this challenge by designing our grants to United Way of Central Indiana and Indiana community foundations with matching incentives to encourage more unrestricted giving.

While I believe it is important to make the case for unrestricted giving to well-run charities so they can more effectively do their work, we must be mindful that the forces for targeted giving are very strong. These forces are often strengthened by social media. The ice water campaign for ALS is certainly an example. It showed the power of social media to drive resources to a particular cause. Buckminster Fuller said, "Don't fight forces, use them." Those of us working in more traditional philanthropy need to figure out how to take better advantage of these new communication and rallying channels. I hope we can find ways, however, that leverage these forces for the most compelling causes and the most effective organizations.

When I am working with my colleagues at Lilly Endowment on our grant-making strategies, I often use as one of my organizing frameworks the four traditions of philanthropy that Susan Wisely sets forth in her article, which I have already mentioned. The four traditions she lifts up are (1) charity, (2) improvement, (3) social reform, and (4) convening. By charity, Susan means compassion or relief—alleviating human suffering. Improvement relates to the development of human potential. The principal way that is done is through education, helping people to become self-sustaining. This tradition is illustrated by the "teach a man to fish" metaphor. The social-reform tradition encourages social change.

Proponents of social change believe that societal circumstances often shape human destiny and create barriers to the thriving of individuals and certain segments of society. They believe that philanthropy must help to change societal circumstances. The support from foundations for the development of and changes in public policy is an example of the social-reform tradition. The initiation and funding of research and pilots relating to significant societal issues such as poverty, global warming, crime, and education and healthcare reform also exemplify this tradition. With respect to the social-reform tradition, while Susan appreciates the positive aspects of this tradition, she notes the risk that foundations can become tantamount to private legislatures or shadow governments. Susan describes a fourth tradition, which involves the ability of a foundation to convene. She encourages them to provide hospitable spaces where people from diverse perspectives can reflect on important issues and engage in moral discourse. I believe this notion of providing hospitable spaces for reflection can be done in a number of ways—in a physical sense or a virtual sense and by a foundation itself or through its funding of intermediaries that convene key stakeholders around an issue.

As I said, I have found these four traditions to be a helpful framework for thinking about Lilly Endowment's grant-making strategies from time to time. We are engaged in all four traditions to various degrees. The extent to which we engage in a particular tradition often relates to our view of what is happening in the contexts of the causes to which we are dedicated. For example, during the Great Recession a few years ago, we put more emphasis than usual on charity. People were falling through the cracks. It just seemed that society's systems were failing them. Among other efforts, we worked with United Way and other funders in Indianapolis to launch the Community Economic Relief Fund to alleviate suffering and address urgent needs.

Another example of how the four traditions guide our work relates to the efforts the Endowment is supporting to bring together several public and private sector organizations and resources to build a more robust capacity in the state for data collection and analysis, with the hope that by having access to better information the public and private sectors can make better policies to address society's challenges and evaluate whether past policies and programs are succeeding. We are hopeful that advances in information technology can enable significant enhancements in our ability to gather important data, assemble and format the data, and analyze them in productive ways.

While Lilly Endowment obviously appreciates the need for good data and analysis in our work, I do want to offer a caution. I am concerned that some place too much emphasis on quantitative analysis of philanthropic efforts. From time to time, I hear statements such as "don't fund what you can't measure." Does that mean that programs that can't be measured with numbers should not be funded? How would that affect funding in religion? How about in the arts? If a foundation had funded the commissioning of a new symphonic work, would the best measure of success be how many people came to the premiere? Sure, that would be a piece of evidence, but would the most significant measure of success be that or would it be what the composer's peers thought about the piece? On the other hand, over the centuries the contemporaries of artists often did not praise their work. Their acclaim came from later generations. In my experience, requiring quantitative outcomes for every program or effort can be counterproductive and, at times, not worth the cost of measuring them. I think a blend of quantitative assessment and qualitative evaluation, which considers the intangibles and key informant feedback, is preferable in many contexts.

I would like now to focus on some thoughts I have about the future of Indiana and role philanthropy could play in making that future brighter. Given my deep Hoosier roots and dedication to Indiana, I must say that it distresses me to see the challenges that Indiana faces. It consistently ranks among the least healthy states on many indicators. We rank forty-first in overall health according to the United Health Foundation's 2015 rankings. According to those rankings, we rank forty-fourth in both obesity and smoking, and we rank forty-seventh in the level of air pollution. According to the Annie E. Casey Foundation's 2015 Kids Count Profile, we rank thirty-second overall on several indicators relating to the well-being of children and youth. The Indiana Youth Institute reported last year that Indiana ranked first in the percentage of teenagers who have thoughts of suicide and second in the percentage that attempted suicide.

Indiana ranks as the fourth highest state in the percentage of the adult population that has only a high school degree. We rank forty-third in the percentage of adults twenty-five to sixty-four with a bachelor's degree or higher according to STATS Indiana, and our per capita income rank is thirty-nineth. Especially alarming is the trend that our per capita income rank has declined over the past twenty years from twenty-eighth to thirty-ninth.

Obviously, we must intensify and expand the good efforts underway by our state to educate and train more residents to meet today's workforce needs. We also must devise and support creative ways to foster the development of more jobs that are appealing to college graduates with a bachelor's or higher degree. Far too many of our talented college graduates leave the state because they cannot find appealing jobs or careers here. This exodus negatively affects our per capita income ranking and overall quality of life.

While these statistics are indeed sobering, there are positive signs for Indiana. In Forbes's 2015 rankings of the best states for business, Indiana ranked eighth. In CNBC's 2015 ranking for America's Top States of Business, we ranked thirteenth. If one assumes that having an attractive business climate will result in increased wealth for the state, some of which can be used to address the negative statistics I just noted, perhaps there is some reason for optimism. But those resources will have to be marshaled effectively to address our challenges.

While I am deeply concerned about the future prosperity of Indiana and its residents, I also am hopeful. Indiana has an impressive legacy of philanthropy throughout the state as evidenced by the generous support for Indiana's community foundations and United Ways. Major philanthropy from Indiana's more affluent families also is exemplary. Think about the Foellingers and Dekkos in northeast Indiana, the Cooks in Bloomington, the Miller family in Columbus, the Ball family in Muncie, the Calvins in South Bend, and the Ogles in southern Indiana. Along with the Lilly family, the Simons, Efroymsons, Fairbanks, Pulliams, Goodriches, Clowes, Glicks, Basilles, Mays, Eskenazis, and Christel DeHaan and Yvonne Shaheen, among many others, have contributed enormously to the quality of life in Indianapolis. And we are seeing that successful entrepreneurs in the IT cluster also are engaging in important philanthropy. Examples include Scott Dorsey, Scott Jones, Mark Hill, David Becker, and Kelly Pfledderrer.

Moreover, there are some encouraging initiatives underway that are supported by the business community and the public sector. The Indiana Chamber of Commerce and several local chambers are pursuing many promising efforts, as are the initiatives under the Central Indiana Corporate Partnership. The Indiana Biosciences Research Institute and the 16 Tech Innovation Community, Agrinovus, BioCrossroads, TechPoint, and Conexus are especially noteworthy. The state's Regional Cities initiative has stimulated many good ideas and connections for regional development in areas around the state, and several Indiana colleges and universities, such as IU, Purdue, Rose Hulman, Notre Dame, UIndy and Butler, among others, are enhancing and accelerating their tech transfer endeavors and their efforts to build the state's intellectual capital.

What can the charitable or philanthropic sector do to help address these negative statistics? An obvious thing is to provide grants for efforts that seek to address these challenges in more strategic ways. While some progress can be made through more effective grant making, some of the problems are so widespread and embedded in the state's culture that there are not enough philanthropic resources to address them adequately. So I would like to suggest an additional approach. It builds off of Susan Wisely's fourth tradition of philanthropy I mentioned a few minutes ago—convening. Community foundations, United Ways, private and family foundations, colleges and universities, and other charitable organizations across the state could make more robust and urgent their efforts to bring stakeholders from diverse perspectives together in their communities to discuss what they view as the key challenges that prevent their residents from having the quality of life to which they aspire. The Thriving Communities, Thriving State project of the IU Public Policy Institute is a good start.

I worry that the forces I mentioned earlier that result in more targeted or special-cause philanthropy have a negative impact on place-based or community initiatives. These forces are affecting communities all over the country—not just in Indiana. In fact, the theme of the annual conference of the Council on Foundations in Washington, DC, in April 2016 is "The Future of Community."

Connecting or mediating organizations like community foundations, United Ways, colleges and universities, and other charitable organizations that are embedded in a given community must make the case for thoughtful philanthropy that is targeted on strengthening the community. How can building community in a given locale be promoted as a special cause? This may require compromise and finding common ground. Good research and analysis may be needed. What are the key reasons the challenges exist? What strategies, if any, are being pursued to address them? How successful are they? What would be needed to make them more successful? What has worked in other communities in the state or throughout the country? Are the highest priority issues in your community similar to those in other communities in your region or throughout the state? Would working with them to mobilize a broader set of stakeholders be worthwhile?

What can be appropriately initiated or funded by the private sector or philanthropy and what needs public funding or public policy changes? New approaches could be piloted with philanthropic support and then the results of the pilots could be shared with the broader public. Engage the elected officials that have responsibilities for your communities at the local, state, and federal level. Let the public officials know that you find these negative statistics unacceptable. Let them know that your community cares about the future quality of life of its residents and what you think stands in the way of the quality of life you envision. Communicate with them about what the philanthropic sector cares about and is funding in your community and learn what the public sector funding streams, initiatives, and polices are with respect to an issue you care about. Too often I have observed a lack of understanding on the part of public sector officials at all levels of government of what the nonprofit sector is doing relating to a particular issue and vice versa. Better alignment between the public sector and nonprofit sector could yield better results.

While private foundations are not allowed to lobby, they can support nonpartisan research that is broadly disseminated. Public charities, like community foundations and United Ways, can engage in a limited amount of lobbying. Engage your Chamber of Commerce. Chambers can lobby. Check with your legal counsel to see to what extent you can engage in advocacy. As these efforts are undertaken, I encourage community leaders to engage young people. They are more adept at using social media and will be able to help engage their peers in developing and participating in strategies to strengthen their communities. The Youth Philanthropy Initiative of Indiana housed at the Indiana Philanthropy Alliance is one resource that should be engaged more. Another resource is the Campus Compact initiative that operates on many Indiana college campuses. MCon is another resource for information about how millennials engage and communicate. Headquartered in Indiana, it is led by Derrick Feldmann.

As I close my remarks today, I am reminded of a poem that used to be published often in the *Indianapolis News*, which I delivered for five years when I was a teenager. Written by William Miller Herschel, an Indiana journalist who wrote for the *News* at the time of Indiana's centennial, it's entitled "Ain't God Good to Indiana." While I believe, indeed, that in many ways God's been good to Indiana, I also believe that God helps those who help themselves. For future generations to agree with William Herschel that God's been good to Indiana, we have got some work to do. I spoke earlier today about the view that Lilly Endowment acts from two contrasting convictions: that tradition is an important resource and that fundamental rethinking is often necessary to respond to new challenges and circumstances. Well, I believe now is a time for fundamental rethinking about how we help ourselves to chart a brighter future for our state, and I urge us all to intensify and make more urgent our efforts to do so.

HOOSIER
PHILANTHROPY

—⚭—

INTRODUCTION

GREGORY R. WITKOWSKI

HOOSIER PHILANTHROPY ANALYZES CHARITABLE GIVING
in Indiana over the first two hundred years of statehood, from
1816 to 2016, presenting the development of philanthropic giving
and the nonprofit sector in a distinct geographic, cultural, and
legal environment. Historians have long outlined how philanthropy and charitable institutions create parallel power structures to government institutions.[1] These structures are especially
important to analyze in a state like Indiana, where donors have
supported nonprofit networks and Hoosiers have emphasized
voluntary action—as opposed to government policy—to advance the public good. The introduction and separately authored
chapters indicate that Indiana philanthropy is supported by a
broad and diverse donor base, well networked to make collective and collaborative decisions, and focused on adopting and
adapting proven methods for the benefit of many Hoosiers, but
especially those in the middle class.

Hoosier Philanthropy differs from other nonprofit and philanthropic studies books in three ways. First, it analyzes one state, a
rarity in this field. The US political system leaves the states latitude in making public policies, and philanthropic giving has historically focused on local needs, which indicates the advantage

1

of a state-level study. Second, *Hoosier Philanthropy* focuses on the entire gift process for both individual and institutional actors. Philanthropic foundations have been at the center of numerous scholarly studies. This book includes engagement by foundations, individual donors, and beneficiary nonprofit organizations. Finally, few historical texts break down the effects of giving on subsectors, for example, higher education and medical research. Such an approach allows for a more differentiated understanding of the effects of philanthropic giving and a better appraisal of the beneficiaries, who have often been wealthier than the poor traditionally identified as recipients of charitable aid. While a great deal of literature has deconstructed the advantages that philanthropy brings to the wealthy, few studies have pointed to the benefits of such giving across classes, especially to the middle class.[2] This book indicates that the middle class has long benefitted from philanthropy.

Drawing on established scholars and emerging voices, this book brings together multiple perspectives on the history of philanthropy in Indiana. Part one traces the development of philanthropic practices by examining five examples: civic engagement, religious giving, social services, higher education, and medical research. These subfields represent the most significant areas of philanthropic engagement nationally, with religion, public societal benefit, human services, education, and health and medicine accounting for 76 percent of all donations in 2020 according to *Giving USA*.[3] The 1956 Giving USA report, which had fewer categories, indicated that 94 percent of giving went to these causes.[4] While there are other areas of philanthropic engagement, such as the arts or international assistance, these five subfields represent the majority of philanthropic giving since measurements began.

Part one reveals that each area of philanthropic engagement, or nonprofit subsector, has its own history based on different funding models, client needs, institution sizes, and societal expectations. Therefore, it is essential to talk about the nonprofit sector and these different subsectors because government policies, budgets, beneficiaries, and so on vary by subsector. For example, the GI Bill (1944) transformed universities before Medicare and Medicaid (1965) influenced medical care. Each subsector has its own historical trajectory.

Part two consists of case studies of specific philanthropic or nonprofit activities. These include histories of donors and their gifts, examinations of funding for nonprofit organizations that provide social services and religious instruction, and the creation of networks aimed to advance social innovation and local funding. Combined, these show in their details just how varied philanthropic giving can be and how philanthropy has influenced so many parts of Indiana's history.

The essays in part two also indicate that many current debates about philanthropy have long histories. Three short examples illustrate this point. The Indianapolis Chamber of Commerce developed a rating system for local charities in the early twentieth century. Evaluating the effectiveness of nonprofit work goes to the heart of charitable activity and remains a contentious part of an ongoing discussion about measuring success. Another long-term trend is the need to adapt to changing societal and donor needs to maintain organizational mission and serve clients. For instance, social pressures on the Wheeler Mission in Indianapolis and the Neighborhood House in Gary placed both under additional financial stress, leading the Neighborhood House to shut its doors. Understanding why charitable institutions succeed and fail remains a critical element of our contemporary study as well. Finally, more recently, public-private partnerships defined Indianapolis's bid to become an amateur sports capital in the 1980s and its innovative cultural trail in the new millennium. As philanthropists seek to leverage their assets for maximum impact, securing partnerships and pursuing innovation remain challenges.

This introduction outlines the characteristics of giving in Indiana, starting with the donor and moving to the recipient, covering both a philanthropic approach and method. The attributes of Hoosier philanthropy include a broad group of donors of both time and money, an emphasis on collaborative donor and nonprofit networks as a means, an approach that focuses on the adaptation of proven methods, and a broad beneficiary group centered around middle-class interests. These characteristics are not exclusive to Indiana but indicate an approach to philanthropy that Hoosiers embrace.

A STATE HISTORY OF PHILANTHROPY

Historians prize understanding the unique context of each state's development, while also recognizing that local histories reflect national trends. Perhaps the most cited early theorist of American democracy, Alexis de Tocqueville, famously declared that "wherever, at the head of a new undertaking, you see the government in France and a great lord in England, count on it that you will perceive an association in the United States."[5] Tocqueville linked civic participation in associations with democracy and thereby acknowledged the importance of charitable institutions in advancing the public good. While this viewpoint endures, especially on the political right, American history shows all three groups Tocqueville referenced became public agents: voluntary associations, the wealthy, and government.

Historically, voluntary associations have played numerous roles in the United States and, when combined with the more formal nonprofit organization or charitable institution, reflect the strong tradition of US voluntarism. On the other hand, although America had traditionally lacked an official noble class, it nevertheless created elites who wielded significant influence in society. American "lords" were the men and women starting in the late nineteenth century who financed railroads and commerce, developed medicines and treatments, and, more recently, created innovative information technology. Many of these ultra-wealthy also became philanthropists. In addition, twentieth-century American political leaders created government-sponsored initiatives like the New Deal and Great Society to provide for individual needs. In this way, by Indiana's bicentennial, associations and formal nonprofit organizations, wealthy individuals and institutions, and government policies and programs have all played a role in providing for the public good.

While Tocqueville's quote no longer defines the US approach, Hoosiers have continued to embrace Tocqueville's view that civic engagement is better than government policy, leading to an emphasis on limited government. Indiana thus represents one archetypal approach to providing for the public good in the United States.

Philanthropy in Geographic Context: Literature Review

Historian Jon Lauck has called the Midwest a "lost region" because scholars see it broadly as part of the United States' development even as they overlook the detailed history of the region.[6] Other historians argue that midwesterners also have seen themselves as the quintessential Americans because they have not had peculiar identities like those in the South or Northeast.[7] *Hoosier Philanthropy* uncovers the history of one state of the "lost region" and illuminates it both on its own terms and in relation to broader national developments.

Indiana, firmly within the Midwest, has long been studied as an American archetype as much as an individual example. In the early twentieth century, Robert and Helen Lynd chose to study Muncie, Indiana. They argued the town served as a microcosm for American beliefs and lifestyles because it was primarily White, Protestant, and native-born. The Lynds claimed that the lack of distinction and diversity made Muncie representative of the whole country. While this focus on mainstream whiteness has been rightly critiqued, the Lynds' "Middletown" studies achieved broad popularity and raised Muncie as an example of a typical American town.[8] When journalist Peter Jennings went "in search of America," he included Muncie. Jennings argued "Middletown" remained a "barometer of American life" and described it as a place "where people embrace their typical Americanness."[9]

Hoosier Philanthropy is one of the few state-level histories of philanthropy. Most historical studies of philanthropy have centered on either cities or nations, with little attention devoted to states.[10] Three exceptions include the celebratory *For the Benefit of All*, a comprehensive study of charitable giving in Michigan, *Colorado Givers*, and the more scholarly *Foundations of Texan Philanthropy*, which focuses exclusively on philanthropic foundations in the Lone Star state.[11]

Efforts to define giving traditions and cultures below the national level have been more regional in outlook. Kathleen McCarthy outlined differences between North and South in antebellum period.[12] Peter Dobkin Hall saw midwestern giving as an overlap of private and public institutions and funding mechanisms. John Schneider advanced a similar view of giving. He built on Joseph Ellis's political cultures that labeled Indiana "individualistic," which means that individual interest is seen as part of the community good. Indiana thus privileges private actions to advance the public good with charitable institutions that supplant government support. Schneider argued that charities are held to standards of efficiency like businesses or state institutions.[13] While these definitions help us understand mainstream philanthropy in the nineteenth century, they neither represent the traditions of minoritized groups, like African Americans and Native Americans, nor trace developments through the twentieth century when government played a much more significant role in nonprofit activity.[14]

This book finds support in the work of Hall and Schneider but moves beyond donors to also trace the means used, approaches or strategies, and beneficiaries of philanthropy. This more encompassing approach allows for a greater understanding of the traditions and cultures of giving in the state. By focusing on one locale, this book centers the history of philanthropy in a particular political and social environment. As such, *Hoosier Philanthropy* builds on some of the best histories of the past while taking a new approach to increase our understanding of philanthropic practice.

Indiana: Limiting Government Action

Indiana is a good case study because it is an archetypal example of an American state that limits government responsibility for the public good. In fact, Indiana has maintained an ideological focus on private action even as federal programs have led to more government spending over the last century. While *Hoosier Philanthropy* is a history of Indiana, the lessons learned have relevance in a region and nation that has often embraced this approach to the public good.

Hoosiers' focus on small government started early in the state's history. For example, Indiana lagged behind its neighbors in establishing state social welfare before the Civil War.[15] Instead, Hoosiers relied on private means to provide for social needs. By the late nineteenth century, the state created a Board of Charities to "investigate the whole system of public charities and correctional facilities," including settlement houses, orphanages, prisons, and asylums. These included a mixture of state-run and private charitable organizations and, as was typical for the era, grouped criminality and corrections with charity and need.[16] The board reduced the number of recipients of poor relief but did so at the cost of care for the needy.[17] In 1897, one in every thirty-one inhabitants received aid, while in 1907, one in seventy-one received assistance. In absolute numbers, the total supported dropped from 82,235 to 37,724 over that decade. In placing the burden for poor relief on the local townships, the state board oversaw a race to the bottom, leading to a decrease in costs from $630,000 in 1895 to under $250,000 by 1905.[18]

Even as national public spending increased substantially in the twentieth century, Indiana leaders were caught between their commitment to limited government and the need to provide for their poorest constituents. During the expansion of federal programs to combat the Great Depression, Indiana's legislators proclaimed that the state "needs no guardian and intends to have none," but nonetheless took all the federal aid offered as part of the New Deal. The rhetoric of curtailing spending was used effectively by Indiana's leaders to achieve political success and became a conservative trope. For instance, despite nationally low taxes, ranking forty-third in 1982 and forty-ninth in 2000, Hoosiers sought to limit state collection of money and focused on private provision and individual responsibility.[19] Over the course of the twentieth century, Hoosiers still placed their trust in nonprofit organizations more than other institutions. A survey of local public officials found that they declared it more likely that nonprofit organizations will "do the right thing" than government offices.[20] This approach to the public good of limiting government action and responsibility has been embraced on the national level by the political right. As such, this history speaks to nationally relevant trends and Indiana's development.

HOOSIER PHILANTHROPY: DEFINING CHARACTERISTICS

Indiana's philanthropic history includes four core elements that combine to form a Hoosier philanthropic tradition. First, a diverse group of donors, defined by race, gender, class, and religion, gives in Indiana. Second, over the past two centuries, the state has developed broad networks of individuals and institutions willing to work together to achieve pragmatic policy solutions to social issues. This defines one means by which philanthropy has had an impact on the state. Third, Indiana's nonprofits have been early adopters of new forms of philanthropic engagement present elsewhere in the United States but at the cost of developing solutions that arose from local innovation. This approach to philanthropy is a more conservative but effective one and puts the state at the forefront without placing it in a leadership position.

Fourth, the focus on limited government has led to philanthropic benefits representing middle-class individuals and values, perhaps at the expense of the neediest in society. Who benefits from philanthropy is much broader than often realized and historically closer to who has benefited from government programs, namely the middle class.

These four points indicate that from donation to public impact, Indiana has developed traditions, practices, and strategies that define Hoosier philanthropy historically and today. Throughout this section, I draw on the rich histories presented in the subsequent chapters. I analyze the donors, their approaches and means, and the beneficiaries, presenting an encompassing view of philanthropic giving.

Donors: Diverse Individuals and Interests

A broad range of Hoosiers belonging to many socioeconomic classes, ethnicities, religious traditions, and genders have given philanthropically. This section will begin to explore some of this diverse mix, starting with the archetypal wealthy philanthropist and moving to the everyday donor of lesser means. The breadth of philanthropic participation is significant because it indicates that philanthropic giving is one means that Hoosiers use to participate in public life and contribute to their visions of the public good.

Indiana certainly has had a history of wealthy men who succeeded in business and gave back.[21] In her chapter, Nicole Etcheson analyzes Calvin Fletcher of Indianapolis as a forerunner of the major donors of the twentieth century. Fletcher's roles as a leading organizer of charities, actor in benevolent movements, and philanthropic donor demonstrates the overlapping nature of different modes of charitable engagement during this crucial half century, which saw the rise of important reform movements such as asylums and public schools, temperance, and slavery.[22] In his day, Fletcher was so ubiquitous within Indianapolis charitable circles that Etcheson compares him to Eli Lilly.

The Lilly family founded Lilly Endowment Inc. (LEI, Endowment) in 1937 for the "promotion and support of religious, educational and charitable purposes."[23] Over its history, LEI has become one of the wealthiest general-purpose foundations in the United States. The Endowment has helped maintain a vibrant nonprofit sector in Indiana. As of the Indiana bicentennial, over eighty years, LEI has disbursed $9.4 billion to over ninety-four hundred nonprofit organizations, spurred urban development plans in Indianapolis, and funded educational and nonprofit networks. About 40 percent of grant dollars went to education, 37 percent to community building, and 34 percent to religious institutions. In 2016, LEI split donations in Indiana equally between greater Indianapolis-based organizations (including statewide organizations) and organizations headquartered in other counties.[24] The level of local funding (68 percent of its grants in 2016) by one of the nation's largest foundations is exceptional. It has created strong, trust-based partnerships with local nonprofits and also given the Endowment significant leverage within the state. It would be impossible to explain Indiana's nonprofit landscape without referencing the Lilly family and LEI.

The Eli Lilly Corporation's success, especially with insulin production, secured wealth for the Lilly family and top corporate leaders. Elizabeth Van Allen focuses on the philanthropy of these leading families, discussing their philanthropic approach, the causes funded, and the influences they had on one another. As Van Allen indicates, the wives of many of these corporate leaders, including Ruth Lilly, were highly engaged in their family's philanthropy. Studies of philanthropy have focused on more significant donations by wealthy men but Van Allen shows that in Indiana, these gifts were often given with the input, if not leadership, of women.[25]

Moving beyond the wealthy businessmen, women have played a leading role in creating social change. Women supported and made possible the formation of the Indianapolis Museum of Art and the Evansville History and Art Museum, to name just two institutions. In fact, May Wright Sewell turned the ceremonial first spade on the construction of the first building to house the Indianapolis Museum of Art.[26] Women constituted most of the volunteers for the Charity Organization Society (COS) in Indianapolis, visiting the homes of those in need and evaluating the level of care needed. Beyond these volunteers, women also took leadership roles. In Gary, Kate and Jane Williams launched the Neighborhood House to provide housing for recently immigrated workers. In Evansville, Albion Fellows Bacon led the way in creating better housing conditions to fight poverty and prevent the spread of tuberculosis. She called for better housing through a public-private partnership in the progressive era.[27]

Madame C. J. Walker continued in this tradition and defined her own path. As the nation's first self-made female millionaire, she used her corporate model and money to finance a variety of philanthropic projects. Tyrone Freeman examines her philanthropy, which emerged "out of her experiences as a poor, Black, female migrant from the Jim Crow South." Walker relied on the philanthropic infrastructure of Black civil society in the Midwest, both institutions and individuals, who mentored her and enabled her to become a financially independent, yet community-minded entrepreneur and donor. Her subsequent giving positions her philanthropy as distinctive from the dominant paradigm of wealthy Whites and more with that of other African Americans.[28]

There is less historical data about other minoritized groups, but as David King shows, diverse religious communities also developed their own philanthropic traditions. Religious affiliation separated most social services in Indianapolis. These charities received support from within their faith communities and provided aid for specific groups of congregants. For instance, Jews in Indianapolis supported social service organizations that were distinct from Christian organizations and represented different ethnic Jewish (e.g., Hungarian and German) and religious (e.g., orthodox and reformed) denominations. Jewish donors, of course, also crossed over into broader philanthropic engagement. For instance, the Glick and Efroymson families took leadership roles in several Indianapolis charitable institutions.[29]

The nature of historical documentation means it is easier to write about wealthy philanthropists, but individual gifts of time and money to associations indicate the support that everyday donors provided. Hoosiers have been joiners, using associations not only for social engagement but also for civic activity. Hoosier men, women, girls, and boys have repeatedly embraced civic clubs and organizations. A survey of Muncie in the 1970s indicated that 90 percent of men and 82 percent of women belonged to at least one association, including unions, social groups, and voluntary associations for charitable purpose.[30] Throughout the state, Hoosiers joined chapters of national organizations such as the Odd Fellows, Shriners, Boy Scouts, or the Elks and formed local organizations such as the Camp Fire Girls in Angola.[31] A large number even embraced the Ku Klux Klan in the 1920s, a dark moment of Indiana's associational history and an indication that not all voluntary action positively affected society. Many Hoosiers, especially women, normalized the Klan's extreme activities by focusing on the social aspects of the organization.[32]

Hoosiers of varied religious, ethnic, class, and gender backgrounds have engaged in charity and philanthropy in formal and informal giving. There is a continuing need to explore more donor histories to understand the entire tradition of giving in Indiana, particularly among minoritized groups often excluded from historical studies of philanthropy. Still, this book indicates already that a broad base of donors gave in Indiana.

Means: Working Collaboratively—Focus on Networks

Indiana's major donors have led the way in creating networks of collaboration, including matching grants, donor networks, and nonprofit collaboratives. These groups raise community voices and create buy-in for projects but also mask the power of major donors' influence. While not exclusive to Indiana, networks mediating gifts and coordinating nonprofit activity is a state characteristic. LEI has used networks to distribute its substantial assets, consistently among the largest in the United States. As Thomas Lake, CEO of LEI, declared in 1990, "We believe the best way to assist Indiana communities is to help them generate local solutions to local problems."[33] The Endowment has long made unrestricted grants to nonprofits, trusting its grantees to make the best use of its gifts. LEI has also funded collaborative networks across many subsectors. These networks create local decision-making bodies that define the public good. No other state has such a large foundation interested in supporting local initiatives at this scale. As a result, Indiana may be closest to creating a genuinely parallel nonprofit structure to government agencies. LEI deserves credit for supporting these networks, but they built on a history of collaborative giving within Indiana.

Matching gifts provide an informal means of creating a donor collaborative. Perhaps the greatest historical example is the Carnegie library match. Pittsburgh steel magnate Andrew Carnegie provided funds for building libraries while local communities donated land and set aside money to operate them. Indiana accounted for almost a tenth of the 1,679 libraries built nationally. Hoosiers embraced this approach so much that 155 Carnegie libraries were built throughout the state, leaving only five towns with a population above three thousand without a public library.[34] Carnegie's success may have inspired Hoosier donors to follow a similar strategy.

In 1911, the Ball family used a matching grant to support the YMCA in Muncie.[35] They supported Ball Memorial Hospital and, in 1918, founded Ball State University in partnership with the state. The Balls institutionalized their philanthropic commitment with a $3.5 million gift to create the Ball Brothers Foundation. The first major general-purpose foundation in Indiana, its mission was "to promote religious, education, and charitable purposes, or all of them, within the State of Indiana."[36] The foundation has remained an essential local funder and has also used matching grants to generate more philanthropy. The foundation provided a $1 million matching grant in 1985 to help form the Community Foundation of Muncie and Delaware County. Following the prototypical community-foundation model, this institution has leveraged local assets and provided social services. Through the Indiana bicentennial, both the Ball Brothers Foundation and the community foundation remained essential drivers in their community networks, as their support for local innovation centers indicated.[37]

LEI employed networks to mediate the distribution of its gifts and has been the primary driver of this means of organizing philanthropic activity. The Endowment granted its first donation to the United Way and has continued to support nonprofit infrastructure and encourage nonprofit networks to share knowledge and coordinate programming. LEI funded the Associated Colleges, today Independent Colleges of Indiana, to represent all the state's independent colleges in 1948. This association was the first of its kind and became a national model.[38]

The most comprehensive effort to create a network was the GIFT (Giving Indiana Funds for Tomorrow) initiative, analyzed by Xiaoyun Wang in her contribution to this volume. Started after the success in Muncie, this program aimed to help local communities address their own needs. In addition to the matching funds provided to build endowments in these community foundations, the GIFT initiative issued special community grants of up to $100,000 to fund a diversity of local needs, such as recycling efforts or a community center.[39] The initiative led to the establishment of many countywide community foundations and, as of 2022, represented a total of ninety-four organizations throughout the state. The initiative also propelled the organization of what later became known as the Indiana Philanthropy Alliance, which acted as an active consultant to these community foundations.[40] As such, LEI leaders recognized the significance of their organization and divested themselves of some grant-making decisions by funding networks that functioned as intermediaries.

Smaller foundations have also influenced local nonprofit networks. For instance, Fort Wayne's Foellinger Foundation began with a $5,000 gift in 1958 and, through investments and additional gifts (drawn from the sale of the *News Sentinel*), grew its assets to $162 million over the next four decades. The foundation has granted more than $130 million over its existence, primarily to Allen County.[41] In the 1990s, the Foellinger Foundation made a conscious effort to support collaboration, which it described as the "formal sharing of power and resources" in order to strengthen local nonprofits' capacity, a strategy it continues to employ.[42]

While philanthropic generosity has led to the creation of several supportive networks in Indiana, the approach can also bring with it the danger of losing organizational independence or moving away from core values. Philip Byers describes how philanthropic support moved the Yokefellows from a small grassroots fellowship ordered around a set of common religious disciplines to a formalized movement. Between 1956 and 1961, LEI contributed more than $75,000 to the Yokefellows, being especially interested in the idea of creating a "laymen's seminary." While the Yokefellows themselves had an informal ethos, the philanthropic support created organizational structure. In this way, philanthropic support not only helped the Yokefellows grow but changed aspects of its approach.[43]

A lack of funding could be just as influential on an organization's development. As Ruth Hansen describes in her chapter on the Neighborhood House in Gary, a once well-networked organization that lost donor support when it sought to address issues of racial injustice. Instead of growing as many social service nonprofit organizations did in the 1960s, the Neighborhood House was compelled by its funders to join a network whose members had little interest in being socially active. As Hansen outlines, this approach proved neither helpful in advancing social change nor providing for local needs. Many Hoosiers remained cautious supporting progressive causes.[44]

Indiana's focus on collaborative networks is not singular in the United States and networks may increase in importance as a means to leverage more know-how and institutional assets. These networks provide the means to give voice to significant donors and local interests. But they may also drive out more revolutionary approaches, as networks tend to crowd out the most radical voices. This more conservative approach to change is discussed in greater depth in the next section but serves as a warning of unintended consequences of using networks to make decisions.

Approach: Adoption, Adaption, and Innovation

Hoosiers have been early adopters of new methods, taking innovations from their peers in other regions and adapting them to fit the state's needs. This approach has resulted not only from crowdsourced decision-making through networks but also the more conservative nature of Hoosiers. Clay Robbins, chairman and CEO of LEI, referred to the Endowment's tradition of balancing prudence and creativity in its grantmaking in his foreword, and I would argue that represents a Hoosier approach to philanthropy.[45] Indiana's philanthropic leaders have historically minimized risk and captured the upside of innovation by quickly adapting proven methods from other places.

Starting in the late nineteenth century, when many charitable innovations began, Hoosiers were among the first to take advantage of such trends. Indianapolis progressives created one of the first COS chapters in the United States in 1879, only two years after Buffalo started the first US chapter and only eight years after British leaders created the association in London.[46] Indianapolis also formed one of the first community foundations in 1916, adapting the model only two years after Cleveland.[47] An effort to boost efficiency in Indianapolis came with the formation of a "Community Chest," which facilitated unified fundraising efforts among philanthropic organizations. In Indiana, like much of the country, it was inspired by a "War Chest" collected for the American Red Cross after the United States entered World War I. Exceeding the goal of $300,000 and raising $500,000 in Indianapolis, this wartime success led to a greater focus on collaborative fundraising in peacetime.[48] To be sure, such efforts had been organized already in other cities and in Indiana within organizations such as the Jewish Federation. Nevertheless, the Community Chest represented a broad-based, nondenominational effort at federated giving, continued through the United Way.[49]

Advancement radiated out from the Circle City, as Hoosiers in other cities and towns quickly adopted these models too. Less than a decade after the creation of the Indianapolis COS, Richmond leaders started their own chapter. A big step for a small place looking to maximize its charitable impact.[50] Fort Wayne, one of the state's largest and historically significant cities, formed a community foundation in 1922.[51]

From the early stages of formal philanthropy in Indiana, evaluating the effectiveness of a gift also proved a crucial part of philanthropic practice, as the chapter by Katherine Badertscher shows. She traces the evolution from the COS, which centered on improving philanthropic delivery, to progressive era reviews of charitable agencies by the Indianapolis Chamber of Commerce, which provided a rating system, to the Community Chest, which oversaw fundraising and mediated the distribution of social service funds. But a focus on evaluation and "scientific philanthropy" also raised problems, as the chapter by Amanda Koch indicates. Wheeler City Rescue Mission had long been a member of the Indianapolis Community Fund. Still, by 1945, after more than a decade of declining appropriations and wrangling with the businessmen in charge, Wheeler Mission was ready to leave the fund altogether. This conflict stemmed from the two organizations' deeper ideological divide over how best to achieve social change. Wheeler Mission's religious approach held that individual spiritual conversion was the only means of transforming humanity. At the same time, the Community Fund represented a philanthropic strategy that increasingly looked to science and business, rather than religion, for methods to change society as a whole.

The Indianapolis Foundation likewise adapted new methods to advance its mission, using program-related investing to further community interests. As indicated in the chapter by Peter Weber and Chen Ji, this approach, while at the cutting edge of philanthropic trends, emerged organically in Indianapolis out of a desire to reduce risk. Indianapolis leaders did not become bolder in their vision until the late twentieth century. The public-private effort to make Indianapolis the amateur sports capital of America, in which LEI played an essential role in funding civic projects from the 1980s, proved to be a turning point for the city and state. More recently, the Central Indiana Community Foundation and the Glick family birthed the well-regarded cultural trail, which has spread throughout downtown Indianapolis.[52]

These recent philanthropically supported civic projects place the Circle City in the position of leading innovation, but on the whole, the history of Hoosier philanthropy points to a more conservative, early-adopter approach. It is undoubtedly the case that, by definition, there are a limited number of innovators. In this sense, Indiana is representative of mainstream trends in US philanthropy because most institutions in Indiana and elsewhere adopted from the few select innovators. Still, Hoosiers are early adopters, implementing new approaches shortly after they have been proven and therefore on the forefront of change and innovation.

Beneficiaries: Middle Class and Beyond

Recognizing who benefits and who is left out is important to understanding the impact of philanthropy. While it is tempting to think of philanthropic giving as supporting the most vulnerable in society, middle- and upper-class individuals benefit as well.

Giving statistics point to this reality. According to *Giving USA*, welfare agencies nationally received more (23 percent of total giving) in 1955, than education (11 percent) and health (9 percent) combined. By 1964, before Great Society programs had an impact on government funding, education (17 percent) had already moved ahead of welfare agencies (14 percent) and health (11 percent) as priorities for donors.[53] By 1995, with a more diverse grouping of categories, human services had dropped to (8 percent) narrowly ahead of the arts (7 percent) and behind health and education. While certainly the neediest benefit from more than just human services, the other sectors do have broad based impact. A survey of Indiana donors conducted in 1995 found that while Hoosiers gave frequently to human services (46 percent reported doing so), the average estimated gift ($208) trailed religion ($1,141), education ($307), arts and culture ($261), and even recreation ($211).[54] This statistical overview, indicating a broad range of beneficiaries, is further supported by the details of Indiana's philanthropic history.

Badertscher and Crocker argue that Protestant belief and market mechanisms have historically combined to limit services provided to the poorest Hoosiers. Crucial debates characterize the history of Indiana social services, including the respective roles of philanthropy and government in determining recipients' eligibility and how best to intervene in order to meet social needs. Historically, gender, racial, and religious discriminations have limited philanthropy across these divides and further compounded inequalities as much as alleviated them. Often, voluntary associations replicate middle- and upper-class interests. For instance, when the GIFT program started, one of the fundraising experts with a background in social justice wanted to use the program as an opportunity to create more inclusive community engagement. As Wang chronicles, this fundraiser was replaced as local dignitaries wanted to focus on the more powerful in their communities.[55]

While religious giving has been a vital part of Indiana's philanthropic history, donations from parishioners to congregations are not just for the poor. Certainly, religious giving is more than "membership dues" for congregants, as some have called it. Still, moving beyond donations to congregations, religious institutions have aided believers across class differences through their services and by funding colleges for middle-class beneficiaries, as well as services for the poor through organizations like the Salvation Army and Heifer International.[56]

Philanthropic support for secular and sectarian higher education benefited middle and upper classes the most. As Pribbenow and Crowley indicate, from the beginning, one of the core reasons to form Indiana University was to "develop an elite group of educated men."[57] This focus on educating an elite, whether for the benefit of the state or a religious institution, is one important component of college missions. The Ball family and John Purdue made major gifts, creating two of Indiana's largest public universities. From the founding of private colleges to the incorporation of state universities, philanthropy has played an essential role in creating colleges and universities and the direction higher education has taken in the last two centuries. The Independent Colleges of Indiana provided an advocate and network for many of the smaller colleges. As Pribbenow and Crowley show, this association raised money from corporate donors to keep numerous private colleges afloat in the face of changing expectations for higher education. LEI also gave independently to colleges and even started a scholarship program to increase college attendance.

Nonetheless, these philanthropic efforts have fallen short of benefiting poorer Hoosiers. While colleges and universities greatly expanded their reach in the twentieth century to include a diversity of genders, ethnicities, and economic classes, they have remained an exclusive club—in Indiana and nationally. College degrees have also become, as Connolly indicates, markers of socioeconomic status, with those without a bachelor's degree facing a multitude of health and economic challenges leading to a lower life expectancy.[58]

One of the most dramatic changes in public social welfare over the last two hundred years has been in health care. The first increase in care came around the turn to the twentieth century, as the number of hospitals nationally jumped from 178 in 1873 to 4,000 in 1909. In Indiana, these trends started with Bobbs Free Clinic in Indianapolis in 1873. They included the religiously affiliated St. Vincent's in Indianapolis, St. Joseph's in Fort Wayne, and St. Mary's in Evansville. William Schneider analyzes the impressive record of funding hospitals, medical research, and training in Indiana, showing how these institutions relied on a mix of local government support, philanthropic gifts, and fees for services. Throughout the twentieth century, public health and health care shifted more to government programs (Medicare, etc.) and for-profit corporations. Following these trends, philanthropic support began to focus more on medical research. As Schneider indicates in his chapter, the Regenstrief, Showalter, and Walther foundations have been the most consistent supporters of medical research in Indiana.[59]

The US health care system, however, leaves many individuals without insurance coverage. Thus, medical research and health care advances help those with the means to take advantage of them. Indiana has been among the worst states in public health measures, largely because since 1980 counties have funded local health departments at the center of public health initiatives and preventative care. Not surprisingly, nationally, those counties that receive more funds have better health outcomes. Since 1990, Indiana has ranked in the bottom half of all states. It has dropped into the bottom ten states at times in terms of public health outcomes such as infant mortality, mental health mortality, obesity, suicide, and smoking. Nationally, these diseases fall largely on the poorer populations so that the benefits of philanthropy in the medical field are not reaped evenly across classes.[60]

As Van Allen indicates, the development of insulin at the Eli Lilly Corporation represented not only the most important medical development in the state but also strongly influenced Hoosier philanthropy. Yet the Lillys, Cloweses, and Noyeses supported cultural institutions more than public health outreaches.[61] Such institutions likewise skew toward those with the leisure time to engage them and often struggle to reach diverse communities.[62]

Philanthropic giving suffers from a misconception that it is for those most in need, when in reality, it often supports mainstream middle-class or upper-class practices and people. Hoosiers remained committed to a limited government, in which the compulsory redistribution of wealth through taxes is replaced with a focus on individuals' generosity, which neither reaches the scale of support in other states nor redistributes wealth to the same degree.[63] Hoosiers' reliance on philanthropy to provide for the public good further privileges individuals who have already benefited from the political and economic systems.

CONCLUSION

This history traces the philanthropic process from the donors to the beneficiaries, indicating a Hoosier approach to giving. Hoosier philanthropy has included a search for innovation as early adopters and has focused on leveraging giving through networks. Early adoption minimizes risk compared to innovation and has often placed Indiana organizations at the forefront of philanthropic debate and practice. While all states have donor and nonprofit networks, Hoosiers' embrace of limited government and Indiana's major donors' focus on local grant making has made this an especially important means for philanthropic activity. The strength of the nonprofit sector nationally lies in the diversity of its ideas and practices that allows it to meet diverse social needs. But as networks, like the ones often created among Indiana's philanthropies, helped to decide those needs, the sector has focused more directly on the widest common denominator and not those of marginalized groups. It is an unexpected outcome of an effort to democratize giving through networks and raises the question whether philanthropic giving is truly serving the entire public good or certain class and ethnicity-based understandings of that public good.

This research indicates that philanthropic giving informed by a limited-government ideology has supported middle-class interests more than challenging them or advancing social justice and change. Philanthropy and charitable institutions may form a parallel structure to the government, but in a limited government state like Indiana, both private and public action serve similar interests, challenging many of the nonprofit theories that focus on charitable giving providing for the public good in ways different than public policy. Contemporary giving trends indicate this phenomenon may occur beyond Indiana as well. In the year of Indiana's bicentennial, less than one out of eight dollars donated nationally went to nonprofit organization engaged in human services, providing primarily for the neediest.[64]

While much of the academic and public critique of philanthropy has focused on the power of the wealthy, this history indicates that philanthropy has historically served middle-class individuals and interests. This reality, clear when viewed across the multiple nonprofit subsectors, challenges a narrative of philanthropy as a hierarchical giving relationship of the wealthy or middle class for the poor. Instead, middle-class individuals and interests are advanced through philanthropic means. Many who style themselves as donors to the poor may be unwitting beneficiaries of philanthropic giving—for instance, to their alma maters. Failing to recognize the full breadth of beneficiaries undermines the societal value of philanthropy across class divides and disguises the depth of inequality. The disconnect between the rhetoric of serving the disadvantaged and the reality of benefiting the middle class has broad repercussions as it also moves people away from the conception of charitable giving as mutual aid and focuses on the hierarchical nature of philanthropy. Thus philanthropy helps to reify the distinctions in status as opposed to overcoming difference through solidarity. Philanthropic giving—politics by other means—separates as well as unites.

This history of Indiana reveals a number of key points about philanthropy more generally that have often been downplayed in scholarship: many ideas considered new or contemporary have a much longer history; the breadth of donors including various ethnic, religious, class, and genders; the importance of adaptation to complement innovation in philanthropy; the ways that networks can leverage assets and quickly spread services but also may limit the most radical solutions; and the way that the middle class has benefitted from philanthropic giving in contrast to the most common narratives of a focus on meeting the needs of the poor or preserving the authority of the wealthy. These themes became apparent only by looking at the two-hundred-year history of Indiana philanthropy, looking beyond the contemporary and focusing broadly enough on the impact of giving. In analyzing one state, where there is a common legal framework and even a common approach to public policy, it is easier to see the essential elements of philanthropic giving generally as well as the distinctive elements of giving in Indiana. There is a need for more state-level studies to truly understand the national variability, but this history of a state considered part of the American mainstream development already indicates that scholarship needs to further engage how philanthropic giving supports the public good in our communities.

NOTES

1. Kathleen McCarthy, ed., *Lady Bountiful Revisited: Women Philanthropy and Power* (New Brunswick, NJ: Rutgers University Press, 1990);

Daphne Spain, *How Women Saved the City* (Minneapolis: University of Minnesota Press, 2001). For a work that shows voluntary organizations working with the state, see Elisabeth Clemens, *Civic Gifts: Voluntarism and the Making of the American Nation State* (Chicago: University of Chicago Press, 2020).

2. Linsey McGooey, *No Such Thing as a Free Gift* (New York: Verso, 2015); Megan Tompkins-Stange, *Policy Patrons* (Cambridge, MA: Harvard University Press, 2016); Robert Reich, *Just Giving* (Princeton, NJ: Princeton University Press, 2018). One book that took a broader view of beneficiaries in the 1990s was Charles Clotfelter, ed., *Who Benefits from the Nonprofit Sector?* (Chicago: Chicago University Press, 1992).

3. *Giving USA 2021: The Annual Report for the Year 2020* (Chicago: Giving USA Foundation, 2021)23. This percentage includes all of education and all of health and medicine.

4. *Giving USA: Facts about Philanthropy* (New York: American Association of Fundraising Counsel, 1956), 6.

5. Alexis de Tocqueville, *Democracy in America*, edited and abridged by Richard Heffner (New York: New American Library, 1984), 198.

6. Jon Lauck, *The Lost Region: Toward a Revival of Midwestern History* (Iowa City: University of Iowa Press, 2013). Lauck has led efforts to refocus research on the Midwest. For a discussion of differences in the Midwest, see James Madison, ed., *Heartland: Comparative Histories of Midwestern States* (Bloomington: Indiana University Press, 1990).

7. Andrew Cayton and Peter Onuf, *The Midwest and the Nation: Rethinking the History of an American Region* (Bloomington: Indiana University Press, 1990).

8. James Madison, *Indiana through Tradition and Change: A History of the Hoosier State and Its People, 1920–1945* (Indianapolis: Indiana Historical Society, 1982), 6.

9. Peter Jennings and Todd Brewster, *In Search of America* (New York: Hyperion, 2002), xvii–xviii as quoted by Bruce Geelhoed, "The Enduring Legacy of Muncie as Middletown," in *The Other Side of Middletown: Exploring Muncie's African American Community*, eds. Luke Eric Lassiter, Hurley Goodall, Elizabeth Campbell, and Michelle Natasya Johnson (Walnut Creek, CA: AltaMira, 2004), 27.

10. David Hammack and Steven Smith, *American Philanthropic Foundations: Regional Difference and Change* (Bloomington: Indiana University Press, 2018); David Hammack, *Power and Society in Greater NY* (New York: Russell Sage Foundation, 1982); Kathleen McCarthy, *Noblesse Oblige: Charity & Cultural Philanthropy in Chicago, 1849–1929* (Chicago: University of Chicago Press, 1982).

11. Sandy Fugate, *For the Benefit of All: A History of Philanthropy in Michigan* (Battle Creek, MI: Kellogg Foundation, 1997); Thomas Noel, Stephen Leonard, and Kevin Rucker, *Colorado Givers: A History of Philanthropic Heroes* (Niwot: University Press of Colorado, 1998); Mary Kelley and Mary Scheer, *The Foundations of Texan Philanthropy* (College Station: Texas A&M University Press, 2004).

12. Kathleen McCarthy, *American Creed Philanthropy and the Rise of Civil Society 1700–1865* (Chicago: University of Chicago Press, 2005).

13. Richard Ellis, *American Political Cultures* (New York: Oxford University Press, 1993); John Schneider provides a nice overview in "Philanthropic Styles in the United States: Toward a Theory of Regional Differences," *Nonprofit and Voluntary Sector Quarterly* 25, no. 2 (June 1996): 190–210.

14. Peter Hall, *"Inventing the Nonprofit Sector" and Other Essays on Philanthropy, Voluntarism, and Nonprofit Organizations* (Baltimore: Johns Hopkins University Press, 1992),146–49.

15. James Madison, *Justin Walsh. The Centennial History of the Indiana General Assembly, 1816–1978* (Indianapolis: Select Committee on the Centennial History of the Indiana General Assembly, in cooperation with the Indiana Historical Bureau, 1987), 103.

16. "First Report of the Board of State Charities, 1890," 4–5 and appendix 3: "An Act to Establish." Indiana Department of Public Welfare, the Development of Public Charities and Correction in the State of Indiana, Jeffersonville: Indiana Reformatory Printing Trade School, 1910, accessed March 26, 2017, https://babel.hathitrust.org/cgi/pt?id=hvd.li2ick;view=1up;seq=7; Amos Butler, *A Study of the Development of Public Charities and Corrections* (Indianapolis: Indiana State Board of Charities, 1916), 2–4; Sheila Kennedy, "The Poor You Have Always with You," in *The Encyclopedia of Indianapolis*, eds., David Bodenhamer and Robert Barrows (Bloomington: Indiana University Press, 1994).

17. Indiana Department of Public Welfare, *The Development of Public Charities and Correction in the State of Indiana* (Jeffersonville: Indiana Reformatory Printing Trade School, 1910), 125; and Kennedy, "The Poor You Have Always with You," 96.

18. Frank Hanly, "Efficiency in State Charitable and Correction Facilities," in *Proceedings of the National Conference of Charities and Correction at the Thirty Third Annual Session held in Philadelphia, 1906*, ed., Alexander Johnson (Boston: Fred Herr, 1906), 409.

19. Madison, *Hoosiers*, 305, 308; Kennedy, "The Poor You Have Always with You," 97; Madison *Centennial History*, 558–60

20. Kirsten Groenbjerg et al., "Indiana Government Officials and Trust in Nonprofits," Spring 2016, accessed March 2022, https://nonprofit .indiana.edu/doc/publications/localgov/local-govt-trust-nonprofits.pdf.

21. For biographies of wealthy Hoosier families, some of which are sponsored or written by interested parties please see Earl Conn, *Beneficence: Stories about the Ball Families of Muncie* (Muncie: Minnestrista Cultural Foundation, 2013); Dane Starbuck, *The Goodriches: An American Family* (Indianapolis: Liberty Fund, 2001); James Madison, *Eli Lilly, A Life: 1885–1977* (Indianapolis: Indiana Historical Society, 1989); Alexander Clowes, *The Doc and the Duchess: The Life and Legacy of George H. A. Clowes* (Bloomington: Indiana University Press, 2016).

22. See Etcheson chapter in this volume for more on Fletcher.

23. Lilly Endowment Inc., "Annual Report 1950," 2.

24. Lilly Endowment Inc., "Annual Report 2016," 30.

25. See Van Allen's chapter in this volume for more.

26. Heidi Gealt, "The Arts in Indiana," presented at Hoosier Philanthropy Conference, February 18, 2016; Mary Marley, *A Short History of the Indianapolis Museum of Art* (IUPUI Ruth Lilly Special Collections); Jane Graham, *The Story of the Indianapolis Museum of Art* (Indianapolis: Indianapolis Museum of Art, 1998); Kathleen McCarthy, *Noblesse Oblige*.

27. See Ruth Hansen's chapter in this volume for Gary. For Evansville, see Robert Barrow, *Albion Fellows Bacon: Indiana's Municipal Housekeeper* (Bloomington: Indiana University Press, 2000).

28. See Freeman's chapter in this volume; Tyrone Freeman, *Madam C. J. Walker's Gospel of Giving: Black Women's Philanthropy during Jim Crow* (Champaign: University of Illinois Press, 2020); Sevinc Sevda Kilicalp Iaconantonio, "A Conservative Settlement House in Indianapolis: An (Un) usual Case in the Progressive Era," unpublished paper; Norma Erickson, "A Practical Philanthropy: African American Hospitals in Indianapolis, 1907– 21", presented at the Hoosier Philanthropy Conference, February 19, 2016.

29. Judith Endelman, *The Jewish Community of Indianapolis: 1849–present* (Bloomington: Indiana University Press, 1984); Mary Mapes, *A Public Charity: Religion and Social Welfare in Indianapolis, 1929–2002* (Bloomington: Indiana University Press, 2004); and King's chapter in this volume.

30. Theodore Caplow, Howard Bahr, Bruce Chadwick, Reuben Hill, and Margaret Hlmes Williamson, *Middletown Families* (Minneapolis: University of Minnesota Press, 1982), 84.

31. Harvey Morley, ed., *The 1955 History of Steuben County, Indiana: An Historical, Pictorial, Complete County Atlas and Biographical County Album*

(Harvey W. Morley, 1956), 260–307. See also Connelly's chapter in this volume.

32. Leonard Moore, *Citizen Klansman* (Chapel Hill: University of North Carolina Press, 1991), 70–75; Kathleen Blee, *Women of the Klan: Racism and Gender in the 1920s* (Berkeley: University of California Press, 1991), 1–2.

33. Lilly Endowment Inc., *Lilly Endowment Announces $47 million Effort to Help Indiana Communities* (Indianapolis, Indiana: Lilly Endowment Inc., June 24, 1990). As cited by Wang in this book.

34. Paula Jenkins, "The Creation of Carnegie Libraries in the State of Indiana," presented at Hoosier Philanthropy Conference, February 19, 2016; Abigail Van Slyke, *Free to All: Carnegie Libraries & American Culture, 1890–1920* (Chicago: University of Chicago Press, 1995), 1–7; Robert S. Martin, "Introduction," in *Carnegie Denied: Communities Rejecting Carnegie Library Construction Grants, 1898–1925* (Westport, CT: Greenwood, 1993), vii.

35. Conn, *Beneficence*, 216–17. It is unclear if Carnegie was an inspiration. His shadow loomed large, but most philanthropists from the era went their own way, see Gregory Witkowski, "Captains of Philanthropy? The Legacy of Pittsburgh's Most Famous Donors," by Kathleen Buechel, ed., *A Gift of Belief: Philanthropy and the Forging of Pittsburgh* (Pittsburgh: University of Pittsburgh Press, 2021).

36. Edmonds, Anthony, and Bruce Geelhoed, *Ball State University: An Interpretive History* (Bloomington: Indiana University Press, 2001), 59–62; Articles of Incorporation, Ball Brothers Foundation; Marina Harper, "Beneficence, Stewardship, and Reciprocity in Muncie," presented at Hoosier Philanthropy Conference February 19, 2016; *The Community Foundation of Muncie and Delaware County Celebrating 25 Years.*

37. Interview Douglas Bakken, August 18, 1995, GIFT Program, Ruth Lilly Archives, IUPUI, 3–13; "85 Years Later, Unfinished Business," Ball Brothers Foundation Annual Report 2010.

38. See Pribbenow and Crowley's chapter in this volume.

39. Interview with Charles Johnson, July 10, 1995, Pioneer Ruth Lilly Archives, IUPUI, 25–28.

40. Clay Robbins, "Philanthropic Variety: Perspectives from an Indiana Practitioner," presented at Hoosier Philanthropy Conference, February 18, 2016.

41. "Foellinger Foundation 1998 Annual Report" and "Foellinger Foundation 2016 Annual Report" (Fort Wayne: Foellinger Foundation).

42. "Innovation: Getting Things off the Ground" (Fort Wayne: Foellinger Foundation, 1995), 14.

43. See Byers's chapter in this volume.

44. See Hansen's chapter in this volume. The Columbus Irwin Sweeney Miller Foundation did provide support for racial justice nationally. Merriman Cuninggim, *Private Money and Public Service: The Role of Foundations in American Society* (New York: McGraw Hill, 1972), 154; Irwin Sweeney Miller Foundation Annual Report 1974.

45. Clay Robbins's foreword in this volume.

46. See Badertscher's chapter in this volume.

47. Katherine Badertscher, "Organized Charity and the Civic Ideal in Indianapolis, 1879–1922" (PhD diss., Indiana University, 2015); Marc Hardy, "A History of the Formative Years of the Indianapolis Foundation, 1915–23," presented at the Hoosier Philanthropy Conference, February 19, 2016.

48. Marie Cecile and Anselm Chomel, *A Red Cross Chapter at Work* (Indianapolis: Hollenbeck, 1920), 48.

49. Katherine Badertscher, "Organized Charity and the Civic Ideal in Indianapolis, 1879–1922" (PhD diss., Indiana University, 2015); Robert Payton and Patricia Dean, "Philanthropy," in Bodenhamer and Barrows, *Encyclopedia of Indianapolis*, 155–57; Marc Hardy, "A History of the Formative Years of the Indianapolis Foundation, 1915–23," presented at the Hoosier Philanthropy Conference, February 19, 2016.

50. Emily Welker McNew, "A History of the Associated Charities of Richmond, Indiana 1889–1899" (MA thesis, Indiana University, 1955).

51. "The History of the Community Foundation of Greater Fort Wayne," Community Foundation of Greater Fort Wayne, accessed March 28, 2017, https://cfgfw.org/about/history/. Fort Wayne's community foundation spent down during the Great Depression so that it was disbanded in 1941 and reformed in 1956.

52. Weber and Ji's chapter in this volume.

53. *Giving USA: Facts about Philanthropy*, 6; *Giving USA: Annual Report of 1965*, 13.

54. *Giving USA 1996*, 13; Dwight Burlingame et al., *Indiana Gives* (Indianapolis: Indiana University Center on Philanthropy, 1996), 12; *Giving USA 2020*, 23.

55. Amanda Porterfield, *Corporate Spirit: Religion and the Rise of Corporate America* (New York: Oxford University Press, 2018); Badertscher and Crocker's chapter in this volume; Wang's chapter in this volume.

56. King's chapter in this volume.

57. Pribbenow and Crowley's chapter in this volume.

58. Robert Topping, *A Century and Beyond: The History of Purdue University* (West Lafayette, IN: Purdue University Press, 1988); Edmonds and Geelhoed, *Ball State University*, 2001; Connolly's chapter in this volume. For national data, see Anne Case and Angus Deaton, *Deaths of Despair and the Future of Capitalism* (Princeton, NJ: Princeton University Press, 2020).

59. Schneider's chapter in this volume.

60. Paul Halverson and Valerie Yeager, "Indiana Public Health System Review," December 2020, 16, 27, 29–30, 47–48. See also Clay Robbins's chapter in this volume.

61. Van Allen's chapter in this volume.

62. Diane Grams and Betty Ferrell, *Entering Cultural Communities: Diversity and Change in the Nonprofit Arts* (New Brunswick, NJ: Rutgers University Press, 2008).

63. Julian Wolpert, *Patterns of Generosity in America* (New York: Twentieth Century Fund, 1993).

64. *Giving USA 2017 Annual Report for the Year 2016* (Chicago: Giving USA Foundation, 2017), 30. For scholarship that makes this point about contemporary giving, see William Diaz, "For Whom and for What? The Contributions of the Nonprofit Sector," by Lester Salamon, ed., *The State of Nonprofit America* (Washington: Brookings Institution Press, 2002), 517–35; Angela Eikenberry, *Giving Circles* (Bloomington: Indiana University Press, 2009).

GREGORY R. WITKOWSKI is a Senior Lecturer of nonprofit management and affiliate faculty at the National Center for Disaster Preparedness at Columbia University. He taught history for six years at Ball State and philanthropy for seven years at Indiana University, helping launch the Lilly Family School of Philanthropy. He is the author of *The Campaign State: Mobilizing the Masses in East Germany, 1945–89* and *Germany Philanthropy in Transatlantic Perspective: Perceptions, Exchanges, Transfers.*

PART I

OVERVIEWS OF PHILANTHROPIC
AREAS OF ENGAGEMENT

ONE

—◊◊◊—

INDIANA'S PHILANTHROPIC HISTORY

A Continuing Legacy

JAMES H. MADISON

HOOSIERS HAVE BEEN THEIR BROTHERS' and sisters' keepers for two centuries. The story is complicated and beset with challenges. There is little good scholarship and many stories, emanating from a jumble of overlapping, episodic, and diverse forms of philanthropy. It may be premature to identify patterns in two hundred years of Indiana philanthropy, but nonetheless, here are some possibilities.[1]

Indiana's 1816 Constitution includes some of the finest words ever penned on Indiana soil. The delegates gave to the state legislature the duty to care "for those persons, who by reason of age, infirmity, or other misfortunes, may have a claim upon the aid and beneficence of society." They also stipulated that the new state would have, as soon as possible, a system of public education, "ascending in a regular gradation, from township schools to a state university, wherein tuition shall be gratis, and equally open to all."[2]

The first Constitution set down a magnificent foundation of civic obligations and citizen responsibility to provide for the less fortunate, including children, and look to the future. Here was pioneer optimism and the forward-looking idealism of the founding generation at a time when most Hoosiers lived in crude log cabins. Abe Lincoln's family arrived on the Indiana frontier in 1816 and later recalled "a wild region, with many bears and other wild animals, still in the woods." And he added, "If a straggler supposed to understand latin, happened to sojourn in the neighborhood, he was looked upon as a wizzard."[3]

Of course, pioneers were overly optimistic. Indiana has not yet created universities where tuition is free or met other promises made in 1816. Such failures reflect Hoosier distrust of government, a tradition that runs through two centuries of public policy. Hoosiers have always preferred small government. If there must be government, it should be local, close to the people. There must be no taxes or if necessary, low taxes. Moderate public services have usually been the Indiana way.

Small government has meant that Hoosiers have placed very large burdens on private philanthropy. For the first several generations, government seldom touched Hoosier lives. Citizen volunteers were usually the only players, offering immense opportunities and obligations for designing and securing the public good. Religion claimed the largest philanthropic space in nineteenth-century Indiana. Religious belief and action set the foundations of the state's philanthropic traditions.[4]

Indiana's great diversity of religious belief and practice included disbelieving Hoosiers. A good example is the Owenite community that settled New Harmony in 1825. These communitarian innovators not only denied religious faith but also waged a battle against religious institutions. At the same time, their sophisticated commitment to the public good led them to push for schools, libraries, and other marks of civilization. Elsewhere across the new state, more ordinary pioneers chose not to claim a religious faith. Voters elected at least two acknowledged agnostics to the Indiana Constitutional Convention of 1851.[5]

Most Hoosiers professed some belief, but the tangled variety of churches and denominations ensured great diversity, rivalry, and conflict. Some, particularly the "Hardshell" Baptists, opposed evangelizing and missions. That is, they opposed do-gooders who wished to lift the human condition. Such work was not the responsibility of earthly beings. Other church people took up the fight against wickedness, outside the church as well as within. As the Indiana economy grew and towns developed, the opportunities to sin seemed more visible. Among the battles joined, as an old-timer recalled, were "drinking, Sabbath Desecration, and sexual bundling of the uneducated youth."[6]

Quakers and Presbyterians most aggressively engaged in good works. Even before statehood Quakers acted on their philanthropic traditions. Most notable were their missions to redeem Native Americans. Despite strenuous efforts to civilize, educate, and Americanize Indians, their noble efforts proved largely a failure.[7]

Presbyterians had the sharpest tools to shape a civilized society on the Indiana frontier. Their denomination sent educated clergy with Yankee reform orientations to the new West. They discovered an appalling ignorance, including, one lamented, "a total abstinence from literature."[8] Presbyterian respect for learning also led to social action and all manner of benevolent associations, including those addressed to temperance, antislavery, and education. Driven by the need to teach young people to read and be civilized, as well as religious, they established hundreds of schools. They created colleges, including Hanover and Wabash, even in some ways Indiana University in Bloomington, where the presidents from the beginning in 1820 to 1884 were all Presbyterian clergymen. Other denominations joined the cause of advancing the common good. Few expressed concern over separation of church and state. Many lobbied local and state government, particularly for schools.[9]

Indiana's greatest lobbyist and school reformer was Presbyterian minister Caleb Mills, who settled in Crawfordsville. His five messages to the state legislature, entitled "One of the

People," are among the best assessments and recommendations ever written on subject of public education. At the foundation was a conviction that public education for all was a right and necessity of citizenship and godliness. Mills pointed to the 1840 US census, which revealed Indiana's poor ranking in literacy. He diagnosed the causes of the state's backwardness: "want of competent teachers, suitable school books, a proper degree of interest in the community on the subject, adequate funds, and the method of procuring such funds." He urged the necessity of a state and township school tax, for "there is but one way to secure good schools, and that is to pay for them." The core of his message would be repeated to the twenty-first century.[10]

Some Hoosiers thought Presbyterians and other reformers pushy and elitist—a charge often made against philanthropists. It was not their business to interfere in such private matters as a child's education or mix with the government. Here individual freedom and distrust of elites and do-gooders sometimes meant disagreement about definitions of the common good.

Friction among religious groups gave way by the mid-nineteenth century to cooperation among Methodists, Baptists, Disciples of Christ, and others, though not Catholics or Jews. One outcome was the Sunday school. A Sunday school opened in Corydon as early as 1814. They spread across the state, with thousands by the end of the nineteenth century. Some were interdenominational. All had more than a religious purpose. While teachers introduced children to religion, particularly the Bible, instruction also focused on reading, writing, and preparation for citizenship. Sunday schools were often the only instruction a child received outside the home. They filled the space between the promise of a public education made in 1816 and the reality of the state's slow creation of public schools.[11]

Many Sunday school teachers were women. Religion provided a special place for women, increasingly so during the late nineteenth century. From their churches women made pathways outside the kitchen and nursery and into the public sphere. They created women's missionary societies, Bible societies, temperance groups, and other voluntary associations that combined religious, social, and philanthropic purposes. During the Civil War, women took on farm duties at home and nursing duties in the field.

By the end of the Civil War, pioneer ways had passed. A growing economy brought railroads, factories, and cities. US Steel, Studebaker, Ball Brothers, and Eli Lilly and Company rose to corporations of national stature in the late nineteenth century. Extraordinary economic growth extended to farming as well. New agricultural machinery and methods created an abundance of corn and hogs. The late nineteenth and early twentieth centuries brought a new prosperity to Hoosiers. Indeed, along with its neighboring states, Indiana was part of the new American heartland, an economic growth machine that had no peer anywhere else in the world.[12]

Economic growth meant new resources for the public good. Greater abundance enabled creation of high schools and colleges, hospitals, medical schools, museums, and places for music and theater. Among the outstanding new institutions were public libraries, particularly Carnegie libraries. Hoosiers in the first two decades of the twentieth century created more Carnegie Libraries than any other state. Many of these temples of civilization still stand as reminders of what local citizens can accomplish.

The new prosperity also provided means to help those less well off, and there were lots of them by 1900. Industrialization created a working class, a lower socioeconomic order, where fathers, mothers, and children all labored in order to survive. Hoosiers offered individual and institutional responses to these great changes. Religious motivations continued to spur action, but the growing cities and the large numbers of newcomers overwhelmed resources and methods of traditional religious-based philanthropy. New organizations appeared, as did new leaders and new partnerships between the public and private sectors.[13]

The best example is Oscar McCulloch, joined by his wife, Alice. Perhaps the most studied philanthropist in Indiana history, and deservedly so, McCulloch served as minister at Plymouth Congregational Church in Indianapolis, where he preached the social gospel of aggressive outreach to the community and engagement in public policy issues, including abolition of child labor and creation of ethical business practices. McCulloch was at the forefront of a wider movement toward organized charity intended to make welfare systematic and scientific. His leadership created the Indianapolis Charity Organization Society. It is true that McCulloch for a time focused on degenerates, lifetime paupers whose deficiencies he thought biological rather than environmental. These were the undeserving poor, represented by the so-called tribe of Ishmael, which so attracted McCulloch's interest. But McCulloch transitioned to appreciate environmental influences on poverty, and he moved toward calls for social justice for all the poor. McCulloch challenged Indiana's deeply held distinction between the worthy and unworthy poor, the latter best left to their own devices, many thought.[14]

McCulloch's generation created philanthropic partners beyond the churches. Especially important were volunteers from the business community. A good example was the Indianapolis Commercial Club, created in 1890 and led by Colonel Eli Lilly, a Civil War veteran who entered the pharmaceutical business a few years earlier. Lilly and his business colleagues organized to lift the city economically and address social and cultural needs.[15]

In addition to business leaders, professional social workers joined the cause of benevolence. Often new college graduates, they partnered with churches to create a different kind of philanthropy, one more systematic and, they claimed, more efficient in identifying and serving those most in need of help.

Professional social workers, church people, and business leaders nurtured booming reform movements in the first two decades of the twentieth century. Citizens rushed to build new community institutions and address the negative consequences of industrial and urban growth. Many of the laborers in progressive reform were women.

In Evansville Albion Fellows Bacon learned of tenement housing in her hometown and later took her crusade across the state and into the statehouse. Most communities had counterparts. Mothers worried about impure milk and joined Indiana's rapidly expanding public health movement. Others pushed for better schools and compulsory education.[16]

In many cities women led in creating settlement houses. Two young graduates of Butler University established Christamore House in Indianapolis in a working-class neighborhood. In Evansville, Gary, Fort Wayne, and other cities, new settlement houses often employed professional social workers, partnered with local churches, and recruited business leaders to their boards. Some settlement houses served a particular ethnic group or neighborhood. Christamore accepted only White clients. Indeed, when the African American population grew around Christamore, the settlement moved to Haughville rather than integrate.[17]

African Americans moved in the great migration north to settle in Indiana's growing industrial cities. Searching for jobs, the newcomers faced all the challenges of the working poor, exacerbated by race. Racial issues run through the history of philanthropy. Segregation meant Black-only institutions, such as Flanner House, the Senate Avenue YMCA, and Crispus Attucks High School in Indianapolis, became centers of African American life separate from White organizations. African American women's groups formed also, such as the Indianapolis Women's Improvement Club, which provided care for those suffering with tuberculosis. Across the state branches of the National Association for the Advancement of Colored People toiled with determined effort to alleviate some of the impediments to jobs, education, and social justice.[18]

White Hoosiers offered occasional philanthropic gestures toward African Americans. Among the most important was the antislavery movement before the Civil War. Quakers played a leading role in Indiana's Underground Railroad. After the war Quakers founded the Indianapolis Asylum for Friendless Colored Children, at a time when there were few orphanages for children of any color—and none for Black children.[19]

Individual racial, ethnic, and religious groups organized their own voluntary associations. Ethnic churches, many of them Catholic, and the large numbers of African American congregations were bulwarks in their communities. Dozens of German-American mutual aid societies formed in cities. In the Calumet region, a rainbow of ethnic groups created voluntary associations providing legal aid, life and health insurance, cultural activity, and places of comfort in a world often skeptical of their claims of being Americans. In Indianapolis, the Jewish Welfare Federation did important work on the south side, where East European Jews had settled.[20]

Progressive reforms included eugenics, one of the era's most regretful efforts to advance the general well-being. Some of the state's respected citizens accepted the notion that heredity ordained one's destiny and that there were defective Hoosiers who by law should be prohibited from procreating. Reformers pushed the state to pass a eugenics law in 1907 that permitted involuntary sterilization of defectives. Most were rural White Hoosiers, written off as the least of the unworthy poor.[21]

Another citizen reform group that determined to uplift Indiana also left a harsh legacy. The Ku Klux Klan attracted Protestant, White, native-born Hoosiers who believed themselves to be America's best people. The organization was anti-Catholic, anti-Semitic, anti-Black, and anti-immigrant. But the Indiana Klan's broader self-described agenda was to save America from its decline into immorality and godlessness. Closely partnered with many Protestant churches, this voluntary association marched to the racially charged "Onward Christian Soldiers" as it placed well-publicized financial offerings on church alters. The Klan also lobbied state and local government to enforce prohibition, police adultery and sexual promiscuity, and raise Protestantism to a central place in public life. Most Klan members were every-day Hoosiers, including businessmen, lawyers, doctors, church-women, and Protestant ministers. Some of the same people active in other benevolent causes joined the Klan.[22]

By the 1920s organized and systematic philanthropy was becoming the norm in Indiana cities. There was still space for churches, small voluntary associations, and individual assistance, especially in small towns and rural areas, but professional so-cial workers employed by formal agencies were increasingly ac-tive. Most welfare and other philanthropic organizations were directed by a board composed of business and community lead-ers. Often an interlocking network of such leaders directed new Community Chests and foundations, such as the Indianapolis Foundation. Most preferred private rather than public charity, with minimal government intrusion. As late as 1939, for example, nongovernmental agencies employed over half the public health nurses in the state.[23]

This Indiana way of philanthropy was tested by the Great De-pression. The 1930s challenged traditional notions of individualism, self-reliance, and small government. By 1932 some communities faced unemployment rates above 25 percent. Breadlines and soup kitchens increased service, but the state's networks of private chari-ties were plainly unable to meet minimal needs. In Fort Wayne one anxious citizen predicted that "the time is not far distant when we are going to be confronted with riots and violence."[24] Occasionally, there were panicked choices later regretted. One was the Mexican-American repatriation in Lake County. The local American Legion post and Community Chest joined the township trustee to assist unemployed Mexican-Americans to move to Mexico. Initially the migration was voluntary, but by 1932 it had become forced, as officials rounded up families and put them on trains heading south. In Johnson County, problems of unemployment caused some to talk of sterilization of those judged unfit.[25]

Across the state, neither private nor public welfare was up to the challenge of the Great Depression. State and local government welfare in 1932 meant mostly the township trustee, one of the best examples of the Indiana tradition of small government. Trustees were locally elected and served with minimal oversight. They were close to the people and claimed to know from personal experience those worthy and unworthy of assistance.

A new governor took office in 1933. Paul V. McNutt called on Hoosiers to "prove that government may be a great instrument of human progress."[26] McNutt set out to eliminate township trustees and Indiana's antiquated welfare system. He increased state and federal assistance and instituted more professional approaches to social welfare. The New Deal in Indiana and the nation stimulated significant change but not a revolution. Private and public aid continued to mix as Hoosiers resisted state and federal welfare programs long after the New Deal. The blurred lines remained, perhaps even intensified, with the faith-based programs encouraged by federal policies in the 1990s and early twenty-first century. And township trustees continued a role in welfare into the current century in spite of an effort by Governor Mitch Daniels to eliminate them.[27]

In health care and housing, Hoosiers remained reluctant to engage with federal programs, aggressively so in the 1950s when Senator William Jenner harshly attacked federal intrusion. Indiana continued its close attachment to private philanthropy, voluntary associations, and partnerships among philanthropy, business, and government. A prime example was the Greater Indianapolis Progress Committee, which began in 1964 to push immense changes in the capital city.[28]

There were always individual philanthropists. Calvin Fletcher in the mid-nineteenth century had his hand, and dollars, in just about every good project in Indianapolis. Later Colonel Eli Lilly embarked on lifting up the city. His son and especially his eldest grandson, Eli Lilly, continued the family tradition.

Eli Lilly (1885–1977) deserves a special mention. Dozens of institutions in Indiana thrive because of his philanthropy. He led in the creation of Lilly Endowment Inc. in 1937 and oversaw it until his death in 1977. The endowment very much reflected his particular understanding of philanthropy, an understanding that fit firmly with Indiana's traditions. His legacy extends, for example, to today's community foundations, thriving in all Indiana counties as they seek to improve the quality of work, education, and culture. Among Eli Lilly's many interests was his Episcopal church, Christ Church on the Circle. In 1957 Lilly led the hiring of Paul Moore as the new dean and rector. With the enthusiastic support of his wealthiest parishioner, Moore soon began a program of social action that extended to African Americans. Here was an unusual crossing of the color line, blended with Indiana's tradition of religious action.[29]

Other individual philanthropists have blessed Indiana, for instance Ian Rolland in Fort Wayne, Richard Ford in Wabash, J. Irvin Miller in Columbus, and Bill and Gayle Cook in Bloomington. And there have always been uncounted numbers of little-known philanthropists who have given gifts of time and talent as well as money. Even Indiana's most notable public philanthropists seldom gave only their money. Most, like Eli Lilly, engaged their intellects and their passions as they created, built, and led their communities upward toward their understanding of public good.

Indiana's two hundred years show a long tradition of philanthropy that sparked action, beginning with religious belief. From 1816 too was a belief in individual freedom and self-help, which has sometimes been a double-edged sword, opening up innovation and opportunity but also impeding action. Another bedrock tradition is distrust of government, which persists into the twenty-first century. Many Hoosiers long believed that only the worthy poor deserved help, although few Hoosiers remained enamored with eugenics. At times even children have been treated as unworthy poor as reflected in reluctance to expand public health care and education opportunities for all. Indiana's strong commitment to small government and low taxes created greater space for private resourcefulness even as private initiatives partnered with government.

In recent years a new challenge has emerged as Hoosiers seem to be drifting toward two Indianas. The first Indiana is well off, the second struggling. The poorer Indiana has lagged further and further behind in jobs, schools, libraries, art, social services, and community cohesion—even craft breweries. Here may be the largest policy issue facing Hoosier philanthropy in the twenty-first century.[30]

Once upon a time, there was one Indiana, albeit with racial and gender differences. A century ago small towns were not much different from Indianapolis. The ninety-two county seats buzzed with retail stores and offices, chiming bells from First Methodist and other churches off the square, and, farther from downtown, the smoke of new factories. And there were engaged citizens—businessmen, doctors, lawyers, schoolteachers, Rotary Club presidents, and others who cared deeply about their community. Many men and even larger numbers of women volunteered. They invested in their community's future. The late twentieth century brought a waning of this tradition, especially in the second Indiana.

Some may think that those in the first Indiana can thrive without the rest of the state, that they can pick what they need in the way of low-cost labor and tax revenues, pull out the talented few, and transition toward a colonial mother country relationship. They are very likely wrong.

It is good that sprinkled across the old Indiana are islands of light. Warsaw provides one bright spot, Jasper and Columbus others, as do the Japanese auto factories booming where cornfields once stood. Signs of revitalization in towns like Kokomo and South Bend offer hope. Our community foundations do superb work, capturing some of the best Hoosier traditions. But too many places are not contenders for the varsity basketball team. Some are not even sure which end of the court is theirs to score.

One tradition that endures for Indiana is a rich sense of place. The state's people share an identity as Hoosiers, built on a two-hundred-year history. They can see themselves as part of an imagined community of citizens with obligations to each other and the common good. That sense of community is our past, our present, and our hope for the future.[31]

NOTES

1. General contexts are in James H. Madison, *Hoosiers: A New History of Indiana* (Bloomington and Indianapolis: Indiana University Press and Indiana Historical Society Press, 2014).

2. Charles Kettleborough, *Constitution Making in Indiana: A Source Book of Constitutional Documents with Historical Introduction and Critical Notes*, vol. I (Indianapolis: Indiana Historical Commission, 1916), 114.

3. William E. Bartelt, *"There I grew up": Remembering Abraham Lincoln's Indiana Youth* (Indianapolis: Indiana Historical Society Press, 2008), 1.

4. L. C. Rudolph, *Hoosier Faiths: A History of Indiana Churches & Religious Groups* (Bloomington: Indiana University Press, 1995).

5. Donald F. Carmony and Josephine M. Elliott, "New Harmony, Indiana: Robert Owen's Seedbed for Utopia," *Indiana Magazine of History* 76 (September 1980): 161–261; Robert M. Taylor, "The Light of Reason: Hoosier Freethought and the Indiana Rationalist Association, 1909–1913," *Indiana Magazine of History* 79 (June 1983): 109–32.

6. Aaron Wood, *Sketches of Things and People in Indiana* (Indianapolis: J.M. Olcott, 1883), 36.

7. Bernard W. Sheehan, *Seeds of Extinction: Jeffersonian Philanthropy and the American Indian* (Chapel Hill: University of North Carolina Press, 1973).

8. Rudolph, *Hoosier Faiths*, 128.

9. Timothy L. Smith, "Uncommon Schools: Christian Colleges and Social Idealism in Midwestern America, 1820–1950," in *Indiana Historical Society Lectures* (Indianapolis, 1979), 2–72.

10. Scott Walter, "'Awakening the Public Mind': The Dissemination of the Common School Idea in Indiana, 1787–1852," in William J. Reese, ed., *Hoosier Schools: Past and Present* (Bloomington: Indiana University Press, 1998), 1–28; Madison, *Hoosiers*, 113–14.

11. Grover L. Hartman, "The Hoosier Sunday School: A Potent Religious/Cultural Force," *Indiana Magazine of History* 78 (September 1982): 215–41.

12. Clifton J. Phillips, *Indiana in Transition: The Emergence of an Industrial Commonwealth, 1880–1920* (Indianapolis: Indiana Historical Bureau and Indiana Historical Society, 1968).

13. Robert V. Robinson, "Making Ends Meet: Wives and Children in the Family Economy of Indianapolis, 1860–1920," *Indiana Magazine of History* 92 (September 1996): 197–234; Joan E. Marshall, "The Charity Organization Society and Poor Relief for the Able-Bodied Unemployed: Lafayette, Indiana, 1905–1910," *Indiana Magazine of History* 93 (September 1997): 217–43; Milton Gaither, "The Rise and Fall of a Pedagogical Empire: The Board of State Charities and the Indiana Philosophy of Giving," *Indiana Magazine of History* 96 (December 2000): 336–46.

14. Genevieve C. Weeks, *Oscar Carleton McCulloch, 1843–1891: Preacher and Practitioner of Applied Christianity* (Indianapolis: Indiana Historical Society, 1976); Elsa F. Kramer, "Recasting the Tribe of Ishmael: The Role of Indianapolis's Nineteenth-Century Poor in Twentieth-Century Eugenics," *Indiana Magazine of History* 104 (March 2008): 36–64; Brian Siegel, "Tales of the Tribe of Ishmael: A Research Note," *Indiana Magazine of History* 106 (June 2010): 189–96; Brent Ruswick, *Almost Worthy: The Poor, Paupers, and the Science of Charity in America, 1877–1917* (Bloomington: Indiana University Press, 2013); Brent Ruswick, "The Measure of Worthiness: The Rev. Oscar McCulloch and the Pauper Problem, 1877–1891," *Indiana Magazine of History* 104 (March 2008): 3–35.

15. A starting point for this and other Indianapolis subjects is David J. Bodenhamer and Robert G. Barrows, eds., *The Encyclopedia of Indianapolis* (Bloomington: Indiana University Press, 1994).

16. Robert G. Barrows, *Albion Fellows Bacon: Indiana's Municipal Housekeeper* (Bloomington: Indiana University Press, 2000); Jennifer Burek Pierce, "Indiana's Public Health Pioneer and History's Iron Pen:

Recollecting the Professional Idealism of John N. Hurty, 1896–1925," *Indiana Magazine of History* 106 (September 2010): 224–45.

17. Ruth Hutchinson Crocker, "Christamore: An Indiana Settlement House from Private Dream to Public Agency," *Indiana Magazine of History* 83 (June 1987): 113–40; Mina J. Carson, "Agnes Hamilton of Fort Wayne: The Education of a Christian Settlement Worker," *Indiana Magazine of History*, 80 (March 1984): 1–34.

18. James H. Madison, "Race, Law, and the Burdens of Indiana History," in David J. Bodenhamer and Randall T. Shepard, eds., *The History of Indiana Law* (Athens: Ohio University Press, 2006), 41–43; Earline Rae Ferguson, "The Woman's Improvement Club of Indianapolis: Black Women Pioneers in Tuberculosis Work, 1903–1938," *Indiana Magazine of History* 84 (September 1988): 237–61.

19. Thomas W. Cowger, "Custodians of Social Justice: The Indianapolis Asylum for Friendless Colored Children, 1870–1922," *Indiana Magazine of History* 88 (June 1992): 93–110; Ellen D. Swain, "From Benevolence to Reform: The Expanding Career of Mrs. Rhoda M. Coffin," *Indiana Magazine of History*, 97 (September 2001): 190–217.

20. Robert M. Taylor Jr. and Connie A. McBirney, eds., *Peopling Indiana: The Ethnic Experience* (Indianapolis: Indiana Historical Society, 1996); Eva Mendieta, "Celebrating Mexican Culture and Lending a Helping Hand: Indiana Harbor's sociedad Mutualista Benito Juárez, 1924–1957," *Indiana Magazine of History* 108 (December 2012): 311–44; Judith E. Endelman, *The Jewish Community of Indianapolis: 1849 to the Present* (Bloomington; Indiana University Press, 1984); Richard Moss, "Creating a Jewish American Identity in Indianapolis: The Jewish Welfare Federation and the Regulation of Leisure, 1920–1934," *Indiana Magazine of History* 103 (March 2007): 39–65.

21. Alexandra Minna Stern, "'We Cannot Make a Silk Purse out of a Sow's Ear': Eugenics in the Hoosier Heartland," *Indiana Magazine of History* 103 (March 2007): 3–38; Alexandra Minna Stern, "Improving Hoosiers: Indiana and the Wide Scope of American Eugenics," *Indiana Magazine of History* 106 (September 2010): 219–23; Kendra Clauser-Roemer, "'What Indiana Can Do': The Influence of Female Field Workers on the Indiana Committee on Mental Defectives, 1915–1924," *Indiana Magazine of History* 106 (September 2010): 246–71; Robert Osgood, "Education in the Name of 'Improvement': The Influence of Eugenic Thought and Practice in Indiana's Public Schools, 1900–1930," *Indiana Magazine of History* 106 (September 2010): 272–99.

22. Madison, *Hoosiers*, 234–53; Leonard J. Moore, *Citizen Klansmen: The Ku Klux Klan in Indiana, 1921–1928* (Chapel Hill: University of North Carolina Press, 1991); Allen Safianow, "The Klan Comes to Tipton," *Indiana Magazine of History* 95 (September 1999): 203–31; Safianow, "'You Can't Burn History': Getting Right with the Klan in Noblesville, Indiana," *Indiana Magazine of History* 100 (June 2004): 109–54.

23. Bradford Sample, "A Truly Midwestern City: Indianapolis on the Eve of the Great Depression," *Indiana Magazine of History* 97 (June 2001): 129–47.

24. James H. Madison, *Indiana through Tradition and Change: A History of the Hoosier State and Its People, 1920–1945* (Indianapolis: Indiana Historical Society, 1982), 105.

25. Robert S. and Helen Merrell Lynd, *Middletown in Transition: A Study in Cultural Conflicts* (New York: Harcourt, Brace, and World, 1937), 102–43; Francisco Arturo Roslaes and Daniel T. Simon, "Mexican Immigrant Experience in the Urban Midwest: East Chicago, Indiana, 1919–1945," *Indiana Magazine of History* 77 (December 1981): 333–57; Chad Berry, *Southern Migrants, Northern Exiles* (Urbana: University of Illinois Press, 2000), 31–81.

26. Madison, *Hoosiers*, 254.

27. Dean J. Kotlowski, *Paul V. McNutt and the Age of FDR* (Bloomington: Indiana University Press, 2015), 127–201; Robert G. Barrows, "The Local Origins of a New Deal Housing Project: The Case of Lockefield Gardens in Indianapolis," *Indiana Magazine of History* 103 (June 2007): 125–51; Mary L. Mapes, *A Public Charity: Religion and Social Welfare In Indianapolis, 1929–2002* (Bloomington: Indiana University Press, 2004); Indiana Commission on Local Government Reform, *Streamlining Local Government* (Indianapolis: Indiana University Center for Urban Policy and the Environment, 2007).

28. Kathi Badertscher, "A New Wishard Is on the Way," *Indiana Magazine of History* 108 (December 2012): 345–82.

29. James H. Madison, *Eli Lilly: A Life, 1885–1977* (Indianapolis: Indiana Historical Society, 1988).

30. James H. Madison, "Drifting toward Two Indianas?" *BizVoice: Indiana Chamber*, January/February 2015, 14.

31. *The Bicentennial Visioning Project: A Collection of Big Ideas for Indiana's Future* (Indiana Bicentennial Commission: Indianapolis, 2016). Document available at https://www.in.gov/ibc/files/BicentennialBookWEB posting.pdf.

RELIGION AND PHILANTHROPY

Indiana's Traditions

DAVID P. KING

SURVEYING THE INDIANA LANDSCAPE DEMONSTRATES
the pervasiveness of religious institutions throughout the state.
By the latter nineteenth century, spires of five of the most prominent Protestant churches rose above all other buildings located
on Monument Circle in the heart of downtown Indianapolis.
Most other religious communities located their buildings within
a few blocks of the circle.[1] Religion was literally at the center of
the city and at the geographic and symbolic center of the state.
To be clear, all congregations were not represented. Indiana's
religious establishment was a White Protestant one defined primarily by denominations such as Methodists, Presbyterians,
Disciples, Lutherans, and Episcopalians. Evangelical revivalists
played a significant (and growing) role as did large minority traditions, such as the Roman Catholics and a firmly established
albeit small Jewish community. Yet, there could be no mistake
that this Protestant mainstream served as a religious establishment comfortable not only among coreligionists but also among
the influential voices shaping the political, commercial, and philanthropic establishments. The churches surrounding Monument
Circle helped to define Indianapolis, but similar landscapes depicted much of Indiana. In tiny towns and county seats, religious

49

congregations have often continued to serve as leading civic, social, and philanthropic community agents.

The history of religious philanthropy in Indiana at times illustrates and at other times initiates larger trends in philanthropy.
Congregations and the numerous religious institutions they
spawned (denominations, mission societies, ecumenical groups,
and charitable agencies) remain at the heart of religious philanthropy. Yet, religious philanthropy in the Hoosier state has also
had its major benefactors. The full history cannot be told without
the stories of Episcopalian Eli Lilly and the growth of Lilly Endowment Inc.; Cummins Engine CEO and Disciples of Christ layman
J. Irwin Miller; or Jewish leader and Indianapolis businessman
G. A. Efroymson. Yet, most often religious philanthropy highlights the mass philanthropy of individual citizens and their gifts
to local faith communities. The interplay between major and mass
philanthropy is one story to highlight in Hoosier philanthropy.

Another theme is the role of religious institutions as both
recipient and agent of philanthropy. Up until the late 1980s, charitable giving to congregations made up over half of all Americans' philanthropy. Congregational and denominational giving
remains at 28 percent of Americans' giving in 2020. Beyond the
philanthropic gifts that remain within congregations to support
internal religious practices—such as worship and faith formation—a significant (but unknown) portion of these funds are
also passed on to social services, education, and various philanthropic causes.[2] People of faith are also led to give out of
religious motivations to causes and organizations outside of their
faith communities or houses of worship. The story of Hoosiers'
religious philanthropy must be told not only by examining what
comes to religious institutions but also by attending to the when,
why, and how these religious traditions and their many adherents
have engaged their broader communities.

Of course, the full philanthropic impact of religious communities goes far beyond finances. When considering service,

volunteering, advocacy, sharing communal resources, and cultivating a civil society, religious actors and institutions become even more significant. They provide the preponderance of volunteer hours, develop community leaders, and often serve as central gathering spaces for voting precincts, neighborhood associations, Boy Scout troops or Alcoholic Anonymous meetings. Faith remains the motivating factor for the volunteering and civic engagement of many Americans, and their diverse religious institutions often serve as the avenue through which they demonstrate their motivation and engagement.

In the past, religious actors often found themselves at the center of debates over philanthropy's purpose. Was philanthropy primarily meant to take care of those within one's own community (most often defined by culture or religion) or was it to serve the larger society? Questions of who should help whom, whom should one help first, and what were the boundaries around one's giving often defined religious giving in Indiana. Even the proper terms were up for grabs: Should *charity* be abandoned for professionalized *philanthropy*? Questions of the role of philanthropy also often followed: Was philanthropy simply to provide for basic needs or promote institutional change? Should religious giving seek to develop an individual's character and shape the morality of society, or were such purposes off limits in respecting individual agency and a pluralist society?

Most of Indiana's religious philanthropy was local—supporting individuals and institutions in their own neighborhoods and cities. It sometimes provided opportunities for cooperation among religious communities. Engaging across theological, economic, or political lines allowed Hoosiers to work together in promoting communal benevolence, support for America's wars, or civil rights. Religious philanthropy promoted common values, but at times, it also fostered deeper divisions. Sometimes, such philanthropy led to fierce competition as various traditions duplicated services, fought with one another over control or market share, and even used philanthropy to compare themselves to one another for recognition and prestige. Yet, philanthropy also served to expand the vision of local Hoosiers. Supporting international missionaries, raising animals to ship to those in need overseas, supporting troops, working for peace, or supporting the nation of Israel brought various communities of religious Hoosiers together with their fellow faithful across the United States while also serving as Indiana's window to the world.

Focusing on philanthropy broadens our histories. While the focus might be on the wealthy philanthropic corporate titan or the clergy leading religious communities, it also cannot ignore the women who continue to make up the majority of attenders and volunteers in religious communities. Perhaps the majority of religious philanthropy remains hidden, unnoticed by fellow citizens much less historians. Indiana's religious philanthropy has accomplished great good even if it occasionally promoted distasteful actions. Across history and a broad religious spectrum, however, religious philanthropy has always remained a vital part of the state's civil society.

RELIGIOUS HOOSIERS

In many ways, the religious makeup of Indiana exemplifies much of the Midwest with a few exceptions. Christians predominate (72 percent), and the majority of those are Protestant. Within that Protestant majority, however, a multitude of diverse traditions operate. Today 31 percent of Hoosiers identity as evangelical Protestants, while 16 percent belong to denominations defined as mainline Protestants. Hoosiers are more evangelical than their midwestern neighbors (averaging 26 percent) and fall only slightly behind their Southern neighbors (averaging 34 percent). Five percent are members of historically Black Protestant churches. Eighteen percent of Hoosiers are Catholic. Jews represent 1 percent of the population and other religious traditions are each less than 1 percent. These numbers have remained relatively steady throughout the state's history with the exception of the Protestant mainstream fracturing into differentiated evangelical and mainline contingents.[3]

Indiana's tongue-in-cheek reputation as the southernmost midwestern state has some truth when comparing its religious demographics. Indiana is also atypical from its midwestern neighbors (Indianapolis in particular) in the size of its Catholic population. While Catholics make up half or more of the church-going population in Cincinnati or Chicago, in Indianapolis that number is only slightly over 20 percent. From the beginning, Indiana has been home to the major Protestant denominations, most of which now identify as mainline. Baptists, Presbyterians, and Methodists (Black and White) were first. Disciples, Lutherans, and Episcopalians arrived later. While small, other groups also found a home in Indiana in larger proportions than elsewhere in the nation, such as the Quakers, Mennonites, and Church of the Brethren. Indiana experienced immigration and migration, but it never saw a significant influx of ethnic communities that seriously shaped its religious landscape like several other neighboring states, especially in the Northeast and West.[4] Even as particular religious and ethnic communities did form, there simply were not enough German Lutherans, Irish Catholics, or Scotch-Irish Presbyterians to sway Hoosier's religious culture in any particular direction. Instead, a patchwork quilt of religious communities emerged over time to undergird and sometimes challenge the broader Protestant consensus.

Of course, many Hoosiers did not affiliate with or attend any religious community, but the business and political elite most often did. These White Protestant mores often defined Indiana's civic life and much of its philanthropy. Yet, the influence of this Protestant mainstream establishment also evolved over time. In the second half of the twentieth century, evangelicals who often became defined less by denominational affiliation and more through independent churches or loose networks have not only grown in numbers but also in wealth, popularity, and public influence. While a Protestant mainstream may still hold, evangelicals and mainline Protestants share the limelight today. At the same time, throughout Indiana's history, large minority traditions, such as Roman Catholics, have been influential first in funding and operating institutions parallel to those of the Protestant establishment (such as schools, social services, and hospitals) and expanding their influence to integrate these institutions into the larger fabric of the community. As a much smaller minority, the Jewish community has similarly funded and built institutions that demonstrate not only self-care for fellow Jews but also their significant philanthropic and civic roles in the larger community. How these majority and minority religious traditions supported themselves, engaged one another, and saw their roles in shaping their larger communities is a significant story amid the landscape of Indiana's religious philanthropy.

RELIGIOUS PIONEERS

In Indiana's pioneer years, religious philanthropy often became a key tool in taming the wilderness, building community, and shaping a moral civil society. Many of the established East Coast traditions sent missionaries to convert the Native Americans and bring order and faith to the new settlers. The Presbyterians stood out as an example, sending over three hundred fully funded missionaries and ministers to Indiana. Henry Ward Beecher, one of the first ministers of the Second Presbyterian Church in Indianapolis and a member of one of the most well-known religious families in America, was just one of these missionary ministers. Leaving Indiana to take the pastorate of the Plymouth Congregational Church in Brooklyn, New York, Beecher would later become one of the most prominent ministers in the nation, but first he sought his calling in taming the wilderness by bringing civilizing agencies of morality and social order to the Hoosier state. In a series of lectures delivered in 1843 and 1844 and later published as *Seven Lectures to Young Men*, Beecher lamented the temptations that faced young men in the city and urged churches to take up the responsibility of rooting out evil in society.[5]

While some ministers and missionaries came with intentions of taming the Indiana wilderness with moral instruction and institutions, others simply brought a white-hot gospel. Camp meetings—long-lasting open-air revivals—were the social event of the season for many on the frontier. With limited options, Hoosiers would gather to hear whatever revivalist was passing through—Methodist, Baptist, or Disciples. As these traditions took root in the Indiana soil, revival often mixed with reform, and the voluntary agencies that formed often initiated much of the philanthropy and institutions that emerged.

One example of early religious philanthropy was education. The American Bible and Tract Societies brought cheap Bibles, books, and tracts to Hoosiers, who often had little access to religious reading material. Sunday schools appeared in Indiana by 1810, bringing both Christianity and education to the frontier. Before there was public education, these Sunday schools founded and funded by clergy and lay men and women served as the only outlet for learning. This soon expanded to a number of religious colleges. All of Indiana's earliest colleges had ties to religious denominations: Hanover, Wabash, Indiana Asbury (DePauw), Franklin, Earlham, Notre Dame, Butler, and even Indiana University itself. As the state sought to develop public education, religious advocates often served to prod the state to take action. Many of these early philanthropic leaders preached that access to education was a civic, moral, and religious good.[6]

Pioneer religious philanthropy was not only tied to education; it often worked to shape a culture toward reform through many volunteer hours. While Protestants sought to regulate plenty of behaviors, the temperance movement served to unite them the most. Religious Hoosiers spent significant money, time, and influence in the 1830s and 1840s urging sobriety, or at least the curbing of overindulgence. Issues such as temperance demonstrated the leading role that Protestants could play in shaping society (often at the expense of Catholics or other religious minorities). By the mid-nineteenth century, despite continued competition, a shared evangelical Protestant culture emerged as the religious establishment in Indiana. As reform movements, philanthropic giving, and institution building continued, this Protestant ethos often defined the issues at hand.

On some particular issues, the Protestant establishment avoided consensus. One of the most pressing issues of the nineteenth century was abolition. Few Hoosiers actively defended the institution of slavery, but even fewer worked aggressively to promote abolition. Most often, the Protestant establishment simply avoided the issue and their complicit role in it. The exception was Indiana's relatively significant Quaker population. While never large, the number of Quakers in areas of the state, such as Richmond, was larger than many other parts of the country, and they were influential in those communities. At certain points in Indiana history, their size allowed them to function on the edge of the Protestant establishment. Differences of opinion existed on abolition even within the Society of Friends, but a number of Quakers worked to support the Underground Railroad in the state and raise support for abolition. They also worked for prison reform and other progressive causes. Hoosiers often trailed the significant philanthropic impulses that defined religious philanthropy in many parts of the North during the 1840s and 1850s; the Quakers served as an exception.[7]

Well outside the religious establishment were Indiana's nineteenth-century utopian communities. Those who settled in New Harmony often brought new economic models to the frontier. The original Harmonists, or Rappittes, turned their farm into the most successful economic enterprise in Indiana and shared these resources among their egalitarian community but rarely did their profits spill over to their neighbors. As they left Indiana by 1824, another community, the Owenites, moved in. They sought to build a community to uplift humanity and share all resources equally. Their community failed financially, but it attracted a number of intellectuals who left their impact on the state. They arrived with their founder, Robert Owen, after sailing down the Wabash in their boat, the *Philanthropist*. While their community was short-lived, they left legacies in education, reform, and even financial resources. At his death, Owenite William Maclure left money to support 144 workingmen's libraries throughout the state.[8]

ESTABLISHING MASS RELIGIOUS PHILANTHROPY

These exceptions aside, an Anglo-Protestant establishment came to define religious philanthropy even more in the latter half of the nineteenth and early twentieth century as Indiana moved beyond its pioneer beginnings. As the state reached its first centennial celebration, its philanthropic and charitable institutions were well established, even as they began to undergo change.

The congregation became the primary charitable outlet for a majority of Hoosiers, both to give and receive aid. Scholars have often debated the true philanthropic impact of giving to congregations. Some resist considering congregational giving as philanthropic and claim that it most often benefits those within the community and should be considered more like membership dues than philanthropy. Others disagree wholeheartedly and point to the significant outlay of philanthropic support congregations offer outside their own walls, both through funds given and hours volunteered. In sociologist Ram Cnaan's late-twentieth-century study of historic urban churches in Indianapolis, he calculated that each congregation contributed an average of $144,000 into the local community in cash and services.

Congregations specifically budgeted an average of $33,000 in actual cash for community work. Based on the number of estimated congregations in Marion County at the time of Cnaan's study in 1997, this comprised almost $20 million. And the number of congregations and their investments in Indiana has continued to grow over the past two decades.[9] These resources perhaps represent only a small percentage of the funds that local, state, and federal governments invested in social services, but it does demonstrate the community investment of the majority of local congregations. The data also reinforces the impact of religious philanthropy throughout history. Individuals in congregations are most often the lifeblood of religious philanthropy even as they spawn various auxiliaries, nonprofits, federations, denominations, and ecumenical groups. As congregations evolved over time, relocated as neighborhoods changed, and even migrated to the suburbs, they continued to shape the way in which religious philanthropy was delivered. Congregations were never simply independent institutions. They operated in a larger ecology of voluntary agencies and communities. Individuals helped one another through informal aid; women's auxiliaries provided food, blankets, or funding for the local children's hospital; and local civic groups met in church basements.

It is true that this chapter may overemphasize the impact of urban philanthropy in the state and it may also overprivilege the capital, Indianapolis; however, Indianapolis serves as a good test case. As opposed to America's largest metropolises, twice as many Americans live in cities of populations between two hundred and fifty thousand and one million as those in populations over one million. More and more Americans have moved from rural farms and small towns to cities and their suburbs.[10]

In Indianapolis in the late nineteenth century, a number of faith-based organizations joined congregations to address what they often referred to as "urban ills." One of these first additions was the Young Men's Christian Association (YMCA). Coming to

Indianapolis in 1854, this Protestant institution gave newcomers a place to eat and sleep, accompanied with job training, religious instruction, and moral guidance. Another model of urban religious philanthropy was the Salvation Army, which has provided food, clothing, shelter, and religious guidance to the destitute in Indianapolis since 1889. As both church and charity, the Salvation Army saw conversion as the highest form of philanthropy. For the army, saving souls often led to reformed lives. Similarly, a few years later in 1893, William Wheeler opened an unpretentious rescue mission that housed and fed men in need. It continues to operate today as the Wheeler Mission serving meals and providing shelter and job training to the unhoused of Indianapolis.

These religious charities largely sought to take care of basic needs. Fraternal societies followed suit but more from the perspective of mutual aid. As historian David Beito has noted, by the early twentieth century "more Americans belonged to fraternal societies than any other kind of voluntary association, with the possible exception of churches."[11] For African Americans migrating northward from the South and ethnic immigrant communities, it was most common to rely on mutual aid to take care of their own. In 1867, immigrants from the German Zion Evangelical Church founded the German Protestant Orphan Home. A few decades later, in 1883, a mutual Bible society of St. Paul and Trinity Lutheran churches founded Lutheran Child and Family Services with the mission "of asylum for orphans and aged people" in their community.[12] Among ethnic and religious minorities, such as Catholics and Jewish communities, throughout the state, formal diocesan efforts and more informal mutual aid societies serviced those within their own communities.

At the same time, however, the Protestant consensus developed a broader network of community philanthropy. Founded in 1835, the Indianapolis Benevolent Society (IBS) sought to meet the temporary needs of individual Hoosiers. While not church-based per se, Protestant elders and religious communities served as the agents gathering the resources and volunteers to provide clothing, firewood, and money to assist strangers "down on their luck." This sentimental approach continued through much of the nineteenth century until the emergence of "scientific philanthropy," which infiltrated the models of traditional charity. Scientific philanthropy condemned traditional almsgiving as haphazard and destructive. Instead, it said philanthropy should be strategic, working for societal change, and focusing on the deserving poor—those whose poverty was perceived as no fault of their own.

Too often histories have pitted scientific philanthropy against religious charity, but in fact, the two often worked in concert with one another.[13] The social gospel was not only a ripe theological movement in the late nineteenth and early twentieth century with prominent national personalities such as Washington Gladden and Walter Rauschenbusch but it also had enormous impact at the local level on the practice of institutions focused on the broad social dimensions of Christianity. Most often social gospelers were leading advocates for the changes proposed by scientific philanthropy. They felt it was more Christian to help individuals break their patterns of dependence than continually alleviate reoccurring need. Such was the case in Indiana.

In 1877, Oscar McCulloch came to Indianapolis to pastor Plymouth Congregational Church. With his own social gospel leanings, he was keen to shepherd his church and the city's charitable institutions in new directions. McCulloch convinced the IBS they should reorganize relief away from the "merely sentimental stage of alleviating want without question, into the scientific method of reformation and prevention."[14] The result was a reorganized benevolent society, renamed the Charitable Organization Society (COS) in 1879 and emerging with a new mission. Instead of distributing resources indiscriminately to those in need, professionals were now assigned cases to investigate, determine need, and coordinate any assistance with local agencies. Rev. McCulloch served as president of COS from 1882 until his death in 1891 and even received national attention as the president of the National Conference of Charities and Correction in 1890. While such approaches led McCulloch toward embracing eugenic models popular for a time that skewed who he determined was worthy of help, his impact was felt throughout Hoosier philanthropy—from his religious reasons for scientific philanthropy to his support for federated fundraising. The COS served as one precursor to the Community Chest and United Way of Central Indiana.[15]

McCulloch's approach modeled a growing trend in religious philanthropy that also saw a transition from pastors to professionals as new fields such as social work developed. Indianapolis's Christamore House serves as just one example. An early settlement house begun in 1905 by two local women trained at Chicago's evangelical Moody Bible Institute, the early settlement house soon became a "sociological laboratory" for social work students from Butler and Indiana University after the founders resigned in 1911 and the religious ethos disappeared.[16] Likewise, the Flower Mission began in 1876 as a Christian women's group to brighten the days of patients in City Hospital with fresh-cut flowers. It soon professionalized to sponsor a long-term medical facility treating tuberculosis, raise funds for the Eleanor Hospital for Sick Children, and a training school for nurses.[17] Women's auxiliaries and Sunday school classes from many local churches often supported these social ministries with their time and money. As the benevolent societies, settlement houses, and local ministries they supported evolved, their own understandings of charity often evolved as well.

Of course, not all religious actors bought into either scientific philanthropy or federated community philanthropic institutions. Few churches shuttered their charitable ministries in order to send all funds to the COS with its efforts to eliminate dependency by distributing only to the deserving poor. Most often religious philanthropy was a patchwork of multiple approaches. Many local congregations felt compelled to continue direct support. Rescue missions fretted that scientific philanthropy sacrificed saving souls for social Christianity. Ethnic and religious minorities still found it necessary to take care of their own. Others did not care to give up their own religious identity to a single communal organization.

Through the early twentieth century, however, support grew among Protestants for more formally united institutions. Founded in 1912, the Church Federation of Indianapolis was a lay-led association of the leading White Protestant churches that focused attention on the social and moral issues of the day. One of the first six church federations in the country, it soon developed a social service department to relate social agencies with congregations. While it first fought against declining public morality, by the 1920s, it became a leading advocate on race relations in the city. While its influence has declined today, for much of the early twentieth century, it served as a chief advocate and a united front for the Protestant consensus.[18] Other agencies followed the same trend. Church Women United brought together multiple philanthropic women's church groups at the turn of the century and gathered over fifteen hundred women together in Indianapolis by 1908 at its annual anniversary event.[19] Religious philanthropy sometimes served to bring disparate or competing communities together.

OUTSIDE THE PROTESTANT CONSENSUS

In the early twentieth century, not all religious communities had the option to join the religious mainstream. Religious philanthropy often illustrated the evolving boundaries between religious communities, government, and civil society. Even as the largest single religious tradition, Roman Catholics often found themselves outside of the Protestant consensus.

The prominence of the Ku Klux Klan in the 1920s and their influence within many White Protestant communities certainly did not help. Some pockets of southern Indiana, symbolized today by St. Meinrad Seminary and School of Theology, or northern Indiana surrounding South Bend and Notre Dame have maintained significant Catholic populations for many years, but they still function as minority traditions almost always creating parallel institutions alongside Protestant ones as they did throughout the United States. Local Catholic communities often came together through philanthropy to build the schools, hospitals, and orphanages that served Catholic populations throughout the state. Mutual aid served as a powerful fundraising tool. Unpaid labor of women religious often staffed these institutions by serving as school teachers, for instance at Indianapolis schools such as Ritter, Cathedral, and Brebeuf, or as nurses at the St Vincent Infirmary. Laymen came together in societies such as the Knights of Columbus to support these institutions.[20]

In 1919, Bishop Joseph Chartrand founded Catholic Community Center (forerunner to Catholic Social Services, CSS) to provide food and clothing for the poor and destitute. In the 1920s and 1930s, CSS added a home for unmarried mothers and children's foster care. As a charter member of the Indianapolis Community Chest, CSS received allotted funds "to take care of their own."[21] Through the traditional theology of subsidiarity, Catholics had no problem accepting federal or state support to provide such aid with professional expertise, but at the same time, they promoted the vital religious nature of their charity. In 1937, director of Catholic Charities Reverend August Fussenegger claimed the Catholic social worker was unique because she "brings the technical skills of the nonsectarian worker plus a deep sense of spiritual values. Here is a religious approach based on Catholic philosophy, principles and ideals."[22] In the second half of the twentieth century, CSS embodied the tensions of many religious nonprofits. As they grew in size, they professionalized and found less need to emphasize their unique Catholic identity. No longer did they simply serve the Catholic community but they grew to meet needs throughout the state without regard to religious or ethnic identity. Finally, as they saw their percentage of government funding rise, they faced questions internally and some criticism externally about how dependent they remained on the private philanthropy of their religious communities.

Albeit small, the Jewish community also served an important part of the history of religious philanthropy in Indiana. Jewish families had settled in river towns throughout Indiana by the 1840s. Enough Jews came together in Fort Wayne to organize their first congregation in 1848. Indiana Jews seemed to concentrate in urban centers with 80 percent of the population living in five cities: Indianapolis, Gary, South Bend, Fort Wayne, and Evansville. Indianapolis itself hosted 40 percent of the state's Jewish population. The Jewish community has remained steady at 1 percent of Indiana's population for much of the century, and from early on, they have often produced leading figures not only in their own religious community but in business and civic life. Entering the twentieth century, G. A. Efroymson served as the leading garment manufacturer in the capital city, and Sol Kiser was its leading banker. Both men served not only as community leaders in such organizations as the Indy Commercial Club (forerunner to the Chamber of Commerce) but also of their synagogues and the Jewish Federation.[23]

The earliest Jews to Indiana were Ashkenazi German immigrants in the Reform tradition. As they prospered in Indianapolis, they followed many others to the north side to settle. None other than Isaac Meyer Wise, leading American rabbi of the Reform movement, came to dedicate the Indianapolis Hebrew Congregation in 1868.[24] Like other religious minorities, the local Jews established parallel organizations to communal charities, such as the Indy Hebrew Benevolent society, the B'nai B'rith lodge for men, and the Hebrew Ladies Benevolent Society for women, to meet the needs of their community. As immigration to America increased dramatically at the turn of the century, Indiana's Jews agreed to help in resettling the overflow of immigrants arriving on the East Coast. Of Eastern European origin, more Orthodox in their religious practice, and often in much greater need of charitable support, these new immigrants settled on the more economically depressed south side.

In 1905, the established German Reform Jewish community created the Jewish Welfare Federation as one of the first Jewish Federations in the country with two main purposes: to "establish a unified method of fund raising" and "utilize the collected funds to support local and Jewish organizations dedicated to the relief of the deserving poor, the prevention of want and distress, the discouragement of pauperism, and the provision of education facilities for deserving Jews."[25] The immediate need was providing for many of these immigrants, and Jewish philanthropy continued the model of mutual aid by taking care of the needs of their own religious community; however, their approach began to follow the larger trends in evolving from traditional charity to scientific philanthropy. Morris Feuerlicht led the Reform synagogue, Indianapolis Hebrew Congregation, as head rabbi from 1907 to 1946. Following a generation after Hoosier social gospeler Oscar McCulloch, he served a similar role in the Jewish community. In drafting the federation's constitution, he focused Jewish giving less on traditional charity (or *tzedakah*, justice or aid for the poor in Jewish tradition) and more on systematic and institutional change.

The federation successfully raised support in its early years, but south-side Jews sometimes resented the professionalized philanthropy that they felt was forced upon them by the German Reform communities. They would rather leave coal or groceries on the doorstep of a neighbor in need rather than submit to interviews and case management of the Jewish federation. Even within the same religious tradition in the same town, approaches to religious philanthropy differed.[26]

As immigration largely stopped by the 1920s with anti-immigrant sentiment locally exemplified by the Klan and nationally through repressive federal legislation, the Jewish Federation transitioned from resettlement and meeting local social needs to resource the Jewish community more broadly at home and around the world. By the 1940s, the federation was supporting a number of constituent agencies: the Jewish Education Association, the Jewish Community Center, Jewish Social Services, Jewish Family and Children's Services, and the Hooverwood Home for the Aged, along with the newly formed Jewish Community Relations Council. With a centralized fundraising platform, the federation positioned itself as *the* institution providing support and structure for the local Jewish community. Many leading Jewish philanthropists appreciated having a single Jewish organization asking for their support, but the single ask came with the assumption that gifts to the federation's annual campaign were necessary to be a Jew in good standing in the community.

Much of these funds went to support the larger Jewish community in the United States and abroad through the United Jewish Appeal (ranging from 45 percent to 70 percent of the total funds raised).[27] Yet, in the 1950s and 1960s, there was also a renewal of interest in local synagogue membership across the country. The trend was particularly true in Indianapolis. By far the two largest congregations in town, Indianapolis Hebrew Congregation and Reconstructionist congregation Beth-EL Zedeck, both dedicated new temples in 1958. The new United Orthodox Hebrew Congregation opened in 1966. Fundraising goals for these new buildings were met quickly.[28] The federation was no longer the only primary outlet for Jewish philanthropy; local congregations also engaged in fundraising. A number of social causes have drawn the *tzedakah* of Jewish philanthropists. Like most religious communities, the options have grown as religious giving has diversified.

Indiana's Muslim community also serves as another significant story of minority religious philanthropy. The first Muslims in Indiana appeared to settle in Michigan City in 1914 with an early mosque present by the 1920s. While Indiana has a long history of Muslims in the state, they remain a small minority—under 1 percent of the state population. Only since the 1960s has the state exhibited multiple thriving local Muslim communities.[29]

The unique Indiana philanthropic story, however, is the growth of Plainfield, Indiana, as a hub of Islamic associations and the nation's most prominent service center for several million American Muslims. In 1976, the Islamic Society of North America (ISNA) bought 123 acres near Plainfield and developed the land to house the organization's headquarters and its partner associations, such as the Muslim Students Association (MSA). The MSA is an example of the philanthropic impulse of many similar associations that were founded to support the likes of American Muslim engineers, social scientists, and doctors. These associations were vital in supporting the faith of Muslims while helping them assimilate into the American system of voluntary societies. Today these associations have come together under one banner, ISNA, to claim the largest voice for American Muslims. ISNA's location just outside of Indianapolis has also bolstered other local Islamic institutions, such as mosques and Islamic schools. Religious philanthropy has served as an important factor in preserving distinct communities and traditions while also enabling newer Hoosier religious communities to assimilate into America's mainstream.[30]

Another smaller but significant group in Indiana were African American Christian communities. While sometimes the recipient of religious philanthropy, they were as often active givers too. Like the fraternal societies mentioned earlier, much of this came through self-help, often undocumented mutual aid, as individuals simply took care of neighbors. In more traditional charitable models, local churches often became the clearinghouse for providing aid to those in need in the surrounding community. Sometimes tall steeple churches stood out for their role in philanthropy and social action. As the oldest and arguably most prominent African American church in Indianapolis, Bethel AME (founded

1836) stood at the heart of the vibrant African American community on Indiana and Vermont Avenues. Known as a stopover on the Underground Railroad, it was the birthplace for the Indianapolis chapter of the National Association for the Advancement of Colored People (NAACP) and a public meeting space for the African American community.[31]

Beyond local churches, Indianapolis had vibrant African American chapters of the YMCA and YWCA, which illustrated community philanthropy. Founded in the late nineteenth century, the YMCA, and later YWCA, movement was infused with Christian social ethics that addressed increasing urbanization and ideals of masculinity and womanhood. The movement also often served as a training ground and network for local and national leaders.[32] In a segregated world, African American men initiated their own local Indianapolis Y branch in 1910 to accomplish enormous amounts of charitable work throughout the city. That same year, wealthy Sears, Roebuck and Co. businessman and renowned philanthropist Julius Rosenwald offered to contribute $25,000 to every African American YMCA able to secure $75,000 for their own building across the nation. Within ten days, local Y members in Indianapolis raised over $100,000, and Booker T. Washington made the trip to dedicate the resulting Senate Avenue YMCA in 1912. The Senate Avenue Y maintained the largest membership of any African American branch in the country for its first fifty years. Like Bethel AME, not only did it provide charity but it brought national voices to Indianapolis, such as W. E. B. DuBois, Adam Clayton Powell, and Thurgood Marshall.[33] African American women met similar fundraising success a few years later when they dedicated the Phyllis Wheatley YWCA in 1929. Both institutions later closed after the Ys officially fully integrated, but they modeled a number of African American religious institutions that shaped philanthropy and advocacy in Indiana.[34]

These institutions often served as forerunners of later organizations that embraced philanthropic ideals for civil rights. Reverend

Andrew J. Brown, pastor of St. John's Baptist Church in Indianapolis, fought for civil rights and against poverty as the chair of the local Southern Christian Leadership Conference (SCLC) in Indiana. Others across racial and religious lines sometimes joined in. To combat Indiana's handling of federal funding generated from President Lyndon B. Johnson's War on Poverty legislation, which simply sought to funnel additional resources into traditional social service providers without reconsidering approaches or inviting input from local communities, Christian clergy across denominational lines formed the Christian Inner City Association (CICA). The CICA president, twenty-six-year-old Miller Newton was the White minister at Fletcher Place Community Center.[35] While a general Protestant consensus still held among the business, government, and civic life in the state, at certain times issues such as poverty or race relations led groups to fund and focus their efforts to work against the establishment. Religious philanthropy often maintained the status quo, but sometimes philanthropic engagement worked to create change as well.

MAJOR RELIGIOUS PHILANTHROPY

While much of the focus has remained on the story of mass religious philanthropy, several major Hoosier philanthropists/ philanthropies figure prominently in the religious history. Lilly Endowment Inc. stands above all others. Founded in 1937 by Eli Lilly, his father, Josiah K. Lilly, and his brother Josiah K. Lilly, Jr. in order to continue their charitable commitments while retaining family control of their pharmaceutical company, Lilly Endowment Inc. (LEI) grew to become, and remains one of, the largest foundations in the country. By the 1950s, LEI was making grants totaling an average of $2 million each year. That grew to $50 million by the mid-1970s. In 2020, it made grants of $773.2 million. Of that number, $210.5 million went to religious projects both in and outside Indiana.[36]

Since the 1950s, LEI has formalized its key focus areas as education, community development, and religion. LEI is relatively unique among foundations in its continued high level of commitment to religion. Since its founding in 1937, it has contributed $3.1 billion to religious causes (26 percent of all Lilly Endowment Inc.'s philanthropy) and that total does not include the significant and long-term support of many of the state's religious-based liberal arts colleges or the funding of faith-based social agencies as a part of its education and community development grants.[37]

Eli Lilly himself was a man of deep faith. As an Episcopalian, he personally supported several Episcopal churches in Indianapolis and around the state as well as the local diocese. He was personally active in Christ Church and served as one of its chief benefactors in restoring the church building, assisting in its being named the diocesan cathedral, and stipulating it remain downtown. Today it is the only congregation left around Monument Circle.[38] As Eli Lilly initially operated the endowment out of his desk drawer, the foundation funded countless organizations, like local churches, the YMCA, and the Church Federation. Many other grantees were simply pet projects of Eli Lilly. Of particular importance to Lilly were religious education and character formation. He poured significant funding in these areas through multiple yearlong projects that were popular at the time but may not have yielded long-term return.[39]

As LEI grew, it professionalized and moved away from funding individual churches and Eli Lilly's personal causes to broader initiatives. While for a short period in the 1960s it became swayed by a particular conservative political and religious agenda, it rarely found itself in broadly controversial religious causes.[40] It often modeled the Protestant consensus, particularly the Protestant mainline tradition. While LEI invested in many initiatives, it may have had the greatest impact in cultivating religious leaders. LEI supported lay ministry as well, but there was a central focus on the work of the minister from his or her training through theological education, to their formation for work in the church or parish, to their effective leadership and care throughout their career. Funding theological schools, denominations, and sabbatical programs helped ensure the vitality of religious institutions. Only the religion division of LEI provided significant support for programs outside of Indiana, but it has not overlooked religious communities at home. Local ministers and religious institutions in the state continue to reap the benefits of local grant programs as the endowment continues to bolster the well-being of Indiana. As Lilly Endowment Inc. continues to leverage its resources and broaden its partnerships in an increasingly plural Christian and religious culture, the faith of its original donor guides its philanthropic motivations broadly, even as it undergirds its focused commitment to support religious causes directly.

Another major Hoosier philanthropist motivated by faith was J. Irwin Miller. As the head of Cummins Engines Company, Miller was one of the most successful businessmen in Indiana. He was also the grandson of two Disciples of Christ ministers. As a committed Disciples layman, his faith guided much of his philanthropy and social action. Miller reportedly gave away 35 percent of his own income and committed 5 percent of Cummins' profits to charity annually.[41] Locally, he was well-known for his commitment to architecture in his hometown of Columbus. That included church architecture as well. Completed in 1942 under Miller's funding and initiative, First Christian Church in Columbus was known as the first modern church building in America. He also helped commission Columbus's North Christian Church, dedicated in 1964.

In addition to architecture, Miller's religious philanthropy extended to a passion for ministerial training. With the influence and philanthropy of his extended family before him, the Millers established the School of Religion at Butler (originally a Disciples university) to train ministers. In 1921, the Miller family established the Christian Foundation with the express purpose of building and funding the School of Religion. Ultimately, Irwin Miller and family members urged separation from Butler, and the School of Religion became its own independent entity, Christian Theological Seminary (CTS) in 1958. The Millers' Christian Foundation then began to designate 90 percent, and later 100 percent, of its undesignated income for the operational support of CTS. More recently, the Miller family supported the building of the modern Sweeney chapel on CTS's campus dedicated in 1987. Over the years, the Miller family has contributed over $11 million to support CTS.[42]

Miller saw Cummins' role as a socially conscious business defining its home base of Columbus as part of his philanthropy, but he also exhibited that commitment nationally. In the 1960s, Martin Luther King, Jr. called Miller the "most socially responsible business man in the country."[43] Miller saw part of his vocation as philanthropist and advocate spending months each year maintaining his commitments as a trustee for the Yale Corporation and the Ford Foundation, but in the religious realm, his trusteeship was most remarkable in his role with the National Council of Churches (NCC), the leading ecumenical body for much of the twentieth century. Miller served as the first layperson to chair the NCC, from 1960 to 1963. He had a hand in organizing the March on Washington and was a national advocate on issues of civil rights through the NCC. Miller's philanthropic impact was felt in Indiana by many religious institutions, but his faith commitments motivated him to become a national spokesperson without leaving his Hoosier roots behind.

TAKING INDIANA'S RELIGIOUS PHILANTHROPY GLOBAL

Indiana has had its major religious philanthropists; it also has its unique religious philanthropic stories. The state has always maintained a small but relatively significant Anabaptist population. Church of the Brethren supported the Bethany Theological

Seminary in Richmond and the Mennonites built its college and headquarters in Goshen. It was in a Church of the Brethren gathering on farmland in northern Indiana that Dan West, founder of Heifer International, got the initial vision to send livestock overseas instead of short-term aid in order to move recipients from dependency to self-sufficiency. With its original motto, "a cow, not a cup," Heifer has become one of the most well-known and respected development-oriented nonprofits.

In serving as a missionary and relief worker after the Spanish Civil War, Dan West knew there had to be a better way to do charity. His idea was to provide livestock so that those in need would have milk and food, and through breeding the animals, they would create a continuous, self-sufficient source of income and support. West shared his idea with the superintendent of animal husbandry at Goshen College, and he suggested sending heifers to Europe. Amid World War II, he proposed his plan at a congregational gathering in northern Indiana. One farmer called out to West, "Have faith." West replied he was trying but needed tangible help as well. The farmer replied, "No, Dan, I mean have my calf, Faith. That's her name." Soon other men volunteered to feed and care for the animal. The Goshen City Church of the Brethren donated two other calves named Hope and Charity. The project took root in Indiana but soon spread across the American heartland. By the end of 1942, the Heifers for Relief Committee brought together Mennonites, Presbyterians, Methodists, Lutherans, and Amish for the work. Farmers raised heifers specifically for the hungry and donated them to the cause.[44]

Young men, known as "seagoing cowboys," would care for the animals and accompany them on the ships overseas. The first seagoing cowboy, Claire Stine, was a sixteen-year-old farm boy from Goshen, Indiana. As these young men delivered livestock overseas, they were confronted with the devastation wrought by the Second World War.[45] As members of historic peace churches, many of these young men volunteered for these posts as alternatives to service. In addition to the outgrowth of Heifer International, many local Hoosiers have served through the Mennonite Central Committee or through the Mennonite Board of Missions and Charities as alternatives to military service or simply as volunteers around the world.[46]

Several national and international religious bodies also have their headquarters in Indiana. With the influence of the Mennonite Board of Missions and Charities founded in Elkhart in 1906, the Mennonites consolidated their other agencies into denominational offices located in Goshen in 1988. Mennonite Mutual Aid, now known as Everence, continues to provide financial resources and investments for the Anabaptist community and is located in Goshen as well. The headquarters of the Church of God, Anderson are located in Anderson, Indiana, along with Anderson University. The Disciples of Christ have their national operations headquartered in Indianapolis. While each of these individual religious communities are strong within the state, their institutional structures provide broad philanthropic impact well beyond Indiana. In many ways, Indiana's motto, "Crossroads of America," is true for its religious philanthropy. It may predominantly focus its efforts at home, but it often serves to promote philanthropic change on a national and international scale.

CONCLUSION

What does the history of religious philanthropy tell us about our current and future contexts? We will continue to see the interactions between mass and major religious philanthropy. Likewise, we will continue to see religious individuals and institutions as both the agents and recipients of philanthropy.

Times may be changing and the landscape of religious giving may be evolving, but religious philanthropy is not going away. While some lament the decline of religion's influence in America and the rise of Americans disaffiliating from religious institutions, the philanthropic impact, particularly in Indiana, where religious institutions have been supported by significant philanthropy such as LEI and local giving, will remain strong. Institutions, however, may look quite different as local congregations may close or sell their buildings or find additional ways to reuse or open space even more intentionally as a philanthropic resource and partner in the community. Shifting demographic patterns may find religious institutions repurposing space for new ethnic congregations or forming partnerships with congregations with resources in the suburbs in an effort to seek ways of engaging their philanthropy and mission locally in places of need in the city. Of course, all religious communities are not in decline in terms of numbers, budgets, or buildings. A Mormon temple consecrated in 2015 in Carmel just north of Indianapolis is an example of both major and mass religious philanthropy necessary for the construction of such a prominent building. New religious communities outside the Protestant and even Christian mainstream are also emerging all through the state. Buddhist shrines and Hindu temples are examples of new Hoosiers' religious philanthropy.

Finally, new forms of philanthropy and public service may lead religious institutions to partner in different ways but rarely has it meant retrenchment into their individual communities. Just as religious philanthropy's debates over traditional charity and scientific philanthropy led to multiple perspectives, the same is true as faith-based funders debate partnering with government and secular institutions. Do they accept federal or state funding along with private donations? Does the comingling of resources and acceptance of certain stipulations on activity inhibit their mission or does faith-based philanthropy and social service sometimes produce better results and greater impact? Indiana has served as a test case and model for faith-based partnerships in the past several decades. Attention over the Religious Freedom Restoration Act (RFRA) brought renewed attention to the state in 2015.

Without exhausting the history of religious philanthropy or making claims to understand the future, religious philanthropy clearly has and will continue to be a major agent for sustaining and shaping the Hoosier state.

NOTES

1. Arthur E. Farnsley II, *Sacred Circles, Public Squares* (Bloomington: Indiana University Press, 2004), 2–3; Jan Shipps, "Religion," in *Encyclopedia of Indianapolis*, eds. David J. Bodenhamer and Robert G. Barrows (Bloomington: Indiana University Press), 172–73.

2. Giving USA 2021: The Annual Report on Philanthropy for the Year 2020.

3. "Religious Landscape Study," Pew Research Center, Religion and Public Life, accessed December 10, 2017, http://www.pewforum.org/religious-landscape-study/state/indiana/.

4. Arthur E. Farnsley II, *Rising Expectations: Urban Congregations, Welfare Reform, and Civic Life* (Bloomington: Indiana University Press), 27.

5. James H. Madison, *Hoosiers: A New History of Indiana* (Bloomington: Indiana University Press), 104; Henry Ward Beecher, *Seven Lectures to Young Men* (Indianapolis: Thomas B. Cutler, 1844); Clifford E. Clark, Jr., "The Changing Nature of Protestantism in Mid-Nineteenth Century America: Henry Ward Beecher's Seven Lectures to Young Men," *Journal of American History* 57 (March 1971): 832–46.

6. Madison, *Hoosiers*, 110–14.

7. Ibid., 105–10.

8. Ibid., 116–17.

9. Ram Cnaan, "Social and Community Involvement of Religious Congregations Housed in Historic Religious Properties: Findings from a Six-City Study," Final Report to Partners for Sacred Spaces, 1997. Farnsley, *Rising Expectations*, 33–34; U.S. Religion Census, "Marion County, Indiana Membership Report," Association of Religion Data Archives, accessed March 22, 2022, https://thearda.com/rcms2010/rcms2010a.asp?U=18097&T=county&Y=2010&S=Name.

10. Farnsley, *Rising Expectations*, 5.

11. David Beito, *From Mutual Aid to the Welfare State: Fraternal Societies and Social Services, 1890–1967* (Chapel Hill: North Carolina Press, 2000), 2.

12. James Hudnut-Beumler, "Religion and Philanthropy," in *Encyclopedia of Indianapolis*, 1107–9.

13. Robert L. Payton and Patricia A. Dean, "Philanthropy," in *Encyclopedia of Indianapolis*, 153–60; Robert A. Gross, "Giving in America: From Charity to Philanthropy," 29–48 and Judith Sealander, "Curing Evils at Their Source: The Arrival of Scientific Giving," 217–40, both in *Charity, Philanthropy, and Civility in American History*, eds. Lawrence J. Friedman and Mark D. McGarvie (Cambridge, UK: Cambridge University Press), 2003.

14. "Yearbook of Charities, 1889–1890," quoted in "Charity Organization Society," in *Encyclopedia of Indianapolis*, 402.

15. Katherine E. Badertscher, "Organized Charity and the Civic Ideal in Indianapolis, 1879–1922" (PhD diss., Indiana University Lilly Family School of Philanthropy, 2015); Payton and Dean, "Philanthropy," 157; Hudnut-Buemler, "Religion and Philanthropy," 1108.

16. Ruth Hutchinson Crocker, "Christamore House," in *Encyclopedia of Indianapolis*, 414–15.

17. Katherine Mandusic McDonell, "Flower Mission," in *Encyclopedia of Indianapolis*, 585–86; Hudnut-Buemler, "Religion and Philanthropy," 1107.

18. Edwin L. Becker, *From Sovereign to Servant: The Church Federation of Greater Indianapolis, 1912–1917* (Indianapolis: The Church Federation of Greater Indianapolis, 1987).

19. Joan Cunningham, "Church Women United," in *Encyclopedia of Indianapolis*, 423.

20. James J. Divita, "Catholics," in *Encyclopedia of Indianapolis*, 389–91.

21. Thomas N. Gaybrick, "Catholic Social Services," in *Encyclopedia of Indianapolis*, 388.

22. August Fussenegger, "Catholic Charities Bureau of the Diocese of Indianapolis, Annual Report, 1937 in *A Public Charity: Religion and Social Welfare in Indianapolis, 1929–2002*, ed., Mary Maples (Bloomington: Indiana University Press, 2004), 27.

23. Judith E. Endleman, *The Jewish Community of Indianapolis: 1849 to the Present* (Bloomington: Indiana University Press), 1984.

24. Endleman, *Jewish Community*, 30.

25. S. B. Kaufman, "The Jewish Federation of Indianapolis," *Indiana Bulletin of Charities and Correction* (December 1909): 420–23; Endelman, *Jewish Community*, 97.

26. Endelman, *Jewish Community*, 102.

27. Ibid., 190.

28. Ibid., 198.

29. L. C. Rudolph, *Hoosier Faiths: A History of Indiana Churches & Religious Groups* (Bloomington: Indiana University Press, 1995), 633–34.

30. Ibid., 635–40.

31. Michael D. Hale, "Bethel AME Church," in *Encyclopedia of Indianapolis*, 318–19.

32. For background on the YMCA and YWCA movements across the racial divide, see Nancy Marie Robertson, *Christian Sisterhood, Race Relations, and the YWCA, 1906–46* (Urbana: University of Chicago Press, 2007) and Nina Mjagkij and Margaret Spratt, eds., *Men and Women Adrift: The YMCA and the YWCA in the City* (New York: New York University Press, 1997).

33. Nina Mjagkij, "Senate Avenue YMCA," in *Encyclopedia of Indianapolis*, 1249–50.

34. Etta Russel, "Phyllis Wheatley YWCA," in *Encyclopedia of Indianapolis*, 1114–15.

35. Maples, *A Public Charity*, 67–69.

36. James H. Madison, *Eli Lilly: A Life* (Bloomington: Indiana University Press, 2006), 189–223; James H. Madison, "Lilly Endowment," in *Encyclopedia of Indianapolis*, 914–15; Lilly Endowment Inc., *Annual Report*, 2020, accessed March 22, 2022, https://lillyendowment.org/2020-annual -report/.

37. Lilly Endowment Inc., *Annual Report*, 2020.

38. Madison, *Eli Lilly: A Life*, 225–38.

39. Ibid., 192–204.

40. Ibid., 215–18.

41. Charles E. Mitchell Rentschler, *The Cathedral Builder: A Biography of J. Irwin Miller* (Bloomington, IN: AuthorHouse, 2014), x.

42. Rentschler, *The Cathedral Builder*, 139.

43. Ibid., 82.

44. Glee Yoder, *Passing on the Gift: The Story of Dan West* (Elgin, IL: Brethren Press, 1978).

45. Peggy Reiff Miller, *Seagoing Cowboy*, (Elgin, IL: Brethren Press, 2016).

46. L. C. Rudolph, *Hoosier Faiths: A History of Indiana Churches & Religious Groups* (Bloomington: Indiana University Press, 1995), 302.

THREE

—ᴍ—

SOCIAL SERVICES IN INDIANA

KATHERINE BADERTSCHER AND
RUTH C. CROCKER

THIS CHAPTER TRACES THE DEVELOPMENT of social services in Indiana since its statehood in 1816. Social services are
organized efforts to supply the basic needs of shelter, food, and
income to Indiana residents—a fundamental charitable mission and a foundation of the nonprofit sector. Since Indiana's
statehood, social service delivery for basic human needs has
formed the core of philanthropy, usually labeled "benevolence"
or "charity." Philanthropy is one of several possible responses to
fundamental human problems and can compete, complement,
or collaborate with self-help, mutual aid, business, or government systems. Crucial, intertwined debates characterize the
history of Indiana social services: the respective roles of philanthropy and government in service delivery, the determination
of recipients' eligibility, and how best to intervene. Could charitable effort deter individuals from self-help or organizing help in
their communities? Social scientists, ministers, and economists
debated whether relief sapped individual effort and "character"; they argued how to define "need" and how to determine
eligibility for assistance; they worried over whether relief of
poverty—a traditional obligation of religious communities—
might actually lead to moral decline or prompt unruly demands
for entitlements; finally, they struggled to raise sufficient funds

from donors to support social services for a growing population. These debates have shifted throughout the last two centuries, at times in favor of individual relief and character development and at other times with a focus on reforming entire societal structures.

Donating today encompasses a variety of public purposes. Close examination of donating to social services illustrates universal questions in philanthropy more than any other sector: empowerment or effectiveness of recipients, public or private provision of basic needs, and humanitarian compassion or community service. Indiana, in general, is slow to change—what James Madison calls "evolution, not revolution"—but at times has been an early adopter of new social service delivery models. Challenges to provide for basic needs "or even defining what 'basic needs'" are have persisted throughout Indiana's history and remain with us today, for example, as we debate whether access to health care is a universal right, a social good, or a commodity.

ORIGINS OF INDIANA SOCIAL SERVICES

When Indiana was admitted to the Union in 1816, Congress authorized the donation of four square miles of public land for the state capital. Four years later, when Indiana's State Capital Selection Committee chose to move the capital from Corydon to Indianapolis, the city consisted of only about fifteen White families. It became the seat of government in 1825, and people migrated from around the state to settle there.

Indiana inherited an older relationship, one of general tolerance and minimal regulation of charities between government and philanthropy. English common law, from which the US legal system was largely derived, gave wide latitude to donors in creating charitable trusts if three elements were present: assets or property, evidence of intention to create the entity, and devotion to charitable purpose. Poor laws required church parishes to care for the poor within their borders and permitted local government, usually a parish or county, to levy taxes to care for them.[1] Poor laws also codified the worthy/unworthy poor distinction, which has permeated social services ever since. The so-called worthy—widows, children without parents (or functional parents), the ill, incapacitated, elderly, or disabled—deserved assistance. The so-called unworthy—the able-bodied who refused work—did not deserve assistance. American poor laws thus reflected an uneasy application of English charitable law, classical economic theory, which argued against interfering with poverty as a natural state, and the Protestant theology of salvation through hard work and morality.[2]

Americans in the early Republic did not adopt English charitable law wholesale. Care for the poor became the responsibility of the local, and at times state, government and formally separated from the church.[3] By the time of Indiana statehood, all aspects of charitable trusteeship and its testamentary, institutional, and fiduciary aspects were in place.[4] Taken together, this body of law formed the basis for trust law that was eventually adopted in most US states. Midwestern pioneers, moreover, adapted concepts from both Adam Smith's free hand of the market and Christian benevolence to provide limited social services that would not dampen individual efforts to achieve economic success.[5]

Nineteenth-century government spending on "dependent" care reflected the assumption that the federal government should only assume a limited role in social welfare. Local government thus funded nonprofits to provide social services, with social policy aimed at assisting the putative truly "dependent." Territorial law, and subsequently state law, provided for the appointment of two overseers of the poor in each township with responsibility for poor relief supported by taxes.[6] Overseers of the poor bore the legislated responsibility to assure citizens' basic needs of food, clothing, and shelter in their jurisdictions.[7] Poor laws' jurisdiction reflected the worthy/unworthy distinction. Those considered worthy encompassed a wide range of dependent people, not only low-income families or individuals but also the ill, infirm, aged, orphaned, widowed, and "every idiot, lunatic, and insane person who is or shall become a pauper."[8]

Governmental poor relief in nineteenth-century Indiana assumed several forms: outdoor relief, indoor relief, contracting, farming out, and apprenticing of children.[9] Outdoor relief, or direct monetary assistance outside of an institution and in the normal place of residence, was available only on a small scale. Authorities generally viewed outdoor relief as a temporary measure to be used until the recipient could become self-sufficient or until some other solution developed.[10] Indoor relief meant gathering the poor, including the ill, into poorhouses, asylums, or poor farms. Poor asylum care represented the earliest form of indoor relief, or care of the indigent within an institution, in Indiana. As counties built and established poorhouses, public employees assumed the superintendent's function. The able-bodied, employable poor could also be farmed out to work for private individuals who offered the lowest bid.[11] If families were willing to part with their children or if children did not have functional parents at all, minors could be apprenticed or "bound out."[12] Overseers of the poor, in addition to their other responsibilities, possessed the authority to control a child's destiny.

The legal structure and its patchwork approach to social welfare changed little in Indiana through the nineteenth century. In general, citizens frowned on public assistance and viewed it as a last resort. The image of Indiana as America's heartland represented a land of abundant resources and virtually unlimited opportunity. While residents looked sympathetically on victims of circumstances, they simultaneously believed that anyone who wanted to could gain independence through work. The poor relief debate revolved around which strategy best achieved the goals society believed were paramount, such as quality of care or the lowest possible cost and whether philanthropic or public entities, or some hybrid, should carry out the majority of poor relief.

Religious ferment also shaped the contours of antebellum philanthropy in the United States. Religion informed how people shaped their public lives and understood duty toward one another.[13] Indiana's religious configuration quickly followed national trends, with mainline Protestant denominations having the greatest number of churches and members throughout the nineteenth century. Closely connected to religious expression was a culture of voluntary association. Alexis de Tocqueville in the 1830s observed that Americans freely associated to get things done, for example build churches, hospitals, and meeting places and distribute books. In Indiana, neighbors banded together for barn raisings, quilting sessions, assistance with ailing family members, and various other tasks of daily life.[14]

Neighborhood benevolence formed the core of social services, but a coterie of families guided the city in economic, political, social, and philanthropic circles. On Thanksgiving Day, 1835, James Blake, Calvin Fletcher, and other city fathers formed the Indianapolis Benevolent Society (IBS) "to relieve the necessities of the poor of the city of Indianapolis . . . by means of voluntary contributions."[15] The organizers had been personally supplying the needy with food, clothing, and sometimes money to supplement Marion County's limited allocation of public funds for poor relief and now sought to create a more systematic method of collecting donations and aiding neighbors.[16] The society's mission encompassed broader notions of community: to help individuals and families with personal problems and "to strengthen family life."[17] Indianapolis's church network supported the IBS by hosting meetings, running special fund drives, and including the IBS in special charity sermons. Members of the IBS—both men and women—comprised, donated to, and operated the all-volunteer charitable society. The IBS innovated to develop a social welfare system that adopted voluntarism, a district system of both clients

and visitation, moral instruction, centralization, and coordination with churches, charities, and municipal officials. It never
claimed to eliminate poverty but provided palliative relief to the
town's poor, sick, and occasional travelers.

Social services became increasingly specialized according to
classes of dependents. IBS members created the Widows and Orphans Friends' Society in 1850 "to relieve the physical, intellectual and moral wants of the widows and orphans of the city."[18]
The IBS and Friends' Society advocated for Indiana's first child
welfare law (passed in 1852, which was early relative to other
states) to establish orphanages. It mandated the removal of children from poorhouses. The orphanage, the state's first example
of a private, yet quasipublic, benevolent institution and managed primarily by the women of Indianapolis, demonstrated
that, seventy years before they could vote, women could run a
complex business, fundraise, and partner with government. The
society later became the Indianapolis Orphan Asylum; today it
operates as the Children's Bureau and its mission has changed
substantially over time.

Government and philanthropic leaders continued to debate
the relative strength of individual moral failings versus societal
failings as explanations for dependence and poverty. By the mid-
nineteenth century, US state and local governments operated
systems of confinement for the dependent and delinquent. Charity and corrections became virtually one and the same. State and
local government's role in caring for society's truly dependent
and delinquent rose steadily. As the state capital, Indianapolis
obtained the Indiana State Asylum for Deaf and Dumb (1843),
Indiana State School for the Blind (1847), and Indiana State Hospital for the Insane (1848). States built correctional facilities to
separate the delinquent from the ill or poor, and state-run correctional institutions emerged on the Indiana landscape by the
1870s.[19]

THE CIVIL WAR AND POSTWAR DECADES

The Civil War (1861–1865) altered virtually every aspect of American life, including social services. The postwar Freedman's Bureau marked a large expansion of federal welfare responsibility for those emerging out of slavery by providing relief and education. However, bureau agents also imposed work requirements so that aid recipients often remained on plantations as sharecroppers. Federal war pensions supported the widows and survivors of Union soldiers and constructed the US National Soldiers' Homes for disabled veterans. Soldiers' and Sailors' Orphans Homes, such as Knightstown, Indiana's home, opened to shelter Civil War families left without a male head of household.[20]

Many soldiers and their families settled in Indianapolis after the war, and the composition of the state's population continued to change. New residents without the ready means to become self-sufficient strained philanthropic resources. Those included newly freed but destitute African Americans who migrated to Indiana from the upper South and single women who flocked to Indianapolis during the war, sometimes in search of missing male family members. The city's YMCA branch helped to found the Home for Friendless Women in 1866. Established in Indianapolis in 1854, the YMCA had taken over the spiritual needs of the poorhouses and the Hospital for the Insane. YMCA members volunteered at the jail to conduct religious services on Sundays on their way home from their own church services. Men and women already involved with the IBS, the orphanage, or the YMCA became aware of the number of women released from jail with nowhere to go. Just as the orphanage managers hoped to rescue children from the poorhouses, the women's home managers sought to rescue women from the brothels or jails. The Home for Friendless Women still exists today as the Indianapolis Retirement Home.

Township trustees from all over Indiana who could be viewed as fiscally responsible, savvy, or cunning shipped their relief applicants to the capital city, exacerbating poverty in Center Township. By exporting their poor in this manner, other counties rid themselves of a fiscal problem, declaring that "Indianapolis was such a benevolent city."[21] Large numbers of indigent, unemployed men, commonly known at the time as "tramps," meandered into the city with no promise of jobs or housing.

The postwar years, punctuated by a depression in the 1870s, severely tested the social service system, which relied heavily on voluntarism and public/private partnerships. The IBS saw donations plummet as requests for aid reached an all-time high. Questions about the respective roles of men and women in philanthropy and uncertainty about the responsibilities of philanthropy, business, and government in assisting the poor swirled in the press. The menacing symbol of the dependent pauper emerged as the person unwilling to work, who chose to live on government relief and charity.[22] American civic and charitable leaders recognized that the existing kaleidoscope of churches, benevolent associations, asylums, and poorhouses could not keep pace with the rapidly changing industrial economy and related societal problems, especially urban poverty. The able-bodied who depended on assistance, now in addition to the traditional orphans, widows, elderly, ill, disabled, and the unemployed or "tramps," became increasingly stigmatized as people to be identified and driven away, not nurtured.

LATE NINETEENTH-CENTURY SCIENTIFIC PHILANTHROPY

Taken together these changes provided the setting for the late nineteenth-century scientific philanthropy movement based on several fundamental concepts: use of businesslike procedures to tackle societal problems, emphasis on data and root-cause analysis, and strategies of prevention rather than relief. For several decades, Indiana led the country in social service expansion and experimentation, making it an influential state in national debates over recipients' empowerment and philanthropic effectiveness. Some historians equate scientific philanthropy with either charity organization societies (COSs) or benevolent trusts. Philosophy more than structure signaled the broader movement, and it encompassed a range of orderly and systematic approaches to giving, including many charity organization societies and, after 1900, federated giving, community foundations, and the early twentieth-century foundations of Carnegie, Rockefeller, and Sage. The movement's methods melded voluntarism, noblesse oblige, religion, and social Darwinism and promised simultaneous benefit to donor, recipient, and community.[23]

Confident and ambitious COSs assumed full purview over social services in most US cities. Reverend Stephen Humphreys Gurteen (1836–1898) integrated aspects of the German and British models and Darwinian concepts when he established the Buffalo Charity Organization Society in 1877, the first in the country. Gurteen visited Indianapolis and within only three days the city created its own COSs, subsuming the IBS. The merger created the largest private, nonprofit, social service organization in Indianapolis.[24] The COS of Indianapolis quickly became the model for COSs, or associated charities, across Indiana and the United States. Within a decade any city with a population over ten thousand had such a structure. Indiana's COSs conducted the majority of social service investigation and relief, rendering township trustees a resource of last resort.

COSs centralized case records and summary reports, called exchanges, to meet multiple goals: facilitate communication among agencies, eliminate the inefficiency of multiple investigations, and expose overlapping aid requests. Exchanges promised to build over time the most effective weapon in the struggle to end pauperism, never before available to charities: the power to uncover the root causes of poverty. COSs could accumulate data, analyze them, and link cause and effect in a truly scientific manner. Aid applicants therefore became specimens in a massive social experiment to improve the quality of life in all communities that organized charity.

THE SETTLEMENT MOVEMENT

The settlement movement emerged in US cities around the same time as organized charity. The movement's national leaders, including Jane Addams and Lillian Wald, emphasized the difference in philosophy and practice from COSs, but at the local level—including in Indianapolis—the two movements often cooperated. Settlement houses quickly emerged as striking features of America's philanthropic urban landscape, responses to the interconnected problems posed by growing urban populations, inadequate public health and housing, and limited public welfare.[25]

The Indianapolis settlement houses, Flanner House (f. 1898), Christamore (f. 1905), and American Settlement (f. 1909), reveal how philanthropic effort could supply social services not provided by local, state, or federal government. The settlement house turned social work inside out. Settlement workers rented or purchased homes in a poor neighborhood and "settled" there to serve. They called themselves neighbors, not social workers, and settlement houses became their homes.

Indianapolis settlement worker Anna Stover, founder of Christamore, purchased a house in the Atlas district, a White, working-class neighborhood, just as Jane Addams had purchased Chicago's Hull House and met its expenses for decades. Christamore resembled Hull House, though with closer ties to Protestantism (Church of Christ) than the more famous agency, which modeled an internationalist, multicultural approach on Chicago's south side. In the years before World War I, settlement houses joined reform campaigns that resulted in regulatory legislation,

especially at the state and local level. In a decade when tuberculosis, diphtheria, and typhoid still devastated crowded urban
communities, public health advocates sought allies in a campaign of education and prevention. An important public-private
partnership was forged when Christamore joined the Pure Milk
movement—a national effort to require tighter regulation of pro-
ducers and shippers of milk.[26] Christamore residents also worked
for housing reform. Like the Pittsburgh settlement workers, who
compiled the statistics for the famous *Pittsburgh Survey*, or the
Hull House residents, whose maps and social statistics filled
Hull-House Maps and Papers, Indianapolis settlement workers
gathered data in their immediate neighborhood on crowding,
sanitation, and safety conditions to catalyze reform legislation.[27]

Often barred from tax-supported social services, African
Americans had to make do with separate and inferior institutions in this period. Frank Flanner, an active public citizen and
successful mortician, donated a cottage for children as a Black
branch of the White settlement house run by the COS. The history of Flanner House and other Black settlements reminds us
of the limits of Progressive-era reform. Far from encouraging
integrated social services, White social experts generally saw racially and ethnically mixed populations as a sign of degeneracy
and a call for action. In fact, Flanner House's integrated board secured significant leadership from Black professionals, including
the Kings Daughters (teachers), the Women's Improvement Club
(middle-class Black women), and Black physicians and nurses,
who at that time were limited to practice in the Black community. The settlement tried to tackle the problem of unemployment
through training programs and opened an employment agency
where "fallen" women could find domestic work. After 1920 Flanner House health services included a day nursery, which took in
the children of working mothers.

Immigrants were moving into industrial centers, such as Indianapolis and Gary, posing additional challenges for settlements.

Settlements that served immigrant families pursued multiple goals: Americanization, religious teaching, and improving families' health and housing.[28] American Settlement (today Mary Rigg Neighborhood Center) offered classes, a day nursery, and educational and recreational activities for mothers and children.

A different situation was more critical in northwest Indiana, where U.S. Steel, America's first billion-dollar corporation, launched an industrial complex in 1906 that rapidly drew thousands of immigrant workers. Unskilled workers, many of them foreign, lived outside the planned area of straight streets and middle-class housing. Gary's south side became notorious for its two hundred plus saloons and streets full of men from a dozen nations, rootless, brawling, and disorderly. In response—and to bolster its own image—U.S. Steel subsidized a plethora of social welfare agencies, including settlements, to temper the volatility of its workforce and encourage stability, loyalty, and Americanization.

All four Gary settlement houses had strong denominational identifications. The Christian Women's Board of Missions opened Campbell Friendship House (f. 1914) as a bold program of religious social work. The settlement opened a day nursery; its nurse conducted home visits to advise on health and domestic problems. Later it added a community hall with a welfare department, serving European immigrants and Mexican, African American, and White families. Neighborhood House (f. 1909), affiliated with the Presbyterian synod, similarly combined religious teaching and social work. Like Campbell House, it became known as both a mission and a settlement.[29] Stewart House (f. 1920), affiliated with the Methodist Episcopal Church, served African Americans. Like Flanner House, its board included prominent White and African American citizens.

By 1916, 64 percent of Gary's churchgoing population identified as Catholic, largely immigrants from Croatia, Slovakia, and Italy.[30] The Catholic hierarchy sought to establish a strong presence in Gary in part to forestall Protestant mission work; one strategy was its Gary-Alerding Settlement (f. 1923). The forty-room community center included living quarters for the Sisters Catechists and a chapel, Our Lady of Guadalupe, the first Mexican parish in the Midwest, serving Italian, Spanish, and Mexican families. In its prime, Gary-Alerding was Gary's largest and most elaborate settlement house, although it only operated until the end of the 1930s.

WORLD WAR I AND INSTITUTIONAL PHILANTHROPY

Nineteenth-century men and women had freely joined to form associations for every kind of social service, from Flower Missions to homeless shelters, children's aid societies to visiting nurse associations, charity organization societies to settlements. Elite and middle-class women pursued an active philanthropic career by defining what they did as within "a sphere of usefulness."[31] Delegating their household work to servants, they became the managers, board members, and treasurers of multiple voluntary associations of social welfare. Black and White, middle-class and wealthy women united in voluntary associations in the years before suffrage to tackle a range of public issues, including the condition of the streets, prostitution, alcoholism, and child labor.

World War I brought an age of organization and consolidation, and the visionary nineteenth-century idealism of prior generations waned. Social work was on its way to professionalism and the place of the volunteer was now as a subordinate to the trained worker. Middle-class women with disposable time no longer staffed social agencies. Nor was there an oversupply of college-educated single women with time on their hands and barred from jobs in academia, government, and business as there had been in the 1880s and 1890s.

The scientific philanthropy movement gave way to new strategies in social service theory and practice after World War I.

Community funds, or Community Chests, stemmed from both World War I "War Chests" and the Cleveland Chamber of Commerce. Cleveland had piloted a community-wide fundraising campaign as an outgrowth of its interest in organized charity work. Cleveland's chamber created a "federation" to make a coordinated appeal and allow donors to designate their gifts to particular charities. Almost four hundred War Chests had formed across the country but all but thirty-nine disbanded after 1919. The federated fundraising apparatus, however, did not disappear. Communities repurposed the federated concept to social welfare fundraising so that by the mid-1920s over three hundred coordinated campaigns existed.[32] Again Indiana remained ahead of national trends as Indianapolis conducted its first community-fund drive in 1920. Community funds promised to enhance cooperation among agencies, avoid duplication of effort, and reduce fundraising expenses. The federation, or "federated giving," technique is very much alive today, best known through the example of the United Way.

Community Chest / fund development also coincided with the evolution of corporate philanthropy. Chests therefore pursued businesses and employee pools as sources of funds that charities had accessed previously on a limited, ad hoc basis.[33] Chests became the primary fundraising organ for social services, and social service charities received the majority of chest allocations. Moreover, charities had to relinquish their own fundraising efforts in order to receive a chest allocation. Community funds did not, however, grapple with questions of empowerment or effectiveness. Community leaders, through their fund leadership, instead signaled social service agencies' trustworthiness by including them in the local federations.[34]

In a related development, service clubs, such as Kiwanis, Lions, and Rotary, allowed smaller businesses to combine in order to participate in community endeavors.[35] Both Community Chests / funds and businessmen's service clubs had emerged throughout

Indiana during the 1920s. In 1929, the Lynds' *Middletown* recorded their dominance: Secular social service agencies had risen rapidly, were backed by the "big men in town," relied more on professional staff than volunteers, and received the majority of their donations via the Community Chest.[36]

The Cleveland Chamber of Commerce also stimulated the development of the community foundation, a grant-making nonprofit with multiple purposes: to provide community leadership, promote local development, teach philanthropy, and provide a vehicle for strategic giving for those without sufficient resources to create an independent foundation. The Indianapolis Foundation formed in 1916, making it one of the nation's oldest community foundations. All but two US cities with populations of three hundred thousand or more had community foundations by 1929.[37]

THE GREAT DEPRESSION AND THE NEW DEAL

The 1929 stock market crash increased demand for social services while reducing donations to nonprofit organizations. Unlike previous economic slumps, however, the ensuing 1930s Great Depression produced legislation that redefined the relationship between government, business, and philanthropy and transformed the United States into a welfare state. Between 1929 and 1931, relief spending quadrupled and overtaxed existing capacity to provide relief. Many private welfare efforts crumbled; an astounding one-third of nonprofits in the country closed their doors.[38] Community funds were hit especially hard. The turmoil of the Great Depression challenged many aspects of social service delivery. Newly established community funds had formed on the basis of building communities by developing the character of citizens, not on the basis of poor relief. Funds had no choice but to shift back to relief during the Depression. The Indianapolis Community Fund, for example, in 1932 distributed over 80 percent of its funds to agencies providing direct relief. Charity organization societies, the institutional archetypes of scientific philanthropy, fell out of favor. Many reorganized, restructured, or merged into family welfare agencies. Some agencies, including most of the newly formed family welfare agencies, questioned the need for community funds at all. Critics argued that the funds had short and uneven performance records and represented unnecessary overhead.[39]

President Roosevelt's 1932 National Recovery Administration (NRA) ramped up federal involvement in relief and formalized cooperation among government, business, and philanthropy.[40] Subsequent New Deal legislation created a veritable alphabet soup of relief initiatives backed by government spending that would allow nonprofits to retrench and permanently involve the federal government in public welfare.[41] Signature elements of the New Deal included work relief programs, a federal-state unemployment system, and the Social Security Act (SSA). The SSA included two main platforms: contributory social insurance and public assistance (Old-Age Assistance and Aid to Families with Dependent Children). New Deal programs changed the lives of the elderly, widows, the blind and disabled; put a safety net under the unemployed; supported farm economies (but not poor farmers); and established a new contract between labor, business, and government. Much of the administrative burden of work relief, unemployment, and public assistance fell to the states. Most states focused on assimilating these new programs and abandoned their now arcane poor relief function of township trustee offices. Indiana retained its township trustee poor relief function to maintain local control over relief and keep expenditures low. This township trustee function continues to this day.[42]

When the National Conference of Charities and Correction (NCCC) returned to Indianapolis in 1937, some attendees viewed with nostalgia the state of social work and poor relief that had prevailed when the 1891 NCCC conference had taken place. Much had changed. By the 1930s, social welfare policy leaders recognized the interdependence of poverty with living and working conditions. Philanthropy's limited scale to address massive unemployment was abundantly clear by 1937. The country, still mired in the Great Depression, had witnessed waves of New Deal welfare programs, which rendered the turn from charity to the welfare state irretrievable. "The charities and correction trappings are gone," one social worker noted, "but new panoplies of security and social work have taken their place."[43] The Depression's financial-assistance programs caused family welfare agencies, successors of COSs, to shift away from poor relief completely. Family welfare agencies therefore refocused their missions on all families, regardless of socioeconomic class. Their range of services expanded to include adoption, care for unwed mothers, and marriage and family counseling, all designed to keep traditional family units intact.[44] The COS of Indianapolis, later the Family Welfare Agency, today operates as Families First.

WORLD WAR II, THE 1960S, AND THE GREAT SOCIETY

World War II shifted local, state, and national attention to the war effort. Government spending accelerated for national defense. Federal spending, coupled with New Deal programs already underway, allowed social services to move away from direct relief and back toward building character and family life. The Indianapolis Family Service Association, for example, noted in its *Handbook for Members* that "most social ills have their roots in family life."[45] To bolster the home front, therefore, social service agencies and community funds returned to counseling and casework for all families regardless of socioeconomic status. By the 1950s, the shift was complete. Direct relief had become the purview of government to be shared among all levels: local, state, and federal.

By mid-twentieth century, Indiana no longer led trends in social service models and mirrors national patterns to this day. The 1960s ushered in tremendous change in federal-government involvement in social welfare and accordingly in demand funding of nonprofit organizations. Before the 1960s, the federal government played virtually no role in funding nonprofit organizations, and state funding of selected social welfare institutions was relatively circumscribed. Government provided some services, and philanthropy filled some gaps. Nonprofit organizations that delivered health and human services relied most heavily on the twin pillars of the nonprofit sector: voluntarism and private donations, including endowments and federated giving. Between the mid-1960s and mid-1970s, President Johnson's Great Society programs caused federal participation in nonprofits to increase dramatically. Medicare, Medicaid, the Community Action Program, and amendments to Social Security for health and human services, when taken together, profoundly affected the relationships among federal and state governments and nonprofits. Government substantially expanded programs by supporting the nonprofit sector, thereby tapping into existing resources without adding as much to government bureaucracy as these programmatic changes would have otherwise necessitated.

Federal spending on social welfare services rose from $1.14 billion in 1960 to $13.5 billion in 1980. State spending rose in lockstep, from $2.6 billion in 1975 to $4.8 billion in 1980. Even with the dramatic change of pace of state spending, federal spending by 1980 exceeded total state spending by a factor of two to one.[46] These changes in spending patterns affected nonprofit organizations in three ways. Traditional nonprofits were slow to embrace government funding but were ultimately transformed to expand client services and become highly dependent on government funds. Government-sponsored nonprofits emerged rapidly as alternatives to state social service agencies, especially community-action agencies that provided day nurseries, Head Start classes, employment training, mental health treatment, and substance abuse treatment. Treatment centers emerged in sync with dein- stitutionalization of the mentally ill and closure of state mental hospitals around the country. New volunteer-driven nonprofit agencies also proliferated, especially shelters for the homeless and domestic violence survivors and programs for the develop- mentally disabled. Successful small start-up nonprofits eventu- ally grew from reliance on private donations to dependence on government funds to sustain them.[47] Whether traditional or new, the plethora of community nonprofits completely replaced the social settlement model of the early twentieth century.

1980S AND 1990S—"DEVOLUTION" AND CHARITABLE CHOICE

Even as the Reagan and Bush administrations of the 1980s and 1990s curbed federal spending on social services, government involvement in social welfare and nonprofit funding has not sig- nificantly abated. Economist Burton Weisbrod noted what he called the "retrenchment" of government, the withdrawal of gov- ernment from direct service delivery and increased reliance on the nonprofit sector through the 1990s.[48] In 1995, government was still the largest funder of nonprofit human service agencies, even after twelve years of conservative federal administration. Passage of welfare reform legislation known as Personal Responsibility and Work Opportunity Reconciliation Act of 1996 (PRWORA) set in motion a new wave of government funding and contract- ing relationships to state and local governments and nonprofit organizations, collectively known as "devolution."[49] PRWORA abolished the New Deal's Aid to Families with Dependent Chil- dren and capped federal aid to the states in exchange for greater flexibility for the states to administer welfare programs. Devo- lution intensified the challenge to nonprofit organizations that provide services for low-income populations to find new ways to alleviate poverty, encourage employment, strengthen families, and reduce long-term dependence on welfare.

Bipartisan federal legislation known as Charitable Choice passed in phases between 1996 and 2000, embedded in PRWORA welfare reform. Charitable Choice aimed to create equal competitive footing for religious and secular social service agencies, allow congregations to act as social service providers on behalf of government, reduce barriers for clients on welfare to access social services, and encourage faith-based organizations to offer holistic services to underserved populations. Locally, Indianapolis mayor Stephen Goldsmith (1992–2000) piloted the Front Porch Alliance to encourage clergy to become more active in their neighborhoods, an initiative reminiscent of the late nineteenth-century Social Gospel. Indiana governor Frank O'Bannon (1997–2003) created FaithWorks, a statewide system modeled after the Front Porch Alliance, to assist congregations participating in Charitable Choice.[50]

SOCIAL SERVICES AT THE BICENTENNIAL

Federal funds today continue to flow into nonprofit organizations through several channels. Federal agencies remunerate nonprofits through grants and contracts, federal agencies fund states that in turn execute grants and contracts, and federal agencies act as payers for services rendered by nonprofits and received by individuals. State, local, and nonprofit organizations—and at times for-profits—thus deliver most social services on behalf of government. This government/philanthropic partnership is especially evident in Indiana. Fewer than 1 percent of the 27,300 employees in social service agencies in the state work for the government; the vast majority work for nonprofit organizations.[51]

Social services today encompass vocational rehabilitation, individual and family services, childcare services, and emergency disaster relief. The pastiche of programs support communities by meeting basic needs, helping the unemployed and under-employed secure and retain jobs and maintaining standards of living. Social service nonprofits have fared relatively well since the 2008 economic downturn. Unlike the Great Depression, which forced so many nonprofit closures, Indiana social service nonprofits stayed in business, formed new organizations, and increased staff despite the Great Recession of the twenty-first century.[52] Social service nonprofits, therefore, fulfill an essential role in Indiana communities by serving those in need and protecting at-risk populations. Their ability not only to survive but to expand in challenging economic times is a testament to Indiana philanthropy. Over one thousand foundations, including ninety-four community foundations, sixty-one United Way funds, and thousands of individual donors together support over two thousand nonprofit organizations around the state.

Indiana has grown and modernized in two hundred years, but questions of public welfare persist. The past still invades the present and shapes policy. For providers, the fear that income support will perpetuate poverty and encourage the undeserving remains a strong deterrent to effective action to end poverty. That fear would be familiar to an earlier generation. In other ways the debates are strikingly familiar: empowerment or effectiveness of recipients and public or private provision of basic needs. Indiana communities will always debate how best to care for those in need, whether through government, business, philanthropy, family, or some combination. We have not discovered all the answers to questions of public welfare, but fortunately Indiana philanthropy will not cease while Hoosiers search for them.

NOTES

1. Marion Fremont-Smith, *Governing Nonprofit Organizations: Federal and State Law and Regulation* (Cambridge, MA: Belknap Press of Harvard University Press, 2004), 26–28; David C. Hammack, ed., *Making the*

Nonprofit Sector in the United States, A Reader (Bloomington: Indiana University Press, 1998), 9.

2. Walter I. Trattner, *From Poor Law to Welfare State*, 6th ed. (New York: Free Press, 1999), 50–55.

3. Hammack, *Making the Nonprofit Sector in the United States*, 87–90.

4. Peter Dobkin Hall, *Inventing the Nonprofit Sector and Other Essays on Philanthropy, Voluntarism, and Nonprofit Organizations* (Baltimore: Johns Hopkins University Press, 1992), 170–71.

5. Michael B. Katz, *In the Shadow of the Poorhouse: A Social History of Welfare in America*, rev. ed. (New York: Basic, 1996), 38–40; Trattner, *From Poor Law to Welfare State*, 55–56.

6. "Many Volunteer Welfare Agencies Serve City's Unfortunate Today," *Indianapolis Star*, September 27, 1953, 41; Louis Rosenberg, "Overseeing the Poor: A Legal-Administrative Analysis of the Indiana Township Assistance System," *Indiana Law Review* 6, no. 3 (1973): 386–87.

7. Amos W. Butler, *A Century of Progress: A Study of the Development of Public Charities and Correction, 1790–1915* (Indianapolis: Indiana State Board of Charities, 1916), 2.

8. Emma Lou Thornbrough, *Indiana in the Civil War Era, 1850–1880* (Indianapolis: Indiana Historical Society, 1992), 576.

9. Alice Shaffer, Mary Wysor Keefer, and Sophonisba P. Breckenridge, *The Indiana Poor Law, Its Development and Administration with Special Reference to the Provision of State Care for the Sick Poor* (Chicago: University of Chicago Press, 1936), 30. A recent treatment is David Wagner, *The Poorhouse: America's Forgotten Institution* (Lanham, MD: Rowman and Littlefield, 2005).

10. Shaffer, Keefer, and Breckenridge, *The Indiana Poor Law*, 4.

11. Alexander Johnson, "A State Aged 100," *Survey* 36 (April 22, 1916): 97; Shaffer, Keefer, and Breckenridge, *The Indiana Poor Law*, 12.

12. Shaffer, Keefer, and Breckenridge, *The Indiana Poor Law*, 30, 52; Frances Doan Streightoff and Frank Hatch Streightoff, *Indiana: A Social and Economic Survey* (Indianapolis: W. K. Stewart, 1916), 179.

13. Kathleen D. McCarthy, *American Creed: Philanthropy and the Rise of Civil Society, 1700–1865* (Chicago: University of Chicago Press, 2003), 49.

14. Robert G. Barrows and Leigh Darbee, "The Urban Frontier in Pioneer Indiana," *Indiana Magazine of History* 105, no. 3 (September 2009): 276.

15. "Indianapolis Benevolent Society," *Indianapolis Journal*, December 17, 1872, 4.

16. Weintraut & Associates Historians, *For the Children's Sake: A History of the Children's Bureau of Indianapolis, Inc., 1875–2001* (Indianapolis: Children's Bureau of Indianapolis, 2000), 3.

17. "Many Volunteer Welfare Agencies Serve City's Unfortunate Today," *Indianapolis Star*, September 27, 1953, 41.

18. Children's Bureau of Indianapolis, "Act of Incorporation, 1851," CBI Records.

19. Indiana Reformatory, Jeffersonville (1821); Indiana Boys' School, Plainfield (1851); Indiana State Prison, Michigan City (1859); Indiana Reformatory Institution for Women and Girls, Indianapolis (1869); and the Indiana Women's Prison, Indianapolis (1869).

20. Butler, *A Century of Progress*, 22–31; Max R. Hyman, *Hyman's Handbook of Indianapolis: An Outline History* (Indianapolis: M. R. Hyman Company, 1909), 85–92; Theda Skocpol, *Protecting Workers and Mothers: The Political Origins of Social Policy in the United States* (Cambridge, MA: Harvard University Press, 1992).

21. COS Historical Sketch ca. 1910, box 3, folder 5, FSA Records.

22. Nancy Fraser and Linda Gordon, "A Genealogy of *Dependency*: Tracing a Keyword of the U.S. Welfare State," *Signs* 19, no. 2 (Winter 1994): 316.

23. Bremner, *American Philanthropy*, 91–95 and 97–98; Peter Dobkin Hall, "The Community Foundation in America, 1914–1987," in *Philanthropic Giving: Studies in Varieties and Goals*, ed. Richard Magat (New York: Oxford University Press, 1989), 183; Judith Sealander, "Curing Evils at Their Source: The Arrival of Scientific Giving," in *Charity, Philanthropy, and Civility in American History*, eds. Lawrence Friedman and Mark McGarvie (New York: Cambridge University Press, 2003), 218.

24. COS Historical Sketch ca. 1910, box 3, folder 5, FSA Records.

25. On the settlement movement, see Allen F. Davis, *Spearheads for Reform: The Social Settlements and the Progressive Movement, 1890–1914*, 2nd ed. (New Brunswick, NJ: Rutgers University Press, 1984); Judith A. Trolander, *Professionalism and Social Change: From the Settlement House Movement to Neighborhood Centers* (New York: Columbia University Press, 1987). For a recent assessment, see Rebecca Edwards, *Americans in the Gilded Age, 1865–1905* (New York: Oxford University Press, 2011), 212–14.

26. Ruth Hutchinson Crocker, *Social Work and Social Order: The Settlement Movement in Two Industrial Cities, 1889–1930* (Urbana: University of Illinois Press, 1991), 32; Clifton Phillips, *Indiana in Transition, 1880–1920* (Indianapolis: Indiana Historical Bureau and Indiana Historical Society, 1968), 163; Helen Worthington Rogers, "A Modest Experiment in Foster Motherhood: The Work of the Pure Milk Commission of the Children's Aid Association of Indianapolis," *Survey* 22 (May 1, 1909): 176–83.

27. Leander M. Campbell Adams, "An Investigation of Housing and Living Conditions in Three Districts of Indianapolis," *Indiana University Studies* 8, no. 8 (1910); Crocker, *Social Work and Social Order*, 255n13.

28. Crocker, *Social Work and Social Order*, 103; "*Forward!*" 1 (December 1909), 2–3.

29. Crocker, *Social Work and Social Order*, 140.

30. Ibid., 165.

31. Ruth Crocker, *Mrs. Russell Sage: Women's Activism and Philanthropy in Gilded Age and Progressive Era America* (Bloomington: Indiana University Press, 2006), 113–14.

32. Eleanor L. Brilliant, *The United Way: Dilemmas of Organized Charity* (New York: Columbia University Press, 1990), 23.

33. Peter Dobkin Hall, "Business Giving and Social Investment in the United States," in *Philanthropic Giving: Studies in Varieties and Goals*, ed. Richard Magat (New York: Oxford University Press, 1989), 227–32.

34. Roy Lubove, *The Professional Altruist: The Emergence of Social Work as a Career 1880–1930* (New York: Atheneum, 1983), 180; Morrell Heald, *The Social Responsibilities of Business: Company and Community, 1900–1960* (New Brunswick, NJ: Transaction, 1988), 117.

35. Hall, "Business Giving and Social Investment in the United States," 232.

36. Robert S. Lynd and Helen Merrell Lynd, *Middletown: A Study in Modern American Culture* (New York: Harcourt Brace & Co., 1957), 464.

37. Eleanor W. Sacks, *The Growing Importance of Community Foundations* (Indianapolis: Lilly Family School of Philanthropy, 2014).

38. Katz, *In the Shadow of the Poorhouse*, 217; Trattner, *From Poor Law to Welfare State*, 273.

39. Mary A. Mapes, *A Public Charity: Religion and Social Welfare in Indianapolis, 1929–2002* (Bloomington: Indiana University Press, 2004), 19.

40. Peter Dobkin Hall, "A Historical Overview of Philanthropy, Voluntary Associations, and Nonprofit Organizations in the United States, 1600–2000," in *The Nonprofit Sector: A Research Handbook*, 2nd ed., eds. Walter W. Powell and Richard Steinberg (New Haven, CT: Yale University Press, 2006), 50.

41. Robert H. Bremner, *American Philanthropy*, 2nd ed. (Chicago: University of Chicago Press, 1988), 146–47; Trattner, *From Poor Law to Welfare State*, 294.

42. Mapes, *A Public Charity*, 30.

43. Russell H. Kurtz, "Back to Indianapolis: National Conference Brings 1937 Social Workers to an Old Stamping Ground," *Survey* 73 (May 1937): 154.

44. Mapes, *A Public Charity*, 32–34.

45. Mapes, *A Public Charity*, 38.

46. Steven Rathgeb Smith and Michael Lipsky, "The Political Economy of Nonprofit Revenues," in *Making the Nonprofit Sector in the United States*, ed. David C. Hammack (Bloomington: Indiana University Press, 1998), 459.

47. Smith and Lipsky, "The Political Economy of Nonprofit Revenues," 461–65.

48. Burton A. Weisbrod, "The Future of the Nonprofit Sector: Its Entwining with Private Enterprise and Government," *Journal of Policy Analysis and Management* 16, no. 4 (Autumn 1997): 543.

49. Carol De Vita, "Nonprofits and Devolution: What Do We Know?," in *Nonprofits and Government: Collaboration and Conflict*, eds. Elizabeth T. Boris and C. Eugene Steuerle (Washington, DC: Urban Institute, 1999), 215.

50. Mapes, *A Public Charity*, 10.

51. Kirsten A. Grønbjerg et al., *Indiana Nonprofit Employment: Trends in Social Assistance, 1995–2009* (Bloomington: Indiana University School of Public and Environmental Affairs, 2012), 1–4, 8.

52. Grønbjerg, *Indiana Nonprofit Employment*, 3.

FOUR

—ᴍ—

IN SEARCH OF THE ETHICAL SOCIETY

A History of Voluntary Associations in Indiana

JAMES J. CONNOLLY

IN *MIDDLETOWN*, AN IN-DEPTH STUDY of community life in 1920s Muncie, Indiana, Robert and Helen Lynd looked back nostalgically at the activities of the city's Ethical Society during the 1890s. The Ethical Society was a discussion club devoted to political and cultural issues. It was the group's members as much as the topics they addressed that attracted the Lynds. "Week after week in the nineties," *Middletown* reported, "baker and nailmaker sat side by side with banker and doctor, discussing such questions as the 'Ethical Life of Man,' . . . 'Physical Culture for Our Children in Schools,' 'Free Silver,' or 'The Meaning of Evolution.'" For the Lynds, these gatherings captured the character of civic life in a preindustrial community. They were lively and inclusive, generating a strong sense of citizenship. By contrast, they found Muncie's associational life during the 1920s—dominated by the Rotary, the Woman's Club, and similar organizations—to be status-oriented, intellectually limited, and segregated by social class.[1]

The Lynds' admiration for the Ethical Society aligns with many of the principles promoted by present-day theorists of democracy and civic life. Discussions allowed the "utmost freedom of speech." Organizers welcomed participants from "all denominations and political complexions" and all social backgrounds.

Even women attended in an era when female participation in pub-lic activities was relatively uncommon. Positions were advanced through rational argument rather than relying on the status or prominence of the advocate. Discussions addressed important civic issues: Free silver and the social implications of evolutionary theory were among the hottest topics of 1890s public life. Sessions attracted broad participation, with as many as seventy-five to one hundred people attending meetings. Perhaps most important, the Ethical Society was but one example of discussion, engagement, and sociability among many according to the Lynds, a reflection of the robust and open civic life of preindustrial Middletown.

The Lynds' nostalgic tone also prefigures that of more recent commentaries about the civic character of the United States. Most, though not all, contend that both the quality and quantity of associational and voluntary activity in America have dimin-ished and that this decline has weakened Americans' sense of citi-zenship. They point to a golden age of clubs, fraternal groups, and churchgoing that stretched from the middle of the nineteenth century to the middle of the twentieth. These endeavors, a num-ber of scholars have suggested, bred good citizens by producing healthy social relations, teaching participants how to cooperate and organize, and cultivating interest in public affairs. The de-cline of associational activity in recent decades, they contend, has undermined civic life.

Not all analysts of American civic history subscribe to this narrative of declension nor is there full agreement among those who do. For some observers, there have been major changes in the ways Americans engage with one another to address common concerns, but these shifts do not necessarily constitute a decline so much as a transition. We may be "bowling alone" more often, to borrow a phrase made popular by Robert Putnam's study of the same name, but many more are also "kicking in groups," a reference to the proliferation of youth soccer clubs that Nicholas Lemann cited as one example of new kinds of shared activity.[2]

Even among those who argue that civic decay has occurred, there is disagreement about why it happened and what to do about it. For Putnam, the loss of social capital and social trust that had been cultivated by face-to-face collective activities is a crucial concern. Particularly important are organizations that cultivate "bridging" social capital—connections that cut across class and group lines—as opposed to "bonding" social capital, which strengthens in-group ties. Both types of civic links have diminished, Putnam insists, a development that he argues has impoverished public life. Theda Skocpol, another leading voice in this conversation, describes civic change over the past seventy years in a somewhat different way. She sees a precipitous drop in participation in a specific kind of group: multiclass, translocal organizations. Fraternal bodies, such as the Odd Fellows, the Elks, and the many woman's groups that joined the General Federation of Women's Clubs, provided opportunities to forge close ties locally while also creating national networks that could be mobilized for political purposes. As these groups faded after World War II, expert-run lobbying organizations filled the void, Skocpol contends. These newer associations often relied on grassroots financial support but operated in a top-down manner that did not cultivate meaningful forms of civic engagement among ordinary citizens.[3]

Indiana's experience provides evidence to support all of these perspectives, and for the most part, the state's civic evolution has followed national patterns. There has been a decline in what Putnam calls "serious volunteering" through formal associational activity among Hoosiers, but other forms of voluntary action and engagement have persisted and even increased. As in the rest of the country, voter participation in Indiana has dropped dramatically from where it was a century or more ago. Today, Hoosiers are a little less likely to vote and about as likely to volunteer as the average American. On other measures, including participation in group activities, church membership, and the maintenance of social connections, Indiana does slightly better than the nation as a whole.[4]

This essay aims to examine the history of civic life in Indiana from the state's formation in 1816 through the early twenty-first century. It focuses in particular on ways that the state's distinctive social, economic, and geographic characteristics have shaped voluntarism and associational activity. Three features have had noticeable impact. The first is the importance of manufacturing to the state's economy after the Civil War. Industrial production grew tremendously beginning late in the nineteenth century and became the principal economic activity in the state by 1920. Even today, manufacturing remains an unusually large part of Indiana's economy.[5] As a result, the recent decrease in factory jobs has had an outsized impact on Indiana's civic affairs. The second is the state's settlement pattern. More than most states, Indiana's landscape is dotted by small and midsized cities, most of them agricultural market towns that became industrial centers. These settings were especially fertile ground for the associational activities that flourished during the nineteenth and early twentieth centuries.[6] Odd Fellows, women's clubs, Rotaries, and other voluntary groups thrived in these communities and remained active longer than they did elsewhere. Finally, Indiana has been comparatively homogenous in a racial and ethnic sense. Immigrants and African Americans have been an important presence in some communities, particularly Indianapolis and the cities near Chicago, but racism and ethnocentrism have strongly influenced Indiana's civic life, which has not been particularly inclusive for most of the state's history.

In surveying Indiana's civic past, it is useful to keep the standard set by the Lynds in sight. Ideally, a healthy civil society is inclusive and deliberative; it promotes interaction among people of varied backgrounds and social positions, fosters democratic social relationships, and encourages respectful discussions of issues and concerns affecting communities. As is the case in the rest of the United States, civic engagement in Indiana has not always met these lofty standards. Nevertheless, they serve as a useful measuring stick as we consider the history and present condition of voluntarism and associational activity in the state.

Indiana remained sparsely settled and chiefly agricultural from its organization as a state in 1816 through the Civil War. Substantial numbers of White migrants began arriving during the late eighteenth century in search of land. The newcomers started forcing Native Americans out of the state, a process that was largely complete by the 1840s. Indian removal was rooted in hostility to non-Whites, an outlook that would continue to define the parameters of Hoosier civic culture for two centuries. Religious faith provided another key building block of the state's early voluntary life. It facilitated stronger social and civic bonds, both in small towns and the countryside. Revivals and camp meetings staged by itinerant Methodist and Baptist preachers generated opportunities for sociability and education, as well as worship. More formal organizations, particularly Methodist, Baptist, and Presbyterian churches and associated voluntary groups, gradually developed in the state's scattered towns. The slow growth of urban settlements also influenced the state's civic character, as did the cultural inheritances of the newcomers. The development of the party system during the 1820s and 1830s, which to a considerable degree mapped onto broader cultural patterns, provided a second set of institutions that drew people together and generated public engagement.

The different groups of White migrants who came to Indiana shaped its initial civic development. The earliest arrivals, mainly from Virginia and North Carolina, began entering Indiana even before it became a state in 1816. They were predominantly subsistence farmers who spread widely across the southern tier of the state, a settlement pattern that discouraged town formation and thus limited opportunities for civic engagement. They also brought with them a set of beliefs that emphasized personal liberty, egalitarianism, and skepticism of government activism. These precepts left them less inclined to develop formal voluntary groups in the pursuit of civic improvement. Later arrivals from the mid-Atlantic states and New England populated the central and northern sections of Indiana and were more likely to live in towns and cities. They displayed greater enthusiasm for government and were more prone to organize institutions designed to advance the moral character of people and communities.

Clashes between these two outlooks gave shape to civic life before the Civil War. As Andrew Cayton has explained, "The men and women who wanted to reform Indiana had to limit their activities largely to voluntary activities in urban areas." Reform-minded activists, almost all of them Protestant members of an emergent urban middle class, created a temperance society in Indianapolis in 1826 and formed the Indianapolis Benevolent Society in 1835. Religious groups in the city began organizing educational institutions as well, such as a Sabbath school in 1823 and the Indianapolis Female School in 1830. Similar institutions emerged even in small towns, but the slow pace of urban settlement in Indiana limited the impact of this kind of civic engagement. More importantly, reformers faced fierce resistance from the state's rural residents, who rejected efforts to uplift them to town standards.[7]

The cultural antecedents of the state's early White settlers also shaped the agenda of voluntary life before the Civil War. The temperance movement, a staple of Protestant-driven reform through most of the northern United States, thrived in Indiana. Even smaller towns usually featured at least one organization devoted to that cause, and many communities passed laws regulating the sale of alcohol. While members of the state's principal Protestant denominations rarely expressed support for slavery, they displayed less enthusiasm for its abolition before 1850 than did comparable groups in most other states, a disposition at least in part attributable to traditions of segregation and discrimination brought by settlers from the upland South. Only the Quakers, a small minority of religious Hoosiers, actively aided African American efforts to ferry escaped slaves to freedom through the Underground Railroad.[8]

Another demographic pattern that would shape Indiana's civic character in the long term, the relatively limited presence of religious and ethnic minorities took shape before the Civil War. The state attracted fewer immigrants than most of its northern counterparts, in part because it had comparatively few cities and less industrial development. Small pockets of Catholics and Jews lived in Indianapolis and other towns and these groups did develop a parallel network of voluntary institutions, but Protestants dominated. One exception to this pattern was Fort Wayne, which drew a substantial influx of Germans after 1840, including Catholics, Jews, and Lutherans. These settlers built churches, synagogues, turnvereins, and other organizations that distinguished the city from other nineteenth-century Hoosier communities. The relative absence of these groups through most of the state meant that interethnic tensions around moral reform efforts, such as temperance—which in other places often targeted Catholics and Jews, were comparatively modest, while frictions between town and country were particularly salient.

Civic organizations less formally tied to religious life also developed during the early nineteenth century. Utopian reformers established the New Harmony settlement in southwestern Indiana in 1814, a community first run by members of the Harmony Society, a dissenting sect of German Lutherans headed by George Rapp. The Rappites sold the town to mill owner and socialist Robert Owen in 1825, and it became a center of educational and philosophical activity. The settlement attracted influential thinkers and activists and established the first free library and school in Indiana. Although in many ways distinct from the principal thrust of civic culture in early Indiana, it did produce several influential figures in the state's public life, including the reformer Robert Dale Owen, son of Robert Owen, and William MacLure, the noted geologist who left a bequest that established workingmen's libraries across the state.[9]

By the mid-nineteenth century, as Indiana began to urbanize, fraternal organizations became a significant presence in Hoosier civic life. In most communities, fraternal groups and other voluntary bodies emerged as towns grew. Masons organized in Indianapolis in 1824, just three years after its streets were laid out. They established a lodge in Muncie in 1842, when the town barely had five hundred residents. Soon most towns of any size had one or more fraternal lodges. These groups had both practical and civic purposes: They served as mutual-benefit societies that provided an early form of insurance for their members and they also provided a setting for developing social connections and organizing collective action.[10]

The other influential voluntary groups that drew people together and generated public engagement in early Indiana were political parties. The second-party system, which pitted Democrats against Whigs, took shape during the 1820s and 1830s throughout the United States. It featured spectacular campaigning in the form of parades and rallies and mobilized large swaths of the electorate. Partisan newspapers proliferated, urging support for platforms and candidates. Turnout reached 85 percent of eligible (White male) voters by 1840, and it would remain high for the rest of the century, averaging more than 90 percent after the Civil War. In many respects the two parties expressed the civic and cultural divisions that defined the state's public life in this era. Whigs advocated public improvement and moral uplift, attracting support from evangelical Protestants in towns and cities, while Democrats stressed limited government and individual liberty, drawing strong support in southern parts of Indiana, where

migrants from the upland South had settled. These commitments
would largely carry over into the postwar period, with Republi-
cans inheriting much of the ideology propounded by Whigs and
most of their supporters.[11]

THE INDUSTRIAL ERA, 1880 TO 1960

A survey of Indiana's civic life from the late nineteenth century through the first half of the twentieth century reveals the
deepening fault lines of an industrial society. Associations proliferated from the late nineteenth century to the middle of the
twentieth, including an extraordinary array of fraternal groups,
women's clubs, ethnic societies, Granges, and, eventually, labor
organizations. As the state's manufacturing sector began to grow
during the latter part of the nineteenth century and its population became more urban, class and cultural tensions sharpened.
Civic life evolved to reflect these divisions, with an increasingly
exclusive vein of organizational activity undertaken by middle-
class, native-born Whites, while parallel associations formed by
African American and ethnic groups. Cultural cleavages were
especially sharp during the 1920s, when the Ku Klux Klan (KKK)
briefly emerged as the dominant civic organization in the state.
Members of the industrial working class were increasingly cut
off from many facets of this associational life until the formation
of unions during the 1930s provided them with a civic and social
infrastructure that increased their levels of engagement.

As in the preindustrial period, church life remained closely
tied to civic affairs during the late nineteenth and early twentieth
centuries. Religious congregations of all denominations engaged
in charitable work. Organizations such as the Indiana Benevolent
Association, the YMCA, and the Salvation Army were prominent
elements of the civic landscape in Indianapolis at the end of the
nineteenth century. Oscar McCulloch, pastor of Plymouth Congregational Church, spearheaded a variety of philanthropic work,

including the formation of Indianapolis's Charity Organization Society and the Plymouth Institute, which provided educational and cultural opportunities for the city's residents. Religiously inspired campaigns for Sabbatarianism and temperance figured prominently in public debates through the late nineteenth century and into the twentieth. The Women's Christian Temperance Union (WCTU), a national organization formed in 1878, had a prominent presence in Indianapolis and other cities. Catholics and Jews launched parallel charities, mutual-benefit groups, and social organizations, particularly in Indianapolis, Fort Wayne, and South Bend.[12]

Voluntary activity also intensified in smaller towns and rural settings during the decades following the Civil War. Fraternal organizations multiplied and dispersed so much that one could find numerous lodges not only in substantial cities but even in the smallest of settlements. In Delaware County, lodges formed in the tiny hamlets of Gaston, Cowan, Albany, Daleville, and Wheeling during the 1860s and 1870s, a pattern that repeated itself across the state. Women's literary societies and reform groups increased in number and membership totals during the 1870s and 1880s, not only in cities but in communities of every size. A survey of the WCTU's work in late nineteenth-century Allen County found branches in the little towns of Hoagland, Maysville, and Monroeville—although its antialcohol agenda earned it little traction in heavily German Fort Wayne. These associations were tied to national networks that integrated their members into the wider society and, along with religious denominations and political parties, gave them the institutional means to exercise power.[13]

The Granger movement, a network of organizations that one historian dubbed "the only rural fraternity in the world," dominated civic life in much of rural Indiana. Formed as an advocacy group and social organization for agricultural interests, the National Grange of the Patrons of Husbandry, as it was officially known, thrived throughout the Midwest beginning in the 1870s.

Early in that decade, every eighteen square miles in Indiana had a Grange. These bodies met regularly, usually once or twice a month, and their meetings featured lectures, debates, and entertainment, along with opportunities for sociability. A typical meeting of Grange number 189, in tiny Olive, Indiana, in 1888 included discussions about government's ability to sell land and tax sugar. The same group held periodic neighbors' nights, in which members exchanged visits with Granges in nearby communities. Participation declined gradually after the 1870s, but the Grange remained a significant element of civic life in rural Indiana well into the twentieth century.[14]

Another important development during the closing decades of the nineteenth century was a shift toward greater civic activism among middle-class clubwomen. Literary societies once devoted to the discussion of books transformed into aggressively reformist organizations, a process that gave women increasingly substantial public roles, even before they had earned the vote. Indianapolis featured an extensive array of such groups at the turn of the century. Fort Wayne had sixteen according to one list, while Muncie had at least a dozen. Women in smaller communities, such as Cambridge City (the Helen Hunt Club), Greencastle (The Women's Club), Frankfort (the Tourist Club), and New Albany (the Amaranth), organized in this fashion, as did female residents in rural settings, such as those who launched the Mary-Martha club in 1891. This Delaware County group limited its membership to those not residing in the area's towns or cities. In urban settings, including Indianapolis, Fort Wayne, and Muncie, activist women organized federated bodies that united various clubs. Many groups joined the Indiana Union of Literary Clubs and the General Federation of Women's Clubs, becoming part of an extensive network of coordinated voluntary activity.[15]

By the turn of the twentieth century, Indiana's roster of fraternal groups had also expanded significantly. An 1897 survey of these organizations reported more than two-dozen national bodies with a significant presence in Indiana, several of which claimed tens of thousands of members. The largest was the Independent Order of Odd Fellows, with almost forty-two thousand enrollees across the state. Other substantial organizations included the Freemasons, the Knights of Pythias, and the Grand Army of the Republic. Most of these groups had formed during the middle decades of the nineteenth century as mutual-benefit societies and were thriving as the new century began. Although the majority were male-only societies, many had parallel women's organizations. Numerous other, smaller, Indiana-based bodies popped up during the 1890s, including the Light of the Ages, a benefit society that quickly converted into a life insurance company, and groups such as the Tribe of Ben-Hur, designed to capitalize on the tremendous popularity of Hoosier author Lew Wallace's novel of the same name.[16]

Scholars disagree about the civic impact of fraternal groups during this period. Some historians, most notably David Beito, point to these organizations as powerful examples of cross-class social activity that bound communities together. By providing social insurance through mutual-benefit schemes, these bodies insulated members from the risk endemic to an industrial society while also creating ties across socioeconomic lines that fostered social stability. The economic security provided by fraternal bodies became less significant as the modern American welfare state emerged during and after the New Deal. As a result, membership declined over the second half of the twentieth century, and the communal ties such groups formed diminished as well. Jason Kaufman is among the scholars who dissent from this view. He contends that the predominance of fraternal groups that attracted blue-collar and white-collar members and highlighted ethnic and cultural differences ultimately had detrimental civic effects. These groups helped block the political mobilization of workers on the basis of their class interests, encouraged interest group activism, and helped shape a state that was more attuned to business and middle-class interests and less responsive to the needs and demands of ordinary industrial workers.[17]

The history of fraternal bodies in Indiana complicates both interpretations. It suggests that the cross-class sociability that was once a significant feature of such groups began to fade well before the New Deal era. Class divisions became clearer and more salient as the economy changed and cities grew. Older, cross-class fraternal organizations lost some of their popularity while new more socially exclusive societies formed. When queried about lodge life in 1929, an anonymous leader of an Indianapolis fraternal association reported that "it ain't what it used to be," and statistics showing that active participation in such groups had "dwindled considerably" support this impression. The Lynds saw a similar pattern in Muncie, pointing to the rise of groups such as the Rotary, which was limited to business and professional men and drew the middle class away from traditional fraternal groups that had, at one time, united participants across class and group lines. While clubs of this sort engaged in philanthropic work, in the Lynds' judgment, they functioned as much to reinforce socioeconomic distinctions as they did to improve the community.[18]

As had been the case since the state's founding, it was almost impossible to separate the associational and philanthropic activity of industrial-era Indiana from its religious life. Most fraternal groups and women's clubs were nondenominational, but they were nonetheless religious. Men who joined the Odd Fellows, Masons, or Elks engaged in quasireligious rituals, professed faith in God, and often opened meetings with prayer. Charitable activities, such as poor relief, were closely tied to churches during the nineteenth century and remained so even as antipoverty efforts grew more scientific and philanthropic groups organized on a more formal basis during the early twentieth century. Religious ideals formed a key part of the motivation for the women reformers who organized settlement houses in Indianapolis, Gary, and

Terre Haute during the century's first two decades. They aimed to assist the poor, including African Americans and immigrants, and incorporate them more fully into American life. For some, the best way to achieve this goal was to convert them to more respectable forms of Christianity. While these efforts represented sincere attempts to improve the lives of impoverished Hoosiers and bring the most marginalized into the state's civic fold, the religious and cultural agendas of settlement workers often made it difficult for them to earn the trust of those they aimed to help.[19]

The mix of civic, socioeconomic, and religious agendas that characterized Hoosier associational life received unsettling expression through the brief but intense popularity of the KKK during the 1920s. The Klan of this period differed from the more recent manifestation of the organization and its Reconstruction-era predecessor. Though avowedly racist, anti-Semitic, and anti-Catholic, its members displayed greater concern for improving the civic and moral health of their communities. They were especially alarmed about many aspects of modern life, including increased ethnic diversity, the corrupting influence of alcohol, the loosening of sexual mores, and the rise of a cosmopolitan urban cultural order. The Klan operated along the lines of other fraternal organizations, complete with quasireligious rituals and women's auxiliaries. Indiana's first Klavern formed in Evansville in 1920 and recruited its members from church groups and fraternal orders. It spread rapidly, achieving a massive membership of more than three hundred thousand across most of the state by 1923. Near its peak in 1925, it enrolled more than a quarter of all adult White men in Indianapolis, Terre Haute, Muncie, Kokomo, Anderson, Elkhart, and Logansport and had healthy participation in all but a handful of the state's counties. Close analysis of its membership reveals that the largest share of its rank and file came from the middle of the economic spectrum—grocers, bank tellers, insurance agents, and skilled workers—but lower-skilled manual workers were well represented and a handful of elite businessmen joined. Although these numbers began to drop rapidly in 1925, particularly in the wake of a scandal surrounding D. C. Stephenson, the Klan's leader in Indiana, for a short period of time the KKK was the preeminent civic organization in the state.[20]

In important respects the Klan of the 1920s reflected developments in Indiana's associational culture. The state's club life had become more exclusive and the Kluxers' desire to limit themselves to a White, Protestant, and respectable membership fit with that trend (although it drew from a wider socioeconomic spectrum). There were also religious overtones to the Klan's rituals and agendas, much as there were in many other voluntary groups. The Klan engaged in charitable work and encouraged its members to be active in civic and political affairs. Of course, it was also openly hostile toward immigrants, particularly those who were Catholic and Jewish, blaming them for a perceived decline in the civic and moral fiber of American society. Although it did not directly engage in violence toward African Americans and immigrants, its activities contributed to a hostile atmosphere in the state.

Despite its popularity, not all Hoosiers shared the Klan's outlook. During the 1920s, some communities established institutions that sought to cultivate a form of civic engagement that drew people of varied backgrounds together instead of exploiting differences. One such effort was the Open Forum movement, a campaign to promote democratic discussion reminiscent of Muncie's Ethical Society. It offered an alternative vision of public life to that espoused by the Klan. The idea was to invite prominent speakers to discuss the pressing issues of the day followed by open discussion of the topic from all points of view. Organizers set up forums in Evansville, Indianapolis, Terre Haute, and Hammond. Of these, Hammond's was the most durable, lasting into the 1940s, when the wartime shortages of World War II brought it to a close.[21]

Hammond's ethnic character helps explain the success of the Open Forum movement there. It was part of the industrial cluster of communities near Chicago that drew substantial numbers of immigrants. Although it was also the scene of some Klan activity, including a twelve-thousand-person rally in 1922, its immigrant community was large enough to sustain an alternative approach to civic affairs. The city's Jewish community, led by Rabbi Max Bretton and members of the Temple Beth El congregation, started a forum in the fall of 1924. Its first lecturer was the Reverend John Ryan, a well-known Catholic advocate of social justice causes. The next speaker was an Indian journalist discussing eastern religions, followed by a historian examining "race prejudice" (and criticizing the KKK). In later years, W. E. B. DuBois, socialist leader Norman Thomas, and Eleanor Roosevelt spoke. Despite the forum's willingness to explore controversial topics, it earned the support of a cross section of the community. Even the Chamber of Commerce eventually backed it, citing it as evidence of the city's "civic development."[22]

The democratic openness of Hammond's forums was hardly characteristic of Indiana civic life during the first half of the twentieth century. As the Klan's success indicates, racism and hostility to immigrants was strong, and the patterns of associational activity reflected that reality. Outside groups, including African Americans, Jews, Catholics, and various immigrant populations, organized separate clubs and fraternal bodies that produced parallel civic networks. In some cases, such as the activity of Jewish groups in Indianapolis and Hammond or Germans in Indianapolis and Fort Wayne, these organizations facilitated the integration of their members into White middle-class society. But racial barriers were too steep for African Americans to overcome, so they maintained separate organizations that often mirrored the civic activities of Whites. There were Black versions of fraternal groups such as the Masons and the Knights of Pythias, a network of Colored Women's Clubs, and a range of church-based activities that enabled the modest population of African Americans in the state, concentrated increasingly in the steel-producing cities of northern Indiana, to sustain community life and demand civil rights in the face of pervasive discrimination. Other groups, such as the small cohort of Mexican laborers drawn to work in the steel factories in East Chicago and Calumet between 1915 and 1930, formed mutual aid societies that advanced their interests.[23]

There is no systematic evidence examining trends in working-class civic life during the first half of the twentieth century. What testimony we do have suggests that industrial operatives and manual laborers engaged in less associational activity than their middle-class counterparts and that they were comparatively isolated. Lodge life continued, as did church membership, but participation in these activities gradually diminished and they no longer brought manufacturing workers into contact with members of the middle and upper classes on a regular basis. Partly this was the product of the rise of factory labor, which required twelve-hour shifts, six days a week. While middle-class men worked shorter hours and their wives benefited from labor-saving household technologies (or, for the most affluent, servants), blue-collar men and women had comparatively little time for civic and leisure activities.[24]

These circumstances changed as Indiana's industrial workforce began to unionize during the second half of the 1930s. On the eve of World War II, most workers in the state's steel factories and auto-parts plants had organized, and those in other industries followed suit over the next decade. While the impact of the United Auto Workers, the United Steel Workers, and other unions on wages, benefits, hours, and working conditions is well documented, scholars have not fully appreciated their powerful effect on working-class civic engagement. Unions not only mobilized workers politically, they expanded their social networks, encouraged voluntary activity, and honed civic skills. After World War II, labor representatives began to serve on the boards of local philanthropic groups, such as the United Way. Oral history interviews with union workers suggest that these organizations cultivated in their members a sense of connection to the community as a whole that encouraged confidence in institutions and a belief that they had some control over their lives.[25] They did not always defuse class tensions, as Indiana's business community remained notably hostile to unionization.[26] Nor were unions especially quick to integrate racially or incorporate women. But organized labor gave many workers a sense of belonging and means of exerting civic influence that helped integrate them into the civic life of their communities.

If increasingly divided in socioeconomic and cultural terms, associational life in Indiana nevertheless remained robust through the middle decades of the twentieth century. A 1929 report on organizational activity in Indianapolis found 171 formal groups staging more than four hundred meetings in a single month, a level of activity that persisted (and, for workers, increased) during the period after World War II. These included gatherings of church groups, service clubs, union locals, business associations, university alumni, and a host of fraternal orders. Even small-town Indiana maintained a rich array of formal voluntary activity: In 1939 tiny Brookston, with a population of fewer than a thousand, had thirty-nine active clubs, a figure that does not include several church groups.[27] But midcentury associational life had changed from fifty years earlier. There was less mixing across class lines than there had once been, especially in cities, and ethnic and religious differences were more salient than ever. These divisions lessened the bonds that united different elements of the community, even as substantial numbers of Hoosiers of all classes and backgrounds still participated in the state's voluntary life.

THE POSTINDUSTRIAL ERA, 1960 TO PRESENT

Economic and cultural changes reshaped Indiana's civic life during the closing decades of the twentieth century. Manufacturing remained a central element of the state's economy, but the proportion of Hoosiers working in factories diminished, as did union membership and the civic benefits tied to it. The success of the civil rights movement helped break down many of the barriers dividing African American and Whites, but race (and class) still mattered when it came to patterns of civic engagement. The character of leisure also changed in post–World War II America, as television and suburban living encouraged private activities and reduced the attraction of the lodge meeting, Rotary lunch, or woman's club lecture. Membership in these groups, and especially in the cross-class fraternal organizations so prominent in the associational life of the early twentieth century, declined precipitously. In place of these institutional forms of civic engagement, new forms of voluntary action arose. Directed through churches, nonprofit organizations, and in a few instances, large-scale civic initiatives, these efforts became a significant form of public engagement for many Hoosiers. As was the case during the industrial period, trends seen in Indiana generally matched those of the entire nation, but they continued to be shaped by Indiana's distinctive economic, demographic, and cultural character.

The most significant change in Indiana's civic life, and in the nation's, after 1960 was the greater incorporation of African Americans and other minority groups. Although civil rights campaigning by African Americans centered on the South during the 1950s and early 1960s and in major urban centers such as Chicago and Detroit during the late 1960s, Indiana saw the passage of civil rights laws in 1961 and 1963 that put it ahead of the curve in a legal sense. Residential segregation and other forms of discrimination remained powerful elements of everyday life in the state nonetheless. Racial tensions in Indianapolis remained high, particularly in regard to schools and housing, while the economic decline of Gary and other northwestern Indiana steel cities left masses of African Americans trapped in poverty and decaying urban environments.[28] While these difficulties have persisted and racial inequality remains a stubborn fact of life in Indiana, formal barriers to civic participation for minority groups diminished considerably after 1960. Associational life was no longer segregated, which had the unintended side effect of reducing participation in Black-only fraternal groups and clubs, while African American voting and office holding increased.[29]

Another shift in the state's voluntary life was the decline of membership-driven organizations, such as fraternal groups and women's clubs.[30] The Masons, Elks, and Odd Fellows endured through the twentieth century, but membership had dropped to a few thousand of each by the 1990s. As late as 1970, the Lafayette Elks had more than two thousand members; by 2014 it had just 322, most of them retirees.[31] These groups were more service oriented than they had been a century before, when they functioned as mutual-benefit associations and influential civic bodies. More significant, they no longer brought substantial numbers of community members together across class lines to make shared civic experiences possible.

Changes in the economic landscape of Indiana further sharpened the civic salience of class differences. Although manufacturing remained a core part of the state's economy, industrial employment began to decline over the final years of the twentieth century as a result of globalization and technological developments. The state lost two hundred thousand manufacturing jobs between 1970 and 2007 despite a population increase of more than a million people during that period.[32] Union membership among industrial workers had an even sharper decline as older plants with organized workforces closed and newer nonunion plants opened. In civic terms, this development lessened working-class voluntary activity. Research on the connection between union membership and civic engagement shows a strong correlation between the two. Workers without ties to organized labor are considerably less likely to vote or participate in other facets of public life. This union-civic engagement connection is especially strong when it comes to political participation, including voting, lobbying, and joining protests. There is no clear evidence that union membership generates greater cross-class social capital.[33]

Churches are one type of institution that has continued to nurture strong social ties and healthy levels of civic engagement. Even during and immediately after the upheavals of the 1960s, when activists challenged all manner of American institutions, religious faith and practice remained strong in Indiana.[34] Although churchgoing has declined somewhat recently, both in Indiana and nationally, the state still ranks among the most religiously active, and 60 percent of its residents still say that religion is an important part of their lives (in comparison to 56 percent of all Americans). The state's religious scene is overwhelmingly Christian. Nearly three-quarters (72 percent) of Hoosiers describe themselves as such, while just 2 percent report allegiance to a non-Christian faith. The remaining 26 percent claim no religious affiliation. As has been the case throughout the state's history, religious institutions have generated civic engagement and voluntary action. Indeed, participation in associations tied to churches and other religious institutions accounts for the largest share of voluntary group activity in the state and is a dimension of civic life in which Hoosiers continue to do considerably better than the national average. Without it the state would probably lag behind national levels on a number of measures of engagement.[35]

The effects of Indiana's strong and durable religious tradition on the evolution of its civic life are complex. Churchgoing has long been positively associated with volunteering, charitable work, voting, and other forms of civic engagement. Religious participation also makes it more likely that a person will establish connections with people of different social backgrounds, in part because they are more engaged generally. It is also worth noting that, historically, religious institutions have been at the forefront of efforts to alleviate poverty and promote social justice in Indiana. But religiously motivated altruism at times fostered inequitable social relationships in which the beneficiaries were expected to assume a subordinate status relative to those providing help.

There is also mixed evidence about the civic impact of evangelical religion, which expanded significantly during the late twentieth century and drew the allegiance of nearly a third (31 percent) of all Hoosiers in 2014. Survey evidence from the 1990s indicated that fundamentalist churches encouraged their members to vote but also cultivated civic and social ties that focused inward on other members of a congregation rather than toward the wider community. More recent data highlights the fact these churches draw members from a wider range of social backgrounds than do mainline Protestant denominations and other religious groups. Strong ties within evangelical congregations thus produce a form of cross-class exchange that generates sympathy and support for fellow churchgoers, regardless of background, an important feature in a state such as Indiana, where class differences are especially acute. But attendance at an evangelical church does not foster similarly strong engagement with outsiders. More generally, this effect is limited because there has been a steeper drop in working-class churchgoing in recent decades. Thus, in some respects, the resurgence of evangelical religion in Indiana appears to have introduced new social cleavages that run along religious lines even as they help bridge an older divide.[36]

Two other areas of civic life where Indiana compares somewhat favorably to national norms are in the percentage of adults who volunteer and the percentage who give to charity. In 2013, 26.9 percent of the state's residents reported engaging in volunteer activity. Just over half (50.9 percent) of Hoosiers indicated that they had donated at least $25 in the previous year. The state ranked

slightly above the national average in both measures, a modest increase over the previous measurement in 2010. Churches or other
religiously inspired or faith-based organizations, such as Habitat
for Humanity, facilitated a considerable portion of this activity.
The state government also put resources into the promotion of
civic engagement through an Office of Faith-Based and Community Initiatives, formed in 2005, which aimed to coordinate
the work of voluntary organizations.[37]

Another measure of the state's relatively healthy and durable
ethic of volunteering is the support generated for large sporting
events in Indianapolis. Civic and business officials successfully
attracted thousands of volunteers to help the city stage the 1982
National Sports Festival. This experience provided the model
for the city when it hosted the 1987 Pan Am games, a multisport
competition that drew athletes from thirty-eight countries. Organizers recruited thirty-seven thousand volunteers to staff the
event (as compared to three hundred paid staffers). Another
major sporting event staged in the city, the National Football
League's 2012 Super Bowl, drew the support of eight thousand
volunteers who provided one hundred and fifty thousand hours
of service (and another five thousand offered to participate but
were not needed). These impressive mobilizations of volunteers
both reflected the city's strong level of civic engagement (especially among younger adults) and sought to increase it. The chairman of the host committee argued that "once people get involved
initially in something bigger than themselves, assuming it goes
well, they love it and develop an appetite to do more." In the
aftermath of the Super Bowl, the Indiana Sports Corporation,
which had been maintaining a database of Indianapolis-area
volunteers since the 1980s, reported that the list now included
seventeen thousand names.[38] These efforts appeared to bear fruit
as Indianapolis climbed to become the tenth-ranked large city in
the country for percentage of volunteers in 2015, up from nineteenth in 2011.[39]

It is impossible to compare these behaviors with those of a century ago in a quantitative sense, but there are notable qualitative differences. Voluntary efforts in the early twentieth century were largely membership oriented. Civic engagement beyond direct political participation typically entailed working with a church group, fraternal body, or club. Although there were undoubtedly an untold number of informal activities taking place during this era, the formal links provided through associations helped knit communities together. At the opening of the twentieth century, many of these associations were cross class in character, although that quality diminished over time. By contrast, a larger share of contemporary volunteering is individualized and focused on single events, as was the case with the volunteering around the Super Bowl. While that mobilization appears to have generated new enthusiasm for volunteer work, it is not the sustained, institutionalized activity that once prevailed. This kind of civic engagement appears to be increasingly significant in Indiana. As the "exalted ruler" of an Elks lodge in Lafayette recently explained, many younger people lack the time to engage in the sustained organizational work that a fraternal group or service club demands. They are more likely to participate in "one and done" activities, "such as running a 5K."[40] That sort of engagement, whether it is participation in a race, a couple of Saturday hours unloading a truck at a food pantry, or helping stage a spectacular sporting event, does not produce the kind of intense connectivity among citizens of all backgrounds that most analysts argue is a necessary element of a healthy civic life.

The social patterns associated with various forms of voluntary activity in contemporary Indiana highlight this gap. By almost every conventional measure of civic engagement, Hoosiers with college degrees participate at far higher rates than those with little or no education. Nearly half of college graduates report volunteering in some form, while fewer than 20 percent of those with just a high school diploma do. Higher levels of education also correlate with stronger rates of voting, charitable donations, and participation in groups of various types. In a state where barely one in five people have completed college, educational attainment is clearly a rough proxy for socioeconomic status, and these behavioral gaps illustrate the socioeconomic divide that continues to define the state's civic character.[41]

CONCLUSION

Observers of contemporary American civics tend to bemoan its decline. Whether fretting about a loss of social capital or pointing to the rise of interest groups, most commentators lament the passing of an earlier era in which voter turnout was higher, organizational culture was more robust, and popular knowledge of, and engagement with, public affairs was supposedly deeper. Conservatives and liberals share these concerns, although they attribute them to different causes and seek different solutions. Scholars such as Putnam and Skocpol may disagree about precisely how and why the quality of American civic life had declined, but they agree that is worse now than it once was. One can certainly find evidence from Indiana to fuel these worries, and yet there are also reasons to temper our sense of alarm. A 2015 assessment of developments related to the state's civic health strikes an appropriate tone: "Some of these trends are positive and things on which Hoosiers can continue to build, while others are cause for concern and areas we need to improve."[42] It is also worth noting that a narrative of decline requires a relatively positive assessment of the starting point. Looking back on Indiana's civic history, there is evidence of strong communal bonds and substantial engagement in the past. But there are also indications that the social ties of earlier eras were not always so substantial. A close analysis of a single block in Bloomington in 1939 found only modest levels of connectivity, similar to those detected in contemporary surveys of social networks.[43]

One potential source of strength is Indiana's enduring settlement pattern. The state's dispersed urban network remains a distinct element of its geography. Indianapolis has grown into a sprawling metropolis, an urban form generally not considered conducive to robust civic connections. But the rest of Indiana's cities are of a modest size and are dispersed relatively evenly across the state. The scale of these communities and their proximity to rural districts may provide fertile ground for efforts to bridge the racial and cultural divisions that have become a pervasive feature of American public life.

More generally, it is important not to romanticize the civic life of the past as we strive to enhance it in the present. Citizens residing in a state in which the KKK constitutes one of the most robust historical examples of civic engagement, however briefly, would be well served to ask how much the seemingly close-knit, well-integrated communities of the past owed to the state's homogeneous, often intolerant, social character. Finally, it is worth noting that a key civic challenge facing Indiana today—the integration of its large population of poorer, less educated workers and minorities—is far from a new one. Fortunately, despite its dark moments, the state's history includes enough examples of successful efforts to generate the inclusive, ethical civic life that most Hoosiers seek.

NOTES

1. Robert S. Lynd and Helen Merrell Lynd, *Middletown: A Study in Modern American Culture* (New York: Harcourt, Brace, Jovanovich, 1959), 300.

2. Robert D. Putnam, *Bowling Alone: The Collapse and Revival of American Community* (New York: Simon and Schuster, 2001); Nicholas Lemann, "Kicking in Groups," *Atlantic Monthly*, 277, no. 4 (April 1996): 22–26.

3. Theda Skocpol, *Diminshed Democracy: From Membership to Management in American Civic Life* (Norman: University of Oklahoma Press, 2004); Michael Schudson, *The Good Citizen: A History of American Civic Life* (New York: Free Press, 1998).

4. Ellen Szarleta et al., *2015 Indiana Civic Health Index* (Indianapolis, 2015). Indiana ranks 25th among states (and the District of Columbia) in percentage of people who volunteered in 2015. "State Rankings by Volunteer Rate," Corporation for National Service, accessed December 22, 2017, https://www.nationalservice.gov/vcla/state-rankings-volunteer-rate.

5. James H. Madison, *Hoosiers: A New History of Indiana* (Bloomington: Indiana University Press, 2015), 175, 290.

6. Gerald Gamm and Robert D. Putnam, "The Growth of Voluntary Associations in America," *Journal of Interdisciplinary History* 29, no. 4 (Spring 1999): 511–57. Scholarly examination of the relationship has been limited to studies of contemporary community life in the United States. The results of these investigations, while mixed, generally indicate that smaller communities generate closer social ties and greater civic engagement. See Christine A. Kelleher and David Lowery, "Central City Size, Metropolitan Institutions, and Political Participation," *British Journal of Political Science* 39, no. 1 (January 2009): 59–92; Eric Oliver, "City Size and Civic Involvement," *American Political Science Review* 94 (2000): 361–73.

7. Madison, *Hoosiers*, 56–63; Andrew R. L. Cayton, *Frontier Indiana* (Bloomington: Indiana University Press, 1996), 295.

8. Madison, *Hoosiers*, 108–10.

9. Ibid., 115–17.

10. Kevin Corn, "Fraternal Organizations," in *The Encyclopedia of Indianapolis*, eds. David J. Bodenhamer et al. (Bloomington: Indiana University Press, 1994), 599; General William Harrison Kemper, *A Twentieth-Century History of Delaware County*, vol. I (Chicago: Lewis Publishing Company, 1908), 501, 507.

11. Madison, *Hoosiers*, 98, 131, 216.

12. David P. King, "Religion," Hoosier Philanthropy Conference, 6–9; Genevieve C. Weeks, "Oscar C. McCulloch Transforms Plymouth Church, Indianapolis, into an Institutional Church," *Indiana Magazine of History* 64, no. 2 (June 1968): 87–108.

13. Kemper, *A Twentieth-Century History of Delaware County*, 509–10; Russell Pulliam, "Temperance and Prohibition" in *Encyclopedia of Indianapolis*, 1440; Peggy Seigel, "Winning the Vote in Fort Wayne, Indiana: The Long, Cautious Journey in a German American City," *Indiana Magazine of History*, 102, no. 3 (September 2006): 442–44.

14. Charles Milo Gardner, *The Grange, Friend of the Farmer: A Concise Reference History of America's Oldest Farm Organization, and the Only Rural Fraternity in the World, 1867–1947* (Washington, DC: National Grange,

1949); Dennis S. Norden, *Rich Harvest: A History of the Grange, 1867–1900* (Jackson: University Press of Mississippi, 1974), 87, 112.

15. Jane Cunningham Croly, *The History of the Women's Club Movement in America* (New York: Henry G. Allen Company, 1898), 440, 443.

16. Albert C Stevens, *Cyclopaedia of Fraternities* (New York: Hamilton Printing, 1897), 114–15, 190.

17. David T. Beito, *From Mutual Aid to the Welfare State: Fraternal Societies and Social Services, 1890–1967* (Chapel Hill: University of North Carolina Press, 2000); Jason Kaufman, *For the Common Good?: American Civic Life and the Golden Age of Fraternity* (New York: Oxford, 2003).

18. Lynd and Lynd, *Middletown*, 301–2.

19. Ruth Hutchinson Crocker, *Social Work and Social Order: The Settlement Movement in Two Industrial Cities, 1889–1930* (Urbana: University of Illinois Press, 1992), 54–57.

20. Leonard J. Moore, *Citizen Klansmen: The Ku Klux Klan in Indiana, 1921–1928* (Chapel Hill: University of North Carolina Press, 1991), 13, 57, 60–70.

21. Arthur S. Meyers, "'A Sturdy Core of Fact Seeking Citizens': The Open Forum Movement and Public Learning in Terre Haute and Hammond, Indiana, in the 1920s," *Indiana Magazine of History*, 99 (December 2003): 353–69.

22. Meyers, "A Sturdy Core of Fact Seeking Citizens," 367.

23. Giles R. Hoyt, "Germans," in *Peopling Indiana: The Ethnic Experience*, eds. Robert M. Taylor and Connie A. McBirney (Indianapolis: Indiana Historical Society, 1996), 146–81; Carolyn S. Blackwell, "Jews," in *Peopling Indiana*, 314–35; Emma Lou Thornbrough, *Indiana Blacks in the Twentieth Century* (Bloomington: Indiana University Press, 2000), 97–235; Eva Mendieta, "Celebrating Mexican Culture and Lending a Helping Hand: Indiana Harbor's Sociedad Mutualista Benito Juarez, 1924–1957," *Indiana Magazine of History* 108, no. 4 (December 2012): 311–44.

24. Lynd and Lynd, *Middletown*, 53–72.

25. See Muncie Organized Labor Oral History Project, 2005–2006, Archives and Special Collections, Ball State University, Muncie, Indiana; and Indiana Labor History Project, 1996, Center for the Study of History and Memory, Indiana University, Bloomington, Indiana.

26. David M. Anderson, "'Things Are Different Down Here: The 1955 Perfect Circle Strike, Conservative Civic Identity, and the Roots of the New Right in the Industrial Heartland," *International Labor and Working-Class History* 74 (Fall 2008): 101–23.

27. James H. Madison, *Indiana through Tradition and Change: A History of the Hoosier State and Its People, 1920–1945* (Indianapolis: Indiana Historical Society, 1982), 345–46.

28. Richard Pierce, *Polite Protest: The Political Economy of Race in Indianapolis, 1920–1970* (Bloomington: Indiana University Press, 2005), 26–84; Thornbrough, *Indiana Blacks in the Twentieth Century*, 163–206.

29. Theda Skocpol et al., *What a Mighty Power We Can Be: African American Fraternal Groups and the Struggle for Racial Equality* (Princeton, NJ: Princeton University Press, 2006), 60.

30. Kirsten A. Grønbjerg and Deb Seltzer, *Indiana Nonprofit Employment, Trends in Membership and Related Organizations, 1995–2011* (Bloomington, IN: Indiana University School of Public and Environmental Affairs, 2014), 35.

31. Corn, "Fraternal Organizations," in *The Encyclopedia of Indianapolis*, eds. Bodenhamer et al., 598–99; Taya Flores, "Fraternal, Service Groups Battle Declining Membership: Elks, Rotarians, Freemasons and Other Fraternal Groups Struggle to Attract Younger Members," *Lafayette Journal Courier*, October 11, 2014, , accessed March 23, 2022, https://www.jconline.com/story/news/2014/10/11/fraternal-service-groups-battle-declining-membership/16874977/.

32. Srikant Devaraj, *Indiana's Manufacturing Employment Trends* (Muncie, IN: Center for Business and Economic Research, Ball State University, 2010), 2.

33. Jasmine Kerrisay and Evan Schofer, "Union Membership and Political Participation in the United States," *Social Forces* 91, no. 3 (March 2013): 895–928.

34. Theodore Caplow et al., *All Faithful People: Change and Continuity in Middletown's Religion* (Minneapolis: University of Minnesota Press, 1983).

35. "Adults in Indiana," Pew Research Center Religious Landscape Study, accessed January 27, 2016, http://www.pewforum.org/religious-landscape-study/state/indiana/; Szarleta et al., *2015 Indiana Civic Health Index*, 7.

36. Robert Wuthnow, "Mobilizing Civic Engagement: The Changing Impact of Religious Involvement," in *Civic Engagement and American Democracy*, eds. Theda Skocpol and Morris Fiorina (Washington, DC: Brookings Institution, 1999): 331–63; Robert D. Putnam and David E. Campbell, *American Grace: How Religion Divides and Unites Us* (New York: Simon and Schuster, 2010), 253–54.

37. Szarleta et al., *2015 Indiana Civic Health Index*, 8.

38. Delores J. Wright, "Pan American Games," in *The Encyclopedia of Indianapolis*, eds. Bodenhamer et al., 1074.

39. "City Rankings by Volunteer Rate," Corporation for National and Community Service, accessed December 22, 2017, https://www .nationalservice.gov/vcla/city-rankings-volunteer-rate.

40. Flores, "Fraternal, Service Groups Battle Declining Membership."

41. Szarleta et al., *2015 Indiana Civic Health Index*, 15.

42. Ibid., 2.

43. Karen Campbell, "Networks Past: A 1939 Bloomington Neighborhood," *Social Forces* 69, no. 1 (September 1990): 139–55.

FIVE

INDEPENDENT TOGETHER

*Historical Highlights of the Links
between Philanthropy and
Higher Education*

PAUL C. PRIBBENOW WITH CAITLIN CROWLEY

ONE OF THE GREAT TREASURES to be celebrated on the occasion of Indiana's 200th anniversary of statehood is its robust and diverse higher education community. From great public universities to flagship research institutions, from leading liberal arts colleges to faithful and high-quality sectarian institutions, the state of Indiana is home to a remarkable legacy of higher education.

The evolution of Indiana's higher education community over the past two hundred years is a story of passionate individuals and communities seeking to ensure a citizenry and a body politic in which education is a vital public good. At the same time, it is a story of generous and often strategic philanthropy ensuring that various institutions—public and private—can pursue their missions with both a fierce independence and a willingness to work across sector and institutional boundaries.

In what follows, we highlight five themes related to the history of higher education in Indiana and the role philanthropy played in the founding and flourishing of colleges and universities in the state. The five themes include: (1) the founding of Indiana University; (2) the role of faith communities in establishing colleges and universities; (3) the legacy of the Lilly family, company, and endowment in supporting higher education in Indiana; (4) the pioneering work of the Associated Colleges of Indiana (ACI) in soliciting corporate support for private higher education; and (5) the founding of Indiana University-Purdue University in Indianapolis (IUPUI) and its role in the life of a major metropolitan area. This selective approach means that much will be left unsaid about this history, but we argue that the chosen themes provide a fitting framework for exploring this history and understanding its central dynamics.

HIGHER EDUCATION AND PHILANTHROPY

Two core beliefs, common to the history of higher education in the United States, guide the story of philanthropic giving to colleges and universities in Indiana. The first is that "giving is a response to divine blessing";[1] it is motivated by the belief that everything we are given, including wealth, is a gift from God and should be used in God's honor. Those who held this belief founded many of Indiana's higher education institutions. These funders made it their explicit goal to educate new generations of Christian men and women with the firm conviction that those leading religious lives should also have an educational foundation on which to base their understanding of Christianity. Even the founding of nonsectarian and public institutions was often premised on the spread of religious values and parallel civic virtues.[2]

The second core belief stresses "social need and a horizontal movement of benefits among humans."[3] Those who worked to found Indiana's colleges and universities and those who supported them did so to improve the knowledge and lives of people in their communities. Philanthropists like Eli Lilly, full of pride for their home state and for whom higher education was a symbol of the American Dream, gave to Indiana colleges to keep the state flourishing for Hoosiers in years to come.

An expansive understanding of philanthropy defined by Robert L. Payton, founding director of the Center on Philanthropy at Indiana University, as "voluntary action for the public good,"[4] suggests that the founding and flourishing of colleges and universities is, at its core, the result of philanthropic intent and activity. Higher education, whether focused on the formation of individual values or the betterment of society, is a public good supported by the many forms in which philanthropy is practiced. Indiana led many of these philanthropic practices aimed at securing a vital higher education community.

A GREAT PUBLIC UNIVERSITY: FOUNDING
INDIANA UNIVERSITY

As Indiana's leaders gathered in Corydon in the summer of 1816 for the constitutional convention; education became a core aspect of the new state's responsibility: "It shall be the duty of the General Assembly, as soon as circumstances will permit, to provide by law for a general system of education ascending in a regular gradation from township schools to a State University, where tuition shall be gratis, and equally open to all."[5]

We argue that the very claim on the state to create a public educational system is the philanthropic intent to make education a public good in Indiana. What did these members of the constitutional convention have in mind when they made this claim? Historian Thomas Clark in his *Indiana University: Midwestern Pioneer* suggests three main purposes: (1) to develop an elite group of educated men who could lead the new commonwealth; (2) to spread the Protestant religion in this pioneer part of the country; and (3) to train men in scientific and technical skills to meet the physical and economic challenges of a growing state.[6] In this way, these Indiana leaders reflected a tradition inherited from the Puritans of New England, who prioritized education since landing in the Americas.[7]

Two congressional ordinances—promulgated in 1785 and 1787—provided a foundation for this commitment to education in the Northwest Territories. Both ordinances included the provision of public lands for schools (and further, for religion and morality) and thereby reflected the belief that schools and churches would be the foundation upon which communities would gather, property would be purchased, and economies would emerge.[8] Given these, perhaps mercenary, motives for the provisions of education, the ordinances pointed to a higher purpose. For example, in the third article of the Ordinance for the Government of the Northwest Territory, it states, "Religion, morality and knowledge being necessary to good government and the happiness of mankind, schools and the means of education shall be forever encouraged."[9]

The Act of Congress of April 1816, which provided for the admission of Indiana to the Union, included a similar commitment to a public education system and an offer from the federal government to donate a new township of land "for the use of a seminary of learning."[10] With the commitment to education secured in the new constitution, President James Madison acted just eleven days after the constitutional convention adjourned to designate the seminary township in what was to become a part of Monroe County. Near the geographic center of the state, the designated township was a fertile and desirable property that would serve both as a fitting site for the seminary (and subsequent institutions) and also economically beneficial lands for the farms and businesses that would settle nearby.[11]

With property now secured, early leaders of the new state made the prudent decision to delay selling land and establishing a seminary until 1820, after more of the state had been settled. Hoosier pioneers faced poverty, illness, the difficulties of clearing lands, natural disasters, a lack of goods to support basic needs. These issues, and others, contributed to a challenging existence. And yet these intrepid pioneers stayed the course, staking out towns to build their new lives, including in the new township of Bloomington, which adjoined the seminary township to the north.[12]

Thus, in 1820, when the time came to secure and sell portions of the seminary township land to support a new school, Bloomington was ready. With no direct representative in the state legislature, the people of Bloomington sent Dr. David H. Maxwell as their agent to present their case to the legislature in Corydon. In January 1820, Dr. Maxwell prevailed over skeptical legislators the right to organize the state seminary in Bloomington, gaining approval only with a tie-breaking vote cast by Senate President and Lieutenant Governor Ratliff Boon. The legislation was simple in its charge. It named trustees of the new institution and called for their "perpetual succession." It called for the identification of "an eligible and convenient site" and the selling of any parcels under their sanction. It charged trustees with "the erection of a suitable building for state seminary." The legislation also required trustees to report their proceedings and plans to the general assembly.[13]

In fact, the setup of Indiana University (IU) as a public school with a religious orientation, rather than a private school, might be the result of a contemporary US Supreme Court ruling. In Dartmouth College versus the State of New Hampshire, the school's trustees successfully fought against the state's attempt, in 1816, to take over Dartmouth College and control its operation.[14] The state claimed that because private colleges and other charitable organizations were chartered by the state they could be redefined as public institutions to shore up public funds and services. Dartmouth's trustees argued that its charter, originally issued in 1769 by King George III, conveyed its purposes and governing structures, along with land, and thus could not be altered by the state.

Writing for the majority in favor of Dartmouth College, Chief Justice John Marshall stated that private property "both real and personal which had been contributed for the benefit of the college, was conveyed to and vested in, the corporate body,"[15] thus holding that the original charter, in establishing a corporation and giving it rights to property, could not be altered. Importantly, Marshall went further to argue, in response to a state claim that the educational purposes of the college supported the government's interest in education, that public institutions are not defined by their purposes but by their being part of "civil government."[16]

In other words, the court's ruling established a legal distinction between public and private spheres in American society and thus created the context for "alternative visions of American society" to be pursued and supported in voluntary organizations.[17] Thus public or private entities could pursue the establishment of colleges without interference from the other sector. The 1819 Dartmouth College ruling occurring shortly after Indiana became a state was an important factor in the emergence of both public and private higher education institutions in the state, as the case likely influenced its general assembly.

What may be most striking about the legislation to establish IU is not what it includes but what it omits. There is no mention of an academic program or faculty. And there is no mention of the students to be served or the curriculum. As Thomas Clark suggested, "The intellectual origins of Indiana University had their sources far away from Corydon or Bloomington."[18] Few in Indiana understood what it meant to found a school, let alone set its central objectives.

The fledgling state seminary quickly developed faculty, buildings, and a curriculum following the legislation. The first faculty member was Baynard A. Hall, a Presbyterian minister, and an initial class of ten young men began in early May 1824.[19] With initial training offered only in the Greek and Latin languages, trustees charged Professor Hall with instructing students in English grammar, logic, rhetoric, geography, moral and natural philosophy, and Euclid's geometry—a charge he apparently did not feel compelled nor prepared to follow.

A second professor was soon hired, a mathematics instructor by the name of John H. Harney, who expanded the seminary's curricular offerings.[20]

The next two years saw a significant increase in the number of students and quality of academic offerings. Professors Hall and Harney were beloved by their students, and the seminary thrived, creating a culture of classical learning that would set the foundation for the seminary's 1828 transition to Indiana College, the predecessor institution to IU, which was formally created ten years later.

In his history of the seminary, college, and university, Thomas Clark shows that Indiana's foray into public higher education spans two eras of the broader American experience of higher education. The inherited classical tradition, where Greek, Latin, and traditional liberal arts were central curricular objectives, shaped the early days, while the needs of the new state pointed to educational objectives focusing more on practical arts.[21] Respected historian of American higher education John R. Thelin argues that the primary public policy issue at stake for IU's founders was not academic in nature but rather an effort to diminish denominational squabbles that dominated American higher education at that time.[22] In this way, Indiana University was at the forefront of the movement to create vibrant public universities alongside primarily faith-based colleges that were, until that point, the primary form of higher education in the United States.

It would be some sixty years after founding the seminary when IU president David Starr Jordan (later to serve as president of Stanford University) would move the university toward an academic mission that broke from the classical tradition, emphasizing sciences, engineering, and other professional and technical fields alongside literature and the arts. In Jordan's own words, we understand the philosophy that would define Indiana University: "In like spirit the Morrill Act was framed, bringing together all rays of various genius, the engineer, and the psychologist, the student of literature and the student of exact science, 'Greek-minded' men and tillers of the soil, each to do his own work in the spirit of equality before the law."[23]

Indeed, the Morrill Act not only provided a vision but—thanks to a large gift of $150,000 by John Purdue—it also spurred competition for public institutions by creating a second major public university in Indiana. The act provided land for the creation of universities. Purdue used his own gift to make a successful bid for Tippecanoe County. Purdue required that the university be located in his county, have his name, and include him on the board of trustees. These stipulations brought criticism that Purdue displayed unbecoming vanity; however, his defenders in the legislature were happy to receive funds to advance the university and break what had been a political stalemate over where to locate the school. Founded in 1869, Purdue University (PU), together with IU, became the bulwark of a successful public education system.[24] In 1918, the vision of state leaders and the generosity of individual donors came together, once again, to create Ball State University.[25] From the beginning, the combination of public and private support made Indiana's state-university system a valuable public resource.

FAITH AND HIGHER EDUCATION IN INDIANA

The history of higher education in Indiana is inextricably tied to communities of faith. Longtime University of Notre Dame president Father Theodore Hesburgh once remarked, "All American higher educational efforts, as universities worldwide historically, began with the churches."[26] The same was true for many Indiana institutions of higher education, as will be illustrated through the exemplary stories of Hanover, Earlham, and DePauw. These three are among many colleges and universities that would not have existed or survived without support from churches and church members whose philanthropy was motivated by spiritual intent.

"Gratitude and stewardship," write Thelin and Trollinger, "while not specifically religious terms, are basic tenets of the Judeo-Christian faith."[27] Just as churches played an important part in the formation of higher education in America, religion was a key factor in donor motivations to support colleges and universities, both in their beginning stages and their continuing development and sustenance. The histories of many religious colleges and universities in Indiana are often similar in that many struggled to stay afloat for lack of adequate finances. At the same time, these schools managed to recuperate, flourish, and maintain their independence thanks to the often fierce loyalty of their founding communities of faith.

Hanover, the oldest private college in Indiana, remained close to the Presbyterian Church in hard times. When a tornado destroyed the campus in 1837, Hanover Presbyterian Church turned over to Hanover College "all materials and funds . . . in its possession" to fund a new church for the school.[28] The church and its members remained loyal to Hanover, and contributions from churches, individuals, and the Presbyterian Board of Education made up a large part of Hanover's income.[29] It was perhaps because of the deep commitment to the church that Hanover College, which for "a good part of its first century . . . has had a financial struggle for existence,"[30] rejected the church's suggestion in 1870 to merge with Wabash College, a school founded by Presbyterians that opted to remain nonsectarian.[31]

DePauw University was not always called DePauw. Originally, the school was named Indiana Asbury, after Francis Asbury— "the first American bishop of the Methodist Episcopal church."[32] In 1837, a community in Greencastle, where the college was established, raised $25,000 to convince the Methodists to build their college in what was then a "rough, frontier village."[33] In the coming years, the Methodist Church gave the college "constant support," with most of the "chief" donors being Methodists.[34] When the time had come to move away from traditional courses like theology, those who opposed adding courses in natural science, modern languages, and modern history were told DePauw would be "not unrestrained, but unconstrained" in efforts to move forward.[35] The university would honor and keep the old but not stifle the need for something new.

Earlham College, likewise, formed out of the need for a school expressed by Friends in the Quaker community, who moved to Indiana from the eastern states during "the Great Migration of Quakers."[36] The school, similar to DePauw, was briefly "hindered" by "devout Friends who feared that an increase in general education would lead to a decrease in spiritual life and activity."[37] As the story often goes, however, the prevailing argument was that "the heads as well as the hearts, of hearers and preachers, too, should be cultivated," and the Quakers began a philanthropic quest to build a school.[38]

In Indiana's history of higher education, Father Hesburgh, who served as president of Notre Dame from 1952 until 1987, perhaps best exemplifies the recurring role of Christian communities establishing themselves as bulwarks of faith in the founding and shaping of colleges and universities to further their particular values. Hesburgh's commitment to creating a Catholic university of superb caliber is a more contemporary example of the stories of Christian schools in Indiana whose founders received their charters from the state and established their universities primarily to serve their respective religious communities.

Father Hesburgh believed in the importance of universities that did not rely on federal and state support. In his book, *The Hesburgh Papers*, he writes, "There will, I think, be increasing occasions for us to resist the bureaucratic urge to interfere with the university's essential independence, the move to insist that we do this or that or forfeit the beneficence of the state."[39] And yet, Father Hesburgh states, the university "claims a unique autonomy to criticize the very society that once gave it birth and now gives it financial support."[40] He believed such autonomy was crucial.

Leading Notre Dame, over a century after it was founded in 1844, Father Hesburgh's devotion, independence, and confidence helped him succeed like no one who had come before. His ability to raise funds and support to keep Notre Dame's essential independence, as a priest and theologian rather than a businessperson, was unprecedented and became legendary. During his presidency, he brought Notre Dame's position on the national listing of colleges from fortieth place to fifth.[41]

Over the course of his long presidency, Father Hesburgh increased Notre Dame's endowment "from $9 million to $350 million" and "increased student aid from $20,000 to $40 million."[42] To some he seemed to garner support for Notre Dame with ease. Yet the rhetoric of his speeches to "cultivate alumni philanthropy" were structured and planned in a meticulous manner.[43] One of Father Hesburgh's recurring appeals to alumni stressed that by giving back to their college, they would be able to "serve the world on behalf of the university."[44] This appeal recalls the second core belief guiding philanthropic giving to higher education: the notion of social benefit.

While Father Hesburgh understood that as president he must not be a "spectator in raising funds" for Notre Dame, he also recognized that his duty was to make the best decisions for the university as well.[45] In his own words, "budget officers understandably try to find the most economical solution. It is not always the right one."[46] In this way, a university leader "focuses on what the University has, not what it does not have,"[47] the qualities that can also inspire alumni and others to invest in the mission and work of the institution.

Father Hesburgh, whose ideas exemplify the broader trend of connections between higher education and faith in Indiana, was keenly aware that the ties that benefit could also be seen as "retrogressive" by many.[48] Yet he believed "the Notre Dame community should reflect profoundly, and with unashamed commitment, its belief in the existence of God," so long as this was done "in a spirit of civility as well as of love, in openness as well as in commitment."[49] This spirit lies at the heart of many faith-based colleges and universities founded throughout Indiana's history that continue to thrive in the twenty-first century.

THE LILLY LEGACY: A FAMILY, CORPORATION, AND ENDOWMENT

Lilly Endowment Inc. is currently one of the largest foundations in the United States.[50] The primary focus of the endowment's gifts to higher education was the state of Indiana. The legacy that began with J. K. Lilly, Sr. was continued by his two sons, Colonel Eli Lilly and J. K. Lilly, Jr. and endures within the endowment to this day. "Our Hoosier heritage has influenced the course of our past fifteen years of operation," the endowment stated in 1952. "We are cognizant of our responsibility to projects which are national and international in scope; but following the policy established (at its inception), interest has remained centered in Indiana and has worked its way outward."[51] After Eli Lilly's death, the endowment made a promise to "support a broad range of activities in the field of religion, and to encourage education directed toward ethical, moral and social values," in honor of Lilly, a "reflection of his own deep personal interests."[52] Today, Lilly Endowment Inc. (LEI) continues to support a wide range of higher education institutions in their efforts to inculcate those values, honoring the wishes of Mr. Lilly and his family. For example, in its 2013 Annual Report, LEI stated that "Despite a steady supply of four-year college graduates emerging from Indiana campuses, Indiana ranks very low among the states in the percentage of its adult working-age population that has a bachelor's degree."[53] The Endowment reaffirmed its mission to once again make Indiana a focus of its educational grants.

Colonel Eli Lilly founded Eli Lilly and Company in 1876 in the rapidly growing capital city of Indianapolis, Indiana.[54] The colonel was "dedicated to improving the well-being of the city" and spending, "time and money in charitable and relief activities." He instilled a deep devotion to Indiana in his family, including his grandson Eli Lilly.[55]

The company was among the first to employ scientific methods to production and it grew tremendously.[56] Focus shifted around World War I to large-scale research operations, and Eli Lilly and Company began manufacturing drugs, like insulin, and hiring researchers and chemists to come up with effective synthetic drugs.[57] In the 1930s, the company prospered and the Lilly family became multimillionaires.[58] As president of Eli Lilly and Company, wealth brought Eli Lilly the weight of "new responsibilities and problems"; nevertheless, he began channeling time and money into philanthropic pursuits, which he took seriously.[59] "Philanthropy at a distance" was not for Eli Lilly; he preferred to give his money to institutions led by people he knew personally, a policy that would define his philanthropic giving for years to come.[60]

LEI was created and organized in 1937. In addition to the philanthropic intent of the family, tax laws provided another good reason to set up the endowment. The formation of the foundation allowed Eli Lilly and his brother J. K. Lilly Jr. to avoid paying an inheritance tax on their father's company stock, which would have forced them to sell many of his shares and lose control of the company.[61] The endowment came into being, and Eli Lilly, his wife, Ruth, and his brother J. K. were all named as trustees. "These were commonplace motivations in the formation of America's large foundations," wrote Eli Lilly's biographer, James Madison, "combining genuine charitable impulses with desires to reduce tax burdens and maintain control of family-owned businesses."[62]

The endowment supported both the specific academic interests of the Lilly family and broader support to higher education in Indiana, first focusing on small private colleges and later offering gifts to public universities as well. Eli Lilly's mistrust of increasing government involvement in business is what partially led him to sympathize with colleges and universities with the same concerns. Over the years, Lilly connected with university presidents, such as Frank Sparks of Wabash College, and would focus more on Wabash College than any other small college in Indiana.

In 1953, LEI wrote of Wabash president Sparks that "he has run the gamut of two distinct courses of life."[63] What the foundation and Eli Lilly himself were so impressed by was Sparks's interest in "using adapted business methods," translated from his ventures in industrial enterprise, as president of Wabash College.[64] Though Lilly himself never attended a four-year, private, religious college, he appreciated men like Sparks, who came to the world of higher education with a business perspective. He also appreciated the value of small colleges in Indiana. Lilly's appreciation for Frank Sparks was surely warranted, and at Wabash College the feeling was certainly mutual. As Byron Trippet writes in *Wabash on My Mind*, "If Frank Sparks had done nothing more than winning the interest of Eli Lilly for Wabash, his important place in the history of Wabash can be assured."[65] Mr. Lilly, and by extension LEI, was not interested in giving money to just anyone.

By the 1960s, LEI's numerous gifts to small colleges were scrutinized for ulterior motives, such as bringing conservative scholars to "left-leaning campuses."[66] After a report was published in 1972, which criticized the endowment for losing "its good reputation in the swamps of the far Right," Eli Lilly decided that the endowment should focus on projects broader than just higher education, perhaps seeking to emulate the Rockefeller, Ford, Danforth, and Mellon Foundations.[67] Interestingly enough, the endowment hired Earlham College president Landrum Bolling to initiate changes as executive vice president of the endowment.[68]

In recent years, LEI reaffirmed its strong support for higher education in Indiana. In response to demographic trends indicating a diminishing number of Indiana citizens with bachelor's degrees, the endowment launched a scholarship program for college students in Indiana. The Lilly Endowment Community Scholarship program began in 1998 with 117 recipients, doubling in size to 240 students one year later, allowing excellent scholars across Indiana to attend private or state colleges and universities.[69] The program was created as "part of the larger endowment effort to raise the unacceptably low level of educational attainment in Indiana."[70]

In addition, the endowment developed a series of funding programs enabling private and public colleges and universities in Indiana to make significant investments in academic programs, facilities, community outreach, and alumni engagement. For example, in 2002, the endowment launched a matching grant program to encourage charitable giving from alumni, parents, faculty, and staff.[71] More recently, the endowment made significant grants of $33 million to Indiana University and $40 million to Purdue University for capital projects to strengthen core academic priorities.[72]

The endowment's continued focus "on higher education and on programs designed to increase the percentage of Indiana residents with bachelor's degrees" honors Eli Lilly's legacy and personal ties to colleges and universities in his home state.[73] It also illustrates the legacy of the Lilly family's belief in higher education's ability to inculcate values and enhance social benefits.

SEEKING INDEPENDENCE TOGETHER: THE ACI

Federated fundraising has a long history in America. As early as the colonial period, representatives of charitable and educational organizations traveled together in England and beyond to solicit funds for their organizations.[74] The case to be made for cooperative fundraising was compelling for both donors and recipients. It gave charitable organizations an opportunity to amplify the impact of their common work, even as it offered efficiencies in fundraising. For donors, it was an opportunity to support common work across the sector, even as it lessened the number of solicitations from individual causes.

The Community Chest movement (now the United Way) first launched on a broad scale in 1913 in nearby Cleveland, Ohio.[75] It was perhaps the most impressive model of federated fundraising at the time, primarily supporting local charitable agencies serving a particular community. For colleges and universities, the first large-scale federated fundraising effort was for the United Negro College Fund, which began in 1944 by twenty-seven member colleges, raising an impressive $765,000 in its first year (30 percent came from corporations).[76] This federated fundraising effort quickly drew the attention of the higher education community, especially those concerned about the financial plight of independent private colleges and universities and those who believed that the relationships between higher education and the corporate community could be strengthened.

In Indiana, several higher education, civic, and business leaders shared this perspective. In December 1943, Indianapolis attorney Kurt F. Pantzer hosted many of these individuals at his home to explore ways they might overcome a common concern to ensure the survival of small independent, church-related, non-tax-supported colleges and universities. It was an impressive assemblage, including presidents of Indiana University, Purdue University, DePauw University, Earlham College, Wabash College, and Evansville College, as well as corporate leaders from Eli Lilly and Company, Perfect Circle Corporation, and P. R. Mallory and Company.[77]

Of concern to these men was the possibility that small schools would need to turn to the federal government for support and bear the regulatory control and oversight that might accompany it. The group considered a variety of alternatives and, ultimately, agreed the best option was to pursue cooperative fundraising, particularly from corporations. The meeting's conclusions gave impetus to Pantzer's dream to create what he called the Indiana Institute for the Support of Education, which would serve as the collaborative organization to raise funds and advocate for independent higher education.[78] Though Pantzer's dream never became a reality, it was a helpful blueprint when, years later, the ACI was created.

One of the key architects of ACI was Wabash College president Frank Sparks, who was present at the initial Pantzer meeting and who reflected—in his own background—the nexus of corporate and higher education leadership.[79] Rising in the 1920s and 1930s to lead Noblitt-Sparks Industries, an automotive accessories company in Columbus, Indiana, Sparks retired from the company in 1937, returned to graduate school to receive a PhD from the University of Southern California, and became president of Wabash in 1941, where he served until his retirement in 1956.

In personal correspondence with Eli Lilly in 1944, Sparks seeks Mr. Lilly's endorsement of, and engagement with, the Indiana Institute. Sparks waxes eloquent about the potential of this initiative and concludes that despite his deep attachment to Wabash College his "estimate of the importance of this new venture . . . is the only educational activity of which I have knowledge—the advancement of which I would put ahead of our own institution."[80] Though Mr. Lilly did not immediately endorse the project, the demands of wartime America and other charitable commitments led him to respond to Sparks with these words, illustrative of his personal style: "Your letter of October 28, about Mr. Kurt Pantzer's brilliant idea is much appreciated, and from what you say it must have made as great an impression upon you as it did upon me. I only wish I had the time and ability to help push such things through, but many other things stand first."[81]

But "this brilliant idea" did, in fact, come to fruition, overcoming reluctance among some private-college leaders to form an alliance with businesses, including Mr. Lilly's blessing in early 1947.[82] The effort began informally, with Sparks and Earlham president Jones making a series of joint visits to Indiana corporations in 1948. During those visits, they received two modest gifts totaling $15,000. In 1949, two other presidents joined, and one hundred appeals were made to corporation executives, raising $65,000 from twenty-seven businesses.[83]

The case for corporate support of private higher education was strong. At the time, almost 50 percent of those who pursued higher education in the United States attended private institutions. Corporate contributions, through taxes, paid a large portion of the operating costs of public institutions; however, they gave almost nothing to private colleges that were educating their future workforce. Meanwhile, some industries doubted the associated-college movement and questioned the legality of corporate philanthropy. In 1951, the not-yet incorporated group of private colleges organized a series of meetings across the state to explain the federal law established in 1935 (the so-called five-percent tax privilege), which encouraged corporate giving.[84]

The compelling case for corporate support and advocacy in the corporate community for private higher education propelled the growth of the ACI over the next several years. Four institutions joined in 1950, three more in 1951, and a final inaugural member in 1952, bringing total membership to twelve. And ACI raised almost $150,000 in federated support for operating budgets.[85] In 1952, the ACI was formally incorporated "to encourage and promote scientific, literary and educational purposes within the State of Indiana, and more particularly to further the cause of higher education and culture within the State; to support the Members of the Corporation in a cooperative movement to secure eminent teachers, worthy students, and adequate plants and equipment; to broaden the foundation of higher education and culture in the State of Indiana; and to stimulate interest of the citizens of the State of Indiana in educational and cultural pursuits."[86]

Significant operating support from LEI first granted in 1952 and sustained over many decades created the infrastructure needed to support and expand ACI's work. Within two years, ACI doubled its fundraising to almost $300,000 from 149 corporations and businesses.

Not all private institutions chose to join ACI, believing their reputations and profiles made it better to seek corporate support on their own. For those who did join, corporate support generated through ACI offered an important stream of philanthropic revenue to support their fragile operations and secured a groundbreaking relationship between private higher education and the corporate community.

Over the next twenty years, ACI member institutions reported the impact of increased support from corporations and individuals as faculty salaries were raised, educational programs were improved, urgently needed maintenance was performed, church and alumni support increased (inspired by corporate support), and faculty gained a better understanding of business problems.[87]

By the early 1960s, ACI raised more than $1 million a year from corporate subscriptions.[88] At the same time, however, the costs of higher education were increasing and the percentage of institutional operating budgets covered by income from ACI decreased from a high of 7.4 percent in 1957 and 1958 to 5 percent in 1963.[89]

In the second half of the 1960s, subscriptions continued to increase and reached almost $1.9 million in 1968, aided in part by an innovative state tax credit for education passed by the Indiana General Assembly in 1966.[90] Even with impressive fundraising and policy results, the increasing costs of higher education meant that ACI members were facing the fact "colleges, like businesses, must offset soaring costs with increased income or face cutbacks that can led to second-rate operations and output."[91]

In its last five years, ACI members faced their own economic challenges while experiencing increased countrywide inflation, along with changing patterns of corporate giving (i.e., mergers and the professionalization of corporate giving programs).[92] Despite efforts to change the fundraising strategy, such as partnering college presidents with "business ambassadors" to solicit support, ACI could not keep pace with support provided to colleges by their alumni, church bodies, and private foundations.[93] By 1973, despite having raised more than $24 million for independent colleges and universities in Indiana, it was time for a transition.[94]

In 1973, ACI became the Independent Colleges of Indiana (ICI). Today, ICI represents thirty-one private higher education institutions in Indiana (including several of those who chose not to join in its initial years) and serves both as a cooperative fundraising organization and a public and government advocacy group.[95] Though individual institutions have long since developed their own robust fundraising operations, these federations in Indiana and elsewhere—albeit serving wider purposes—continue to serve as important symbols of an idea first launched in Indiana. The abiding impact of the formation of ACI as the first state federation of private colleges and universities is seen in the rapid growth of such state organizations around the country.[96] By 1958, the Independent College Funds of America, later the Federation of Independent Higher Education (FIHE), now a program of the Council of Independent Colleges (CIC), was formed to support this burgeoning movement. At least thirty-one such state federations exist today, many combining federated fundraising for members with public advocacy for private higher education. And it all began in Indiana with a group of leaders dedicated to ensuring the independence of private higher education through philanthropy.

A CAPITAL CITY NEEDS A PUBLIC
UNIVERSITY: CREATING IUPUI

On December 14, 1968, newly elected Indianapolis mayor Richard Lugar publicly supported efforts by a group of state and local officials who submitted a bill to the 1969 Indiana General Assembly to create an independent state university in Indianapolis.

"A key factor in each great city is the strength of a distinguished city university."[97] Continuing, Lugar lamented the need for the city to benefit from a university whose courses would "foster technology and scientific growth and research" and pointed to the economic needs of the city to support its industries and keep unemployment low.[98] While praising the leadership of two public universities who maintained branch programs in Indianapolis, he suggested that because they were not based there, they were not connected to the local issues and dynamics that demanded dedicated resources of a university.

Concluding with soaring language, Lugar appealed to state pride by stating, "We must think and act as if we truly believe that Indianapolis is the great city destined for much greater years immediately ahead . . . a great city must have at its heart a great university."[99] And with this so-called surprise move, Mayor Lugar set in motion a remarkably speedy and dynamic process that led, in 1969, to the creation of IUPUI.

Building off previous efforts to create a University Quarter, in which IU and PU, both of which sponsored a wide range of academic programs in Indianapolis for decades, would colocate on the west side of Indianapolis, Presidents Joseph Sutton of IU and Frederick Hovde of Purdue huddled shortly after Mayor Lugar's speech to issue a response.[100] Their proposed plan was remarkable by all standards. The agreement called for IU and PU to create a new entity in place of their competing operations in Indianapolis. The union gave IU primary responsibility, through a chancellor, for management functions; assigned academic missions to each university based on its traditional programs and strengths; and called for bringing all operations together in one site on the near west side of Indianapolis.[101]

The agreement, and a phased merger plan, received approval from the boards of trustees of both universities in January 1969. A schedule to enter the first phase of the plan by September 1969 was soon developed. The sitting chancellor of IU campus in

Indianapolis, Maynard K. Hine, DDS, was soon named the first chancellor of IUPUI. He assembled a leadership team from IU and PU campuses across the state. The school needed to merge, consolidate, and integrate disparate programs, personnel, facilities, and cultures of the two institutions.

As background to this unprecedented merger, it is important to note the rather checkered history of both Indiana and Purdue academic programs in Indianapolis. There is evidence of IU offering extension courses in Indianapolis as early as 1891, primarily in response to requests from alumni for continuing education opportunities. These efforts were noteworthy, not simply for their presence in Indianapolis but also as part of a burgeoning extension movement across the country. In fact, one of the key figures in the early days of IU's extension presence in Indianapolis, Robert Cavanaugh, is remembered in the name of the first classroom/office building on the IUPUI campus.

Indiana University's first permanent presence in Indianapolis came in the 1905–1906 academic year, when the new IU medical school in Indianapolis opened its doors. The battle over the creation of the medical school—still the only medical program in the state—is beyond the scope of this chapter, but it points to the genesis of institutional infighting between IU and PU, which also sought to establish a medical school but was thwarted.[102]

In subsequent years, IU established other schools in Indianapolis, primarily through mergers with preexisting proprietary schools. These included the school of dentistry in 1925; the school of physical education in 1941; and the school of law in 1944. All would become important parts of IUPUI after the merger.

After the withdrawal of its short-lived medical college in 1908, PU did not try to organize other academic programs in Indianapolis until the need for technical training—occasioned by World War II—brought them back to the city. Thus, the school established a Division of Technical Studies in Indianapolis in 1943. Purdue University also offered agricultural courses and entered into partnership with the IU Extension Center to offer basic courses needed for undergraduate degrees in technical areas. Later, PU expanded its own course offerings for undergraduates and consolidated its facilities in a new Purdue regional campus.

The primary conclusion to be drawn from this brief survey of IU and PU activities in Indianapolis is that both institutions showed considerable good faith in responding to the educational needs of the capital city. At the same time, disparate locations— IU offered courses at five scattered sites—and a lack of a coordinated academic and management structure clearly created the context for Mayor Lugar's call for a new university. This abiding presence in Indianapolis offered a timely opportunity (and admittedly difficult task) to integrate the work of these two great institutions into one new entity. The success of that effort would ultimately depend upon a remarkable philanthropic act—once again by LEI and other influential philanthropic foundations.

During the first few years of IUPUI's existence, Chancellor Maynard Hine worked tirelessly to get IUPUI established. It was left to his successor, Chancellor Glenn W. Irwin, who served from 1973 to 1986, to take the disjointed campus and cultures of IU and PU and create a "real campus."[103] Former dean of the IU medical school, Irwin was aware of the dynamics of the emerging institution and reported to Chancellor Hine after the initial merger (previously he reported to the IU president). He put his long-standing relationships within the campus community, and the wider power structure of the city, to work on behalf of IUPUI.

His partnership with Indianapolis Mayor William H. Hudnut, III (Lugar's successor) and their nearly coterminous tenure in office demonstrated true leadership in urban transformation around, and within, a university campus. It began with a tennis stadium, part of Hudnut's efforts to make Indianapolis the "Amateur Sports Capital." With land from the university, public funding from the city, and an unprecedented capital matching grant from LEI (one hundred companies each pledged $15,000 to match Lilly's $1.5 million grant), the forty-five-hundred-seat stadium hosted national tournaments and gave IUPUI students a fine facility for exercise and competition. The tennis stadium was shortly dwarfed by a football stadium (the Hoosier Dome, later the RCA Dome), built—once again—with public and private funds (including $25 million from LEI and $5 million from the Krannert Charitable Trust) as part of a civic improvement effort.[104]

While the dynamic expansion was happening, Chancellor Irwin engaged a group of civic and business leaders, known as the City Committee, to share his vision for the IUPUI campus.[105] LEI's decision, in the late 1970s, to focus on revitalizing downtown Indianapolis was the conduit for support of significant facilities projects on campus, including the natatorium, track-and-field stadium, University Place Conference Center, and numerous improvements to the Riley Hospital for Children.

Perhaps even more important than funds provided for the campus transformation was the support from LEI president Thomas H. Lake, who as Irwin recalls it, challenged IUPUI to "think a lot bigger, and build the same things, but build them world class."[106] In less than fifty years, IUPUI became the third largest university, by enrollment, in Indiana. The growing vibrancy in Indianapolis, the commitment to think big and be innovative, and good university leadership all came together to bring about the transformation.

CONCLUSION

Whether in South Bend or Crawfordsville, Indianapolis or Bloomington, Fort Wayne or Anderson, Muncie or Evansville, higher education institutions across the state view themselves as serving important public roles. Certainly, their core mission is educating people for lives of meaning and purpose, many of whom will pursue their work and civic lives in the state. Equally impressive is the role these institutions play as anchors in their communities: economic engines, conveners of important conversations, stewards of place, and so on.

There also is an impressive thread of innovation and nimbleness in the role of colleges and universities in the state. From the pioneer role of Indiana University in carving out a vision of public higher education to the entrepreneurial efforts of Kurt Pantzer and Frank Sparks, who secured corporate funding for private institutions, to the founding of a distinctive urban university in Indianapolis, individuals involved in Hoosier higher education became leaders in key areas of innovation in higher education—often supported by strategic philanthropy.

Finally, throughout the history of the links between higher education and philanthropy, a deep sense of Hoosier pride that often presents itself as fierce independence remains, an aversion even to relinquishing control to others as institutions live out their missions. It seems part of Indiana's character, fierce independence is almost always supported by generous and passionate donors who share the values of the institutions they love. This independence is best extended and enhanced by working across institutional and sector boundaries. Though the shifting sands of higher education financing and oversight sometimes threaten this independence, the principled spirit that characterizes higher education in Indiana ensures that, at its best, there will always be those who stand up and fight to maintain that independence and the sort of education it fosters.

NOTES

1. John R. Thelin and Richard W. Trollinger, *Philanthropy and American Higher Education* (New York: Palgrave Macmillan, 2014), 49.

2. For this point related to the founding of Indiana University and other early public universities, see Thomas D. Clark, *Indiana University: Midwestern Pioneer, Volume I / The Early Years* (Bloomington: Indiana University Press, 1970), 3–4.

3. Thelin and Trollinger, *Philanthropy and American Higher Education*, 50.

4. Robert L. Payton, *Philanthropy: Voluntary Action for the Public Good* (New York: Greenwood, 1988).

5. Constitution of the State of Indiana, 1816, article IX, section 2, accessed January 24, 2016, http://www.in.gov/history/2460.htm.

6. Clark, *Indiana University*, 3–4.

7. Robert S. Robertson, "The Indiana University as Fostered and Developed by Legislation," in *Indiana University: Its History from 1820, When Founded, to 1890*, ed. Theophilus Adam Wylie (Indianapolis: Wm. B. Burford, 1890), 2–3.

8. Wylie, *Indiana University*, 8.

9. Ibid.

10. D. D. Banta, "The Seminary Period (1820–1828)," in *History of Indiana University, Volume 1, 1820–1902*, ed. James A. Woodburn (Bloomington: Indiana University Press, 1940), 3.

11. Woodburn, *History of Indiana University*, 4.

12. Ibid., 6.

13. Ibid., 10.

14. *Trustees of Dartmouth College v. Woodward*, 17 US (4 Wheat), 1819, 518, 658–59.

15. Ibid., 658.

16. Ibid., 658–59.

17. Dwight F. Burlingame, ed., *Philanthropy in America: A Comprehensive Historical Encyclopedia*, vol. II (Santa Barbara, CA: ABC-CLIO, 2004), 303.

18. Clark, *Indiana University*, 7.

19. Woodburn, *History of Indiana University*, 17–18.

20. Ibid., 19–20.

21. Clark, *Indiana University*, xi–xii.

22. John R. Thelin, *A History of American Higher Education* (Baltimore: Johns Hopkins University Press, 2014), 71.

23. Ibid., xiii.

24. Robert Topping, *A Century and Beyond: The History of Purdue University* (West Lafayette, IN: Purdue University Press, 1988), 26–31.

25. Bruce Geelhoed and Anthony Edmonds, *Ball State University: An Interpretive History* (Bloomington: Indiana University Press, 2001).

26. Theodore M. Hesburgh, *The Hesburgh Papers: Higher Values in Higher Education* (Kansas City, MO: Andrews and McMeel, Inc., 1979), x.

27. Thelin and Trollinger, *Philanthropy and American Higher Education*, 53.

28. "About Hanover," Hanover University, accessed January 14, 2016, https://www.hanover.edu/about.

29. William Alfred Millis. *The History of Hanover College from 1827 to 1927* (Hanover, Indiana: Hanover College, 1927), 119.

30. Ibid., 114.

31. "About Hanover."

32. "History of the University," DePauw University, accessed January 14, 2016, http://www.depauw.edu/academics/catalog/university/.

33. Ibid.

34. George B. Manhart, *DePauw through the Years*, vol. II (Greencastle, Indiana: DePauw University, 1962), 404.

35. William Warren Sweet, *Indiana Asbury-DePauw University 1837–1937* (New York: Abingdon, 1937), 153.

36. "Campus and History," Earlham College, https://earlham.edu/about/campus-and-history/.

37. Opal Thornburg, *Earlham: The Story of the College, 1847–1962* (Richmond, Indiana: Earlham College Press, 1963), 29.

38. Ibid., 30.

39. Hesburgh, *The Hesburgh Papers*, 31.

40. Ibid.

41. Peggie Ncube, "A Rhetorical Analysis of Theodore Hesburgh's Fundraising Speeches for the University of Notre Dame" (unpublished PhD diss., Indiana University, 2002), 14.

42. "Fr. Ted's Life: The Notre Dame President," Notre Dame University, accessed January 12, 2016, http://hesburgh.nd.edu/fr-teds-life/the-notre-dame-president/.

43. Ncube, "A Rhetorical Analysis of Theodore Hesburgh's Fundraising Speeches for the University of Notre Dame," 11.

44. Ibid., ii.

45. Ibid., 19.

46. Hesburgh, *The Hesburgh Papers*, 5–6.

47. Ncube, "A Rhetorical Analysis of Theodore Hesburgh's Fundraising Speeches for the University of Notre Dame," ii.

48. Hesburgh, *The Hesburgh Papers*, 44.

49. Ibid., 45.

50. As of the end of 2013, the Lilly Endowment Inc. ranks as the 7th largest private foundation in the United States, based on its assets. See https://www.fundraisingschool.it/wp-content/uploads/2014/12/Top-100-U.S.-Foundations-by-Asset-Size.pdf, accessed March 20, 2022.

51. Lilly Endowment Inc.: A Report for 1952, 4.

52. James H. Madison, *Eli Lilly: A Life, 1885–1977*, 2nd ed. (Indianapolis: Indiana Historical Society, 2006), 204.

53. Lilly Endowment Inc. 2013 Annual Report. 16. accessed March 20, 2022. https://lillyendowment.org/wp-content/uploads/2017/04/annual report2013.pdf.

54. Madison, *Eli Lilly*, 4.

55. Ibid., 5, 7.

56. Ibid., 51.

57. Ibid.

58. Ibid., 89.

59. Ibid.

60. Ibid., 190.

61. Ibid., 205.

62. Ibid., 206.

63. Lilly Endowment Inc.: A Report for 1953, 11.

64. Ibid.

65. Byron Trippet, *Wabash on My Mind* (Crawfordsville, IN: Wabash College, 1982), 57.

66. Madison, *Eli Lilly*, 217.

67. Ibid., 219.

68. Ibid.

691998. Lilly Endowment Inc. Annual Reports Online, 30.

70. Ibid., 31.

71. "Lilly Endowment Launches Philanthropy Initiative for Indiana Colleges and Universities," Philanthropy News Digest (PND), accessed October 12, 2016, http://philanthropynewsdigest.org/news/lilly-endowment -launches-philanthropy-initiative-for-indiana-colleges-and-universities.

72. "Lilly Endowment: Grants for Higher Education," Inside Philan-thropy, accessed October 12, 2016, http://www.insidephilanthropy.com /grants-for-higher-education/lilly-endowment-grants-for-higher-education .html.

73. Ibid.

74. Robert H. Bremner, *American Philanthropy*, 2nd ed. (Chicago: University of Chicago Press, 1988), 22.

75. Ibid., 118.

76. Ibid., 227; Philip K. Sherwood, "A Historical Study of the Associated Colleges of Indiana" (unpublished PhD diss., Indiana University, 1973), 58.

77. Sherwood, "A Historical Study of the Associated Colleges of Indiana," 65.

78. Ibid., 66.

79. Trippet, *Wabash on My Mind*, 40.

80. Sparks to Lilly, October 28, 1944, Wabash College archives.

81. Lilly to Sparks, November 1, 1944, Wabash College archives.

82. Sparks to Lilly, 1947, Wabash College archives.

83. Associated Colleges of Indiana, "A Report of Progress 1948–52," 4.

84. Sherwood, "A Historical Study of the Associated Colleges of Indiana," 70.

85. Ibid., 72.

86. Associated Colleges of Indiana, articles of incorporation, 1952 (article I, section 1, clause (a)), 1.

87. Sherwood, "A Historical Study of the Associated Colleges of Indiana," 80.

88. Ibid.,117.

89. Ibid.

90. Ibid., 123.

91. Ibid.

92. Ibid., 130.

93. Ibid., 139.

94. Ibid., 153.

95. "Independent Colleges of Indiana, History of ICI," Independent Colleges of Indiana, accessed January 14, 2016, ici.edu.

96. Trippet, *Wabash on My Mind*, 74.

97. Ralph D. Gray, *IUPUI—The Making of an Urban University* (Bloomington: Indiana University Press, 2003), 86.

98. Ibid.

99. Ibid., 87.

100. Ibid., 66.

101. Ibid., 88.

102. Elizabeth Van Allen, "History of the IU School of Medicine" (unpublished PhD diss., Indiana University, 2003).

103. Gray, *IUPUI*, 135.

104. See http://www.company-histories.com/Lilly-Endowment-Inc-Company-History.html, accessed January 24, 2016, for a summary of the Lilly Endowment Inc. support for these various capital projects to revitalize downtown Indianapolis.

105. Gray, *IUPUI*, 144.

106. Ibid., 146.

HOOSIER HEALTH PHILANTHROPY

Understanding the Past

WILLIAM H. SCHNEIDER

INDIANA HAS A LONG HISTORY of offering philanthropic support for matters relating to health, with an impressive record of
funding hospitals, medical research and training, and campaigns
that raise awareness about specific illnesses.[1] The state's history
reveals key social and economic transformations throughout the
country regarding health-focused philanthropy—moving from
primarily medical service provision toward medical research—
which influenced a dramatic revolution in health care over the
past two hundred years. The field of health continues to attract a
large proportion of philanthropic giving in Indiana, and for this
reason, understanding this history offers lessons for ongoing and
future work. The following is an overview of the history of health
care philanthropy in Indiana with reference to broader trends in
philanthropic support for health care in the United States.

THE NATIONAL CONTEXT

Private business and government sources far overshadow philanthropic funding for the US health sector. Nonetheless, health
is usually among the top categories of giving by individuals
and foundations, and historically philanthropy has played a

significant role in discoveries and changes in the field. Better health and treatment of illness are universal values, and those wishing to contribute to the public good have for centuries devoted resources toward these shared goals, from medieval aristocrats to the two largest foundations in the twentieth century: Rockefeller and Gates.[2]

Philanthropic giving to hospitals, for curing diseases and other medical research, is extensive. In 2014, according to the Philanthropy 50 list, the wealthiest donors in America gave $400 million to hospitals and medical centers (out of a total of $5 billion given directly to institutions and causes).[3] Organizations that educate the public and lobby for action to prevent and treat specific diseases have grown over the years thanks to past successes by researchers and clinicians in preventing and treating some of the scourges that have plagued humankind. A list showing the top-twenty grant-giving organizations for disease foundations in 2011 shows that over half received more than $100 million in income from investments or donations.[4] An even clearer demonstration of the important role played by private donations can be seen in a 2014 report of the upper Midwest regions of the American Lung Association. While the national association was raising about $500 million annually, the upper Midwest region (including ten states between North Dakota, Wisconsin, Missouri, and Indiana) reported that of the approximately $26 million in revenue in 2014, half came from popular support, including Christmas seals, direct mail, and special events.[5] Philanthropic support for medical research has also increased, especially that which is focused on specific diseases. These last two categories overlap because disease research often takes place at medical schools and hospitals. In addition, most disease foundations combine public education with appeals for donations to conduct research.

Such a significant amount of health philanthropy is not a recent phenomenon. In fact, its growth began in the last half of the nineteenth century, and its importance increased dramatically until the mid-twentieth century, when increased government expenditures on health overshadowed it. The story of health philanthropy in Indiana offers a good example of these broader, national trends.

HOSPITALS AND HEALTH PHILANTHROPY

The nineteenth century, following Indiana statehood in 1816, was a time of major change in both philanthropy and medicine. It was not until midcentury that there were enough doctors in the state (as distinct from healers and quacks, identified by training and self-advertising) to establish an effective medical society in Indianapolis. But, in the last half of the century, almost twenty medical schools, colleges, or institutes were established, thus increasing the number and quality of physicians in the state.[6] These varied greatly but were mostly private for-profit schools, created largely to supplement the income of practicing physicians who started them and taught students on the side. Most frequently these "proprietary" schools, as historians refer to them, were located in Indianapolis, although at least nine were located elsewhere in the state. Until the last part of the nineteenth century, training was short (in months), and although some schools attempted to affiliate with colleges (i.e., DePauw, Butler, Laporte), those relations and most of the schools did not exist for long, nor was philanthropy a part of their support.[7]

Until recently, academic medical research in Indiana was less important than training of physicians and clinical care. As to the root causes of disease, public health only became a medical field toward the end of the nineteenth century, even though Indiana was hit hard by yellow fever and cholera epidemics during that time. Naturally, local and state government authorities took the lead in matters of public health.

Philanthropy had its earliest impact on Indiana health care through the establishment of hospitals. Although the first, and most important, hospitals in Indiana were government institutions, a number of private mostly religious-sponsored hospitals were soon established. All initially cared for the poor. Among the first government hospitals, the Indiana Hospital for the Insane (later Central State Hospital), created in 1848 by the Indiana State Legislature, was located three miles west of Indianapolis. Of note, it was the visit to Indiana, earlier in 1848, by reformer Dorothea Dix that prompted the legislature to take action and establish the hospital.[8] A decade later, in 1859, Indianapolis City Hospital was opened after years of debate and lobbying by doctors and other interested parties in the state capital.[9]

In the last three decades of the nineteenth century, many more hospitals were established in Indiana, in part to serve the poor but also resulting from new developments in medicine—especially in surgery and diagnosis—that required hospital facilities for their practice. The growth statistics are dramatic: In the United States, there were just two hospitals in 1800 and 178 in 1873, but by 1909, there were over four thousand.[10] These numbers did not result from a sudden upsurge of compassion for the poor but rather from dramatic improvement in medical services and practices offered at hospitals. This included new techniques such as anesthesia and antisepsis in surgical operations and new methods of diagnosis using hospital laboratories and equipment, which—by the end of the century—included x-rays. Hospitals, therefore, changed from treating poor patients in large wards supported by charity from donors and local government to the care of individuals in so-called private beds, who paid for their care. The combination of added income from paying customers plus local government compensation for care of the needy supported rapid growth in the construction and expansion of hospitals.

These hospitals also provided patients for the clinical instruction of medical students. One of the earliest examples in Indianapolis was the Bobbs Free Clinic, established in 1873 with $7,000 bequeathed by Dr. John S. Bobbs. The Indiana Medical College ran the clinic along with a medical library that he and eight other doctors had established in 1869. Bobbs was born in Pennsylvania in 1809 and attended Jefferson Medical College in Philadelphia. He moved to Indiana in 1835 to establish a medical practice and later became a professor of surgery, serving as dean of the short-lived Indiana Central Medical School in the 1850s. Bobbs is best known in the medical field for a pioneering operation in 1867 to remove gallstones (cholestcytotomy).[11]

Bobbs was on the original board of commissioners of the new Hospital for the Insane and served in the state senate, where he led support to establish schools for the blind and deaf and City Hospital. After completing military service in the Civil War, he returned to Indiana and was a leader in the establishment of the new Indiana Medical College and the clinic that bore his name. Indiana Medical College was one of two private medical colleges later taken over by Indiana University (IU) to form the IU medical school in 1908. This included the Bobbs Clinic, which shortly thereafter was replaced by Long Hospital, dedicated in 1914.[12]

The better-known St. Vincent Hospital in Indianapolis dates back to the founding of an infirmary that was established in 1881 by four nuns from the Daughters of St. Vincent de Paul. The nuns established the infirmary just three years after Bishop Chatard of Vincennes sent them to the state capital. The bishop himself had trained as a physician before entering the priesthood and soon joined the nuns when he moved the Episcopal See to the rapidly growing city. The move was delayed because of anti-Catholic sentiment, but the St. Vincent's Infirmary was legally incorporated in 1884. The nuns and bishop initially cared for the sick until a house physician joined them in 1885. The number of patients grew, and in 1913, the hospital moved to a larger new, 325-bed facility on Fall Creek, which included a nursing school thanks to a contribution of $60,000 from the St. Vincent headquarters in Maryland. The hospital remained at that location until it moved to the north side of Indianapolis in 1974.[13]

Methodist, another large hospital in Indianapolis, was organized in 1899 and opened in 1908 with sixty-five beds. It was established following the fourth international meeting held in Indianapolis of the Epworth Society in 1899, the official youth organization of the Episcopal Methodist Church. Teenagers from over forty Methodist churches in Indianapolis raised funds for ten thousand members to attend the convention. When it was over, $4,750 remained, and Charles Lasby, pastor of the Central Methodist Episcopal Church, suggested that the cash be used to start a building fund for a Methodist hospital in Indianapolis. The Indiana Conference approved the proposal later that year, and by 1905 the funds were raised. The hospital was dedicated in 1908 at a total cost of $225,000. In 1916, two new pavilions added 185 beds, which made it one of the largest hospitals in the state.[14]

These brief histories represent just a few examples of Indianapolis hospitals founded late in the nineteenth and early twentieth centuries. Others also established during this time included the Protestant Deaconess Hospital and Home for the Aged (1899), St. Francis Hospital (1914), and—perhaps most neglected by historians—hospitals established by African Americans in Indianapolis, including, Lincoln Hospital (1909), Charity Hospital (1911), and Dr. Ward's Sanatorium (late 1910s). These latter institutions were all short-lived since they lacked money and adequate facilities to practice the new hospital-based medicine.[15]

Cities in other parts of Indiana established hospitals in a similar fashion and at the same time as those in Indianapolis. For example, St. Joseph Hospital in Fort Wayne, was established in 1869, following a smallpox outbreak. Initially staffed by a nursing order from Germany, the Poor Handmaids of Jesus Christ, St. Joseph Hospital started out in the sixty-five-bed Rockhill Hotel, which had been built in 1838. In 1870, the city government began paying the hospital to take care of the poor as an alternative to housing them in the city poorhouse. In Evansville, St. Mary's Hospital was established in 1872 in an old marine hospital that had been created in 1856 to care for disabled merchant seamen and serve the wounded during the Civil War. Later, a $25,000 donation from Mrs. William Robert Fergus enabled Bernard Schapker, an Evansville businessman, to invite the Daughters of Charity (St. Vincent de Paul) to run a hospital at that location until it moved to a new building in 1894. A school of nursing was added in 1904.

Not all hospitals were of religious origin. For example, Reid Hospital opened in Richmond, in 1905, with financing from local industrialist Daniel G. Reid. The hospital replaced St. Stephens Hospital, a ten-bed facility created in 1884 by St. Paul's Episcopal Church. Perhaps most ambitious, and following a new philanthropic model of the twentieth century, was the 142-bed, $1.7 million Ball Memorial Hospital in Muncie, which opened in 1929. The hospital succeeded two private hospitals, one begun in 1891 that closed in 1910 and another that opened in 1905 and was replaced by Ball Memorial. Its funding came from the Ball Brothers Foundation, which was created from the estate of the oldest brother, Edmund Burke Ball, who died in 1925.[16]

Philanthropic support for hospital construction in Indianapolis took an unusual turn with the beginning of the IU School of Medicine in 1908. The school was established when two important proprietary medical schools agreed to become part of IU after several failed attempts to affiliate with other colleges in the state, including Purdue. The impetus for the merger was the need to meet rising standards for medical education best represented in a 1910 report by Abraham Flexner.[17] Indiana University was willing to commit resources, as was the state legislature.

The training of doctors required patients for clinical teaching, and these were provided by the Bobbs Clinic and more importantly by City Hospital. Although the latter provided a large number of patients, medical school reformers called for a "teaching" hospital where the quality and variety of care could be controlled. To this end, in 1911 a prominent physician and real estate investor, Robert W. Long, donated property to the university, the sale of

which went to finance a new hospital, with the legislature providing additional funds. The size of the Long donation ($200,000)
was extraordinary; in fact it exceeded the $150,000 John Purdue
gave fifty years earlier to establish the land grant university that
took his name.[18]

The impact of the Long gift is difficult to overestimate. The
hospital was built on the west side of the city, next to City Hospital. Shortly thereafter a new classroom and laboratory building was constructed across the street from Long Hospital to
replace the old downtown, proprietary medical school buildings. The gift determined the location of the medical center,
and the new facilities allowed the school to attract more faculty, which by the end of the 1930s made the medical school the
equal of others in the country. The gift also provided a model
for other donors to contribute. For example, the Riley Memorial Association, created in 1921 to honor the recently deceased
James Whitcomb Riley, raised half a million dollars to build a
children's hospital that opened in 1924.[19] And, in 1926, the Cole-
man family donated $250,000 for a maternity hospital dedicated
the following year.[20]

After 1945, a postwar boom in hospital construction had important consequences for health philanthropy. This paper can only
summarize the underlying reasons, including an acceleration of
new medical practices, especially in diagnosis (e.g., new imaging
and lab testing) and surgery (e.g., open-heart and transplanta-
tion) and demographic changes resulting from the baby boom
and movement to the suburbs, where hospitals soon followed. Of
most immediate importance was the new availability of federal
funding for hospitals thanks to the Hill-Burton Act. Congress
passed this legislation in 1946 as a compromise intended to avoid
more dramatic proposals for socialized medicine. Its most important provisions gave hospitals, nursing homes, and other health
facilities grants and loans for construction and modernization.
In return, these facilities agreed to provide a reasonable amount

of services to persons living in the facility's area who were unable to pay.[21]

Although the primary effect of this dramatic increase in government support was to overshadow private philanthropy, the need for matching funds and ongoing support to hospitals remained. The tradition of individual and community support continued to play a key role, as illustrated in the example of Community Hospital in Indianapolis. In the 1950s, residents and businesses on the east side of the city organized a grassroots campaign to bring needed hospital services to this part of the city that the *East Side Herald* called "the swiftest, most effective fund-raising campaign of our time." Led by Edward Gallahue, a businessman who donated twenty-eight acres of land at Sixteenth Street and Ritter Avenue, the effort successfully broke ground in 1954—with Vice President Richard Nixon in attendance. The three-hundred-bed, $5 million Community Hospital opened in 1956.[22]

COMBATING DISEASE FOR THE PUBLIC GOOD

Just as hospitals changed dramatically over the past two centuries, so too has the general understanding of and response to disease. In the nineteenth century, epidemics of cholera, yellow fever, smallpox, and other infectious diseases periodically struck the United States, including Indiana. By the beginning of the twentieth century, the increased practice of vaccination and discovery of germ theory helped to control epidemics and increase recognition of how and why some widespread diseases continued to harm both individuals and society at large. This led to social movements to educate the public and lobby the government to proactively combat these diseases. Privately organized initiatives provided a model that has been emulated and expanded to this day.

At the time, the three diseases eliciting the most extensive responses—the "social plagues" as they were commonly

termed—included alcoholism, venereal disease, and tuberculosis. Groups based in Indiana participated in these national movements with varied methods and responses. For example, the Indiana Temperance Society was formed in 1830 and the Woman's
Christian Temperance Union began in 1874, arguing that the
consumption of alcohol led to immorality, criminal activity, and
domestic violence.[23] In the twentieth century, prohibition supporters enlisted scientific and medical arguments in their cause.
The broader appeal helped draw together a coalition that eventually led to the ratification of the eighteenth amendment to the
constitution in 1919, which banned the manufacture, transport,
and sale of alcoholic beverages.[24]

Temperance overshadowed medical arguments, but an Indiana antituberculosis movement focused much more on medical
and health causes and prevention of the disease. Local organizations arose in response to this health concern, in part because
statistics revealed that tuberculosis was the most common cause
of death in the United States by the beginning of the twentieth
century: In 1910 tuberculosis was the number one cause of death
(11 percent) in Indianapolis.[25] Efforts in the state to combat the
disease followed an organizational model that was similar to
other movements. In 1904, inspired by international and national
movements, the Indiana Society for the Prevention of Tuberculosis (later renamed the Indiana Tuberculosis Association) was
created, and in 1911 it affiliated with the National Tuberculosis
Association.

The following year, the Indiana Tuberculosis Association
began fundraising efforts that included selling the recently introduced Christmas Seals. In 1911, the Marion County Society
for the Study and Prevention of Tuberculosis (later changed to
Marion County Tuberculosis Association) was established to
lead activities in the state's capital. Although the organization
worked closely with the Indiana Board of Health to educate the
public and lobby the state (e.g., efforts to build the Rockville State

Sanatorium in Parke County), it focused primarily on child education, health awareness, and early diagnosis. One of its first campaigns was for the creation of so-called fresh-air schools, which were eventually built throughout the state. The Indianapolis School Board's construction of Theodore Potter Fresh Air School, in 1924, was the organization's most ambitious project. The school was named after a tuberculosis specialist at IU School of Medicine who died prematurely in 1915. Although the building was later demolished, Public School 74 still bears Potter's name.[26] The medical rationale behind the development of these schools was that fresh air and sunshine were essential to the treatment of tuberculosis.

Education of the broader public was also a high priority of the tuberculosis organizations from the start, and the most important source of funding for public education activities was the sale of Christmas Seals. That practice began in Denmark in 1904 and was adopted three years later by the American Tuberculosis Association. In 1911, sale of Christmas Seals provided the Indiana and Marion County Tuberculosis Associations with funds that represented the overwhelming majority of the two organizations' annual income. This quickly rose from around $5,000 to $15,000 during the First World War and to over $35,000 by the mid-1920s. Public fundraising was a second key feature of the organizations' efforts to combat the disease. When new drugs were developed in the late 1930s and 1940s to treat tuberculosis, it became a less urgent health problem, and the local organizations shifted their focus, as did the national association, to combating other pulmonary diseases.

The pattern of local, state, and national collaboration, along with a focus on children was also reflected in state campaigns against venereal disease. Originally, the "venereal peril" raised a specter that was out of proportion to the incidence of the disease since it was much less prevalent compared with alcoholism or tuberculosis. However, the method of disease transmission, and its symptoms, greatly increased fear, as did its connection to moral weakness, somewhat like alcoholism. In 1907, John Hurty, secretary of the Indiana Board of Health, organized the Indiana Society for Social Hygiene to combat the "sexual plagues," including the recently discovered gonorrhea and syphilis. Its focus was on changing adolescent male behavior, and the main activity of this group was the distribution of one hundred thousand copies of Hurty's pamphlet, *Social Hygiene and the Sexual Plagues*, between 1908 and 1919.[27] The organization did not survive Hurty's death in 1922, in part because his protégé and successor, Thurman Rice, decided to concentrate efforts on education in schools.

During the 1930s, the Anti-Syphilis League of Indiana was created, following a call for such organizations from the American Social Health Association. In 1939, the organization changed its name to the Indiana Social Hygiene Association. Its philosophy was that education about "appropriate sexual behaviors" was primarily the duty of school educators. In 1942, the organization focused its work in Indianapolis, changing its name to the Indianapolis Social Hygiene Association. Over the following decades, it worked with the public schools, Indianapolis Community Chest (later United Way), and the State Board of Health to develop curricula for the schools. After the war, when penicillin became widely available and dramatically reduced incidence of venereal disease, the organization shifted its focus away from disease toward sex, marriage, and the family.[28]

By the late 1930s, and especially after antibiotics to treat infectious diseases became widely available in the 1940s and 1950s, other diseases attracted public attention. Organizations to combat them usually followed the model of a local chapter linked to a national organization with education and fundraising aimed at a mass market. In 1938, the Indianapolis chapter of the National Foundation Against Infantile Paralysis was established. In 1945, chapters of the American Cancer Society and the Little Red Door were created, followed by local organizations concerned with muscular dystrophy (1952), cerebral palsy (1953), and multiple sclerosis (1954). Local chapters focused on fundraising and education, while national organizations focused on granting medical research awards, thanks to the success of local mass fundraising.[29]

MEDICAL RESEARCH PHILANTHROPY

Philanthropic support for medical research was subject to the same underlying influences as giving to hospitals and efforts to combat disease, although it came later. Dramatic changes in the fundamental nature of medicine were the result of advancements in research in the nineteenth century; however, these discoveries were initially made on a small scale, in already established laboratories of hospitals and medical schools. The new model of research, which was established by the Pasteur Institute at the end of the nineteenth century, was on a larger scale and relied on philanthropy, but these institutes were few in number until the 1920s.

The nature of medical education in Indiana in the twentieth century concentrated research in Indianapolis, but it was a much lower priority than the need to educate physicians and care for patients in the new university hospitals of the medical school. There was some external funding for research as early as the 1930s, notably from the Riley Memorial Association and Eli Lilly and Company, but discoveries such as Rolla Harger's Drunkometer (a precursor to the Breathalyzer) were made without external support.[30] Nor was the IU School of Medicine able to take advantage of new national foundations funding health research, notably the Rockefeller Foundation. As with hospitals and disease campaigns, the Second World War marked a dramatic change in medical research, including its sources of funding both nationally and within Indiana. Just as federal support largely financed postwar hospital construction so too did the National Institutes of Health and the National Science Foundation overshadow, but not eliminate, private philanthropic support for medical research.[31]

One of the first major medical research gifts in Indiana after the war came in 1953 from Herman and Elnora Krannert. Their contribution helped establish the Robert M. Moore Heart Clinic at Indianapolis City Hospital. It was later renamed the Krannert Heart Institute of the IU medical school, although the institute continued its collaboration with City Hospital and also brought in Methodist Hospital as a partner. The donation by the Krannerts, whose fortune came from the success of the Inland Container Corporation, was one of numerous gifts they made to colleges in the Midwest for many other purposes, including a Center for the Performing Arts at the University of Illinois and contributions to industrial management education at Purdue University.[32]

Postwar philanthropy by wealthy individuals and spouses in Indiana included other foundations specifically devoted to medical research. Among the most important were the Regenstrief, Showalter, and Walther foundations.[33] All three were the result of fortunes made by their namesakes, one of whom, Walther, was a medical practitioner. Joe Walther created Winona Memorial Hospital in Indianapolis and used proceeds from the 1983 sale of that hospital to launch a foundation that remains dedicated to the prevention and treatment of cancer. Ralph Showalter made his fortune as a lawyer who served as the first head of the international division of Eli Lilly and Company. After his death in 1958, his wife, Grace, made a number of philanthropic gifts, eventually establishing a trust in 1973 that she dedicated to supporting medical and scientific research. Sam Regenstrief established the world's largest residential dishwasher plant in Connersville, Indiana, the income from which enabled him to create a foundation for medical research.

Unlike the Krannerts and other Indiana philanthropists who made gifts to a variety of organizations and causes, including medical ones, these three philanthropists dedicated their gifts specifically to health and medical research. They came to this cause by different means, and used mechanisms that evolved over time, but they shared some features in common. For example, because they changed over time, the overall pattern of their giving can be described as evolutionary; that is, they were flexible and made changes in both the specific purpose and methods of giving. All three developed and maintained strong relationships with their recipients and with the other foundations. In addition, all three provided extensive support to the IU medical school and each expanded giving to include other research institutions in Indiana.

According to the Regenstrief Foundation's history, it began as a result of a suggestion by Sam Regenstrief's nephew-in-law, Harvey Feigenbaum, who was a faculty member at the IU School of Medicine. Sam was not particularly interested in scientific discovery, but as a businessman whose success depended on efficiency, he was struck by the inefficiencies he saw in the US health care system. There were also personal reasons for Sam's philanthropy: He was no fan of the tax code and the Regenstriefs had no children.

During initial discussions in 1967, Feigenbaum's Department of Medicine chair, John Hickam, recommended creation of a Regenstrief Foundation. After it awarded a few research grants, the foundation funneled its support through an institute that used medical school expertise to study the health practices of the adjacent City Hospital (renamed Marion County General Hospital in 1959).[34] Rather than transfer the corpus of the foundation to the institute, the foundation made periodic awards to operate it, and the institute was also expected to obtain grants from government and private industry to support its research. This arrangement enabled the foundation to review and ultimately shift the focus of the institute's research. This story of the foundation's legal structure and its relationship to the Regenstrief Institute and its partners, including the medical school, is complicated. Of note, the arrangement gave the foundation flexibility to shift support and take risks. By the mid-1970s, for example, the foundation began to support the work of Clem McDonald on the Regenstrief Medical Records System, one of the earliest computer-based systems that became the foundation's best-known accomplishment.[35] In addition to providing core support to the Regenstrief Institute at IU for research in aging, health services, and biomedical informatics (electronic medical records work), the foundation now supports the Regenstrief Center for Healthcare Engineering at Purdue. As of 2017 the Regenstrief Foundation assets were approximately $180 million, and in recent years, annual awards have averaged $9 million.[36]

Grace Showalter's philanthropy followed a similar path in some respects. She used the foundation created in her husband's memory to support research at the IU School of Medicine and health-related science and engineering departments and schools at Purdue University. Her motivation to support this work did not initially spring from an interest in medicine.[37] An avid art collector, Grace was best known for the funds she provided after the death of her husband to build a fountain portraying the birth of Venus at the center of the IU Bloomington campus. In the fall of 1967, the fountain became the center of protests against the Vietnam War, and the politically and socially conservative Mrs. Showalter decided to support other beneficiaries from her estate. She instructed her attorney in Indianapolis to approach the dean of the IU School of Medicine and the president of Purdue University about making a donation, not for buildings but for research.

Showalter gave little guidance on the type of research that interested her. This lack of direction and her death shortly after creating the trust explains why it took three years of discussion before the Showalter Research Trust came to be. Foundation trustees decided to divide annual income equally between the two institutions. The medical school and Purdue were both represented on the board and both were required to submit annual requests for support. This made it possible for each to direct funds according to their needs—but always subject to the foundation's approval. Both institutions initially requested support for faculty chairs and other support for key departments. Purdue did so in biomedical engineering, which allowed it to recruit Les Geddes from Baylor University, whose work on regenerative tissue grafting eventually became one of Purdue's most successful research programs in securing external grants and royalty income.[38] The medical school initially requested support for the departments of biochemistry and pharmacology. The trust also reserved some funds to support research at other institutions, including Methodist Hospital; however, this grant and the trust's support for a new Center for Advanced Research were small compared to the Purdue and IU School of Medicine grants.

Like the Regenstrief arrangement, the requirement of annual requests permitted a shift not only in the subject of research but eventually also in the strategy. As medical research costs increased and proposals to federal and national funding sources became more competitive, both Purdue and the IU School of Medicine persuaded the Showalter Trust to provide seed money to begin new research projects that would allow them to apply for larger research grants. Both institutions established internal competitions for research proposals that were evaluated and ranked before forwarding the top proposals to the Showalter Trust for approval. The trust's corpus is around $40 million, and it makes approximately ten awards annually to each institution totaling $1.5 million.

The Walther Cancer Foundation is the most recent of the three medical research philanthropies established in Indianapolis. Joseph Walther was a 1936 graduate of the Indiana University School of Medicine. After much travel before and during the Second World War, he returned to Indianapolis and purchased the Glossbrenner Mansion on Meridian Street, where he set up his practice. Entrepreneurial by nature, Walther showed an early inclination toward enterprise building, including purchasing and managing properties and nearby medical offices. In 1956, Walther opened Memorial Clinic Hospital, which he later renamed Winona Memorial Hospital, adjacent to the Glossbrenner mansion. In 1983, Walther's wife, Mary Margaret, died from colon cancer and his own health was failing. He sold the hospital and, in 1985, established the Walther Cancer Foundation and the Walther Institute with over $100 million in proceeds from the sale.[39]

Walther had one driving goal: the eradication of cancer. In short order, he created a medical research organization and four related legal entities funding a variety of programs on drug development and basic science at five university and hospital campuses.[40] Beyond scientific research, the foundation supported work intended to improve nursing care, the quality of the in-hospital experience, and education and support for family members. Walther also created a charity that sought to raise money from the public to support his efforts, but it proved unsuccessful. Over time, the complex organization was simplified, contracting to a single grant-making foundation. It continues to focus on the prevention, treatment, and cure for cancer. With an eye for innovative talent, the foundation provided early and steady funding to Hal Broxmeyer, a pioneer in stem cell research and the practice of infant-cord blood banking for the treatment of leukemia. The foundation's assets of approximately $145 million allow it to make grants averaging $5 million annually in recent years. These awards are spread more widely than the other two Indianapolis foundations, which concentrate on the IU School of Medicine and Purdue, whereas Walther's beneficiaries include researchers at Notre Dame and the University of Michigan, as well as nursing and bioethics at IUPUI, the Indianapolis campus of IU and Purdue.[41]

CONCLUSION

Long-term trends in health philanthropy in Indiana are similar to national trends. These include the obvious fact that health-related philanthropy has grown, despite being overshadowed by an even more rapid growth in government funding of health care and medical research in the past fifty years. Indeed, the rise of overall health expenditures in the United States, including private funds, rose to 17.5 percent of gross domestic product (GDP) in 2014, according to the Centers for Medicare and Medicaid Services.[42] Most of this provided income for health services at hospitals, including private, government, and nonprofit. That does not mean that health philanthropy and fundraising are irrelevant. Like other philanthropy, it has proven crucial for demonstrating matching support, encouraging innovation, and filling gaps that are not met by private and government funding. Perhaps the most spectacular example of the latter is the Gates Foundation, which funds global health initiatives that have prompted governments and private companies around the world to increase their support for disease eradication, vaccine development, and access to other health services in countries with limited resources.[43]

A subtler purpose served by health philanthropy, especially grassroots and mass fundraising, is the role it plays in education and increasing awareness of both personal and broader social health problems. Local mass fundraising is important for hospital support, but the campaigns against major diseases also collectively help to fund research awards, usually to universities. New discoveries eventually have an impact on the public, but more immediately through advertising, media, and special events, the public learns of the experience and needs of people whose lives are affected by threats to health. Engaging in fundraising is a way for the public to participate.[44] Most agree that the level of expenditure on health in the United States is unsustainable, but health and illness are universal conditions and health philanthropy has disproportionately focused on areas of neglect. Therefore, to the extent that our culture has an altruistic tradition of giving for the benefit of others, health philanthropy will continue to be an important activity, using both well established and new practices.

NOTES

1. There is a great deal of scholarship on health philanthropy in the United States, although it focuses heavily on the largest foundations. In contrast, other than internal and commemorative studies, there is little academic historical research on local efforts. Aside from the entries in the *Encyclopedia of Indianapolis*, eds. David J. Bodenhamer and Robert G. Barrows (Bloomington, IN: Indiana University Press, 1994), this overview of Indiana health care philanthropy is heavily based on research completed by graduate students who taught me a lot over the past years: Kathi Baedertscher, Norma Erickson, Kelly Gascoine, Suzann Lupton, and Angie Potter. Any errors or omissions are of my own doing.

2. William H. Schneider, "Philanthropy: The Difficult Art of Giving," *Nature* 497 (May 15, 2013): 311–12.

3. Maria Di Mento and Idit Knaan, "6 Graphics to Tell You More about the Philanthropy 50," Chronicle of Philanthropy, accessed February 8, 2015, https://philanthropy.com/article/6-Graphics-to-Tell-You-More/151789.

4. Alex Phiilippidis, "Top 20 Grant-Giving Disease Foundations," GEN [Genetic Engineering and Biotechnology News], accessed May 28, 2013, http://www.genengnews.com/insight-and-intelligence/top-20-grant-giving-disease-foundations/77899817/. Some figures are for the 2011–2012 fiscal year.

5. "2015 Form 990 for American Lung Association of The Upper Midwest," accessed March 17, 2022, https://www.causeiq.com/organizations/view_990/204392201/d848d8be27c5497eb463223607e6db24.

6. William H. Schneider, *Indiana University School of Medicine: A History* (Bloomington: Indiana University Press, 2020), 12–33; Walter J. Daly, "The Origins of President Bryan's Medical School," *Indiana Magazine of History* 97 (2002): 266–84; Thurman B. Rice, "History of the Medical Campus," *Monthly Bulletin Indiana State Board of Health* (February 1947): 35–40.

7. Kenneth M. Ludmerer, *Learning to Heal: The Development of American Medical Education* (Baltimore: Johns Hopkins University Press, 1996), 9–28.

8. Evelyn C. Adams, "The Growing Concept of Social Responsibility Illustrated by a Study of the State's Care of the Insane in Indiana," *Indiana Magazine of History* 32, no. 1 (1936): 1–22.

9. Kathi Badertscher, "A New Wishard Is on the Way," *Indiana Magazine of History* 108, no. 4 (2012): 345–82.

10. Charles Rosenberg, *The Care of Strangers: The Rise of America's Hospital System* (New York: Basic Books, 1987), 4–5.

11. Alembert W. Brayton, "Dr. John S. Bobbs, of Indianapolis, the Father of Cholecystotomy," *Indiana Medical Journal* (1905); R. S. Sparkman, "Dr. John S. Bobbs of Indiana. The First Cholecystotomist," *J Indiana State Med Association* 60, no. 5 (May 1967): 541–48.

12. Schneider, *Indiana University School of Medicine*, 34–70.

13. Given its long history and importance, there have been a number of accounts of the hospital. See Terri L. Sinnott, "The $84.77 Hospital—St. Vincent," *Hektoen International Journal* (Spring 2015), accessed March 17, 2022, https://hekint.org/2017/02/24/the-84-77-hospital-st-vincent/; Ryan Hamlett, "A Room with a View—The History of the St. Vincent Hospital Fall Creek Building," accessed March 17, 2022, http://historicindianapolis .com/a-room-with-a-view-the-history-of-st-vincent-hospitals-fall-creek -building/; Marie D'Andrea Loftus, *A History of St. Vincent's Hospital School of Nursing, Indianapolis, Indiana, 1896–1970* (Indianapolis: Litho Press, 1972).

14. Doug Davies, "A Century of Service," The Indiana Methodist Historical Society Newsletter, Spring 2009, 2–3, accessed March 17, 2022, http://www.depauw.edu/files/resources/iumhs-spring-2009.pdf.

15. Norma Erickson, "The Lincoln Hospital of Indianapolis: A Study of African-American Hospitals and Health Care in Early Twentieth Century Indianapolis" (MA thesis, IUPUI, 2015).

16. Keith Roysdon, "Doctors, Hospitals Met Muncie's Health Needs," *Star Press*, March 21, 2015, which is based on the book Wiley W. Spurgeon, *Ball Memorial Hospital: A Legacy of Caring, 1929–1989* (Muncie, IN: Ball Memorial Hospital, 1989).

17. Schneider, *Indiana University School of Medicine*, 62–6. On Flexner, see Kenneth Ludmerer, *Learning to Heal* (Baltimore: Johns Hopkins University Press, 1996) and Thomas Duffy, "The Flexner Report—100 Years Later," *Yale Journal of Biological Medicine* 84, no. 3 (September 2011): 269–76.

18. Schneider, *Indiana University School of Medicine*, 77–95.

19. The James Whitcomb Riley Memorial Association became an important ongoing source of support for the hospital. It raises more than $25

million annually in support. See Elizabeth J. Van Allen et al., eds., *Keeping the Dream, 1921–1996: Commemorating 75 Years of Caring for Indiana's Children* (Indianapolis, IN: James Whitcomb Riley Memorial Association, 1996).

20. Joseph F. Thompson, *"This Important Trust": A History of the Department of Obstetrics and Gynecology, Indiana University School of Medicine and Medical Center, 1909–1992* (Indianapolis: University Obstetricians and Gynecologists, 1993).

21. An example of the enormous literature on this landmark legislation is Harry Peristadt, "The Development of the Hill-Burton Legislation: Interests, Issues and Compromises," *Journal of Health & Social Policy* 6, no. 3 (1995): 77–96.

22. Beth A. DeHoff, "Community Hospitals," in *Encyclopedia of Indianapolis*, eds. David J. Bodenhamer and Robert G. Barrows (Bloomington: Indiana University Press, 1994), 480.

23. Jane Hedeen, "The Road to Prohibition in Indiana," Indiana Historical Society, accessed March 17, 2022, https://indianahistory.org/wp-content/uploads/1d7d71dfbb39529a736fdba5279a5ba9.pdf; Jason Lantzer, *Interpreting the Prohibition Era at Museums and Historic Sites* (Lanham, MD: Rowan and Littlefield, 2015), 56; Jason Lantzer, *Prohibition Is Here to Stay* (Notre Dame, IN: University of Notre Dame Press, 2009), 75.

24. Lantzer, *Prohibition Is Here to Stay*, 75.

25. Kelly Gascoine, "Saving Children from the White Plague: The Marion County Tuberculosis Association's Crusade against Tuberculosis, 1911–1936" (MA thesis, Indiana University, 2010), 1. This is a model for the detailed study of health and philanthropy.

26. "Open Air Schools in Indiana," Gascoine and Indiana State Library, accessed March 17, 2022, http://www.in.gov/library/2482.htm.

27. Angela Potter, "From Social Hygiene to Social Health: Adolescent Sex Education in Indiana, 1907–2013" (MA thesis, Indiana University, 2015).

28. Ibid.

29. On disease organizations' support of research especially after 1945, see Angela Creager, "Mobilizing Biomedicine: Virus Research between Lay Health Organizations and the U.S. Federal Government, 1935–1955," in *Biomedicine in the Twentieth Century: Practices, Policies, and Politics*, ed. Caroline Hannaway (Washington D.C.: IOS Press, 2008), 171–201.

30. "Rolla N. Harger Dies; Invented Drunkometer," *New York Times*, August 10, 1983.

31. William H. Schneider, "The Origin of the Medical Research Grant in the United States: The Rockefeller Foundation and the NIH Extramural

Funding Program," *Journal of the History of Medicine and Allied Health Sciences* 70, no. 2 (2015): 279–311.

32. Nora McKinney Hyatt, "Krannert Charitable Trust," in *Encyclopedia of Indianapolis*, 878-9.

33. Suzann W. Lupton, "Local Foundations and Medical Research Support in Indianapolis After 1945" (PhD diss., Indiana University, 2019).

34. Wendy Ford, *Regenstrief: Legacy of the Dishwasher King* (Indianapolis: Regenstrief Foundation, 1999), 57–67.

35. Ibid., 143–66.

36. "Regenstrief Institute" Department of Medicine, Indiana University School of Medicine, accessed January 13, 2016, http://medicine.iupui.edu/INTM/research/regenstrief and http://www.regenstrief.org/centers/research-resources/.

37. The following is based on an earlier study by Suzann Lupton, "'To Benefit Mankind and Encourage Medical and Scientific Research'; The Ralph W. and Grace M. Showalter Research Trust, 1973–2007" (unpublished paper, 2008).

38. Ibid., 21–23, 42–43.

39. "Walther Cancer Foundation," accessed March 17, 2022, http://www.walther.org/history/beginnings.aspx.

40. Personal communication from Suzann Lupton, January 15, 2016.

41. Ibid.

42. "National Health Expenditure Data," Centers for Medicare and Medicaid Services, accessed January 28, 2016, https://www.cms.gov/research-statistics-data-and-systems/statistics-trends-and-reports/nationalhealthexpenddata/nationalhealthaccountshistorical.html.

43. Kirstin RW Matthews, "The Grand Impact of the Gates Foundation. Sixty Billion Dollars and One Famous Person Can Affect the Spending and Research Focus of Public Agencies," *EMBO Reports* 9, no. 5 (May 2008): 409–12.

44. Some argue that this process of health awareness has gone too far, producing a phenomenon called the "worried well," which is people who have never been healthier yet never more concerned with their health. Others have linked this to the "medicalization" of society, whereby pharmaceutical and other medical interests are stimulating a demand, especially through media and advertising, for their products and services. J. Y. Wick and G.R. Zanni, "Hypochondria: The Worried Well," *Consult Pharm* 23, no. 3 (March 2008):192–94, 196–98, 207–8; Peter Conrad, "The Shifting Engines of Medicalization," *Journal of Health Social Behavior* 46, no. 1 (March 2005): 3–14.

PART II

TRENDS AND INNOVATIONS

SECTION I

MOTIVATIONS TO GIVE

SEVEN

—ༀ—

THE CAUSE OF BENEVOLENCE

Calvin Fletcher as
Philanthropist

NICOLE ETCHESON

CALVIN FLETCHER BECAME ONE OF the most important figures in nineteenth-century Indiana.[1] He left his Vermont home at seventeen, and his earliest letters recorded him being "destitute of money and in debt three dollars." He labored as a farmhand, went to school, and worked in a brickyard, a job he was driven to "by Poverty." He taught school, studied law in Ohio, and moved to Indianapolis. As a young lawyer, he rode the circuit, speculated in land, and dabbled in politics. He established a successful farm and presided over the Indianapolis branch of the state bank for much of the 1840s and 1850s. By the end of the Civil War, "he was the highest income taxpayer" in the Hoosier capital. It is perhaps ironic, given his role as a philanthropist, that much of Fletcher's wealth came from economic misfortune. He noted that the "most profitable part" of his law business was "collecting," that is, collecting the debts of businessmen who had suffered financial reverses. However he gained his money, he believed that "if God prolong my life & give me success in business, I hope to distribute the proceeds to his cause of benevolence to the poor and the benefit of mankind."[2]

Fletcher was both proud of his worldly success and at the forefront of philanthropy in Indianapolis from his settlement there in 1821 to his death after a riding accident in 1866. In some ways, Fletcher's history mirrors that of the more famous twentieth-century Hoosier philanthropist Eli Lilly. Both built successful business careers and devoted large sums of money to good causes. While Lilly came of age during the Progressive period—most associated with the rise of organized institutional giving—Fletcher lived during the period of transition between philanthropy as acts of individual charity to a system of bureaucratized institutions. Again and again, Fletcher helped individuals in need with private donations, but he also participated in and helped establish numerous benevolent and civic associations to aid the unfortunate and improve their quality of life. During the Civil War, some of these associations partnered with the federal government, looking forward to a time when Americans accepted the legitimacy of government help in forming a social welfare state.[3]

A study of Fletcher's career allows for an examination of the development of philanthropy in the nineteenth-century Midwest, showing that Indiana participated in the trends that were occurring nationally. Fletcher's roles as a leading organizer of charities, actor in benevolent movements, and philanthropic giver demonstrate the overlapping nature of different modes of philanthropy during this crucial half century that saw the rise of important reform movements, such as asylums, public schools, temperance, and abolition.

The literature on philanthropy suggests periods in which good works predominated during the colonial period, the voluntary associations that made such an impression on the French visitor Alexis de Tocqueville marked the Jacksonian period, and the Progressive Era saw a transition to more government responsibility for social welfare. This is a vast oversimplification. Kathleen D. McCarthy, in particular, has argued that the division between private and public philanthropy was not as clear-cut in previous eras as twentieth-century observers claimed. For McCarthy, the Civil War is a transitional period in which the government, which had withdrawn from philanthropy during the Jacksonian period, entered into partnership with private associations. David C. Hammack has noted that churches dominated the dissemination of social services such as health care, education, and the arts until the early national period. The Constitution's separation of church and state led to the formation of private, nongovernmental organizations.[4]

Calvin Fletcher's career of giving further challenges any stark periodization of American philanthropy and highlights its religious underpinnings. In the tradition of John Winthrop and Cotton Mather, Fletcher provided assistance to individuals in acts of private charity. When still only twenty-three, he expressed the Puritan sentiment that he could repay God for his own worldly success by "doing good to all my fellow creatures."[5] He participated in the Jacksonian era reform associations, particularly temperance but also agricultural societies and the antislavery movement. He joined the Methodist church and was active in church organizations. Although he had only a brief career in state government, he was an active proponent of public schools. He occasionally gave money for political causes, such as donating $13 to three young men who set off to aid the free-state cause in Bleeding Kansas. And during the Civil War, he worked with the Indiana Sanitary Commission and state officials to care for Indiana troops.[6] Fletcher's philanthropy thus spanned personal acts of charity and organized philanthropy and reform, both in the private and public sphere.

Fletcher's Calvinist roots included a religious emphasis on charity as a way for fellow Christians to care for each other. Fletcher's well-known piety as an adult caused historian John H. Wigger to use him as the exemplar of the nineteenth-century Methodist who combined success in worldly affairs with a "thirst for improvement."[7] But Fletcher disdained the church as "uncouth low bread Methodist whom I despise."[8] However almost a decade after his marriage to Sarah Hill, whose family were Methodists, Fletcher joined the church. In addition to regular church attendance, he began holding family prayers with his children. He also became active in the organizational efforts of the church, including the Preachers Aid Society, sabbath schools, and missionary societies. He frequently presided over meetings of these groups and donated money. Only a year after his conversion, the Bible Society appointed him president. Over the years, he delivered many addresses to sabbath schools. Reverend Allen Wiley persuaded Fletcher to teach in the sabbath school, and soon after Fletcher became one of the sabbath school's superintendents. He helped organize the first Sabbath School Convention.[9]

His increasing wealth made him an important benefactor. Attending the dedication of the Depot Church, he learned that $450 was still owed. Those in attendance subscribed $250, and Fletcher pledged to pay the remainder. He had covered the debts of so many other churches that he wrote, "I have now Capital in every Church in town except the Catholic." In 1848, he estimated that in the previous six years he had given "for churches & church purposes some $1500 or 1800." Typically, he added, "it was the Lords I claim no merit in handing it over & I pray I may have filled his holy will in the distribution."[10]

His religious beliefs caused constant concerns that attention to business impeded his spiritual growth. He described business transactions as "temptations." Those concerns did not cause him to give up business, but they did lead to continual reflection on the state of his soul. He spoke of "clos[ing] up my worldly affairs," or at least circumscribing them. But he believed his wealth had a higher purpose: "It is of no consequence I think to be wealthy unless that wealth makes a better man," he wrote in his New Year's reflections of 1859. "Unsanctified wealth is a curse—made just for self is to miss the great objects for which God gives means

& agents to mortals. . . . May God direct me in the choice of the means to be yet useful in my day."[11]

One way that Fletcher found to be useful was in individual acts of private charity for the needy. As a young and impecunious school teacher, Fletcher "schoold the widows sons and daughters—orphans—and all such as were not able to pay and who would have staid at home had I not told them their tuitions should be gratis if they could not pay." Fletcher regularly took children into his home as apprentices or servants in order to provide for them. In 1836, he entered into a contract with "old Mrs. Walls," apparently a widow with many children, for her fifteen-year-old daughter to live with his family. Judson Benjamin, the orphaned son of a Baptist missionary who lived with the Fletchers, received an exhortation "to make himself a useful man & as one means to rise early & devote every spare moment to books & especially biography." In 1850, two "adopted childrin," Elizabeth Smith and Almyra Thompson, who were living with the Fletchers, died of the cholera. Myra had been "a poor out cast 14 or 15 years of age" when she came to the Fletchers. Fletcher frequently recorded tracts of land for such dependents and women such as a Mrs. Richmond, for whom he entered a quarter section. "So the widow & orphin are provided for," he noted in his diary after such a transaction.[12]

In 1848, former governor James Brown Ray died. Two years later, his widow also passed away. Fletcher visited Esther Ray on her deathbed: "She requested I should take charge of her youngest son Johnny." Fletcher agreed to "see after his property" but felt unable to "take him into my house" given his own large family. A year later, Fletcher officially became the eight-year-old boy's guardian. Johnny did come to live with the Fletchers. He went to school and worked with the Fletcher children on the farm.[13]

Not all the recipients of Fletcher's aid benefited from it. Fletcher's son Miles, a professor at Indiana Asbury University (later

DePauw), encountered Scotch John, drunk on a Greencastle
street. After their chance meeting, a sober John visited Miles,
"cried, said he'd acted foolishly," and "asked for money to get
home." He said he wanted to return to Calvin Fletcher in Indianapolis. After securing a promise that John would not drink,
Miles loaned him the money, noting, "He was very anxious that
you should not know that he had been drinking." The latter comment suggested that Calvin had had similar conversations with
John, offering help on the condition that John reform.[14]

But Fletcher's aid was often gratefully acknowledged. William Hart had borrowed thirteen dollars when he first arrived
in Indianapolis to bury his son, Alexander. The Hart family had
suffered illness on their arrival; their son died and William was
too sick with the plague to work. Having recovered, Hart repaid
the loan, saying, "I hope you will now receive our thanks to you
upon your kindness to us in our distress." The son of an old friend,
W. W. Vance, had asked Fletcher for advice and later wrote, "I
believe you to be the first who was able, that has ever offered
to take me by the hand & lift me from the mire, unactuated by
entirely selfish motives I shal ever feel deeply greatful to you for
the interest that you taken in my welfare."[15]

Fletcher's acts of private charity frequently included African
Americans. He helped protect a Black man named Overhall in
a dispute with a White man who claimed his property. He represented "a poor but honest *colored* man" named Perry who had
been defrauded out of a horse by a young lawyer of a prominent
family. Fletcher concluded that he had "done justice to the poor
African. He gained his cause." He also served as lawyer for a slave
woman and her three children who were claimed by a Virginian.
Although he "spoke in behalf of the woman" in court, he did not
go beyond that. The judge's verdict in the woman's favor was not
popular, and although Fletcher anticipated there might be "violence" or "outrages . . . committed on the poor negroes," he felt
he had "discharged my duty towards them & in accordance with

my own sober convictions."[16] In other words, he was not going to defend them from the mob.

In his dealings with African Americans, Fletcher displayed a strong sense of paternalism. A Black man named Harry sought advice from Fletcher. When Harry's master, Mr. Webb, moved to Indiana from Kentucky, he sold Harry to his son-in-law. Harry asked instead to come to Indiana with Webb, promising to serve him for life. But after some months in a free state, Harry became "dissatisfied." Harry consulted Fletcher, who advised him to continue working for Webb for a year. Webb, meanwhile, was notified by the overseers of the poor that he needed to give the security required under Indiana law for Harry's maintenance. Webb then asked Harry for a binding indenture. After a long "parly" between Harry, Webb, and Fletcher, Harry bought himself from Webb for $200. A man of purer abolitionist sentiment would have argued that Harry owed Webb nothing, but Fletcher was impressed with Harry's "integrity" in feeling bound by his pledge to work for Webb.[17]

Fletcher also deplored stirring up excitement and urged respect for legal proceedings. On July 4, 1845, Fletcher returned home from the sabbath school parade to learn that "ruffians" had murdered John Tucker, "a very peacible colored man," who had lived in Indianapolis for decades. Fletcher helped solicit attorneys to prosecute the murderers and contributed five dollars to fund the prosecution. In addition, Fletcher wrote to the editor of the local Democratic newspaper hoping to gain his aid in protecting Henry De Puy, editor of the abolitionist newspaper, the *Indiana Freeman*. Fletcher and Henry Ward Beecher, whose congregation at Indianapolis's Second Presbyterian Church had heard the mob's attack on Tucker, had interceded with De Puy to prevent him publishing an account of the mob attack. When stories of Fletcher and Beecher's meeting with De Puy appeared in regional newspapers, Beecher replied that they had tried to persuade De Puy to let the courts handle the matter. Fletcher pointed out that the circuit court would be meeting in two weeks. Fletcher's faith in the law was only partially justified: The leading assailant received three years for manslaughter, another was acquitted, and a third was apparently never brought to trial.[18]

Fletcher played a similar kind of role in the famous case of John Freeman. Freeman had lived in Indianapolis for over a decade and owned a restaurant when he was claimed, under the recent Fugitive Slave Act, in 1853. Freeman's wife approached Fletcher, who noted Freeman's long residence, "considerable property," and position as sexton at a Presbyterian church. Fletcher wrote, "I wish not to prom[en]ade a disregard of the law & constitution but if the owners refuse as I am told they do to take a fair price for him I shall not feel greved if he escapes." Fletcher helped finance the defense until it was proven that Freeman was not the runaway Kentucky slave.[19]

Fletcher's support of colonization further complicated his relationship with the African American community. He was elected manager of the Indiana Colonization Society on its organization in 1829. He was aware of criticism of colonization; some of his acquaintances asked him to defend the movement from the charge "that it was a plan to contrive to relieve the slave holders of the obnoxious Black whom they wanted out of the way." After attending a meeting of free Blacks that was "very unanimous not to go to Liber[i]a or Affrica," Fletcher did not change his opinion. He merely hoped "the Lord will open their eyes & direct them back to ther own country." He continued to give the colonization society money even though he disliked its agent, James Mitchell. Nonetheless, his involvement with colonization waned, and by the Civil War, he was working actively with societies to aid the freedmen. Elected presiding officer of the Indianapolis Freedmen's Aid Commission, Fletcher noted that he had not been active in associations for many years. He made an exception for the cause of "protect[ing] the manumitted slaves" as he considered it "a solemn duty reserved perhaps to me as the last public act of my life." Fletcher also provided part of his farm as the muster camp for the Twenty-Eighth US Colored Troops, Indiana's Black regiment.[20]

Fletcher was overstating his withdrawal from associational work when he joined the Freedmen's Aid Commission. In December 1835, he and his wife participated in forming the Indianapolis Benevolent Society. They continued active in the organization, attending meetings and collecting groceries, money, wood, and medicine for the poor. Need increased during the winter or "charity" months and especially during the economic downturn of the late 1850s. Sarah Hill Fletcher had been aiding the poor for years before the Benevolent Society formed, taking "provisions" to a widow with "orphan childrin," nursing the sick, and tending the dying. She continued to manage a large household, help those in need, and work for other charities, such as the church sewing society. She was active in the "female society for the Relief of widows & orphans," an offshoot of the Benevolent Society. By the 1850s, such female societies were well established in American cities. So immersed was Sarah Fletcher in these associations that one night she dreamed she was talking with their son Calvin Jr. when he became angry at an interruption "by some poor women who come for me to get them bonnet's from the benevolent society so they could go to church." In her dream, Sarah told Calvin Jr. "their wants must be tended to."[21]

Sarah, however, disliked making the public solicitations on which these societies relied. Calvin tried to get her "excused" from soliciting for a church fair. When that failed, he "encourg[ed] her to do her duty cheerfully." With her fifteen-year-old son, Ingram, to carry her basket and provide moral support, "she succeeded well." Calvin made such visits routinely, often escorting female members. On one trip for the Benevolent Society, Fletcher and his companion "got some 125 pieces of good clothing in our district & 2 or $3 in mony." On another occasion, Fletcher and William Sheets attended a meeting of the Widows and Orphans

Society "to see if we could not act in concert in collecting old clothes &c." Fletcher accompanied Mrs. J. B. Hollingshead in canvassing local businesses, and they collected $42.[22]

When Sarah Hill Fletcher died, the Benevolent Society adopted resolutions lauding her "attention to the poor" and sick. Calvin hoped that Sarah's "judicious kind aid to the poor ... has conferred a blessing on her family." Fletcher remained active in the organization until his death, including serving on the executive committee and organizing annual meetings. The Benevolent Society, however, was only one of many reform organizations in which Fletcher participated.[23]

The antislavery and colonization movements were types of reform associations considered the signature philanthropic development of the pre–Civil War era. There were numerous other examples, but one of the most prominent reform movements of Fletcher's era was temperance. Abstinence from alcohol appealed to the middle-class values of hard work, self-discipline, and economic progress. Temperance separated men such as Fletcher from the excesses of the working class.[24]

Fletcher grew up in a hard-drinking society. His father drank "regular drams," a practice that did not contribute positively to his "activity mental or physical." His father's drinking, although condoned by custom, may have influenced Fletcher to avoid alcohol. In the Midwest, he noted that when neighbors gathered to harvest together, "they drink a great deal of whiskey & it is not uncommon for them to fight." As a state legislator, he observed the heavy drinking at political gatherings.[25]

Fletcher was involved in the earliest days of organized temperance in Indiana, a movement Emma Lou Thornbrough says Methodists were especially active in. Fletcher called temperance a "great moral reform." The entire Fletcher family signed the temperance pledge, including the children. Fletcher regularly attended temperance lectures and participated in meetings of the temperance association. When Indianapolis organized a children's temperance association, Calvin's oldest son, Cooley, acted as secretary, and Calvin attended to hear a lecture.[26]

Fletcher was vexed that businessmen seemed less interested in the movement. They attended lectures but left early. At one meeting, the society "adopted a temperance plege of non intercourse with such as use whiskey or a[r]dent spirits in the stores or groceries—not to trade with them—nor to vote for those who do not take an open stand against the license laws & for heavy penaltes for making or vending &c."[27]

By the 1850s, the state temperance society was considering whether to endorse a Maine (or prohibition) law. Fletcher was invited to argue in favor of a state law "prohibiting the Importation manufacture & sale of Intoxicating Liquors except for medicinal mechanical & sacramental purposes." Fletcher participated in lobbying the governor for a temperance law. In spring of 1853, the legislature passed a local option law that allowed township voters to decide whether liquor would be sold in that jurisdiction. Fletcher hoped it would "produce . . . salutary cha[n]ges in matters." But the Indiana Supreme Court quickly ruled that the law violated the state constitution because it did not operate uniformly across the state. The legislature passed a stricter, prohibitory, law in 1855, but, again, the state supreme court ruled against it for destroying property rights. After these defeats, Fletcher largely gave up on temperance. The lower classes did not want it and the supreme court and politicians were in the hands of the "Whisky interest."[28]

Fletcher helped organize and participated in a number of associations, including a library, a thespian society, and church groups, but after temperance and antislavery, the agricultural society engaged most of his efforts. As the frontier period ended, there was increased concern about soil fertility and emphasis on introducing scientific principles in agriculture, such as developing better seed varieties, improved stock breeding, and promoting horticulture. Historian Ariel Ron argues that "scientific agriculture" was a

major reform movement in the antebellum rural North intended
to "reinvigorate" northern farming to be "both market and technology savvy." Indiana had formed a state board of agriculture in
1835, but it was largely inactive until a new board was organized
in 1851. The 1851 law included provisions for agricultural fairs that
were becoming major events in other northern states.[29]

As a farm owner producing for the market and a middle-class
reformer, Fletcher was exactly the kind of northerner likely to
engage in agricultural reform. He participated in the Marion
County Agricultural Society and the state agricultural society,
regularly serving as an officer. He was one of the organizers of
a horticultural society and attended its lectures. He helped organize the first state fairs and served as a judge for prizes. During the first state fair in Indianapolis in 1852, plowing matches
on Calvin Fletcher's farm were a featured attraction along with
sewing machines, minstrel shows, a vaudeville troupe, and P. T.
Barnum's Museum and Menagerie.[30]

Although he derived his income from his law practice, banking, and business, Fletcher also had tenants working his farm
under the supervision of his sons Calvin, Jr. and Ingram. In 1864,
the farm produced $1,200 of wheat, $7,500 of hay, $1,500 of corn,
$200 of pork, $500 of wood, and $1,500 of livestock. The Fletchers
stayed abreast of the latest developments in agriculture. Calvin
Jr. attended a fair in Kentucky and wrote back admiringly, "The
exhibition of fruit—flowers vegetables—mechanical implements
&c was limited—but of good quality." Calvin Jr. thought Indiana
superior in "horses and mechanical show" but "far-far behind" in
"fat cattle." The elder Fletcher was certainly interested in improving stock. A. C. Stevenson, the leading agriculturalist in the state,
purchased a fine short-horn bull calf in England for the purpose
of reselling to Fletcher.[31]

In addition to his many private philanthropic activities,
Fletcher believed strongly in the need for government to provide public services and welfare. Scholars of philanthropy have

noted that American churches and private associations provided
so much in the way of human services and support for the arts
because government provided so little. As Hammack has written,
"In most of the world, governments and tax-supported religious
groups continue to provide all—or nearly all—social services,
higher education, health care, and opera, orchestral music, and
museum exhibits." Fletcher certainly thought government could
do more, especially for public education. He not only recorded
his debts and assets in his diary, he also regularly recorded his tax
payments. In 1860, he paid over $1,500 in state, county, and city
taxes. "I pay all taxes cheerfully & consider good tax & a just application for public purposes the best investment a man can make
in a republic." As a school trustee, he wrote an eloquent appeal
to the Indianapolis common council for support of "good public
schools" as promoting citizenship, improving real estate values,
and stimulating economic prosperity.[32]

The editor of his diary maintains Fletcher "had a strong concern for the educational . . . development" of Indiana. While in
the legislature, he professed more concern for the school bill than
other important legislation. He read tracts on education and went
to addresses on the subject, including one by William H. Mc-
Guffey, author of the famous series of readers.[33] When Fletcher
taught school as a young man, it was common for teaching to
serve as a youth's career apprenticeship. During his lifetime,
teaching became increasingly feminized. In Indiana, as well, increasing power to hire teachers passed to district trustees. Before 1837, teachers had to be examined in reading, writing, and
arithmetic before they could be hired. A law passed that year,
however, that waived the examination requirement and left it to
the discretion of the trustees whether to require a job candidate
to take the exam. The district trustees became "the sole judges"
of applicants' qualifications to teach.[34]

Throughout the 1850s, Fletcher served as a school trustee in Indianapolis. The trustees oversaw hiring teachers, the movement

to a graded system, which included opening a high school, school inspections and allocations of limited space, and student examinations. Fletcher described the position of school trustee as "one of the most important offices in the gift of the people." Although pressed with business matters, he made time to attend school examinations and even concerned himself with the problem of tardiness. As he wrote his wife, he wanted to "systematize things." Prospective teachers wrote to him inquiring about the availability of positions and dealing with school trustees. Fletcher's son Miles recommended a Miss Clark, who was teaching in Illinois for $25 per month. Fletcher had said Indianapolis would pay $30 per month for a "firstrate teacher." Miles recommended Clark as "a Christian, a scholar, and a practical successful teacher," presumably qualities he felt his father would find important. Unfortunately, as one correspondent informed Fletcher, Indiana's failure to support the schools with state money impeded recruiting good teachers from the east.[35]

According to one student of education in Indiana, the reforms that Calvin Fletcher and others wanted in Indiana were typical of northern schools. These included graded classrooms, more professional teachers, standardized curriculum, less township control, a state superintendent of education, and the hiring of female teachers to reduce costs and improve instruction. Reformers wanted "a *system* of public education" rather than the private academies that had offered schooling in an earlier period. Indiana's new state constitution in 1851 did provide for a superintendent of public instruction and gave the legislature the power to establish a permanent fund to pay for schools. Although rural areas lagged behind urban ones, by midcentury Indianapolis and other cities in the state had established "fairly centralized school committees" and made progress on the reforms that education experts thought necessary.[36]

In the late 1840s, Fletcher lobbied hard for a bill for "free schools," tax-supported education that would give Indiana children three to six months schooling per year. He doubted that the measure would succeed: "The wealthiest will not consent that is some of them not to pay the tax & the Ignorent have been told by the demagogue that they do not need any further intelligence." He predicted the state would "suffer" for the lack of schools. "I can leave no better inheritence to my childrin than a moral intelligent religious community & I cannot be an indifferent spectator to these matters & to the interests of this my adopted state." In this case, Fletcher's gloom was unwarranted: The voters supported common schools. Fletcher then threw himself into organizing district schools. Keziah Lister, the teacher of the district school Fletcher's children and Johnny Ray attended, boarded with the Fletchers. Fletcher participated in examining the students, noting their improvement and approving writing instruction on slates and the maps the students had made of Indiana. Fletcher reflected, "A just tax for every educated child is a well qualified centenal to watch the whole republic." Unfortunately, the other schools the trustees examined did not fare as well. Mr. Houston's school was "dirty," and the examination did not attain the levels seen at Lister's school: "No composition and no maps made by the students."[37]

But Fletcher continued to push for improved education. Robert M. Payton argues that philanthropists see flaws and take action "to make things better, or to make them less bad." Fletcher saw serious flaws in Indiana schools. Some have romanticized frontier schools, but one Hoosier recalled their "squalor and discomfort." Children squirmed on rough-hewn log benches in rooms that lacked any aesthetic encouragement for learning. Fletcher's son Elijah, a minister in Massachusetts, was reading aloud to his wife an article describing "the broken fences, dry pumps and leaking buildings." Before he read the author's name, his wife announced, "I know your father wrote that." In 1852, the legislature passed a law that allowed townships to levy a tax to support public schools, but the Indiana Supreme Court ruled the law unconstitutional two years later. In 1855, the legislature passed another school law, this time giving towns a taxing power to supplement state funds; once again, the supreme court ruled it unconstitutional. Fletcher wrote that the 1858 court decision was "mischievous" and would "destroy & close our schools." Despite these setbacks, Fletcher did not give up interest in education. In early 1861, he drafted an amendment to a proposed school law to the new state superintendent of public instruction, who happened to be his son Miles.[38]

Fletcher was involved with other government services for public welfare. Historian Robert H. Bremner estimates that only 3 percent of tax revenue went to poor relief in the pre–Civil War period. Under Indiana law, overseers of the poor in each county provided relief for those who could not care for themselves and helped with burial expenses for the poor. By midcentury, more emphasis was put on counties establishing poorhouses and asylums for the deaf, blind, and insane. Only months after moving to Indianapolis, Fletcher was appointed overseer of the poor for townships in Marion County. In 1849, he was a member of a committee that prepared a memorial to the legislature arguing for the creation of a state orphan asylum.[39]

Historians of philanthropy note that caring for those in need had always involved a partnership between private individuals and government. When the Civil War broke out, state officials in Indiana moved immediately to mobilize the private sector. Again and again, Governor Oliver P. Morton called on Calvin Fletcher for assistance. After the firing on Fort Sumter, at Morton's request, Fletcher made a lengthy trip to purchase arms for Indiana troops. Again, at Morton's behest, Fletcher interceded with army officials to allow Indiana's wounded and sick soldiers to be transported home to the state for care. On one occasion, when Fletcher refused one of Morton's requests, a family tragedy resulted. In spring 1862, Morton asked Calvin Fletcher to ensure that sanitary stores from Indiana were reaching Hoosier troops after the battle of Shiloh. Instead, Fletcher sent Miles, who was killed in a train accident on the return trip.[40]

Unsurprisingly, Fletcher played a leading role in the Sanitary Commission, a private organization that coordinated supplies and aid for soldiers that historian Judith Ann Giesberg says "provided critical support to the U.S. Army throughout the war." Although the volunteers were women, the leadership of the Sanitary Commission consisted of elite males, such as Calvin Fletcher. However, the Indiana Sanitary Commission never cooperated fully with the national organization. Governor Morton and others did not want to subordinate their efforts to a national body but wanted to direct the relief supplies coming from Indiana to Hoosier troops. Historian Bremner noted that the Sanitary Commission "made little headway" in states such as Indiana. Fletcher was involved in the organization and direction of the Sanitary Commission in Indianapolis. He presided over the Indianapolis commission's 1864 convention, where Governor Morton was a principal speaker. The reports showed that the organization had collected $100,000 in money and $250,000 in clothing. In addition, Fletcher was involved with the Freedman's Aid Society, which provided not just food and clothing to Black refugees but helped emancipated slaves build educational and religious institutions.[41]

At the end of March 1866, Fletcher took a fall from his horse. He badly hurt his leg and died about two months later. At sixty-eight, Fletcher considered himself an old man, but his activities had not eased. In the months before his accident, he had seen to business for the "Orphen asylum," responded to a request for money from an old acquaintance to educate his son, took pleasure in a religious revival, responded to the appeal of "a negro woman Mrs. Locklier," who requested aid for a Black family down with smallpox by directing the Freedman's Aid and Benevolent societies to provide help, and attended a meeting of the Freedman's Aid Society. In one of his final diary entries, he and his wife "went to buy shoes for Mrs. Locklier (poor colored woman)."[42] To the end of his life, Fletcher continued his pattern of individual acts of charity combined with involvement in associational philanthropy.

His belief that the purpose of wealth was to do good had not altered. When he was in his midfifties, he pondered whether he needed to spend more time on his personal affairs, weighing that desire against the need to attend to public matters. "I feel that I have not been selfish I have devoted much of my life to the care of the public & to individuals During this time God has seen proper to give me [possessions] that are ample if I take care of them—If I let them go uncared for I set a bad example as a citizen & father." Fletcher more commonly lamented his involvement in business and longed for the day when he could devote himself to good works. At the beginning of 1866, after totaling his assets, he wrote, "I feel no amount of means can add to my spiritual wealth—unless it be to do a greater good. May God give me the disposition to so conduct my stewardship that I can serve him acceptably." In his will, Calvin Fletcher left the bulk of his wealth and property to family members. Fletcher had given much to those in need during his life, but he made few individual bequests at its end. He had built numerous associations, but with the exceptions of bestowing his papers on the Indiana Historical Society and $2,000 to the Orphan Asylum, he endowed no philanthropic organizations.[43]

James H. Madison writes of the best-known Hoosier philanthropist Eli Lilly, "Money was important to him. He watched it carefully and did not waste it. But it was not the currency with which he kept score in the game of life." The same could definitely be said of Calvin Fletcher. But Lilly was clearly within the post–Progressive Era of philanthropy. His giving to causes and organizations was more important than the private acts of philanthropy that marked so much of Calvin Fletcher's philanthropic career. Lilly gave to causes that interested him, such as archaeology and history, but he also funded institutions, such as Lilly Endowment

Inc. and the Indiana Historical Society, which carry on his philanthropic work. Unlike Fletcher, Lilly bequeathed much of his fortune to a range of nonprofit organizations. Although Fletcher and Lilly distributed their wealth differently, they agreed on its purposes. Madison, noting that Lilly did not philosophize about his giving, nonetheless places him in the Andrew Carnegie, Gospel of Wealth tradition, which emphasized administering wealth as a public trust. Fletcher also saw having wealth as a "stewardship," although he perhaps invested more religious significance in his philanthropy than Lilly did. Carnegie attributed the acquisition of wealth to "natural superiority in the economic struggle," not to divine providence as Fletcher did. God had blessed Calvin Fletcher with riches, and Fletcher's duty was to use that money wisely for the benefit of his fellow beings. In this Fletcher was a man of his times, situating Indiana philanthropy in the broader trends of nineteenth-century charity. Fletcher's obituary in the Indianapolis *Daily Journal* assessed his philanthropy as a success. He would have made a good politician, the eulogist wrote, "yet for many years he was one of the most prominent persons in volunteer movements for the public benefit, and his name is inseparably connected with the benevolent organizations and schools of the city."[44] It was a summation of his career that Calvin Fletcher might have approved.

NOTES

1. My thanks to Greg Witkowski for arranging the conference from which this essay originated and to Jim Madison for emphasizing Calvin Fletcher's importance and Robert J. Williams for his superb editing and continued support.

2. Gayle Thornbrough, ed., *The Diary of Calvin Fletcher*, vol. I: *1817–1838* (Indianapolis: Indiana Historical Society, 1972), xi, xiii, xxxii, 8, 202; Calvin Fletcher to respected parent, June 27, 1817, folder 1, box 1, Calvin Fletcher Papers, Indiana Historical Society, Indianapolis; Calvin Fletcher to respected father, May 16, 1818, ibid.; Daniel Blake Smith, *Our Family*

Dreams: The Fletchers' Adventures in Nineteenth-Century America (New York: St. Martin's, 2016), 58, 74, 94; Gayle Thornbrough and Dorothy L. Riker, eds., *The Diary of Calvin Fletcher*, vol. II: 1838–1843 (Indianapolis: Indiana Historical Society, 1973), 548; Gayle Thornbrough, Dorothy L. Riker, and Paula Corpuz, eds., *The Diary of Calvin Fletcher*, vol. VI: 1857–1860 (Indianapolis: Indiana Historical Society, 1978), 286.

3. Lawrence J. Friedman, "Philanthropy in America: Historicism and Its Discontents," in *Charity, Philanthropy, and Civility in American History*, eds. Lawrence J. Friedman and Mark D. McGarvie (Cambridge, UK: Cambridge University Press, 2003), 1–21, esp. 8. Eli Lilly played a major role in seeing that Calvin Fletcher's massive diary was acquired, edited, and published by the Indiana Historical Society. James H. Madison, *Eli Lilly: A Life, 1885–1977* (Indianapolis: Indiana Historical Society, 1989), 155–58.

4. Robert H. Bremner, *American Philanthropy* (Chicago: University of Chicago Press, 1988); Kathleen D. McCarthy, *American Creed: Philanthropy and the Rise of Civil Society, 1700–1865* (Chicago: University of Chicago Press, 2003), 4–9; David C. Hammack, *Making the Nonprofit Sector in the United States* (Bloomington: Indiana University Press, 1993), xvii–xviii.

5. Bremner, *American Philanthropy*, 12–14; Robert A. Gross, "Giving in America: From Charity to Philanthropy," in *Charity, Philanthropy, and Civility in American History*, eds. Friedman and McGarvie, 29–48, esp. 31; Thornbrough, ed., *Diary of Calvin Fletcher*, vol. I, 24.

6. Thornbrough, ed., *Diary of Calvin Fletcher*, vol. I, xii, 150–51; Gayle Thornbrough, Dorothy L. Riker, and Paula Corpuz, eds., *The Diary of Calvin Fletcher*, vol. V: 1853–1856 (Indianapolis: Indiana Historical Society, 1977), 569; Gayle Thornbrough, Dorothy L. Riker, and Paula Corpuz, eds., *The Diary of Calvin Fletcher*, vol. VII: 1861–1862 (Indianapolis: Indiana Historical Society, 1980), 340.

7. Gross, "Giving in America," 31; John H. Wigger, *Taking Heaven by Storm: Methodism and the Rise of Popular Christianity in America* (New York: Oxford University Press, 1998), 103.

8. Calvin Fletcher to Father, November 21, 1818, folder 1, box 1, Fletcher Papers (IHS).

9. Thornbrough, ed., *Diary of Calvin Fletcher*, vol. I, 150–51, 175, 266, 337; Gayle Thornbrough and Dorothy L. Riker, eds., *The Diary of Calvin Fletcher*, vol. II: 1838–1843 (Indianapolis: Indiana Historical Society, 1973), 42, 233, 246; Gayle Thornbrough and Dorothy L. Riker, eds., *The Diary of Calvin Fletcher*, vol. III: 1844–1847 (Indianapolis: Indiana Historical Society, 1974), 73; Thornbrough, Riker, and Corpuz, eds., *Diary of Calvin*

Fletcher, vol. V, 17, 79, 83; S. H. Colip to Mr. Fletcher, June 17, 1853, folder 2, box 7, Fletcher Papers (IHS); Grover L. Hartman, "The Hoosier Sunday School: A Potent Religious/Cultural Force," *Indiana Magazine of History* 78 (September 1982): 215–41, esp. 216–17, 219–20.

10. Gayle Thornbrough, Dorothy L. Riker, and Paula Corpuz, eds., *The Diary of Calvin Fletcher*, vol. IV: 1848–1852 (Indianapolis: Indiana Historical Society, 1975), 63; Thornbrough, Riker, and Corpus, eds., *Diary of Calvin Fletcher*, vol. V, 119–20.

11. Thornbrough, Riker, and Corpuz, eds., *Diary of Calvin Fletcher*, vol. VI, 5, 286.

12. Calvin Fletcher to Father, June 18, 1819, folder 1, box 1, Fletcher Papers (IHS); Thornbrough, *Diary of Calvin Fletcher*, vol. I, 291–92, 297, 304, 327.

13. Thornbrough, Riker, and Corpuz, eds., *Diary of Calvin Fletcher*, vol. IV, 59, 207, 208n67, 312, 315, 363; Thornbrough, Riker, and Corpuz, eds., *Diary of Calvin Fletcher*, vol. V, 550.

14. Miles to Father, March 14, 1853, folder 1, box 7, Fletcher Papers (IHS); Miles to Father, March 17, 1853, ibid.

15. Hart to Fletcher, March 8, 1853, folder 1, box 7, Fletcher Papers (IHS); W.W. Vance to Mr. Fletcher, Wabash, March 4, 1853, ibid.

16. Thornbrough, ed., *Diary of Calvin Fletcher*, vol. 1, 167–68, 322 –23, 442.

17. Ibid., 455–56.

18. Thornbrough and Riker, eds., *Diary of Calvin Fletcher*, vol. III, 164–65, 170; Debby Applegate, *The Most Famous Man in America: The Biography of Henry Ward Beecher* (New York: Doubleday, 2006), 188–89.

19. Emma Lou Thornbrough, *Indiana in the Civil War Era, 1850–1880* (Indianapolis: Indiana Historical Society, 1995), 47–51 for the Freeman case. Thornbrough, Riker, and Corpuz, eds., *Diary of Calvin Fletcher*, vol. V, 80–81, 84–85, 110–13, 183.

20. Thornbrough, ed., *Diary of Calvin Fletcher*, vol. I, xxxiii; Thornbrough and Riker, eds., *Diary of Calvin Fletcher*, vol. III, 180; Thornbrough, Riker, and Corpuz, eds., *Diary of Calvin Fletcher*, vol. IV, 303–4; Thornbrough, Riker, and Corpuz, eds., *Diary of Calvin Fletcher*, vol. V, 236; Gayle Thornbrough and Paula Corpuz, eds., *The Diary of Calvin Fletcher*, vol. VIII: 1863–1864 (Indianapolis: Indiana Historical Society, 1981), 200–1; George P. Clark and Shirley E. Clark, "Heroes Carved in Ebony: Indiana's Black Civil War Regiment, the 28th USCT," *Traces of Indiana and Midwestern History* 7 (Summer 1995): 4–16.

21. Robert H. Bremner, *The Public Good: Philanthropy and Welfare in the Civil War Era* (New York: Knopf, 1980), 19–20; Thornbrough, ed., *Diary*

of Calvin Fletcher, vol. I, 467, 477; Thornbrough and Riker, eds., *Diary of Calvin Fletcher*, vol. II, 97n, 150–53, 249–51; Thornbrough and Riker, eds., *Diary of Calvin Fletcher*, vol. III, 291–92; Thornbrough, Riker, and Corpuz, eds., *Diary of Calvin Fletcher*, vol. V, 311, 314–18; Thornbrough, Riker, and Corpuz, eds., *Diary of Calvin Fletcher*, vol. VII, 580; Thornbrough and Corpuz, eds., *Diary of Calvin Fletcher*, vol. VIII, 262; Thornbrough and Corpuz, eds., *Diary of Calvin Fletcher*, IX, 173; Sarah H Fletcher to Husband, June 23, 1853, folder 2, box 7, Fletcher Papers (IHS).

22. Thornbrough, Riker, and Corpuz, eds., *Diary of Calvin Fletcher*, vol. IV, 152, 239; Thornbrough and Riker, eds., *Diary of Calvin Fletcher*, vol. III, 97; Thornbrough, Riker, and Corpuz, *Diary of Calvin Fletcher*, vol. VI, xxiii; J. B. Hollingshead to Mr. Fletcher, January 30, 1853, folder 1, box 7, Fletcher Papers (IHS); Thornbrough, Riker, and Corpuz, eds., *Diary of Calvin Fletcher*, vol. V, 168.

23. Thornbrough, Riker, and Corpuz, eds., *Diary of Calvin Fletcher*, vol. V, 311; Thornbrough and Corpuz, eds., *Diary of Calvin Fletcher*, vol. IX, 174–75. The records of the Indianapolis Benevolent Society have been lost, so much of what is known about it comes from the Fletcher diary. Thornbrough, Riker, and Corpuz, eds., *Diary of Calvin Fletcher*, vol. IV, 349; "The Family Service Association of Indianapolis Records," accessed March 2022, https://indianahistory.org/wp-content/uploads/family -service-association-of-indianapolis-records.pdf.

24. Ronald G. Walters, *American Reformers, 1815–1860* (New York: Hill and Wang, 1978), 140.

25. See W. J. Rorabaugh, *The Alcoholic Republic: An American Tradition* (New York: Oxford University Press, 1979) for drinking habits in the nineteenth century. Thornbrough, ed., *Diary of Calvin Fletcher*, vol. I, xxi–xxii, 6, 85, 191, 302; Calvin to Father, July 25, 1818, folder 1, box 1, Fletcher Papers (IHS).

26. Thornbrough, *Indiana in the Civil War Era*, 29–34; Thornbrough, ed., *Diary of Calvin Fletcher*, vol. I, 153; Thornbrough, Riker, and Corpuz, eds., *Diary of Calvin Fletcher*, vol. V, 182; Thornbrough, Riker, and Corpuz, eds., *Diary of Calvin Fletcher*, vol. IV, 21, 141, 270, 288, 366; Thornbrough and Riker, eds., *Diary of Calvin Fletcher*, vol. II, 18, and image of "Family Pledge" on 22.

27. Thornbrough, Riker, and Corpuz, eds., *Diary of Calvin Fletcher*, vol. IV, 349–50.

28. Thornbrough, Riker, and Corpuz, eds., *Diary of Calvin Fletcher*, vol. IV, 366, 509; Thos. Nichols to C. Fletcher, February 21, 1853, folder 1, box 7, Fletcher Papers (IHS); Thornbrough, Riker, and Corpuz, eds., *Diary of*

Calvin Fletcher, vol. V, 36; Thornbrough, Riker, and Corpuz, eds., *Diary of Calvin Fletcher,* vol. VI, xxiii; Thornbrough, *Indiana in the Civil War Era,* 57–58, 68–69.

29. William M. Reser, "Indiana's Second State Fair," *Indiana Magazine of History* 32 (March 1936): 23–33, esp. 23–25; Ariel Ron, "Summoning the State: Northern Farmers and the Transformation of American Politics in the Mid-nineteenth Century," *Journal of American History* 103 (September 2016): 347–74, esp. 348–51.

30. Thornbrough, ed., *Diary of Calvin Fletcher,* vol. I, 22, 34, 259, 290, 296, 361; Thornbrough and Riker, eds., *Diary of Calvin Fletcher,* vol. II, 220, 268; Thornbrough, Riker, and Corpuz, eds., *Diary of Calvin Fletcher,* vol. IV, 368–69; W. T. Dennis, Sec'y Indiana State Board of Agriculture, to Calvin Fletcher, June 20, 1853, folder 2, box 7, Fletcher Papers (IHS); "First State Fair in Indiana," *Indiana Magazine of History* 3 (September 1907): 144–45.

31. Thornbrough and Corpuz, eds., *Diary of Calvin Fletcher,* vol. VIII, 15, 506; Calvin, Jr. to Father, September 14, 1853, folder 4, box 7, Fletcher Papers (IHS); A. C. Stevenson to C. Fletcher, August 9, 1853, folder 3, ibid.

32. Hammack, *Making the Nonprofit Sector,* xv; Thornbrough, Riker, and Corpuz, eds., *Diary of Calvin Fletcher,* vol. VI, 510, vol. V, 248–49.

33. Thornbrough, ed., *Diary of Calvin Fletcher,* vol. I, 157, 242, 447.

34. Thornbrough, ed., *Diary of Calvin Fletcher,* vol. I, xii, 157, 242, 447; Kathleen A. Murphey, "Schooling, Teaching, and Change in Nineteenth-Century Fort Wayne, Indiana," *Indiana Magazine of History* 94 (March 1998): 2–28, esp. 24–25, 27; Otho Lionel Newman, "Development of the Common Schools of Indiana to 1851," *Indiana Magazine of History* 22 (September 1926): 229–76, esp. 251–54, 261.

35. Thornbrough, Riker, and Corpuz, eds., *Diary of Calvin Fletcher,* vol. V, xvi–xvii; Calvin Fletcher Sr. to Wife, June 8, 1853, folder 2, box 7, Fletcher Papers (IHS); E. Lizzie Gravis [?] to Mr. Fletcher, May 25, 1853, ibid.; E N C Travis to Mr. Fletcher, June 22, 1853, ibid.; Miles to Father, June 22, 1853, ibid.; William Slade to Calvin Fletcher, June 30, 1853, ibid.

36. William J. Reese, "Indiana's Public School Traditions: Dominant Themes and Research Opportunities," *Indiana Magazine of History* 89 (December 1993): 289–334, esp. 302–3; Newman, "Development of the Common Schools of Indiana to 1851," 267–73.

37. Thornbrough, Riker, and Corpuz, eds., *Diary of Calvin Fletcher,* vol. IV, 42–44, 59, 312, 343.

38. Robert L. Payton, *Philanthropy: Voluntary Action for the Public Good* (London: Collier MacMillan, 1988), 119; "The Early Schools of Indiana

from the Papers of D. D. Banta," *Indiana Magazine of History* 2 (March 1906): 41–48, esp. 48; E. L. Fletcher to Father, March 14, 1853, folder 2, box 7, Fletcher Papers (IHS); Thornbrough, *Indiana in the Civil War Era*, 466–68, 472–74; Thornbrough, Riker, and Corpuz, eds., *Diary of Calvin Fletcher*, vol. VI, 172–73; Thornbrough, Riker, and Corpuz, eds., *Diary of Calvin Fletcher*, vol. VII, 54.

39. Bremner, *The Public Good*, 24; Bruce Smith, "Poor Relief at the St. Joseph County Poor Asylum, 1877–1891," *Indiana Magazine of History* 86 (June 1990): 178–96, esp. 179–81.

40. Bremner, *The Public Good*, xv; Thornbrough, Riker, and Corpuz, eds., *Diary of Calvin Fletcher*, vol. VII, xi, xiv, 379.

41. Judith Ann Giesberg, *Civil War Sisterhood: The U.S. Sanitary Commission and Women's Politics in Transition* (Boston: Northeastern University Press, 2000), 7; Thornbrough, *Indiana in the Civil War Era*, 175–76; Bremner, *The Public Good*, 45, 101–2; Thornbrough, Riker, and Corpuz, eds., *Diary of Calvin Fletcher*, vol. VII, 340, 536–37; Thornbrough and Corpuz, eds., *Diary of Calvin Fletcher*, vol. VIII, 344.

42. Gayle Thornbrough and Paula Corpus, eds., *The Diary of Calvin Fletcher*, vol. IX: 1865–1866 (Indianapolis: Indiana Historical Society, 1983), 193, 198, 209, 224, 244, 249, 255–56.

43. Calvin Fletcher Sr. to Wife, June 4, 1853, folder 2, box 7, Fletcher Papers (IHS); Thornbrough and Corpus, eds., *Diary of Calvin Fletcher*, vol. IX, 195, 259–61.

44. Madison, *Eli Lilly*, 89, 167, 190–91, 222–23, 266; Bremner, *American Philanthropy*, 100–4; Bremner, *The Public Good*, 220–22; Thornbrough and Corpuz, eds., *Diary of Calvin Fletcher*, vol. IX, 262.

"THE BIG-HEARTED, RACE LOVING WOMAN"

Madam C. J. Walker's Philanthropy in Indianapolis, 1911–1914

TYRONE MCKINLEY FREEMAN

IN 1915, A GROUP OF nearly sixty Black civic leaders in Indianapolis, Indiana, signed a resolution asking Madam C. J. Walker (1867–1919)—the African American beauty culture entrepreneur and philanthropist who was born to formerly enslaved parents and overcame orphanhood, widowhood, and severe poverty to become known as the first self-made, female millionaire in America—not to relinquish her residency in favor of New York.[1] Walker moved to Indianapolis in 1910 after starting a business selling hair-care products in Denver, Colorado, in 1905 and then expanding into a mail order operation from Pittsburgh, Pennsylvania, in 1907. Her move to Indianapolis was not only hastened by the commercial distribution and logistical advantage the Midwest offered her company but also by the warm and hospitable reception she received from local Black business and civic leaders during earlier visits promoting her emerging beauty company. Walker largely enjoyed her time as a resident of Indianapolis; however, during 1915, she began implementing plans to move to New York, where her daughter had already established an East Coast operation for the company in Harlem. Walker was also constructing a thirty-four-room mansion in Irvington-on-Hudson, a New York suburb whose residents included John D. Rockefeller, the oil magnate and philanthropist. Despite efforts to persuade her to stay, after six years, Madam Walker left Indianapolis for her new mansion. Nevertheless, the Madam C. J. Walker Manufacturing Company of Indiana (the Walker Company) remained headquartered in the city, where Walker's confidant and prominent Black corporate attorney, Freeman B. Ransom, led operations.

Indianapolis was the site of dramatic developments in Walker's life, and as a result, its Black community received the bulk of her philanthropic giving between 1911 and 1914. Even after she left the city, her contributions in Indianapolis continued and were maintained through bequest provisions she made through her estate. To be sure, Walker made donations in other areas of the country, including Black causes throughout the South; however, Walker's affinity for Indianapolis was evident from her philanthropic giving and how she expressed her sense of identity and responsibility in her efforts to uplift the race out of the clutches of Jim Crow.

This essay presents a conceptualization of Madam C. J. Walker's philanthropy based on a letter written on the subject by her closest advisor, Freeman B. Ransom, while he directly administered her giving to a range of causes and institutions in conversation with her to realize her philanthropic wishes. Walker's life was not centered on economic success but rather on racial uplift and community building. While Walker never directly explained her philanthropic philosophy, this analysis of her record of giving over her lifetime and the letter by her confidant provide insight into her approach to philanthropy. Combined, it is possible to gain an understanding of Madam Walker's philanthropy during the years she lived in Indianapolis and identify patterns that guided her giving throughout her lifetime. This article reveals much about how her evolving wealth, celebrity, and sensibilities influenced her giving and what more she might have done had her life not ended prematurely at the age of fifty-one, in 1919.

On arriving in Indianapolis, the local Black community quickly embraced Walker as a favored daughter of the city—and state by extension.[2] In fact, a 1915 resolution presented to Madam Walker to discourage her from leaving the city after rumors began circulating about her potential departure represented the affinity felt by the local Black community of Indianapolis. In the resolution, nearly sixty YMCA leaders, members, and local civic leaders referred to Walker as the city's "daughter," "sister," "comrade," "benefactor," "gracious sympathizer," and "generous mother" and begged her to "always live among us."[3] During her relatively short period of residency in Indianapolis, the local Black community quickly became enamored with Madam Walker and hated the thought of her departure. A campaign was launched to persuade her to stay.

During her lifetime, Madam Walker lived in seven different cities: Delta, Louisiana; Vicksburg, Mississippi; St. Louis, Missouri; Denver, Colorado; Pittsburgh, Pennsylvania; Indianapolis, Indiana; and Irvington-on-Hudson, New York. In Indianapolis, Walker first incorporated her business, established the headquarters of her company, and built the company's first factory. The city became a base from which Walker developed her business, traveling extensively throughout the state to cities, such as Gary, Fort Wayne, Marion, and Terre Haute, to recruit agents and sell products.[4] She set down personal roots by purchasing a home and engaging in community work. Further, while living in Indianapolis, Madam Walker achieved international acclaim, and her wealth grew exponentially. In Indianapolis, her dream for a better life, birthed decades earlier during her difficult childhood and young adulthood, fully came into reality.

Indianapolis provided Walker with the first opportunity to establish the kind of roots that were missing in her life. Walker was born as Sarah Breedlove in Delta, Louisiana, in 1867, to parents freed from slavery just two years prior. As a young child, Sarah left for Vicksburg, Mississippi, in 1878, under the care of her older sister, following the death of their parents. When Madam Walker returned to her birthplace in October 1916 as part of a promotional tour for her company, she reflected on the visit in a letter to Ransom: "Went to my home in Delta yesterday and came back to Vicksburg and gave a lecture at Bethel church to a very appreciative audience [sic] going back Wed. night [sic] lecture at Baptist church."[5] Besides this visit, she did not appear to further engage with these cities. During the early days of her business, Sarah lived in Denver, Colorado, where she first marketed her products and adopted the initials and surname of her third husband, Charles Joseph Walker, to become Madam C. J. Walker. She also lived in Pittsburgh, Pennsylvania. She did not find either of those two cities conducive to long-term relationships and connections. By contrast, she had numerous employees in Indianapolis, Indiana, and close friends like Freeman and Nettie Ransom, Robert and Alice Brokenburr, and Joseph and Zella Ward.[6] As a member of Bethel African Methodist Episcopal Church, Walker was connected to the local Black, middle-class community in Indianapolis and maintained connections with important institutions such as the YMCA, Court of Calanthe, the NAACP, and the *Indianapolis Freeman* and the *Indianapolis Recorder* Black newspapers. Walker and the city of Indianapolis developed mutual and multilayered bonds of affection that endured even after she left the city. While Indianapolis was not where she started her business, it was the place where the return on her laborious efforts became most evident—and where she felt appreciated.

The city not only valued Walker for the employment opportunities she provided to local Black residents during the age of Jim Crow segregation but also for her generosity. In covering Walker's exit from the city in 1916, the *Indianapolis Freeman* reported that Walker would be missed not only for her business contributions but also for her charity as "the big-hearted race loving woman that she is." Many individuals personally helped by Walker contacted her, or visited her home, to express gratitude before her departure.[7] In fact, the clearest picture of the scope and contours of Walker's generosity emerged during her time in Indianapolis.

When Walker moved to the city, her fame and wealth were just beginning their upward climb and, within two years, both skyrocketed. Madam C. J. Walker became a household name in Black communities across the country; meanwhile, her international reputation in the Caribbean, Africa, South America, and Asia were percolating as she launched overseas trips from her midwestern home base. Philanthropy was key to relating to her local Indianapolis community and to Black communities around the world. Consequently, Indianapolis provided the stage for Madam Walker's local, national, and international aspirations for helping oppressed Black people in the United States and around the world.

In 1914, Ella Croker, a Black teacher and activist in Indianapolis, contacted Freeman B. Ransom to ask for a list of Madam Walker's philanthropic activities.[8] As a public school teacher, Croker affiliated with Mary Cable, a well-known local, Black civic leader and school principal who was a member of Walker and Ransom's church, in addition to being founder of the Indianapolis NAACP.[9] Croker's intent for Walker's philanthropy was unclear. Ransom replied to Croker's request with a three-page letter on November 19, 1914, which described several types of gifts Walker had made.[10]

Ransom sent the letter to Croker because he felt "that Indianapolis ought to know a little more intimately the life and works of this friend of the poor and needy."[11] He offered the letter as a means of informing Croker—and, perhaps, the broader public—about Walker's philanthropic work. The letter illustrated the types of gifts Walker made and the kinds of recipients and causes she supported. This analysis uncovers the key motivations for her gifts as reflected in her commitment to Black communities around the country.

As a primary source, the letter was interesting not only for its contents but also for what it represented. Ransom described the list of donations in the letter as being "more or less chronological" and representative of "some" of Walker's charitable gifts. Ransom started the list with Walker's 1911 pledge of $1,000 to the building fund of the local Black YMCA in Indianapolis. His list represented a diverse sample of gifts made by Walker over a three-year period, providing important insight into Walker's conceptualization of philanthropy at least through the fall of 1914.[12] Of course, Ransom was Walker's business manager and caretaker of her and her company's image. As such, the letter represented the standard way in which Ransom described Walker's giving. The phrasing and examples found in the letter frequently showed up in Walker Company publications and newspaper articles about Walker.[13] He was also her legal advisor and confidant to whom she entrusted administration of her philanthropic giving, a role similar to that played by Frederick T. Gates and Edward Rogers Embree for industrial philanthropists John D. Rockefeller and Julius Rosenwald, respectively. Consequently, this letter provided insights into Walker's thinking about philanthropy at a relatively early point in the lifecycle of her business and at a point in which her experience of acquiring and possessing wealth was emerging.

TYPES OF GIFTS

Ransom's letter presented several gifts Madam Walker made between 1911 and 1914 in narrative form. The gifts can be categorized into four areas: monetary, tangible nonmonetary items, employment, and institution building. Together, these gift categories revealed the resources at Walker's disposal for philanthropic uses.

The bulk of Ransom's letter focused on the typical category of monetary gifts as philanthropy. Ransom presented twelve of

Walker's monetary gifts. Amounts were not given for two of the twelve gifts, but the remaining ten ranged from $5 to $1,000 and totaled $1,550 over a three-year period. The $1,000 gift was the famous pledge Walker made for construction of a YMCA for Black youth in Indianapolis, a gift that garnered national attention in the media. It was also an outlier on the list because the other gifts were considerably smaller: Five were for $50 or less and four were for either $100 or $200. It was instructive that Ransom led with this gift to the YMCA as it was clear both he and Madam Walker wanted people to know about it and the significance of not only the amount but also its source—a Black woman who owned a business and used her resources to uplift her race.

Walker tended to make gifts of $50 or less to smaller, locally based organizations, such as Flanner House in Indianapolis, the Star Christmas Fund, the Mite Missionary Society at St. Paul's AME Church in St. Louis, and the St. Louis Colored Orphans' Home. These locally based organizations were vital to their surrounding communities. Faced with gaps in service created by discriminatory practices of White mainstream social service organizations, these Black-serving organizations were essential to survival in Black communities.[14] In 1916, the *Indianapolis Freeman* reported that Walker visited poor families in the city several times a year to "attend to their needs."[15] Her private visits to families and public gifts to charities represented her efforts to combat poverty. Walker appears to have made several small donations to the same organizations over time. Such a pattern likely represented her understanding of the importance of continuous support for vulnerable organizations. A steady stream of smaller gifts better addressed organizations' long-term cash flow concerns compared with one-time gifts of larger sums that often left organizations scrambling to find replacement donations after their expenditures.

Walker tended to make gifts of $100, or more, to relatively larger organizations with regional, national, or international programs. In the case of the letter, gifts went to Palmer Memorial Institute, which educated students from across the state of North Carolina and the South; the "State University" in Louisville, Kentucky; and the International YMCA.[16] Her $200 gift to Charlotte Hawkins Brown's Palmer Memorial Institute covered one teacher's salary.[17] The $100 gift to State University was made in honor of Alice Kelly, Walker's tutor, assistant, and frequent travel companion, who had worked as a teacher in Kentucky, and Lucy Flint, Walker's bookkeeper.[18] These gifts were commensurate with those made by White northern donors and frequently exceeded the aggregate given by Black donors and Southern White donors.[19] These types of monetary gifts were the most represented type in the letter and were complemented by examples of nonmonetary giving that provided added dimension to Walker's philanthropy.

Walker's gifts of nonmonetary, tangible items represented another way in which she strived to meet the needs of individuals and families in her community. First, baskets of food were given to Alpha Home and Orphans' Home in Indianapolis and delivered annually—each contribution worth approximately $50. The Alpha Home cared for elderly Black women and offered an alternative to alms houses given that White elder care facilities denied admissions to aged and infirm Blacks. The gift was consistent with Walker's concern for two of the Black population's most vulnerable groups: elderly and orphans.[20] The gift baskets were the beginning of Walker's ongoing support to Alpha Home, which included chairing a travelogue event in January 1916 after she returned from traveling on the West Coast. At the event, Walker showed slides from her trip to the audience, who paid ten cents for a ticket and a chance to win $5 in gold for selling the most tickets. She narrated her slides, which depicted her travels through Missouri, Colorado, Utah, Montana, Washington, and California, and included pictures of the Salt Lake Temple and Cathedral of the Madeline in Utah, as well as geysers from Yellowstone. The event attracted Eugene Kinckle Jones, of the Urban League, and other Black leaders, as Walker used her travel experiences to raise money and awareness on behalf of Alpha Home.[21] Money from the event was used to clear Alpha Home's debt, which the local paper described as Walker's final charitable gesture as a resident of the city before moving to New York.[22] Walker's identification with the plight of orphans, given her own experience losing both parents before the age of eight, may have informed these gifts and her involvement with Alpha Home.

The second gift was described as a "wheeling chair" provided to a disabled elderly man "who had not been out of his door in sixteen years." It is not clear if this individual, or his representatives, solicited Walker; however, she gave him the gift of mobility, something she had not taken for granted given her extensive travel around the country. The third gift was listed as "milk for sick babies," undoubtedly an extension of her concern for vulnerable youth. The fourth gift was described as a "ticket," given by Walker to a young man "who was afficted [sic] with an incurable disease that he might go to his home at Knoxville, Tenn." In closing his letter, Ransom classified this particular gift as one of "any number of charitable acts of lesser importance."[23] It was unclear whether Ransom represented his own sentiments or those of Madam Walker; however, given her background, this gift likely held more significance for Walker.

As one who experienced the direct generosity of others during her time as a poor Black migrant moving around the South in the late 1800s, Walker depended on small, less-formal gifts of support, no matter their constitution, to survive and adjust. Additionally, Walker knew the importance of being in the right place at the right time, particularly the place of one's origins, for a sense of belonging. At first, desperation sent her from city to city—Delta, Louisiana to Vicksburg, Mississippi to St. Louis, Missouri—in search of better options for living. However, hope and ambition replaced her desperation as she began traveling in pursuit of her dream and new customers and markets helped her fulfill it. A range of gifts given to her by Black individuals and institutions in St. Louis who provided her with food, shelter, daycare and education for her daughter, a church home, and a network of women friends and supporters enabled this transition. Helping a sick young man get "home" when he had no other means for doing so likely was a meaningful act of philanthropy for Walker.[24]

In addition to giving tangible items, Madam Walker made nonmonetary gifts of another sort, evident in Ransom's description of her efforts on behalf of an incarcerated young man:

> One of the more recent charitable acts of Madam Walker, was the securing of a pardon for the only son of aged parents, who had been given a life term in the Miss., state prison for killing a White man. Madam Walker's aide [sic] was sought by the poor boy's mother early in the fall of 1911.... [A] certain Mississippi lawyer was employed and after much expense the pardon was denied December 14, 1913. But nothing daunted Madam Walker [sic] employed an Indianapolis attorney and the boy was pardoned early in August of this year, and the young man is now working supporting his old mother and father.[25]

The details of this gift were clearly laid out in Ransom's statement.[26] The more interesting aspect related to what Ransom did not mention. The young man incarcerated for murder was Willie Powell, Madam Walker's nephew, the son of her sister Louvenia, who cared for Walker in her early childhood and adolescent years immediately following the death of their parents. Louvenia asked Walker to assist her son, and Walker obliged by engaging Ransom to secure Norman Allen, an attorney in Mississippi, to pursue a pardon with the governor. Ransom was an excellent advisor to involve in this process as he reportedly had an interest in criminal law and worked on two other murder cases.[27] In addition to Ransom and Allen, Walker may have hired additional attorneys during the five years it took to accomplish her nephew's release, though it was not clear how much she spent on legal services.[28]

The gift's inclusion on Ransom's list revealed an interesting facet of African American philanthropy.

Generally, White western models of giving viewed gifts only to strangers as being philanthropic.[29] By focusing on the other-directedness of giving, western models hoped to distinguish altruistic motivations from legal or sanguinary responsibilities. However, this particular gift by Walker demonstrated the fluidity that historically defines African American philanthropy, where little distinction exists between gifts to family, friends, and others.[30] African American philanthropy emerged from its West African derivations, its formation in the crucible of American racism, and its orientation toward pragmatism.[31] Because of their shared experience facing racial oppression based on skin color, African Americans developed a collective consciousness comprised of a common sense of identity and the struggle that tied their liberation to collective effort. W. E. B. Du Bois called this collective consciousness, a "double consciousness" based on the "twoness" of simultaneously being American and being Black.[32] For Black women, according to historian Deborah Gray White, the dilemma was tripartite: race, gender, and class, which combined into a ternary consciousness.[33] Because philanthropy emanates from the identity of those performing it, personal worldviews, values, interests, and concerns inform the types of voluntary actions taken, whom those actions are directed toward, and the goals sought.

Because of this shared consciousness and shared status in society, each African American was subject to society's abuse and, therefore, equally in need of liberation. When directing gifts for the purposes of navigating and overcoming the scourge of race, preoccupation with the formal nature of relations between givers and recipients held lesser value in African American philanthropy. This is because African Americans had a broader sense of those to whom they had obligations and maintained responsibilities. The African American concept of extended family, or fictive kin, expanded the boundaries of the nuclear family to embrace distant relatives and nonrelated others who were in need.[34] In this context, any form of gift giving for the purposes of liberation was an act of subversion meant to thwart the status quo and bring about justice in a societal context that was unjust.

Emmett Carson argued that social justice has historically been important to the tradition of African American philanthropy, which operated at three levels to fill the voids created by racism: (1) meeting individual and community needs for direct relief from suffering; (2) building self-help institutions to pursue social, cultural, religious, political, and economic needs and aspirations; and (3) creating social change through the abolition of public policies and structural barriers that made America inhospitable.[35] In this view, Walker's efforts to free her nephew from the criminal justice system, which had long been unfair and hostile to Blacks—particularly Black men—can be considered philanthropy. Walker was fond of her nephew Willie and desperately worked to provide him with opportunities. Later, she made specific provisions in her will to further help him become established as a private citizen. Ransom's listing of her efforts to secure Willie's legal pardon further substantiated the perception of this type of giving—public expressions of privately held values related to justice and opportunity directed against an onerous legal establishment—as philanthropic in the African American tradition, even if traditional western ways of thinking would not recognize them as such.

Walker's gifts of nonmonetary items revealed her concern for the suffering of others. Interestingly, these types of gifts tended not to be publicized as much as Walker's monetary gifts. But they represented an important component of her giving. Walker recognized that there were multiple ways to meet needs. She knew that money was certainly important and vital for the causes she cared about, but she also knew that money could be translated into other forms of giving that would meet felt-needs more immediately and directly. Her gifts of Christmas baskets and Thanksgiving turkeys in Indianapolis became annual affairs deeply appreciated by the local community.

Omissions on the list of items Walker gave as nonmonetary gifts were equally notable. With a growing manufacturing company and an expanding number of agents around the country, it could have seemed quite reasonable for Walker to allocate some portion of products available as gifts to others, perhaps to the women at Alpha Home or the girls at Orphans' Home. However, Violet Reynolds, Walker's longtime employee and Indianapolis resident, recollected that "one of [Walker's] business quirks was that she gave freely of her time and money, but she was never known to give away any of her products."[36] According to Reynolds, Walker was adamant that her goods and services would never be given away as gifts but should always be purchased.

Reynolds attributed this stance to Walker's shrewd understanding of business. She quoted Walker as having said to her, "If anyone wants my products, they must buy them. They are for sale."[37] The products and services produced the resources that enabled Walker to be philanthropic on an increasing scale. She was clear that the fundamentals of her business model had to be preserved for her to continue her work. While Walker did reduce Black women's barriers to entry into the beauty culture profession by occasionally discounting her company's new agent or course registration fees or by absorbing some of the start-up costs for salons around the country, she set to recover these discounts and expenses over time as those agents and salons became profitable. The gifting of products would have reduced inventory, increased the cost of manufacturing, and curtailed revenues. Further, Walker traveled the country extensively and delivered demonstrations of her products and services to large and small audiences. It is not clear how much product she personally consumed while conducting these demonstrations; however, given the frequency of this practice, it is likely that the returns—in the form of new agents, new course registrations, and new customers—readily justified it. The return on gifts of product was likely unattractive to Walker because it would have taken the form of good will, something she more readily and easily cultivated through speeches about her life story and widespread newspaper coverage of her high-profile gifts. Further, the majority of Walker's philanthropy was made prior to legal changes that began to provide tax benefits to donors, particularly corporations.[38] There was likely even more to Walker's steadfast stance on this issue.

Giving away products would only address one aspect of her philanthropy, namely her desire to improve the self-image and self-esteem of Black women by enhancing their personal hygiene and appearance. Product donations would not have advanced Walker's philanthropic interests in social services and educational organizations. More importantly, Walker Company products were symbolic as representations of Walker's dreams of success and a better life. Giving away product donations might have lessened those dreams and diminished the dignity of hard work applied in service to them. Thus, Walker's conceptualization of philanthropy did not include her own products as gifts. Instead, she viewed them as part of the overall business model that she leveraged in multiple ways to be helpful to her community.

In an interesting deviation from more traditional conceptions of philanthropic giving represented in the letter to Croker, Ransom noted that Walker gave "employment to one woman Eighty Five [sic] years old, to another who is deaf and dumb."[39] In the first instance, Walker employed an elderly woman, whose age and associated frailty left her outside the labor market. As an elderly Black woman, she was mainly limited to working in domestic positions that, by their nature, required physical strength, mobility, and fortitude. While Ransom did not describe the woman's physical build or labor skills, he implied that her age represented a physical limitation that made her undesirable in the workforce.

According to Ransom, Walker also employed a person whom he described as "deaf and dumb" (a common reference to muteness at the time).[40] The inability to hear and the associated perceptions of reduced mental capacity imposed on deaf people, likely left this individual with few, if any, viable employment prospects. It is not clear what kind of positions these two individuals were given by Madam Walker. In addition to sales agents, traveling agents, and salon owners employed by the Walker Company, she also employed people in the main office and on the factory floor of the Indianapolis headquarters, as well as in the beauty schools. Due to their limitations, the two individuals were likely placed in one of these latter positions.

By employing the unemployable, Walker made at least two gifts. First, there was the actual job, which was prized in a discriminatory labor market hostile to African Americans because of their skin color. Second, there was the dignity that came with being able to support oneself and perhaps one's family, something Walker diligently searched for when she struggled as a washerwoman in places like Vicksburg, Mississippi, and St. Louis, Missouri. Effectively, Walker gave these gifts not only to the two individuals listed in the letter but to all of her employees—and to African Americans, more generally. Walker was one of an increasing number of Black business owners who created job opportunities for African Americans in a society that rarely thought about their welfare or presented an acceptable or meaningful plan for their uplift. This concept of employing the unemployable resonated with Walker as a form of justice. Implicit in the idea of not employing people because of physical limitations or skin color—natural, genetically based characteristics not under the control of the individual—was a sense of injustice that needed to be righted. Walker's gifts in this area aligned with her overall goal of fulfilling her duty as a Black woman to help her race.

Her stance contrasted with that of Hetty Green (1834–1916), a wealthy White woman who turned a multimillion-dollar inheritance into a $100 million fortune through Wall Street investments. Known to have been closefisted and uncharitable, Green used her provision of jobs as a rationale *not* to engage philanthropy.[41] As a Black woman, such a position was untenable for Madam Walker. Helping others was fundamental to how she understood herself and her responsibilities to the Black community. In a 1916 newspaper interview, she described the rationale for using Black workers to build her New York mansion: "My business is largely supported by my own people, so why shouldn't I spend my money so that it will go into colored homes. . . . By giving work to colored men they are thus able to employ others, and if not directly, indirectly. I am generating more jobs for our boys and girls."[42] She felt compelled to use the resources at her disposal to be as helpful to her race as possible. Providing employment through her company, and through her own personal consumption, was one way she could contribute, but doing so did not absolve her from the responsibility to help in other ways, including institution building.

Madam Walker's philanthropic dream was to build an industrial educational institution in South Africa, modeled after Booker T. Washington's Tuskegee. Ransom wrote in his letter to Croker that Walker "established and maintains an Industrial Mission School at Pandoland, [sic] South Africa."[43] There was no formal record of Walker starting a school, at that time or later, but the reference reflected her loyal support to industrial education and confirmed a public announcement she had made two years earlier. In a well-known, 1912 speech before Booker T. Washington's National Negro Business League's annual meeting in Chicago, Illinois—where she commandeered the floor after being denied recognition by Washington as a speaker—Walker discussed her desire to build an industrial college in Africa. By thinking outside the American context, Walker expanded her identity with, and sense of obligation to, others; consequently, her philanthropy followed suit. Her use of gifts of money, tangible items, employment, and institution building demonstrated her sense of how best to help people and important causes.[44]

RECIPIENTS AND CAUSES

According to Ransom's letter, Walker made philanthropic gifts to both individuals and organizations. Gifts to individuals tended to address immediate needs resulting from poverty or other forms of suffering, such as hunger and lack of mobility. Gifts to institutions had operational or programmatic emphases that addressed various social injustices. The inclusion of both individuals and institutions in Walker's philanthropy was important because, during Walker's lifetime, scientific philanthropy emerged as a prominent model for giving in the United States.

Having started in England in the late nineteenth century with the charity organization movement, scientific philanthropy called for the application of scientific knowledge and methods to eradicate social ills.[45] At the time, anything else was branded a lesser form of charity that might have served an immediate need, such as ending the starvation of a child by giving her food, but it offered no long-term, significant, societal impact because the child would be hungry again the following day. Scientific philanthropy became a dominant model in the early twentieth century, aided by settlement houses, such as Jane Addams's Hull House, and the emerging philanthropic foundations of the period, including those started by Olivia Sage, Andrew Carnegie, and John D. Rockefeller. Among African American–led organizations, some elements of scientific philanthropy's major manifestations could be found in the Black clubwomen's movement and the National Urban League.

At the local level, some Black clubwomen adopted social science methods in their programming, such as Lugenia Burns Hope, who founded Neighborhood House in Atlanta, Georgia.

Hope conducted social science surveys of neighborhood conditions, including housing, health, and sanitation, to inform and
measure her organization's planning and programming to meet
the needs of one of Atlanta's most impoverished and neglected
Black neighborhoods.[46] The National Urban League and its local affiliates deployed these methods at the national level. The
league's cofounder and first executive director was Dr. George
Edmund Haynes, the first Black graduate of the New York School
of Philanthropy, a forerunner of social work and a purveyor of the
application of social science methodologies to social problems.
His sister, Birdye Henrietta Haynes, the first Black graduate of
the Chicago School of Civics and Philanthropy, applied similar
methods in her direction of settlement houses in Chicago and
New York.[47] Examples make clear that the tenets of scientific philanthropy were not lost on African Americans; however, during
this historic period of national organization infrastructure building to advance the struggle for racial uplift and social progress,
African Americans may have interpreted and applied the model
differently given their firsthand experience with the severity of
their oppression and social needs.

For instance, Iris Carlton-LaNey, a social welfare historian,
wrote that Black old folks' homes during the late nineteenth and
early twentieth centuries thought about the "worthy poor" differently than many mainstream White organizations, particularly those influenced by scientific philanthropy.[48] The notion
of "worthy poor" was used to deny services and assistance to individuals believed to be responsible for their own downtrodden
condition; thus, they were seen as unworthy of resources because
their behavior and lack of moral fortitude was perceived as the
cause of—or at least a major contributor to—their plight. As a
result, it was felt that no infusion of resources could overcome
such innate faults. By virtue of their skin color and the concomitant stereotypes and perceptions Whites imposed on and associated with darker hued pigmentation, many White social agencies

often automatically deemed African Americans unworthy of services. Black-run old folks' homes, on the other hand, frequently accepted a good word of reference from a prominent Black citizen or that individual's membership in a fraternal organization, which typically included social insurance benefits, as proxies for prospective residents' worthiness and ability to pay for care. Consequently, while Black-run organizations had to be prudent in exercising their limited ability to provide assistance, they tended to be more lenient given the broader situation of the race.[49]

Scientific philanthropy did not greatly influence Walker. She did not apply formulas to her giving. And she did not deploy social science methods to assess the scope of needs and inform her strategy of meeting those needs. Her giving was rooted in cultural and identity-based perspectives of the African American experience, generally, and the Black women's experience, in particular, which expected all members of the race to help as they were able. To be sure, she was concerned with eradicating the suffering of her race and had no desire for temporary measures that offered no long-term solutions. She wanted racial oppression permanently ended and opportunity expanded for every African American, and, more broadly, for every person of color across the world. Her approach to racial uplift involved supporting Black individuals and institutions that were automatically deemed worthy due to the pervasive racial oppression that required a philanthropic response to meet basic needs for survival and advocate and agitate for broader social progress.

Walker was not foolish in her giving. She admitted having great difficulty turning down appeals when, in 1914, she wrote that public knowledge of her wealth "caused scores of demands for help. Many of whom are so pathetic that it has been impossible for me to turn them down."[50] Ransom took steps to ferret out appeals that were bogus or questionable and was diligent in his role to make sure no one took advantage of Walker's generosity. He also took care to ensure that her benevolence did not form problematic alliances that could call into question her sincerity or reputation, or the Walker Company's stability. Walker's giving was not haphazard; rather, it had focus.

According to Ransom's letter on Walker's gifts, there were two main types of organizational causes Walker supported: education and social services. The education institutions consisted of the Lomax Hannon Industrial Institute, Tuskegee Institute, Palmer Memorial Institute, and State University in Kentucky. The Lomax Hannon Industrial Institute was founded in 1893 by the African Methodist Episcopal Zion Church in Greenville, Alabama. In 1912, the approximate time when Walker donated a scholarship there, Hannon had 232 students, mainly from Alabama, and an annual operating budget of $7,360.[51] In contrast, the Tuskegee Institute served as the archetype of Black industrial colleges and received great favor among White industrialist funders of Black education. Consequently, it boasted an enrollment of 1,527 students from thirty-two states and seventeen countries. The institute had an operating budget of $270,568 and an endowment worth $1.9 million. The exact dollar value of Walker's scholarships at Hannon and Tuskegee is unknown, but according to Tuskegee's 1914 annual report, a donation of $50 covered the annual cost of tuition for one student. For that same calendar year, Tuskegee's annual report listed Walker as having given $10.[52] Newspaper accounts indicated that at least one Tuskegee student supported by Walker was African and that his expenses amounted to $72 per year, which she paid.[53] Charlotte Hawkins Brown led the Palmer Memorial Institute, located in North Carolina. Brown based the institute on her "triangle of achievement," which emphasized education, culture, and religion through an industrial and agricultural curriculum.[54] These gifts demonstrated Walker's penchant for education, generally, and industrial education, specifically. Industrial education was Walker's preferred mode and the model on which she based her company's recruiting, training, and credentialing of agents. The period of giving covered in Ransom's letter represented Walker's initial attempts to cultivate Booker T. Washington's interest in and recognition of her work. Her $10 gift was one of many sent to Tuskegee. This gift did not include multiple gifts her agents later leveraged to support Tuskegee's Booker T. Washington Memorial Fund after his death in 1915. In 1916, Walker pledged $500 toward that fund's $250,000 goal for African Americans.[55] She eventually bequeathed $2,000 to Tuskegee. This estate gift, and smaller gifts to the Memorial Fund, represented Walker's interest in and commitment to industrial education and what Booker T. Washington represented as a race leader, which went beyond cultivation of Washington's personal favor and attention while he was still alive. It remains unclear how, or when, Walker met Charlotte Hawkins Brown, but it was common for Walker to support the institutions of her clubwomen friends.

Walker also made gifts to social services. Her gifts to social services focused on the YMCA and Flanner Guild. Ransom noted, in his letter, that Walker gave to the Black YMCAs in Indianapolis and St. Louis and to the international YMCA. Her gifts to the Black YMCA in Indianapolis went toward the building and general expense funds. Madam Walker was not alone in her staunch and enthusiastic support for the YMCA. Historian Nina Mjagkij showed that African Americans believed, despite discriminatory practices, that the YMCA provided Black men and boys with "the proper environment, stimulation, and role models to build their work ethic and their manhood."[56] They viewed YMCA's programs as conducive to racial uplift, and leaders within the YMCA movement created a national network of Black-operated YMCA associations, which served as a source of pride and development within the community. According to Mjagkij, Black YMCAs provided important vocational and professional training, literacy and educational services, dormitory housing, and recreational and physical activities for Black communities. Their facilities became "community centers" and meeting places for Black professional, civic, religious, and social organizations that symbolized African Americans' "search for cultural self-determination." As independent institutions, the Black YMCAs were a source of pride and attracted financial support from the community.[57] By making her $1,000 YMCA gift pledge—which almost equaled total gifts and pledges made by ninety-nine other donors[58]—and subsequent smaller, more regular donations to local, national, and international Black YMCAs, Madam Walker expressed the value she placed on YMCA as a vehicle for uplifting the race and overcoming prejudice. As a multifaceted organization meeting desperate needs at the local and international level, it was a unique institution that Walker deemed worthy of support and replication in communities of color across the globe.

Flanner Guild was an Indianapolis-based community service center, founded in 1898, that provided employment, training, social services, recreational programming, health services, childcare, and a library. In many ways, it resembled the programmatic array of the YMCA and also focused on meeting the needs of the local Black community. Later known as Flanner House, the organization was part of the settlement movement and figured largely in the response to a tuberculosis outbreak in Indianapolis. Walker did not establish a pattern of making specific gifts to Flanner Guild, but she continued supporting YMCAs and social services more broadly. The gift to Flanner House, referenced by Ransom in the letter, may have been facilitated by his associate, Robert Brokenburr, and his wife, Alice, who served as superintendent and matron of Flanner Guild, respectively, from 1912 to 1914.[59]

CONCLUSION

Ransom's letter to Ella Croker illustrated Madam C. J. Walker's strong sense of place regarding Indianapolis and presented important dimensions of her philanthropy during a blossoming period in her life, when her company was firmly established and her wealth and reputation were on the rise. The majority of gifts contained therein were made to meet needs in Indianapolis's Black community. Her giving took form through multiple channels, including monetary gifts, nonmonetary support, employment, and institution building. It supported Black individuals and organizations in need and emerged from Walker's sense of obligation to be a Black woman who served her community. These characteristics were consistent with Black giving practices around the country.

Walker largely focused her philanthropy on education and racial uplift via social services. This philanthropy was directed to communities with which Walker had a personal or business connection. For Indianapolis, the connection consisted of the roots she was able to set after years as a poor, widowed, single mother migrating around the South and, later, as a more established and ambitious entrepreneur traipsing across the Midwest in pursuit of success. A place to call home was important for the orphan and widow, and Indianapolis was that for Walker.

Moreover, the roots Walker set in Indianapolis gave her not only a base of operation for her company but also a base for developing relationships, networks, and engagements necessary to serve the cause of racial uplift against Jim Crow. Connecting with the YMCA, NAACP, and other local charities and organizations in Indianapolis kept Walker formally and consistently engaged in the national organized struggle for equality, no matter where her business travels took her. Thus, she maintained proximity to the people and the cause she sought to help by residing among them and engaging in philanthropic giving in a practical and versatile manner based on known and observed local needs.

Consequently, Indianapolis offered the right place at the right time in Madam Walker's life for these elements to come together. Conceivably, these developments could possibly have occurred in other cities with significant African American populations.

Walker's giving was steeped in the broader traditions and practices of African American philanthropy, which she observed earlier in life while residing in Vicksburg and learned from Black
churchwomen while in St. Louis. Black-owned businesses flourished in many urban centers during this time. The difference is
that Walker was ready to fully leverage the opportunities afforded
to her by Indianapolis when she arrived. It was a perfect meeting
of needs, conditions, opportunities, and resources. For Walker,
the allure of Indianapolis was its people and their warm hospitality, which appealed to her desire for community.

Although their 1915 campaign to persuade Madam Walker
to retain her residence in Indianapolis failed, the nearly sixty
Black civic leaders of Indianapolis succeeded in at least one
major way: They left an indelible mark on a prominent Black
American citizen of the era. Indianapolis remained a place of
importance to Walker and the Walker Company long after she
moved to New York. To this day, Indianapolis forms the primary
basis for Madam C. J. Walker's legacy nearly one hundred years
after her death.

NOTES

1. The author wishes to acknowledge Nancy M. Robertson, Wilma
Moore, and the staff of the Indiana Historical Society for support of this
research.

2. To this day, Madam Walker is considered by many people in Indiana to have been a Hoosier, the colloquial term for natives of Indiana. She
was posthumously honored with many distinctions, including placement
of a sign representing her likeness on the Cultural Trail in downtown
Indianapolis.

3. Resolution from Indianapolis YMCA, 1915, box 2, folder 7, MCJWP.

4. Freeman B. Ransom to Madam Walker, February 20, 1918, box 1,
folder 8, MCJWP.

5. Madam Walker to Freeman B. Ransom, October 30, 1916, box 1,
folder 5, MCJWP.

6. Walker employed Ransom and Brokenburr but also became quite fond of their families. Dr. Joseph Ward was Walker's physician in Indianapolis, and she became close friends with him and his wife.

7. "Madame Walker Leaves Scene of Her Labor and Success," *Indianapolis Freeman*, February 12, 1916.

8. For information about Croker, see Earline Rae Ferguson, "African American Clubwomen and the Indianapolis NAACP, 1912–1914," in *Black Women in Africa and the Americas*, eds. Catherine Higgs, Barbara Moss, and Earline Ferguson (Athens: Ohio University Press, 2002), 80; Ella Croker to Freeman B. Ransom, November 19, 1914, box 9, folder 1, MCJWP.

9. "Mary Ellen Cable," accessed March 16, 2022, https://indyencyclopedia .org/mary-ellen-cable/.

10. Freeman B. Ransom to Ella Croker, November 19, 1914, box 9, folder 1, MCJWP.

11. Ibid.

12. Ibid.

13. See "America's Foremost Colored Woman," *Indianapolis Freeman*, December 28, 1912, 16; "The Negro Woman in Business," *Indianapolis Freeman*, September 20, 1913, 1; "The Life Work of Mme. C.J. Walker," *Indianapolis Freeman*, December 26, 1914, 1; Robert Lee Brokenburr, "A Negro Woman's Success," *Southern Workman* 47 (December 1918): 70–74.

14. Edyth Ross, *Black Heritage in Social Welfare, 1860–1930* (Metuchen, NJ: Scarecrow, 1978); Joanne Martin and Elmer Martin, *The Helping Tradition in the Black Family and Community* (Silver Spring, MD: National Association of Social Workers, 1985); the Star Christmas Fund was an exception as it was run by the *Indianapolis Star* newspaper.

15. "Madam Walker Leaves Scene of Her Labor and Success," *Indianapolis Freeman*, February 12, 1916.

16. State University referred to the State Colored Baptist University / State University in Louisville, Kentucky, which operated from 1881 to 1918. As a black higher education institution, it offered professional degrees in theology, law, and medicine and was supported by black Baptists in Kentucky. The state reference in its title reflected its origins in legislation that created Kentucky's separate but unfunded public system of schools for blacks. See "Towards Louisville Municipal College," University of Louisville, accessed July 3, 2014, https://louisville.edu/lmc/history1.html.

17. "The Life Work of Mme. C.J. Walker," *Indianapolis Freeman*, December 26, 1914, 1.

18. Madam Walker Leaves Scene of Her Labor and Success," *Indianapolis Freeman*, February 12, 1916.

19. See Charles W. Wadelington and Richard F. Knapp, *Charlotte Hawkins Brown & Palmer Memorial Institute: What One Young African American Woman Could Do* (Chapel Hill: University of North Carolina Press, 1999), 80. Charlotte Hawkins Brown, the founder of Palmer Memorial Institute, raised $5,600 from donors between 1914 and 1915 that included less than $100 each from "African Americans and southern whites" as aggregate groups and gifts of $150 to $500 from white individuals and county school boards.

20. For discussion of the vulnerability of black orphans and the elderly, see Iris Carlton-LaNey, "Old Folks' Homes for Blacks during the Progressive Era," *Journal of Sociology and Social Welfare* 16 (1989): 43–60.

21. For a description of the event, see "For Sweet Charity," *Indianapolis Freeman*, December 25, 1915, 8; "MMe. C.J. Walker's Travelogue a Success," *Indianapolis Freeman*, January 22, 1916, 4.

22. "Madame Walker Leaves Scene of Her Labor and Success," *Indianapolis Freeman*, February 12, 1916.

23. Ransom's use of this phrasing may have been an attempt to pre-empt a solicitation from Croker because the volume of requests for assistance to Walker was steadily increasing. Ransom and Walker referred to these requests as begging letters. Ransom would eventually develop an internal office procedure for processing such requests and keeping them away from Walker because she felt stressed by them and had difficulty rejecting them.

24. Freeman B. Ransom to Ella Croker, November 19, 1914, box 9, folder 1, MCJWP.

25. Ibid.

26. Ransom may have taken license in describing this gift because other correspondence shows that the pardon had not yet been granted in 1914, the time of his letter. Rather, the pardon was granted sometime between August 1915 and January 1916 as the Mississippi governor's term was ending and clemency was being granted. See ibid.

27. "Freeman B. Ransom," *Indianapolis Freeman*, December 25, 1915.

28. A $15 travel expense was mentioned shortly before the pardon was granted. But that expense did not encompass the entire effort. See Norman Allen to Freeman B. Ransom, August 31, 1915, box 9, folder 1, MCJWP.

29. Robert Payton and Michael Moody, *Understanding Philanthropy: Its Meaning and Mission* (Bloomington: Indiana University Press, 2008).

30. Cheryl Hall Russell and Robert Kasberg, *African American Traditions of Giving and Serving: A Midwest Perspective* (Indianapolis: Indiana University Center on Philanthropy, 1997), 11–22.

31. Adrienne Lash Jones, "Philanthropy in the African American Experience," in *Giving: Western Ideas of Philanthropy*, ed. J. B. Schneewind (Bloomington: Indiana University Press, 1996), 153–78.

32. W. E. B. Du Bois, *The Souls of Black Folk* (Chicago: A.C. McClurg, 1903), 3.

33. Deborah Gray White, *Too Heavy a Load: Black Women in Defense of Themselves, 1894–1994* (New York: W.W. Norton & Company, 1999).

34. For discussions of fictive kin in the African American community, see Carol B. Stack, *All Our Kin: Strategies for Survival in a Black Community* (New York: Harper Colophon, 1975), 58–61; Herbert Gutman, *The Black Family in Slavery and Freedom, 1750–1925* (New York: Pantheon, 1976), 20; Joanne Martin and Elmer Martin, *The Helping Tradition in the Black Family and Community* (Silver Spring, MD: National Association of Social Workers, 1985), 5; Andrew Billingsley, *Climbing Jacob's Ladder: The Enduring Legacy of African-American Families* (New York: Simon & Schuster, 1992), 31.

35. Emmett Carson, *A Hand Up: Black Philanthropy and Self-Help in America* (Washington, DC: Joint Center for Political and Economic Studies Press, 1993), 2.

36. Violet Reynolds, "The Story of a Remarkable Woman," box 12, folder 15, MCJWP, 10.

37. Ibid.

38. Paul Arnsberger et al., "A History of the Tax-Exempt Sector: An SOI Perspective," in *Nature of the Nonprofit Sector*, 2nd ed., eds. J. Steven Ott and Lisa A. Dicke (Boulder, CO: Westview, 2012), 126–27. The Revenue Act of 1917 created an individual tax deduction for charitable gifts, and corporations were not able to claim charitable deductions until the Revenue Act of 1936.

39. Freeman B. Ransom to Ella Croker, November 19, 1914, box 9, folder 1, MCJWP.

40. The term has since fallen out of favor and is currently viewed as derogatory.

41. Susan M. Yohn, "Crippled Capitalists: The Inscription of Economic Dependence and the Challenge of Female Entrepreneurship in Nineteenth-Century America," *Feminist Economics* 12 nos. 1–2 (January–April 2006): 91.

42. "Madame Walker Leaves Scene of Her Labor and Success," *Indianapolis Freeman*, February 12, 1916.

43. Freeman B. Ransom to Ella Croker, November 19, 1914, box 9, folder 1, MCJWP.

44. While Walker did not build the school in Africa, she did create a national network of beauty schools in the United States that credentialed thousands of black women in beauty culture for more than seven decades.

45. For discussion of scientific philanthropy see Robert Bremner, *American Philanthropy*, 2nd ed. (Chicago: University of Chicago Press, 1988), 85–99; Judith Sealander, *Private Wealth & Public Life: Foundation Philanthropy and the Reshaping of American Social Policy from the Progressive Era to the New Deal* (Baltimore: Johns Hopkins University Press, 1997).

46. Jacqueline Anne Rouse, *Lugenia Burns Hope, Southern Black Reformer* (Athens: University of Georgia Press, 1989); Cynthia Neverdon-Morton, *Afro-American Women of the South and the Advancement of the Race, 1895–1925* (Knoxville: University of Tennessee Press, 1989), 145–63.

47. Iris Carlton-LaNey, "The Career of Birdye Henrietta Haynes, a Pioneer Settlement House Worker," *Social Science Review* 68, no. 2 (June 1994): 254–73; Touré F. Reed, *Not Alms but Opportunity: The Urban League and the Politics of Racial Uplift, 1910–1950* (Chapel Hill: University of North Carolina Press, 2008).

48. Iris Carlton-LaNey, "Old Folks' Homes for Blacks during the Progressive Era," *Journal of Sociology and Social Welfare* 16, no. 3 (September 1989): 43–60. In their research, Hall-Russell and Kasberg found that "the concept of the 'deserving poor' does not exist in the African-American community as a whole." This may have evolved to be true for African Americans in the twentieth century, but more research is necessary to determine how African Americans have historically viewed worthiness. See Cheryl Hall-Russell and Robert Kasberg, *African American Traditions of Giving and Serving: A Midwest Perspective* (Indianapolis: Indiana University Center on Philanthropy, 1997), 4.

49. The influence and role of scientific philanthropy in black-run organizations is beyond the scope of this paper. However, it represents an area in need of additional research. To be sure, the class conflict inherent among African Americans during this period reflected the range of biases from the larger Victorian milieu and moral code that informed much of scientific philanthropy. These complexities and nuances, and their specific influences on black philanthropy, need further attention.

50. Louis Harlan and Raymond Smock, *The Booker T. Washington Papers Volume 13: 1914–1915* (Urbana: University of Illinois Press, 1984), 14.

51. Henry Willingham, *Annual Report of the Superintendent of Education in the State of Alabama* (Montgomery: Brown & Company, 1911), 316, 320, accessed July 3, 2014, http://books.google.com/books?id=PRgwAQAAM

AAJ&pg=PA332&lpg=PA332&dq=Hannon+Industrial+Institute+in+Gr
eenville,+Alabama&source=bl&ots=v468T6hWvU&sig=YymxMXovYCt
m_3WpjSfoARym9K4&hl=en&sa=X&ei=D4a1U7nnG8eoyASto4CYAw
&ved=0CD0Q6AEwBQ#v=onepage&q=Hannon%20Industrial%20Insti-
tute%20in%20Greenville%2C%20Alabama&f=false. Hannon eventually
became a two-year junior college, but closed in 1984.

52. Tuskegee Institute, *Annual Report of the President* (Tuskegee: Institute Press, 1915): 5, 8, 13, 165, accessed July 3, 2014, http://books.google
.com/books?id=2nisVsoT7VQC&pg=PA6&lpg=PA6&dq=Tuskegee+Insti
tute+budget+in+1912&source=bl&ots=pEHGco3ZMT&sig=pxYBcNfbU
ZyqVuG1SPwlNAvw-ig&hl=en&sa=X&ei=nIy1U4q4GMOhyAT34YHYC
Q&ved=0CB4Q6AEwATgU#v=onepage&q=Tuskegee%20Institute%20
budget%20in%201912&f=false. In a letter to Madam Walker, Booker T.
Washington indicated that students did not pay tuition and that her $50
donations would cover students' other expenses. However, the annual report lists $50 as covering tuition.

53. "America's Foremost Colored Woman," *Indianapolis Freeman*, December 28, 1912, 16; "The Life Work of Mme. C. J. Walker," *Indianapolis
Freeman*, December 26, 1914, 1.

54. Charles Wadelington and Richard Knapp, *Charlotte Hawkins Brown
& Palmer Memorial Institute: What One Young African American Woman
Could Do* (Chapel Hill: University of North Carolina Press, 1999), 133.

55. "Tuskegee Memorial Fund," *Indianapolis Freeman*, March 11, 1916, 6.

56. Nina Mjagkij, *Light in the Darkness: African Americans and the
YMCA, 1852–1946* (Lexington: University Press of Kentucky, 1994), 129.

57. Ibid., 84.

58. "Colored Subscribers to the Building Fund of the Colored Men's
Branch Y.M.C.A.," *Indianapolis Freeman*, May 10, 1913, 8.

59. "History of Flanner House," Flanner House, accessed July 4, 2014,
http://www.flannerhouse.com/about/History-1946/default.aspx.

NINE

—ᴍᴍ—

"TAKE WHAT YOU FIND HERE AND MAKE IT BETTER AND BETTER"

*Eli Lilly and Company, Philanthropy, and
the Impact of the Discovery of Insulin*

ELIZABETH J. VAN ALLEN

BETWEEN 1921 AND 1923, ELI Lilly and Company collaborated
with University of Toronto scientists in the discovery of insulin—
"one of the most dramatic events in the history of the treatment
of disease."[1] Before insulin, those with diabetes were doomed to
misery and death.[2] The role that Lilly took in the isolation and emergence of insulin catapulted the company to national and international fame. Insulin production also generated tremendous wealth
for the Lilly family and other company shareholders, enabling them
to extend their philanthropic reach and influence. This new income
increased the capacity of the Lillys as major donors, most notably
driving them to establish Lilly Endowment Inc. in 1937.

New profits also expanded the philanthropic potential of the
circle of Eli Lilly and Company executives, board members, and
their families. George H. A. Clowes and his wife, Edith Whitehill
Clowes, and Nicholas H. and Marguerite Lilly Noyes were principal among them. They were not only involved in some of the greatest advancements in medicine during the twentieth century but
they also left an enduring legacy to Indianapolis, the state of Indiana, and beyond through their philanthropic endeavors. The Lilly
family allows for exploration of the incubation of philanthropic

242

culture across generations. This essay traces first the advancement of the Eli Lilly and Company pharmaceutical firm, describes the philanthropy of the Lilly family, and then addresses the networks of donors that evolved in this corporate environment.

ELI LILLY AND COMPANY: PRODUCER OF PHARMACEUTICALS AND PHILANTHROPISTS

Founded in 1876, Eli Lilly and Company quickly became one of the few important pharmaceutical firms in the Midwest. By the time that Colonel Eli turned over most of the control of his company to his son J. K. Sr. in the early 1890s, Eli Lilly and Company was already highly profitable. It employed one hundred people and had sales totaling over \$200,000.[3] The third generation led the way in revolutionizing and modernizing the pharmaceutical industry. Born in 1885, Eli Lilly, the eldest of this third generation, instituted many changes that streamlined and mechanized production. He introduced blueprint tickets in the manufacturing process that prescribed drug formulas to ensure quality control, and in 1909, he installed automatic capsule-making machines. Within less than ten years, Lilly had in place "the largest capsule factory in the world," producing 2.5 million capsules per day.[4] These modernized production techniques combined with investment in scientific research and, specifically betting on insulin, paved the way for the firm's financial success.

In 1919, J. K. Sr. hired George H. A. Clowes, a respected biochemist born in England in 1877, to oversee fundamental research that led to the development of efficacious products. By nature, Clowes was not afraid of taking risks. He crossed the Atlantic to research cancer immunity in Buffalo, New York.[5]

In May 1922, Eli Lilly and Company and the University of Toronto forged an agreement that "marked the beginning of a widespread movement of collaborative medical and pharmaceutical research in America."[6] J. K. Sr. and Eli committed up to $250,000 to finance mass production of insulin. The agreement with the University of Toronto granted the company one year of exclusive licensure for the drug, which was hardly ideal from a business standpoint. They, therefore, took a calculated risk that sales of insulin would be profitable.

Within a year, sales and profits dispelled these concerns. Eli Lilly and Company garnered more than $1 million in insulin sales during this time. In 1923, over 50 percent of the company's profits (over $1.3 million) came from insulin. Standardization and upfront costs to implement mass production gave the company dominance in the insulin market, which it maintained for generations. Eli's push for systematic management and mass production and Clowes's expertise and astute assessment of the potential of insulin poised Eli Lilly and Company to become a giant in the pharmaceutical industry. Insulin solidified the reputation of Eli Lilly and Company, and its pioneering collaboration made it attractive to other university researchers.[7]

Two family members also joined the leadership team. Born in 1893, the younger of J. K. Sr.'s sons joined Eli Lilly and Company in 1914. In 1923, J. K. Jr. became vice president of the company. He concentrated on marketing and contributed much to winning respect for the company label worldwide. In 1943, he became president of two Lilly affiliates for foreign operations.[8]

Nicholas H. Noyes married into the family. Born in Dansville, New York, in 1883, Noyes came from a prominent New England family. While visiting Indianapolis, he met Marguerite Lilly, the daughter of Colonel Eli's cousin. The couple married in 1908 and moved to Indianapolis in 1910. Noyes went to work for Eli Lilly and Company as a clerk and accountant. By World War I, he had become a purchasing agent. After the war, Noyes solved a packaging problem by recommending the purchase of a box company. In 1932, Noyes became the company secretary and treasurer, and in 1937, he assumed a vice presidency.[9]

Eli Lilly took over as president of the company at the height of the Great Depression in 1932. The company had sales of $13 million, a drop of 9 percent from the previous year, though a relatively small one. The discovery of insulin greatly protected Eli Lilly and Company from the effects of this financial loss.[10] When the banks closed on March 6, 1933, the company was "fortified by a cash and security reserve of several million dollars accumulated for such a contingency."[11] After insulin, the company introduced many important drugs, including Amytal (a barbiturate), Merthiolate (an antiseptic), and ephedrine (a vasoconstrictor). In 1934, with the discovery and production of a treatment for pernicious anemia, the Lilly family could boast its second Nobel Prize–winning collaboration in medicine in less than a decade.[12]

From 1930 to 1939, Eli Lilly and Company had total aggregate sales of $171,684,000, an increase of nearly 48 percent from the previous decade. When Eli retired from the company presidency in 1948, sales had increased from $13 to $115 million. The number of employees grew from 1,675 to 6,912.[13] The second and third generation of the Lilly family and their associates, including Clowes and Noyes, accumulated a fortune of millions. They became connoisseurs, collectors, and preservationists, and as philanthropists they made great contributions to the cultural and intellectual life of Indiana and the United States. Through their philanthropic activities, they fostered and maintained "a civic culture that supported their values and advanced their cultural ideals."[14]

THE PHILANTHROPIC LEGACY OF
THE LILLY FAMILY

As he turned over the reins of the scientific laboratory of his company to his son J. K. Sr., Colonel Eli imparted his business philosophy: "Take what you find here and make it better and better. No business worthwhile can be built on anything but the best of everything."[15] J. K. Sr. took this tenet to heart, and he and other Lilly descendants did their best to apply this goal to all facets of their lives, including philanthropy. Like many other philanthropists of his generation, Colonel Eli had a keen social conscious and sense of civic responsibility, a mindset passed on to his son and later generations. As Teresa Odendahl pointed out in her landmark anthropological study, privileged individuals encourage social responsibility and obligation and kindle support for worthwhile causes in the public interest within their social networks.[16]

Long before the discovery of insulin, members of the Lilly family were already among the most prominent citizens of Indianapolis and were well-known for their civic-mindedness. The Lillys were like other business elites throughout the United States who formed a "cohesive force for civic development." Competition between Midwest cities was fierce. By investing in infrastructure and cultural, civic, and social institutions, business elites enhanced the image of Indianapolis and drew business, residents, and visitors. Moreover, by celebrating their hometowns, business elites throughout the United States "celebrated themselves."[17]

In 1879 Colonel Eli was one of thirty founding donors to Oscar McCulloch Charity Organization Society (COS), and in 1892 he proposed an extension of COS services, encouraging all Indianapolis religious and secular relief-giving agencies to participate.[18] Following the death of Colonel Eli's daughter Eleanor, Eli Lilly and Company staffed a daily clinic and immunization program for poor children at the Indianapolis Orphan's Asylum. Colonel Eli also donated money to the Flower Mission to establish the first pediatric hospital in Indianapolis. Eleanor Hospital opened in 1895 but proved too expensive to operate; it closed in 1909. While grief may have been a primary motivator for his gifts of Eleanor Hospital and the daily clinic, Colonel Eli's philanthropic endeavors reflected notions of moral obligation and a dedication to the Protestant ideals of character building, self-help, hard work, and independence that were emblematic of the Midwest in the late nineteenth century.[19]

When J. K. Sr. took control of the company, Colonel Eli turned his full attention to his community interests. In 1890, he was the driving force behind the foundation of the Indianapolis Commercial Club, which became the Indianapolis Chamber of Commerce, and served as its first president. The club initiated studies that led to modern street paving, new sewage facilities, improved railroad crossings, and a new natural gas pipeline. Responding to the City Beautiful movement of the 1890s and progressive in their ideals, club members turned away from increasing the city's efficiency, safety, and municipal health to deal with the pressing economic crisis of 1893. Organizing the Commercial Club Relief Committee (CRC), Colonel Eli spearheaded a multisector social welfare endeavor that took control of COS operations. The CRC adopted COS principles as part of its model: "registration, investigation, relief without creating dependence, [and] a work test." Drawing national attention for its scientific management of relief, the CRC was actually a precursor to the more renowned Cleveland Federation for Charity and Philanthropy, founded in 1913, the model for coordinating charitable efforts for the modern United Way.[20]

J. K. Sr. inherited his father's place at the center of power among the elite of Indianapolis. Along with John E. Holliday and William Fortune, J.K. Sr. provided philanthropic leadership and changed little in character from his father's time. As in other cities, J. K. Sr. and his cohort were like-minded individuals who used giving opportunities "to socialize, work together, build friendships, and further their sense of mutual involvement." While the various social service agencies and cultural organizations in Indianapolis worked independently, their boards of advisors were all connected. Their members were friends, shared mutual interests, and belonged to the same institutions. This "shared set of leaders" was typical for growing industrial centers at the time. Indianapolis "civic leaders knew one another intimately, attended the same social functions, had similar backgrounds and interacted frequently."[21]

A selection of Indianapolis civic board members of the 1920s revealed that they were overwhelmingly White male and Republican, had been born in Indiana or surrounding states, and lived in conclaves in the wealthiest neighborhoods. Most were older—on average fifty-two. Greater than two-thirds of them held college degrees, at a time when only 15 percent of the general population were college educated. More than one-third belonged to the Columbia Club, the Athletic Club, or Woodstock Country Club, and most belonged to two or three of these exclusive social organizations. Greater than 50 percent were involved with the Chamber of Commerce.[22]

In this network of elites, J. K. Sr. had some contact with nearly all philanthropic agencies. He held a variety of positions for organizations concurrently. He often held these for long periods of time. Membership between religious and secular philanthropic organizations were also fluid. J. K. Sr. chaired the Indianapolis Foundation while he served as an officer of Christ Church Cathedral. This culture made transfer of information from one board to another easy and led to cohesion and consensus regarding philanthropic matters.[23]

Building on his father's past achievements, J. K. Sr. often embraced new causes and ideas as they arose. In 1907, as president of the Indianapolis Young Men's Christian Association (YMCA), J. K. Sr. proposed construction of a new facility for the organization to rival one being planned for Dayton, Ohio. The building opened in 1909. It featured spacious dormitories that served the primary YMCA mission of the time by providing lodging for young men who came to Indianapolis in search of employment.[24]

The new YMCA filled a need, but it was segregated. African Americans who came to Indianapolis during the Great Migration had no such option. Moreover, few recreational facilities existed for the Black community. In 1910, Sears founder, Julius Rosenwald, offered $25,000 to cities that could raise $75,000 to build YMCAs for their Black populations. Indianapolis became one of seven cities that met Rosenwald's conditions. Along with John Holliday, Madame C. J. Walker, and Booker T. Washington, J. K. Sr. supported the project. The Senate Avenue YMCA opened in 1913.[25] It had the largest African American membership among all Ys in the United States during its first fifty years. Nationally known speakers who participated in its "Monster Meetings" included Paul Robeson, W. E. B. Du Bois, Eleanor Roosevelt, Adam Clayton Powell, and Thurgood Marshall. J. K. Sr. regularly attended these forums to remain current regarding important issues and "to keep his finger on the pulse of the Indianapolis African American community."

While he did not support desegregation of the YMCA, he personally sponsored the "Colored YMCA Quartet," renaming it the "Foster Hall Quartet in honor of Stephen Foster."[26] The Lilly family propagated a philosophy, though often paternal, that upheld humane practices. J. K. Sr. actively sought to increase his knowledge of the plight of African Americans, which did not challenge the system but was more than other business elites did at the time.

Among J. K. Sr. and his business associates, the sense of community ran deep. In 1916, J. K. Sr. and other leaders emulated the pioneering efforts of leaders of the Cleveland Foundation by establishing one for Indianapolis. He not only was a founder of the Indianapolis Foundation but also served as chairman of the board of trustees. One of the earliest in the United States, it followed the Cleveland model, charging the trust to promote "the welfare of persons . . . residing in Indianapolis."[27] The foundation not only provided funds for specific agencies but also for undertaking experimental programs and investigations of community problems. It marked the national progression toward more efficient, scientific, businesslike, secular, and impersonal giving.[28]

Lilly took other leadership roles as well. In 1920, he became organizing president of the James Whitcomb Riley Memorial Association (RMA), dedicating himself to establishing the successor of the pediatric hospital that had been named for his sister Eleanor. During the 1921 session of the Indiana General Assembly, J. K. Sr. and other RMA members worked in partnership with Charles Emerson, dean of the Indiana University School of Medicine, and Albion Fellows Bacon of the Indiana Children's Welfare Association to recommend a bill to Indiana governor Warren T. McCray to build Riley Hospital for Children. Modeled after a law that created a pediatric hospital at the University of Iowa, the bill designated the Indiana University Board of Trustees as the custodian of the proposed facility, with RMA serving in an "advisory capacity."[29] In fact, Emerson and Indiana University president William Lowe Bryan hoped that such a children's hospital would put the Indiana University School of Medicine in line for a large endowment from the Rockefeller Foundation. In June 1922, the Lilly family and other Eli Lilly and Company principal stockholders pledged $25,000 to equip it.[30]

J. K. Lilly Sr. also supported the Purdue Research Foundation. David E. Ross, president of the Purdue Board of Trustees, stressed the importance of carrying out research to attract outstanding students and faculty to Purdue and the benefits it presented for economic development in Indiana.[31] J. K. Sr. was the only other member of the board who joined in Ross's effort to develop the Purdue Research Foundation. In 1930, Ross and J. K. Sr. each contributed $25,000 to initiate the fund, an important step in the development of Purdue's national reputation.[32]

Especially with his involvement in the Indianapolis Foundation, the RMA, and the Purdue Board of Trustees, the philanthropy of J. K. Sr. evolved away from traditional distributive charity. He entered the arena of scientific philanthropy. As one of the few community foundations that existed in the 1920s, the vision of the Indianapolis Foundation became a model for others. Although the James Whitcomb Riley Hospital for Children fulfilled a real need to provide health care to poor children throughout Indiana, J. K. Sr. joined the Rockefellers and Carnegie in bolstering the modern US university medical school. J. K. Sr. also set precedents for his sons Eli and J. K. Jr. by investing in Indiana higher education.

J. K. Sr.'s gifts of $25,000 to his choice institutions were large—sometimes the largest for a given entity. Before the discovery of insulin, his greatest contribution funded Colonel Eli Lilly Base Hospital 32, which operated southeast of Paris during World War I.[33] These gifts, however, were not necessarily atypical. For example, in 1929, the Indianapolis Community Fund depended heavily on the donations of wealthy benefactors. Gifts of $10,000 or more accounted for 22 percent of the total contributed to the Community Fund during that year.[34] Although they never left this local circle, J. K. Sr., Eli, and J. K. Jr. also became separated from it as they joined an exclusive group of nationally recognized philanthropists following Eli Lilly and Company's great economic success with insulin and other new drugs.

In 1934, Eli Lilly became concerned about what would happen to the company when his father died. J. K. Sr. was seventy-two, and President Roosevelt and his treasury secretary, Henry Morgenthau Jr., contemplated changes in tax laws that would result in a dramatic hike in inheritance taxes. Eli began conversations regarding the best course of action. He wanted to make sure that the family retained control of the business.[35]

The Tax Revenue Act of 1935 that went into effect in January 1936 did cause a marked increase in estate taxes, especially for fortunes above $50 million. Eli, J. K. Sr., and J. K. Jr. formed Lilly Endowment Inc. (LEI), in 1937, to rivet "the family hold of the ancestral business" and create a foundation that would link the Lilly "name to a great benefaction for generations."[36] J. K. Sr. served as its first president until his death in 1948. J. K. Jr. was vice president, and Eli became secretary-treasurer. Nicholas H. Noyes joined the governing board, as did Ruth Allison Lilly, Eli's second wife. Eli took responsibility for the day-to-day management of the endowment during its early years. Images of him operating the endowment "out of the left-hand drawer of his desk" have become almost legendary. Eli investigated requests for contributions and made recommendations to the board. In its first decade, LEI was much like many other family foundations. It had no formal programming goals and no staff to carry them out.[37]

At the end of the 1930s, foundations were still relatively few in number. Only 188 existed one year after the Lilly family established LEI. While most foundations were headquartered in the northeast, LEI joined a significant number being formed away from the North Atlantic coast.[38]

In December 1937, LEI board made its first gift of $10,500 to the Indianapolis Community Chest. Such annual contributions continued throughout the first years of LEI's existence. LEI would be among several foundations making grants to community fund and chest campaigns, assuring their survival during the Great Depression, World War II, and postwar decades. In 1953, Eli Lilly committed endowment funds to an extensive examination of the Indianapolis Community Chest and its problems. University of Toronto social scientist John R. Seeley produced "an extraordinarily thorough study of fundraising in Indianapolis." Published in 1957, Seeley's research represents a landmark investigation of federated giving. LEI's support of Seeley's study marked an instance where its funding had national ramifications—in this case for development of the United Way.[39]

Although Eli played a primary role, J. K. Jr. also left his mark on LEI during its first two decades. By 1937, J. K. Jr. was well-known as a collector of rare books and manuscripts. Several early grants that funded compilations of bibliographies reflected this interest. The most significant works of this nature accomplished with LEI money included a catalog of the library of Thomas Jefferson, published by the Library of Congress, and *The Bibliography of American Literature*. With these LEI grants, J. K. Jr. contributed to the institutionalization of cultural authority, especially in shaping the American literary cannon. He donated the entirety of his book and manuscript collection to Indiana University between 1954 and 1957. It formed the foundation of the rare book and manuscript collections at The Lilly Library at Indiana University in Bloomington.[40]

Eli's interests were more wide ranging than his brother's. Because of his passion for archaeology, LEI donated money to the Indiana Historical Society in 1938 for the purchase of Angel Mounds, one of the largest prehistoric Native American sites in Indiana. Eli dedicated much money and time to professionalizing archaeology in the state, much more hands-on than, for instance, John D. Rockefeller Jr.'s relationship with the Oriental Institute of the University of Chicago.[41]

Lilly joined John D. Rockefeller Jr., Henry Ford, and others in fashioning the way the public history of the United States would be told with the development of Conner Prairie Farm Pioneer Settlement.[42] The Eli Lilly Collection of Chinese Art, one of the finest and most comprehensive of its kind, eventually formed the core of the Oriental Department at the Indianapolis Museum of Art (IMA).[43] As secretary-treasurer of LEI, Eli also made sure that such programs as the United Negro College Fund and Planned Parenthood received grants.[44]

When J. K. Sr. died, LEI directors eulogized him for his "wisdom, experience, charity, and intuitive vision [that] set a pattern for the future conduct of the affairs of this organization." Following his death, the endowment continued support of the Foster Hall Collection, which had been one of J. K. Sr.'s passions. With the encouragement of J. K. Jr., he amassed a comprehensive collection of items related to American songwriter Stephen Collins Foster and gave them to the University of Pittsburgh in 1937. The collection was groundbreaking not only for the wealth of material it provided on Foster but also because it became the first center for the study of American music. But of most consequence, J. K. Sr. propelled LEI into an entirely different sphere among US foundations. In 1948, his bequest of Eli Lilly and Company stock, which more than quadrupled its assets from $9 to $39 million, suddenly made LEI a major national philanthropic institution. The total annual giving average increased accordingly—from $200 thousand per year between 1937 to 1947, to $2 million per year between 1948 and 1957.[45]

With increased assets also came greater responsibility. Eli realized that he now needed a full-time staff to manage LEI. He hired his nephew J. K. Lilly III, who produced LEI's first published annual reports. He also formalized the grant process. In the 1950s, LEI grants, thus, relied less on personal pleas than they had before, but Eli and J. K. Jr. still often made decisions informally based on their personal associations and interests. Despite its massive growth in assets, it retained much of the character it had had as a smaller family foundation. It largely remained Eli Lilly's personal enterprise and involved only relatives and close associates in decision-making and operations.[46]

During its first twenty years, LEI granted a total of $18.5 million. Its twentieth-anniversary report revealed that its board had directed $8.8 million (43 percent) to education. LEI considered education the hallmark of its programs. The majority of this money, nearly $7 million, went to Indiana institutions. Most were private. Indiana University was the exception. Other colleges and universities that received LEI grants included the University of Chicago, Cornell, and Princeton. In 1956, its board of directors identified three major fields of interest for its programming: education, religion, and community services. Higher education in Indiana continued to be a priority, although "some projects of regional and national importance" also received funding."[47]

Nielsen, in his 1972 book, *The Big Foundations*, noted that LEI was "distinctive among large foundations for its keen interest in Indiana and religion." Indeed, of the $18.5 million spent between 1937 and 1957, $13 million, or about 70 percent, went to Indiana organizations. Over 50 percent, $6.7 million, of the money designated for Indiana supported institutions in the state capital.

Another $5.2 million went to other US organizations. Less than $500,000, or 2.7 percent, went to foreign entities. The 1957 review of grants explained that most of the money spent abroad had gone toward World War II relief activities.[48]

By the 1950s, LEI was already the largest single US source of philanthropy in the field of religion. J. K. Lilly Sr.'s "devoted interest" in religion guided it into this specialization. Between 1937 and 1957, LEI gave $3.9 million (21 percent) for religion, the social sciences, and humanities, and the twentieth-anniversary report promised "continued and more concentrated activity" aimed specifically toward religion. Although the Lillys followed other wealthy donors making gifts to colleges, universities, and arts organizations, they also retained an interest in Protestant missions through the congregations to which they belonged. The Lilly family's membership to Christ Church Cathedral, located on Monument Circle in downtown Indianapolis, made it and other Episcopal causes a primary focus of LEI grants—and also of Lilly personal philanthropy. While most national foundations focused on large secular, educational, and scientific causes, LEI was a member of a more conservative faction of these institutions. Only a few other foundations concentrated on religion. However, LEI remained centrist. Its significant contributions to religious entities favored mainstream Protestantism and theological education.[49]

For LEI, the organization's activities during the 1960s proved an exception. While J. K. Jr. was chairman of the board, he hired John S. Lynn, who was the nephew of Eli Lilly and Company executive Charles J. Lynn, to be LEI's general manager. During this time, LEI made grants to very conservative political and religious causes.[50] By the time Nielsen released his landmark 1972 study of foundations, LEI was the second largest in terms of assets. He criticized LEI for "becoming highly ideological" and lamented that, as a result, it had "lost much of its good reputation in the swamps of the far Right." Nielsen later surmised that the

Lilly family became angry with liberal Tennessee senator Estes
Kefauver's investigation of the practices of the pharmaceutical
industry, which led LEI to become involved briefly in an anti-
communism campaign. The fate of Eli Lilly and Company's business investments with the takeover of communist governments
in China and Cuba may also have been a factor. These countries
had been the largest focus of its international dealings since the
1920s.[51]

Although some LEI funds were directed to extreme rightwing
causes, the foundation also made substantial gifts to the Indianapolis Red Cross, the Flanner House, the Indianapolis Zoo,
the United Hospital campaign, Marian College, and Butler and
DePauw Universities. Most notably, it made its largest awards in
its history up to that point to the Indianapolis Symphony Orchestra (ISO) and the Children's Museum. LEI pledged $2 million to
the ISO endowment to match a grant from the Ford Foundation
and initiated a $3.5 million challenge grant for the expansion of
the Children's Museum. LEI gifts continued to be connected to
Lilly family interests and often were intended to leverage contributions from individuals and other agencies.[52]

In response to Nielsen's scathing criticisms, Eli forced John
S. Lynn's early retirement at the end of 1972. He replaced him
with Earlham College president Landrum Bolling. With Bolling, LEI operations became professionalized, and it regained
its standing among national foundations. During the 1970s, LEI
reinvigorated its core missions of education, religion, and community and increased giving outside of Indiana. After Eli met
with Mayor Richard Lugar in 1972, LEI also became involved in
major revitalization projects in downtown Indianapolis, continuing its dedication to shoring up its institutions.[53]

Although LEI became the second largest endowment in the
United States during the Cold War, it did not venture to expand
its efforts overseas to aid economic and social development in
developing countries to counteract communism, as did the

Rockefeller Foundation, the Ford Foundation, and the Carnegie Corporation.[54] It remained conservative in its reach. LEI
grants and Eli's personal philanthropy focused on agencies and
institutions that incorporated aspects of character building that
had become internalized as part of the Lilly family ethos. It also
centered primarily on bolstering the reputation of Indianapolis
and Indiana.

THE PHILANTHROPIC LEGACY OF THE NOYESES AND THE CLOWESES

Although Nicholas H. Noyes and George H. A. Clowes were neither Indianapolis natives nor midwesterners, the social elite of
the city quickly accepted them. Noyes represented a special case
since he married into the Lilly family. The society columns of the
Indianapolis Star included a notice of the arrival of the Clowes
family in March 1919; and although the Nobel Prize for insulin
went to Banting and Best in 1930, Clowes's role in the discovery
made him well-known. Each of these men used the male network
of clubs and associations to initiate and cement their positions
in elite business, cultural, and philanthropic groups after they
moved to the city.[55]

The Noyeses' giving tended to be intensely personal, and they
gravitated toward establishing tangible monuments and new
entities that bear the family name. They contributed to higher
education, health, and cultural institutions—then to charity.[56]
Nicholas H. Noyes participated actively in the Indianapolis
Chamber of Commerce. In 1926, he was its president. As a director and executive committee member, he reorganized the
Indiana State Chamber of Commerce in 1938. He remained on
its executive committee until 1947. Noyes also followed in J. K.
Lilly Sr.'s footsteps when he served as campaign chairman of the
Indianapolis Community Fund. Most top Lilly executives took
their turn participating in the chamber and Community Fund.[57]

It seems to have been a sort of rite of passage for Lilly executives. Noyes eagerly filled these roles. Marguerite Noyes (née Lilly) was a member of the Junior League, the Dramatic Club, and the Indianapolis Garden Club. She supported the Children's Museum and international children's agencies, such as CARE and HOPE, while Nicholas served as a national director of the Boy's Clubs of America. The Noyeses, like other families among the Lilly cohort, were strong supporters of the arts, including the symphony and art museum.[58]

Nicholas kept close ties to his alma mater, Cornell University, and his hometown, Dansville, New York. Unlike many midwestern philanthropists of the twentieth century who were self-made men, he came from an old New England family.[59] His mother, Emma Hartman Noyes, was a friend of Clara Barton and charter member of the first local chapter of the American Red Cross in Dansville in 1881. Noyes and his siblings donated their childhood home to the American Red Cross in honor of their mother. It serves as a museum about the early history of the organization.[60] Noyes was president of the Cornell Alumni Association in 1919 and 1920 and was elected a university trustee in 1933. In recognition of Nicholas's fifty years of service to the university, Marguerite gave Cornell the Nicholas H. Noyes Collection of Historical Americana, considered one of the most important founding collections of the university's library.[61]

In 1951, the Noyeses established the Nicholas H. Noyes Jr. Foundation in honor of their son. They contributed money to Vassar College to build a dormitory honoring Emma Hartman Noyes, her alma mater. In 1964, they gave $300,000 to Cornell to endow a professorship in engineering, and one year later, they gave $3 million "to supplement the salaries of selected leading members of the university faculty" and support intercollegiate athletics. The Noyeses also followed the lead of LEI in providing money for higher education in Indiana. Earlham College named the centerpiece of a new science complex for Noyes in 1972.[62]

The Noyeses designated other foundation funds for hospitals in Indianapolis and Dansville. In Indianapolis, they contributed over half of the $4.5 million necessary to build the Marguerite Lilly Noyes Children's Pavilion, which later became part of the Indiana University Health Methodist Hospital campus. The poor condition of the Dansville public hospital drew the attention of Noyeses in the late 1960s, and they donated $100,000 to build a new facility. The Noyes Memorial Hospital opened in 1971.[63]

While Noyes advocated for the Indianapolis business community, various cultural and intellectual groups in Indianapolis attracted Clowes. He joined the Indianapolis Literary Club, where he became acquainted with Indiana authors Booth Tarkington and Meredith Nicholson and university presidents and successful men representing various other professions. By 1926, he was first vice president of the Contemporary Club of Indianapolis. Organized by social reformers Theodore and May Wright Sewall in 1890, the Contemporary Club was open to men and women and aimed to "cultivate sociability and intellectual activity" among its membership.[64]

When the Cloweses moved to Indianapolis, they lived in a modest home in the comfortable north side Meridian-Kessler area. As sales at Lilly skyrocketed, they could afford to buy a larger residence in a more secluded neighborhood. In 1933, they moved to their house in Golden Hill, called Westerly, which was adjacent to the elite Woodstock Country Club. Westerly became the home of the Cloweses' art collection. George began collecting art, "a private endeavor," in which he was now able to indulge with his friend Pulitzer Prize–winning author Booth Tarkington. He also became active in the Indianapolis Art Association, another institution founded by May Wright Sewall.[65]

The association supported the John Herron Institute and Museum of Art. In 1934, Clowes became a member of its board. Born out of the American museum and decorative arts movements that followed the Centennial Exposition of Philadelphia in 1876, the Indianapolis Art Association had offered Sewall and other women like her an entry into the broader cultural arena. However, as art museums became more established and turned away from the decorative arts, men, like Clowes and Tarkington, replaced them on boards. Museums, as affluent institutions, became primarily a male province.[66]

In 1936, the Indianapolis Art Association put Clowes on its Fine Arts Committee, which was responsible for art accessions. His influence on the development of this art collection—eventually housed at the IMA—was immediate. The committee turned away from collecting Postimpressionist paintings and focused on the old masters. Clowes and other wealthy board members determined what works would be purchased and which should be shown. This was just one way that the elite maintained their cultural authority throughout the United States. As an Art Association board member, Clowes applied scientific and bureaucratic principles to professionalize and modernize the Herron, setting new standards of excellence in organizing, curating, and documenting exhibitions.[67]

George Clowes was also heavily involved with ISO. Starting in the late 1800s, American municipalities seized on the symphony orchestra as a source of civic pride. Other men in Clowes's circle, such as J. K. Lilly Sr., Nicholas Noyes, and Booth Tarkington, also supported this cause. Clowes joined the State Symphony Society board in 1933. He became vice president in 1937 and president in 1940. Following the model of the Philadelphia Symphony Orchestra, women formed an auxiliary Women's Committee in 1937. Lila Allison Lilly, J. K. Sr.'s second wife and the sister of Ruth Allison Lilly and Marguerite Lilly Noyes coordinated membership recruitment for the Women's Committee of the ISO to get it established.

The Women's Committee volunteered many hours selling season tickets and organizing concerts in outlying areas.[68] By belonging to women's organizations or women's auxiliaries of men's groups, women not only used their volunteer time in traditional ways but also opened new opportunities for themselves without overtly challenging male prerogatives.

Edith and George spearheaded the movement to replace the building for the Episcopalian Advent parish, which had been established in 1919 to serve the growing community on the north side of Indianapolis. In 1949, they committed to provide money to build a new church tower and convinced others to contribute. The Cloweses wanted to build a church reminiscent of those in North Suffolk, where George grew up. They succeeded. The parish completed the new Trinity Episcopal Church in 1953.[69] At Trinity, Edith was a member of the Women's Advisory Committee for building the new church. With other members of this committee, Edith immersed herself in planning every aspect of the interior design, while George and Edith's son, Allen, belonged to the building committee that administered the project overall. As with the Women's Committee of ISO, such arrangements remained typical of men's and women's organizations during the first half of the twentieth century.[70]

By 1900, a dense network of women's organizations existed on the local, regional, and national levels. Within a few weeks after Edith Clowes arrived in Indianapolis in 1919, she joined the Indianapolis Vassar Club to establish herself in her new environs. The student culture at Vassar had encouraged Edith and others like her to commit to women's social and cultural causes. The Indianapolis club offered an introduction to a group of elite reform-minded women. Edith met several early members of the Indianapolis Vassar Club, including Mary Jameson Judah, who had long been active in women's organizations in Indianapolis. Elizabeth Cady Stanton and Susan B. Anthony had directly influenced another member, Elizabeth Vinton Pierce, while she was a Vassar student.[71]

Edith also joined the Woman's Club of Indianapolis, and she arranged winter sports tournaments at Meridian Hills Country

Club. At each of these venues, she mixed with the business, social, and philanthropic elite of the city. A prominent member of the Woman's Club, Mary Stewart Carey, emerged as a very influential figure in Edith Clowes's circle. Edith became close friends with Carey's daughter, Mary Carey Appel, and by the time she met her friend's mother, she already was a well-established social reformer and civic leader. Carey had been a charter member of the Flower Mission in 1877 and an incorporator of the Propylaeum, the home of the Woman's Club in 1888.[72]

Dissatisfied with the school options that existed for her sons, Edith teamed up with Mary Appel to establish the Indianapolis Progressive Education Association in 1921. Others joined them, including Eli's first wife, Evelyn Fortune Lilly.

Within a year, Orchard School opened in the home of Mary Stewart Carey, located at 5050 North Meridian Street. Organized according to the principles of John Dewey and other outstanding educational reformers of the era, Orchard emphasized "personal freedom, creativity, individualization, and self-control." The curriculum encouraged "direct creative work." Orchard was just one such school. In Chicago, Anita McCormick Blaine built a model private school for educational reformer Francis Wayland Parker in 1898.[73]

Next the Progressive Education Association sought to make a "Museum Available for Children." This idea took off when Mary Stewart Carey visited the Brooklyn Children's Museum in 1924. Among the well-traveled elite, such experiences "reinforced benevolent impulses" and registered "vivid impulses for new undertakings." At the time, only two children's museums existed—the Brooklyn Children's Museum, founded in 1899, and the Boston Children's Museum, which opened in 1915. In 1924, Carey initiated an organization to promote the idea of establishing a museum for children in Indianapolis. Along with Carey, Edith Clowes was among nine original trustees. Unlike most museums, the Children's Museum of Indianapolis began without existing collections, buildings, or bequests of money. Carey gave children agency in creating the museum. She invited them to bring objects that they thought would be of interest to become part of its collections. The Children's Museum of Indianapolis also was never intended to be just a storehouse of artifacts. Early on in its development, museum staff and volunteers sought to interpret its collections to educate children.[74]

The Children's Museum opened in 1925. Marguerite Lilly Noyes also became a strong supporter of the Children's Museum. Ruth Allison Lilly's interest and devotion to it proved to be a major factor in its growth and success. She made many gifts to the museum, and a 1972 LEI grant led it to be recognized internationally for its excellence. For her contributions as a patron and trustee, the Children's Museum named a theater in her honor in 1976.[75]

Edith's interest in charity for women and children had its roots in Buffalo. She had worked at a day nursery, designed to care for the children of women who were widows or had been deserted, that was affiliated with the Buffalo COS. In Indianapolis, she supported the Maternal Aid Society, a COS auxiliary that aided widows and single women with children. The Family Welfare Society, created from the merger of the COS, the Children's Aid Association, and the Maternal Aid Society in 1922 (later known as the Family Service Association), remained one of Edith's favorite causes.[76]

In 1950, Edith was elected to the board of the Maternal Health League of Indianapolis, which later became Planned Parenthood.[77] She was well aware of the plight of poor women and joined because of its mission to empower them. First known as the Indiana Birth Control League, the Maternal Health League aimed to reduce maternal and infant mortality, decrease hereditary disease, and prevent criminal abortions.[78]

By 1956 the Maternal Health League of Indianapolis officially had become the Planned Parenthood Association of Indianapolis. Edith became president, and Lila Allison Lilly also belonged to the board.[79] The national office of Planned Parenthood paid attention to its Indianapolis affiliate, perhaps because of the wealth of these families.[80] Edith corresponded with other officers and employees of the Planned Parenthood Federation in New York. National representatives also came to Indianapolis.[81]

LEI gave $3,500, restricted for "marriage education, the nurses institute and clerical work" but avoided providing money for the more controversial clinics. In part, the involvement of LEI in Planned Parenthood probably reflected the strength of Edith's personal relationship with Eli Lilly. With his interest in character education, he also would have supported the organization's marriage success seminars. Edith hoped that the agency would be endorsed by the United Fund. She spoke with Eli in 1957, but despite his urgings, the United Fund refused membership to the organization repeatedly.[82]

George and Edith Clowes established their own family foundation in 1952 "to support education and literary, fine and performing arts." The fund, however, not only served as an avenue to direct their philanthropy but also to protect their art collection. The Herron Museum had become woefully outdated and inadequate. With no safe place but Westerly to hang their paintings in Indianapolis, they followed the example of Andrew W. Mellon who gave his old master paintings to the Andrew W. Mellon Charitable and Educational Trust but kept them in his private collection with the intent of transferring them later to the US government.[83] The legal mechanisms that made the Mellon Collection the nucleus of the National Gallery of Art would make the Cloweses' collection a keystone of the IMA.[84]

The Clowes Fund did more than make it possible for the family to retain guardianship of the art collection. The Cloweses made donations to social service organizations favored by Edith. They also supported establishment of the Indianapolis Council on World Affairs in 1955 and sent money abroad to the Kiyasoto Educational Experiment, in Japan.[85]

When George Clowes died in 1958, he left one dream unfulfilled—to provide a home for the ISO. The orchestra managed to survive and had achieved national prominence, but its future was in jeopardy because it had outgrown the Murat Theater in downtown Indianapolis. Edith made sure that George's dream came true. She notified the Butler University trustees of her decision to build an auditorium in memory of her husband in 1959. Edith provided $50,000 and $500,000 in income-producing securities from the Clowes Fund to build Clowes Memorial Hall. The concert hall opened in 1963 with much fanfare. The building's design was state of the art. Many compared it to the Lincoln Center.[86] Clowes Hall remained the home of the ISO until it moved to Hilbert Circle Theatre in October 1984. Although Edith devoted much of her time, experience, and skills to women's organizations, she saved her largest gift to fulfill her husband's wishes in support of a university and an elite cultural organization dominated by men.

LIVING LEGACIES

In 1972, Eli and Ruth Allison Lilly received the American Award of the Eisenhower Memorial Scholarship Foundation. The Eisenhower Foundation noted that their philanthropy "had a far-reaching impact on the arts and education in Indiana."[87] The same can be said of other Lilly family members, and the Cloweses and the Noyeses. Over the course of their lives, the interests of the Lilly family and their executives touched nearly every aspect of philanthropy in Indiana in the first half of the century. In fact, their philanthropic interests were so great that it is nearly impossible to cover them all or cover them in-depth.

Without the discovery of insulin, the Lillys and their associates may have just remained part of a local business and philanthropic elite. Until the 1920s, they contributed meaningfully to the welfare and the civic and cultural development of

Indianapolis, but the wealth produced by Eli Lilly and Company also triggered important local and national philanthropy. The foundations that each family created still exist. The Noyes Foundation and the Clowes Fund possess assets ranging from around $50 to $300 million, large in comparison to the forty thousand family foundations nationally. At its fiftieth anniversary in 1987, LEI had $2 billion in assets, making it the fifth largest foundation in the United States. In 2014, Foundation Center statistics revealed that LEI still ranked fifth in total assets with nearly $10 billion and twenty-first in giving among all US Foundations, with grants totaling over $333 million.[88] Like "other great givers" of the twentieth century, the Lilly family, the Noyeses, and the Cloweses also tended to establish institutions that bear their names.[89]

The Nicholas H. Noyes Jr. Memorial Foundation initially directed large amounts of money to New York institutions— Cornell University and Vassar College. They also funded a new hospital in Dansville that has evolved into a "diverse and comprehensive healthcare system."[90] In 2016, the Nicholas H. Noyes Jr. Memorial Foundation had $47 million in assets and distributed over $2.1 million in grants. The foundation still distributes gifts that reflect family interests. Most Noyes grants focused on charitable and educational institutions in Indianapolis, but the foundation also continued to support Noyes Memorial Hospital. In 2013, it provided $75,000 to renovate and expand the emergency care department at the facility.[91]

The Clowes Family Fund broadened and shifted its mission over time. It has become more progressive and liberal. Instead of supporting "education and literary and performing arts" as it did in the beginning, it now "seeks to enhance the common good by encouraging organizations and projects that help to build a just and equitable society, create opportunities for initiative, foster creativity and growth of knowledge, and promote appreciation of the natural environment."

The Clowes Family Fund focuses on New England, where the family had a summer home, as well as Indianapolis. New England institutions received over $1 million, or 55 percent of the nearly $2 million in grants the Clowes Fund gave in 2016. Indiana organizations received $718,000, 36 percent of the total. Although the fund continued to support ISO, IMA, and other educational and cultural ventures in 2016, its board directed the largest proportion of its nearly $2 million in grants, $785,000 or 40.2 percent of the total, to projects that bolstered workforce development. Another 25 percent, $495,000, went toward programs that helped immigrants, refugees, and asylees. Education accounted for $447,000, or 22 percent. Projects labeled "Clowes Legacy" constituted only 11 percent of the total—$228,000.[92] The Clowes Fund always supported some social causes, but it seems that the current generation of the family, descendants of George H. A. Clowes, Jr., has increasingly assimilated the more liberal social-reform ethos of Edith W. Clowes. Their foundation seeks structural reform and social justice.

The other son of Edith and George, Allen Whitehill Clowes, established the Allen Whitehill Clowes Charitable Foundation in 1990 to "preserve the Arts and Humanities" and support many of the cultural, arts, and other charitable institutions that he and his parents supported during their lifetimes. Most were in central Indiana. The foundation continues to support these and similar organizations and causes.[93]

The greatest change came with the Lilly family itself. For most of their history, they gravitated toward cultural institutions, higher education, and hospitals rather than implementing more progressive reforms aimed to alter the social landscape. Although they endeavored to rationalize charity through such institutions as the Community Fund and the Indianapolis Foundation, the Lilly family and its cohort remained loyal to philanthropic principles related to the "creed of individual responsibility and achievement, supplemented by mutual aid," which defined the historic American character.[94]

LEI entered the world of the national foundations with J. K. Lilly Sr.'s bequest. It continues to uphold its traditional trinity of programming focuses—religion, education, and community development. It also encourages projects that benefit youth and promote leadership. Approximately 70 percent of the grants distributed each year go to Indianapolis and Indiana organizations. It is difficult to identify a major Indiana organization that Lilly Endowment Inc. has not touched.[95] In 2012, Indiana University created the Lilly Family School of Philanthropy in honor of the family's philanthropic legacy.

LEI's 2015 Annual Report defined its culture as "conservatively progressive," a legacy of J. K. Sr.'s philosophy. The board of directors constantly balance two contrasting convictions that are indicative of this philosophy: "That tradition is an important resource and that innovative approaches are often necessary to respond fully to new challenges and circumstances."[96] George Clowes, J. K. Sr., and Eli recognized the value of this strategy. They relied on the tradition that Colonel Eli had put in place when he founded Eli Lilly and Company "to take what you find here and make it better and better."[97] His descendants and their associates carried out their philanthropy in the same spirit. Indeed they always were conservatively progressive. They usually patterned their efforts on the models of others while adapting and innovating to make them a better fit for their own circumstances. The foundations these men and women established also endeavor to realize these ideals.

NOTES

1. Michael Bliss, *The Discovery of Insulin*, 25th anniversary ed. (Chicago: Chicago University Press, 2007), 11.

2. James H. Madison, *Eli Lilly: A Life, 1885–1977* (Indianapolis: Indiana Historical Society, 1989), 4–5; James H. Madison, "Lilly, Eli, Col.," in *The Encyclopedia of Indianapolis*, eds. David J. Bodenhamer and Robert G. Barrows (Bloomington: Indiana University Press, 1994), 910–11;

Charles Latham Jr., "Chamber of Commerce," *The Encyclopedia of Indianapolis*, eds., Bodenhamer and Barrows, 399–400.

3. James H. Madison, "Manufacturing Pharmaceuticals: Eli Lilly and Company, 1876–1948," *Business and Economic History*, 18 (1989): 72–73; Harmon W. Marsh, "Glue Jackets for Disagreeable Medicines: How Gelatin Capsules Are Manufactured," *Scientific American*, 117 (15 September 1917).

4. James H. Madison, "Manufacturing Pharmaceuticals: Eli Lilly and Company, 1876–1948," *Business and Economic History* 18 (1989): 72–73.

5. Alexander W. Clowes, *The Doc and Duchess: The Life and Legacy of George H. A. Clowes* (Bloomington: Indiana University Press, 2016), 21.

6. John P. Swann, "Insulin: A Case Study in the Emergence of Collaborative Pharmaceutical Research," *Pharmacy in History* 28 (1986): 3–5.

7. Swann, "Insulin," 65–68, 73; Michael Bliss, *The Discovery of Insulin*, 25th anniversary ed. (Chicago: Chicago University Press, 2007), 240; Madison, "Manufacturing Pharmaceuticals," 76–77.

8. "Josiah K. Lilly Jr. Dies; Private Rites Saturday," *Indianapolis Star*, May 6, 1966, 1, 18; "The Lilly Story: It Began in 1876," *Indianapolis Star*, November 20, 1966, 156.

9. E. J. Kahn Jr., *All in a Century: 100 Years of Eli Lilly and Company* (Indianapolis: Eli Lilly and Co., 1975), 23; "Nicholas Noyes Dies; Civic, Cultural Leader," *Indianapolis Star*, December 26, 1977, 1, 13; "Noyes—Lilly," *Indianapolis News*, November 18, 1908, 7; "Mrs. Noyes Dies; Philanthropist," *Indianapolis Star*, May 18, 1973, 34.

10. Peter Ascoli, *Julius Rosenwald: The Man Who Built Sears Roebuck and Advanced the Cause of Black Education in the American South* (Bloomington: Indiana University Press, 2006), Kindle edition, chapter 10.

11. Kahn, *All in a Century*, 43–44.

12. Kahn, *All in a Century*, 61. Madison, *Eli Lilly, A Life*, 64–67, 94–96.

13. Madison, *Eli Lilly: A Life*, 91–92, 96.

14. Laura Tuennerman-Kaplan, *Helping Others, Helping Ourselves in Cleveland, Ohio, 1880–1930* (Kent, OH: Kent University Press, 2001), Kindle edition, chapter 3.

15. J. K. Lilly, "Reminiscences," 1940, Eli Lilly and Company corporate archives, Indianapolis, Indiana; Gene E. McCormick, "J. K. Lilly, Sr.: The Man (1861–1948)," *Pharmacy in History* 12 (1970): 60.

16. Teresa Odendahl, *Charity Begins at Home* (New York: Basic Books, 1990), 8–24.

17. Kenneth Montague Sturges, *American Chambers of Commerce* (New York: Moffat, 1915), 137–39; Kathleen D. McCarthy, *Noblesse Oblige: Charity*

& *Cultural Philanthropy in Chicago, 1849–1929* (Chicago: University of Chicago Press, 1982), 77, 82.

18. Katherine E. Badertscher, "Organized Charity and the Civic Ideal in Indianapolis, 1879–1922" (PhD diss., Indiana University, 2015), 142, 211.

19. Kahn, *All in a Century*, 28; Madison, *Eli Lilly: A Life*, 5; Michelle D. Hale, "Children's Bureau of Indianapolis," in *Encyclopedia of Indianapolis*, eds. Bodenhamer and Barrows, 409–10; Katherine Mandusic McDonell, "Flower Mission," in *Encyclopedia of Indianapolis*, eds. Bodenhamer and Barrows, 585–86; Bradford Sample, "A Truly Midwestern City: Indianapolis on the Eve of the Great Depression," *Indiana Magazine of History* 97, no. 2 (June 2001): 131; Andrew R. L. Cayton and Peter S. Onuf, eds., *The Midwest and the Nation: Rethinking the History of an American Region* (Bloomington: Indiana University Press, 1990).

20. The Cleveland Chamber of Commerce created its Committee on Benevolent Associations in May 1900. The committee proposed the creation of the Cleveland Federation for Charity and Philanthropy, the forerunner of the United Way, in 1913. Sturges, *American Chambers of Commerce*, 147–53; Cleveland Chamber of Commerce, *The Cleveland Federation for Charity and Philanthropy, as Proposed by the Committee of Benevolent Associations of the Cleveland Chamber of Commerce* (Cleveland, OH: Cleveland Chamber of Commerce, 1913); Badertscher, "Organized Charity," 258–63; Ruth Hutchinson Crocker, "Making Charity Modern: Business and the Reform of Charities in Indianapolis 1879–1930," *Business and Economic History* 12 (1983): 164; George W. and Miriam Geib, *Indianapolis First* (Indianapolis: Indianapolis Chamber of Commerce, 1990), 25; Tuennerman-Kaplan, *Helping Others*, chapters 2 and 3.

21. Sample, "A Truly Midwestern City," 139–41; Tuennerman-Kaplan, *Helping Others*, chapter 3; Badertscher, "Organized Charity," 210–28, 256, 362–71, 415–28.

22. Sample, "A Truly Midwestern City," 139–41; Badertscher, "Organized Charity," 210–28, 256, 362–71, 415–28; Madison, *Eli Lilly: A Life*, 23, 72; Elizabeth J. Van Allen and Omer H. Foust, eds., *Keeping the Dream* (Indianapolis: James Whitcomb Riley Memorial Association, 1996), 76–140.

23. Badertscher, "Organized Charity," 210–28, 256, 362–71, 415–28; McCarthy, *Noblesse Oblige*.

24. Sample, "A Truly Midwestern City," 137, 141; "Details of Plan to Raise $250,000 for Y.M.C.A. Home," *Indianapolis News*, February 6, 1907, 11; "Program Prepared for Y.M.C.A. Dedication," *Indianapolis News*, February 11, 1909, 9.

25. Nina Mjagkij, *Light in the Darkness: African Americans and the YMCA, 1852–1946* (Lexington: University Press of Kentucky, 2015), Kindle edition, chapter 5; Nina Mjagkij, "Senate Avenue YMCA," in the *Encyclopedia of Indianapolis*, eds. Bodenhamer and Barrows, 1249–50; Badertscher, "Organized Charity," 344–45; "Booker Washington to Dedicate Y. M. C. A.," *Indianapolis Star*, July 8, 1913, 15.

26. Mjagkij, *Light in the Darkness*, chapter 5; Mjagkij, "Senate Avenue YMCA"; Badertscher, "Organized Charity," 344–45. Although David Leander Williams in his book *Indianapolis Jazz* identified J. K. Jr. rather than J. K. Sr. as the one who attended these forums at the Senate Avenue YMCA, it was J. K. Sr. who was a director of the Indianapolis YMCA for eighteen years and for whom collecting Fosteriana was a passion. His obituary also listed the YMCA, along with the Riley Memorial Association, as one of his primary philanthropic interests. Moreover, numerous newspaper articles from the 1930s and 1940s identify J. K. Sr. as the quartet's sponsor. Sources regarding J. K. Jr. do not include mention of the YMCA. David Leander Williams, *Indianapolis Jazz: The Masters, Legends and Legacy of Indiana Avenue* (Charleston, SC: History Press, 2014), 39–40; "Ministerial Association to Meet in Foster Hall," *Indianapolis Star*, May 27, 1933, 11; "Stephen C. Foster Four Will Sing at Church," *Indianapolis Star*, January 24, 1942; "Quartet Carries Christmas Spirit to 40 Homes with Carol Singing," *Indianapolis Star*, December 26, 1943, 8; "Philanthropist Responsible for Reviving Foster Music," *Indianapolis Star*, February 9, 1948, 1; "J. K. Lilly Succumbs," *Indianapolis Star*, February 9, 1948, 15; "Josiah K. Lilly Jr. Dies; Private Rites Saturday," *Indianapolis Star*, May 6, 1966, 1, 18.

27. Sample, "A Truly Midwestern City," 137, 141; Van Allen and Foust, *Keeping the Dream*, 114–15; Indianapolis Foundation Records, 1916–2000, Ruth Lilly Special Collections and Archives, IUPUI University Library, Indiana University Purdue University Indianapolis, accessed March 26, 2022, https://special.ulib.iupui.edu/collections/philanthropy/mss049; Tuennerman-Kaplan, *Helping Others*, chapter 3; Olivier Zunz, *Philanthropy In America: A History* (Princeton, NJ: Princeton University Press, 2014), 53–56; Judith Sealander, "Curing Evils at Their Source: The Arrival of Scientific Giving," eds. Friedman and McGarvie, *Charity and Philanthropy*, 217–39.

28. Tuennerman-Kaplan, *Helping Others*, chapter 3; Sample, "A Truly Midwestern City," 137.

29. Minutes, organizational meetings, December 11, 1920, January 26, 1921, January 29, 1921, James Whitcomb Riley Memorial Association (Riley

Children's Foundation), Indianapolis, Indiana; "Committee to Confer To-
day with M'Cray," *Indianapolis Star,* January 29, 1921; Van Allen and Foust,
Keeping the Dream, 14; Albion Fellows Bacon, "The James Whitcomb Riley
Hospital for Children," *Indiana Bulletin for Charities and Corrections* 129
(June 1922): 48–49; Robert G. Barrows, *Albion Fellows Bacon* (Bloomington:
Indiana University Press, 2000), 72, 95–116; Minutes, IU Board of Trustees,
March 21–28, 1921, Indiana University, Bloomington, accessed March 26,
2022, http://webapp1.dlib.indiana.edu/iubot/view?docId=1921-03-27
.xml&chunk.id=d1e119&toc.depth=1&toc.id=d1e119&brand=iubot&text1=
Riley&op1=and&op2=and&field1=text&field2=text&field3=text&from
Month=01&fromYear=1918&toMonth=06&toYear=1922&startDoc=1#.

30. Charles Emerson to William Lowe Bryan, October 23, 1922, box
2, Indiana University School of Medicine records, 1848–2005, Ruth Lilly
Special Collections and Archivesspecial collections and archives, IUPUI
University Library, Indiana University Purdue University Indianapolis.

31. "David Ross—The Purdue Connection," Rostone, accessed March
26, 2022, http://www.rostone.com/david_ross.htm.

32. "David Ross—The Purdue Connection"; Madison, *Eli Lilly: A Life,*
66–67; Purdue Research Foundation papers, Purdue University Libraries,
Archives and Special Collections, accessed March 26, 2022, https://
archives.lib.purdue.edu/repositories/2/resources/613.

33. Benjamin D. Hitz, ed., *A History of Base Hospital* 32 (Indianapolis:
Edward Kahle Post, no. 42, American Legion, 1922), 1–2, 6, 9, 26, 44–46,
58, 94, 96–97.

34. Hitz, *A History of Base Hospital,* 32, 139.

35. Madison, *Eli Lilly: A Life,* 205; Zunz, *Philanthropy in America,*
171–73.

36. Zunz, *Philanthropy in America,* 173; Madison, *Eli Lilly: A Life,* 206.

37. Lilly Endowment Inc., *The First Twenty Years, 1937–1957* (Indianapolis: Lilly Endowment Inc. 1957), 4–6; J. K. Lilly Jr. to Homer Capehart,
June 29, 1950, in Madison, *Eli Lilly: A Life,* 207; Waldamar E. Nielsen, *Inside American Philanthropy: The Dramas of Donorship* (Norman: University
of Oklahoma Press, 1996), 157–79.

38. Zunz, *Philanthropy in America,* 175.

39. Lilly Endowment Inc., *The First Twenty Years,* 4, 22; David C.
Hammack, ed., *Making the Nonprofit Sector in the United States: A Reader*
(Bloomington, IN: Indiana University Press, 1998), 354; David C. Ham-
mack, "Failure and Resistance: Pushing the Limits in Depression and
Wartime," in *Charity, Philanthropy, and Civility in American History,* eds.

Lawrence J. Friedman and Mark D. McGarvie (New York: Cambridge University Press, 2002), 279; John R. Seeley, *Community Chest: A Case Study in Philanthropy* (New Brunswick, NJ: Transaction, 1989); Lester M. Hunt, "Top Experts Rate Hoosiers Less Than Tip Top," *Indianapolis Star,* December 19, 1956, 1.

40. Joel Silver, *J. K. Lilly Jr., Bibliophile* (Bloomington, IN: The Lilly Library, Indiana University, 1993), 8, 11; Lilly Endowment Inc., *The First Twenty Years,* 5; Jacob N. Blanck, Virginia L. Myers, and Michael Winship, *The Bibliography of American Literature,* 9 vols. (New Haven, CT: Yale University Press, 1955–1991).

41. Madison, *Eli Lilly: A Life,* chapter 6; Carl M. Wright, "Avocational Archaeology: Eli Lilly—Leadership & Vision for Indiana Archaeology," *Central States Archaeological Journal* 48 (October 2001): 74–77; "About Us," Angel Mounds, accessed March 26, https://www.indianamuseum.org/historic-sites/angel-mounds/; "History of the Oriental Institute," The Oriental Institute, The University of Chicago, https://oi.uchicago.edu/about/history-oriental-institute, accessed March 26, 2022; Ascoli, *Julius Rosenwald,* chapter 7.

42. Madison, *Eli Lilly: A Life,* 172–82; Jessie Swigger, *"History Is Bunk": Assembling the Past at Henry Ford's Greenfield Village* (Amherst, MA: University of Massachusetts Press, 2014), 5–6, 8; Anders Greenspan, *Creating Colonial Williamsburg: The Restoration of Virginia's Eighteenth-Century Capital,* 2nd ed. (Chapel Hill, NC: University of North Carolina Press, 2009), 8–9; Jeffrey Trask, *Things American: Art Museums and Civic Culture in the Progressive Era* (Philadelphia: University of Pennsylvania Press, 2012), 11.

43. Yukato Mino and James Robinson, *Beauty and Tranquility: The Eli Lilly Collection of Chinese Art* (Indianapolis: Indianapolis Museum of Art, 1983), 7; Gene E. McCormick, "Origins of the Lilly Collection of Chinese Art," in *Beauty and Tranquility,* Mino and Robinson, 9–11; Robert A. Yassin, "Director's Forward," in *Beauty and Tranquility,* Mino and Robinson, 6.

44. James H. Madison, "Lilly Endowment," in *Encyclopedia of Indianapolis,* eds. Bodenhamer and Barrows, 914; G. Harold Duling to Mrs. Gordon [Helen] McCalment, March 23, 1956, folder 7, box 43, Clowes family papers, Indiana Historical Society, Indianapolis, Indiana.

45. Lilly Endowment Inc., *The First Twenty Years,* 4; Madison, *Eli Lilly: A Life,* 206–7; Mariana Whitmer, "Josiah Kirby Lilly and the Foster Hall Collection," *American Music* 30 (Fall 2012): 326, 329–30, 333–34; "History of the Center's Collections," Center for American Music Library, University

of Pittsburgh, accessed March 26, 2022, http://www.pitt.edu/~amerimus
/AboutCollection.htm.

46. Lilly Endowment Inc., *The First Twenty Years*, 4; Madison, *Eli Lilly:
A Life*, 206–7; Nielsen, *Inside American Philanthropy*, 157–79; "Lilly Foundation Helping to Promote Many Causes," *Indianapolis Star*, December 3,
1967, 25.

47. Lilly Endowment Inc., *The First Twenty Years*, 8, 11, 13–14; Waldemar Nielsen, *The Big Foundations* (New York: Columbia University Press,
1972), 171–72.

48. Lilly Endowment Inc., *The First Twenty Years*, 7; Madison, "Lilly
Endowment," 914–16; Nielsen, *The Big Foundations*, 171. Eli Lilly, in fact, received personal recognition for gifts directed to war relief. McCormick, "Origins of the Lilly Collection of Chinese Art," 12n4; Kahn, *All in A Century*, 59.

49. Lilly Endowment Inc., *The First Twenty Years*, 8, 16, 19–20; Nielsen,
The Big Foundations, 171–73; Madison, "Lilly Endowment," 914–16.

50. John S. Lynn previously had worked at Eli Lilly and Company
as assistant director of business planning. "Lynn Made Manager of Lilly
Fund," *Indianapolis Star*, October 17, 1961, 30.

51. Nielsen, *The Big Foundations*, 171–73; Nielsen, *Inside American
Philanthropy*, 201; Paul M. Doherty, "Lilly Endowment, Inc. 2d In Assets,"
Indianapolis Star, December 5, 1971, 1, 10; "Lilly Foundation Criticism Un-
justified, Official Says," *Indianapolis Star*, October 17, 1972, 16; Kahn, *All in
a Century*, 56–57, 59; Melody Petersen, *Our Daily Meds: How the Pharmaceutical Companies Transformed Themselves into Slick Marketing Machines
and Hooked the Nation on Prescription Drugs* (New York: Farrar, Straus and
Giroux, 2013), Kindle edition, chapter 4.

52. "$600,000 Pledged to Symphony by Lilly," *Indianapolis News*, Au-
gust 10, 1971, 3; "Donors Boost Zoo Fund to $1 Million," *Indianapolis Star*,
January 3, 1965, 1, 12; "Lilly Gift Spurs Drive by Red Cross," *Indianapolis
Star*, November 18, 1966; Herbert Kenney, "Grant Is First Gift in $8 Million
Drive," *Indianapolis News*, September 8, 1967, 1, 3; "DePauw Receives Gift
from Lilly," *Indianapolis Star*, November 20, 1969, 40; "Butler, Marian Gifts
Total $150,000," *Indianapolis News*, December 24, 1969, 3; "Children's Mu-
seum Gets Grant," December 14, 1972, 59.

53. "Lilly Fund's Lynn to Retire," *Indianapolis News*, October 2, 1972,
14; "L. R. Bolling to Run Lilly Endowment," *Indianapolis Star*, October 21,
1972, 27; Madison, "Lilly Endowment," 914–16.

54. Gary R. Hess, "Waging the Cold War in the Third World: The
Foundations and the Challenges of Development," in Friedman and Mc-
Garvie, *Charity and Philanthropy*, 319–39.

55. "Personal Mention," *Indianapolis Star*, March 23, 1919, 39.

56. "Nicholas Noyes Dies," 1, 13; McCarthy, *Noblesse Oblige*, 154–55; Sample, *A Truly Midwestern City*, 139–41.

57. Van Allen and Foust, *Keeping the Dream*, 114–15; "Nicholas Noyes Dies," 1, 13; "Plan Recruiting in Civic Effort," *Indianapolis Star*, August 8, 1926, 1, 4.

58. "Nicholas Noyes Dies," 13; "Mrs. Noyes Dies," 34.

59. "Noyes-Sponsored Children's Pavilion Hailed as 'Second to None,'" *Indianapolis Star*, October 29, 1967, 8; "Nicholas Noyes Dies; Civic Cultural Leader," 13.

60. A. O. Bunnell, ed., and F. I. Quick, comp., *Dansville, 1789–1902: Historical, Biographical, Descriptive* (Dansville, NY: Instructor, 1902), 183–85; "Nicholas Noyes Dies," 1, 13; "Plaque Given," *Democrat and Chronicle*, May 26, 1951, 27; American Red Cross Greater Rochester Chapter, accessed March 26, 2022, http://www.dansvillechamber.com/index.php/business-members/clara-barton-chapter-1-american-red-cross/.

61. "Founding Collections, Nicholas H. Noyes '06 and Marguerite Lilly Noyes," Cornell University Libraries, accessed March 26, 2022, http://rmc.library.cornell.edu/footsteps/exhibition/foundingcollections/foundingcollections_5.html.

62. "Nicholas Noyes Dies," 13; "Vassar Residence Is Dedicated at Ceremonies Sunday," *Kingston Daily Freeman*, November 13, 1958, 11; "Drug Executive Gives Cornell $3 Million," *Democrat and Register*, November 20, 1965, 1.

63. "Nicholas Noyes Dies," 13; "Noyes Hospital Receives Accreditation," *Democrat and Register*, September 1974, 12, 49; Nicholas H. Noyes (1883–1977), Dansville, New York, Historical Society, accessed March 26, 2022, https://dansvilleareahistoricalsociety.org/nicholas-h-noyes/.

64. Charles E. Meyer, "Indianapolis Literary Club," in *Encyclopedia of Indianapolis*, eds. Bodenhamer and Barrows, 788; "Club Calendar," *Indianapolis News*, December 6, 1924, 20; "Club Calendar for the Week," *Indianapolis News*, March 19, 1927, 21; Mary Jane Meeker, "Contemporary Club of Indianapolis," in *Encyclopedia of Indianapolis*, eds. Bodenhamer and Barrows, 474; Ray E. Boomhower, *But I Do Clamor: May Wright Sewall, A Life, 1844–1920* (Zionsville, IN: Guild Press of Indiana, 2001), vii, 5, 62, 69.

65. Anne P. Robinson and S. L. Berry, *Every Way Possible: 125 Years of the Indianapolis Museum of Art* (Indianapolis: Indianapolis Museum of Art, 2008), 31–32, 38–39, 103–6, 236; Boomhower, *But I Do Clamor*, viii, x, 62, 63, 69; "Hals Self Portrait Steals Detroit Show," *Indianapolis Star*, January 10, 1935, 7.

66. Robinson and Berry, *Every Way Possible*, 23–32, 38–39, 103–6, 236; Kathleen D. McCarthy, *Women's Culture: American Philanthropy and Art, 1830–1930* (Chicago: University of Chicago Press, 1991), 56, 70–75, 114.

67. Robinson and Berry, *Every Way Possible*, 123–24.

68. Alexander W. Clowes, *The Doc and the Duchess*, 141–43; Booth Tarkington and Josiah K. Lilly, *The Story of the Indianapolis Symphony Orchestra* (Indianapolis: no publisher, 1946?); "400 Are Invited to Meeting of Symphony Group," *Indianapolis Star*, October 13, 1937, 6; "Philanthropist Responsible for Reviving Foster Music," *Indianapolis Star*, February 9, 1948, 1; Madison, *Eli Lilly: A Life*, 189; "Cincinnati Orchestra to Close Fifth Year of Concerts," *Indianapolis Star*, April 10, 1927, 75; Thomas N. Akins, *Crescendo, Indianapolis Symphony Orchestra: 1930–2005* (Indianapolis: Indianapolis Symphony Orchestra, 2004), 76, 79; John H. Mueller, *The American Symphony Orchestra: A Social History of Musical Taste* (Bloomington: Indiana University Press, 1951), 32.

69. Alexander W. Clowes, *The Doc and the Duchess*, 141–43; Charles Latham Jr., "Episcopalians," in *Encyclopedia of Indianapolis*, eds. Bodenhamer and Barrows, 549–51.

70. McCarthy, *Women's Culture*; Kathleen D. McCarthy, "Women and Political Culture," in *Charity, Philanthropy, and Civility in American History*, eds. Friedman and McGarvie, 179–98.

71. "Guest of Vassar Club," *Indianapolis News*, May 17, 1919, 18; "Pioneer Suffragists of Indianapolis to Be Honor Guests at Public Reception," *Indianapolis Star*, June 21, 1919, 18; Badertscher, "Organized Charity," 425.

72. *Indianapolis Woman's Club, 1875–1925*, folder 4, box 38, Clowes family papers; "Club Calendar," *Indianapolis News*, January 30, 1926, 22; "Attractive List of Meets Arranged at Meridian Hills," *Indianapolis Star*, April 21, 1928, 13; Jane Cunningham Croly, *The History of the Woman's Club Movement in America* (New York: H. G. Allen & Company, 1898), 435; "Mrs. John N. Carey, Art Patron Dies; Led Movement to Adopt State Flag," *Indianapolis Star*, June 15, 1938, 1; Alexander W. Clowes, *The Doc and the Duchess*, 123.

73. Articles of Incorporation, Orchard School, 1921, folder 1, box 39, Clowes family papers; Excerpts from the first school bulletin, 1922, Orchard School, 1922, folder 1, box 39, Clowes family papers; "Development of Children's Minds and Characters through Directed Creative Work Aim of New School," *Indianapolis Star*, October 1, 1922, 10; McCarthy, *Noblesse Oblige*, 115.

74. "Plan Step for Pupils, Seek to Make Museum Available for Children," *Indianapolis News*, November 28, 1923, 7; David H. Kenny, *Fifty*

Years Young: The Children's Museum (New York: The Newcomen Society in North America, 1975), 7–14; McCarthy, *Noblesse Oblige*, 156.

75. Kenny, *Fifty Years Young*, 24; "Mrs. Noyes Dies," 34; "Merrill Dedicates New Lilly Theater," *Indianapolis Star*, September 30, 1976, 48.

76. Badertscher, "Organized Charity," 272, 385–87; Alexander W. Clowes, *The Doc and the Duchess*, 139–40.

77. Dorothy McClamroch to Edith W. Clowes, January 27, 1950, folder 10, box 39, Clowes family papers.

78. Planned Parenthood Association of Central Indiana, 1932–1985, Indiana Historical Society, Indianapolis, Indiana, https://indianahistory .org/wp-content/uploads/planned-parenthood-association-of-central -indiana-records.pdf, accessed March 26, 2022.

79. Bylaws of the Planned Parenthood Association of Indianapolis, Inc., folder 1, box 43, Clowes family papers.

80. L. A. Arffman to Mrs. G. H. A. [Edith W.] Clowes, May 27, 1956, folder 7, box 43, Clowes family papers.

81. Winfield Best to Mrs. G. H. A. [Edith W.] Clowes, June 7, 1956, folder 7, box 43, Clowes family papers; Mary Marain to Edith W. Clowes, February 25, 1959, folder 7, box 43, Clowes family papers; Miriam F. Garwood to William Vogt, Re: Work with Planned Parenthood Association of Indianapolis, Inc., November 13, 14, 15, 1956, folder 7, box 43, Clowes family papers; Minutes of the Annual Meeting of the Planned Parenthood Association of Indianapolis, January 23, 1957, folder 1, box 43, Clowes family papers.

82. Brief summary of activities for 1956; Minutes of the Annual Meeting of the Planned Parenthood Association of Indianapolis, January 23, 1957; board of director's meeting, Planned Parenthood Association of Indianapolis, April 25, 1956; Treasurer's budget report, January 1–September 28, 1956; Board of directors meeting, Planned Parenthood Association of Indianapolis, February 27, 1957; box 43, folder 1, Clowes family papers; William L. Schloss to Mrs. G. H. A. [Edith W.] Clowes, August 11, 1959; Helen McCalment to Mrs. G. H. A. Clowes [Edith W.] Clowes, August 20, 1959; folder 7, box 43, Clowes family papers. Eli Lilly supported Christ Church Cathedral rector and dean Paul Moore Jr.'s social programs that included "planned parenthood" classes established within the Christ Church parish. It is unclear whether the Planned Parenthood Association of Indianapolis had any connection to them. Madison, *Eli Lilly: A Life*, 232.

83. Zunz, *Philanthropy in America*, 170–72; Memorandum, "In the first place," no author [ca. 1961], folder 18, box 39; Clowes family papers; "History," The Clowes Fund, A Family Foundation, https://www.clowesfund .org/history/, accessed March 26, 2022.

84. Robinson and Berry, *Every Way Possible*, 236–39; Memorandum, "In the first place," director's report [Carl J. Weinhardt, Jr.], annual meeting of the Art Association of Indianapolis, 1965–1966, folder 2, box 39, Clowes family papers.

85. Alexander W. Clowes, *The Doc and the Duchess*, 140–41, 145; Paul Rusch to George A. H. and Edith W. Clowes, February 10, 1954, folder 13, box 39, Clowes family papers; First draft of articles of incorporation, Indianapolis Council on World Affairs, May 16, 1955, folder 14, box 39, Clowes family papers; Copy of resolution to build Clowes Hall, Butler University, May 28, 1959, folder 1, box 40, Clowes family papers.

86. Alexander W. Clowes, *The Doc and the Duchess*, 143–45, 149; Akins, *Crescendo*, 9; Mueller, *The American Symphony Orchestra*, vii–viii, 37, 50–51, 177–79; "The Laying of the Cornerstone of Clowes Memorial Hall for the Performing Arts," Butler University, Indianapolis, Indiana, November 24, 1961, folder 6, box 40, Clowes family papers; "Clowes Hall Blends Past and Present, *Indianapolis News*, October 10, 1963, 15, folder 17, box 40, Clowes family papers.

87. "Mrs. Eli Lilly Succumbs…" *Indianapolis Star*, March 13, 1973, p. 65.

88. In 2014, 60 percent of family foundations had assets of less than $1 million. Kerry Hannon, "Family Foundations Let Affluent Leave a Legacy," *New York Times*, February 10, 2014, https://www.nytimes.com /2014/02/11/your-money/family-foundations-let-affluent-leave-a-legacy .html, accessed March 26, 2022; Nielsen, *Inside American Philanthropy*, 157; "Our Mission," Nicholas H. Noyes Jr. Memorial Foundation, http://www .noyesfoundation.org/, accessed March 26, 2022; "Clowes Fund Incorporated," ProPublica, https://projects.propublica.org/nonprofits /organizations/351079679 , accessed March 26, 2022.

89. Nielsen, *Inside American Philanthropy*, 67.

90. "Noyes Health History," UR Medicine, https://www.noyes-health .org/about-noyes/noyes-history, accessed March 26, 2022.

91. Nicholas H. Noyes Jr. Memorial Foundation; "Jon Shay Leads Noyes Health Foundation Rejuvenation," About Noyes, https://www .urmc.rochester.edu/noyes/about/news/article/4875/jon-shay-leads -noyes-health-foundation-rejuvenation.aspx, accessed March 26, 2022.

92. The Clowes Fund, http://www.clowesfund.org/, accessed March 26, 2022.

93. Allen Whitehill Clowes Charitable Foundation, Inc., http://www .awclowescf.org/, accessed March 26, 2022.

94. Merle Curti, "American Philanthropy and the American Character," *American Quarterly* 10, no. 4 (Winter 1958): 428.

95. Madison, "Lilly Endowment," 916; "About Us," The Lilly Endowment Inc., http://www.lillyendowment.org/theendowment.html, accessed
March 26, 2022; "History," Lilly Family School of Philanthropy, https://
philanthropy.iupui.edu/about/history.html, accessed March 26, 2022.

96. N. Clay Robbins, "Executive Message," in Lilly Endowment Inc.:
Annual Report, 2015, 2.

97. J. K. Lilly, "Reminiscences," 1940, Eli Lilly and Company corporate
archives, Indianapolis, Indiana.

PART II

TRENDS AND INNOVATIONS

SECTION II

EXPERIMENTS IN SOCIAL CHANGE

THE EMERGENCE OF CHARITY EVALUATION

KATHERINE BADERTSCHER

THIS CHAPTER EXPLORES THE ORIGINS of charity evaluation, such as today's Charity Navigator, and demonstrates that evaluation has had a century-long history in the Hoosier state. Trust and legitimacy are fundamental in philanthropy, to donors, managers, clients, government officials, and the general public. Why donate to a charity, after all, if you cannot expect it will spend your money wisely and for its intended purpose? If trust is absent, organized philanthropy cannot sustain itself. To assure their trust in social service agencies, Hoosiers have turned to so-called watchdog organizations, starting in the late nineteenth century.

The issue of charity evaluation prompts a range of questions in philanthropy, both then and now. Donors, managers, clients, and policy makers all question who qualifies for social service assistance. These stakeholders have different opinions about who should evaluate nonprofit effectiveness and what criteria an evaluator should apply in determining a charity's effectiveness. Donors expect their contributions to produce impact, policy makers demand proof that nonprofit initiatives are effective, managers and staff want to know how to work effectively, and clients participate in nonprofit programs and services with the hope of results that improve the quality of life.

The organized-charity phenomenon rose and fell in tandem with the national Progressive movement. The Charity Organization Society of Indianapolis (COS) (1879–1922), a social service agency in its own right, vetted charities and added legitimacy to those it claimed as subagencies. Looking at the COS through the lens of evaluation, furthermore, places gender dynamics into sharp relief. During its most influential years, the COS marshaled an influential cadre of both men and women to vet applicants, dispense relief, fundraise, and create and manage subagencies. Evaluation between 1879 and 1910 was informal and participatory. As the COS structure waned in legitimacy, in Indiana and across the country, the entirely male Chamber of Commerce emerged as the most powerful authority on charity and social service delivery. The shift from philanthropic self-regulation to external, businesslike evaluation was virtually complete by 1922, when the Chamber of Commerce fully assumed the role of governing the charitable agenda in Indianapolis.

THE CHARITY ORGANIZATION SOCIETY

Evaluation traces its roots to the late-nineteenth-century organized-charity movement. The scholarly debate over the usefulness of social control theory, often ascribed to organized charity, is now well-traveled ground. Charity organization societies (societies), archetypal structures of the American scientific philanthropy movement, do not engender glowing tributes from historians of social welfare policy.

The scientific philanthropy movement fully emerged when charity organizers attempted to integrate a third ideological strand, science, into the two origins of philanthropy: compassion and duty to community. Charity organization societies' critics have found science and philanthropy to be irreconcilable and oxymoronic at best—and cruel at worst. Yet charitable leaders believed personal relationships among givers and receivers, data gathering and interpretation, and elimination of misery's root causes were indeed compatible. Religion undergirded the charitable impulses of societies' boards, donors, staff, and volunteers, just as faith and values continue to animate philanthropic organizations today.

Scientific philanthropy dominated the US social welfare landscape at the turn of the century, and regions of the country adopted the movement to suit their particular needs. Indiana was an early adopter of both scientific philanthropy in general and charity evaluation in particular. The Charity Organization Society of Indianapolis had begun operations as the Indianapolis Benevolent Society (IBS) in 1835. Indianapolis's growth, industrialization, and population heterogeneity all challenged traditional neighborhood benevolence as the primary remedy for assisting the poor. In 1879 Indianapolis was one of the first cities in the United States to establish a COS, and the organization expanded quickly, gaining virtual control over poverty relief.[1] Indianapolis adopted the organized-charity structure early and thus provided a blueprint for the state. Local charity leaders Reverend Oscar McCulloch and Monsignor Francis Gavisk led the National Council on Charity and Correction, the national social welfare debating society.

The COS built a "circle of charities" to unite "in a common effort to strengthen that which is weak and lift up that which is fallen down."[2] For nearly four decades, the COS screened and approved all cases for assistance and then assigned cases with the circle of charities for relief and other types of assistance. The COS described the circle as the continuous network of resource providers that it coordinated, managed, and legitimized. The COS included charities in the circle based on personal relationships and agencies' agreements with organized-charity principles, not on any formal evaluation criteria.

Charities in the COS's circle included women's organizations that provided crucial social services, underscoring that the women of Indianapolis exhibited more agency in their charitable work than is commonly understood during the organized-charity movement. Women, and especially women of means, stayed abreast of issues in philanthropy through their social networks. Dozens of women participated as friendly visitors, as district council and committee members, and several women worked on the COS staff. Many more women, however, created their own charitable agencies and then funded, governed, staffed, publicized, advocated, and volunteered for the Flower Mission, Indianapolis Free Kindergarten Society, Mother's Aid Society, Christamore Settlement, YWCA, Women's Improvement Club, and the Indiana University Social Service Department. Women preferred control over their own charitable missions and activities versus participating in a more circumscribed fashion for the COS. In the city of Indianapolis, women's participation in organized charity complemented men's governance roles. This mixed-gender collaborative pattern, however, shifted to one of male dominance with the rise of the Commercial Club.

THE COMMERCIAL CLUB

Founding COS members directed the organization and brought significant financial resources, both as individuals and on behalf of their businesses. Because the high-profile charter members signed on to the organized-charity concept early, their support lent credibility to the organization—and agencies within the circle of charities—unmatched by any other single philanthropic entity in Indiana. The unified male elite, however, trained its sights on scientific management that eventually overshadowed the early religious infusion.

By the late nineteenth century, Indianapolis desperately needed paved streets, an organized street system, a sewage system, and a myriad of other public works. In 1890, a young journalist named William Fortune wrote a series of editorials promoting a civic organization that would unite business leaders to promote the city's economic growth and infrastructure development.[3] Fortune's editorials caught the eye of Colonel Eli Lilly, who had accumulated considerable wealth and devoted his attention increasingly to philanthropy. Lilly imagined Indianapolis as "the model city of America 200,000 strong" by the turn of the century, complete with smooth roads and sidewalks, shade trees, and enhanced utility systems.[4]

Within weeks of Fortune's editorials, Lilly and twenty-seven other men formed the Commercial Club with a broad civic agenda: "to promote the prosperity and work for the general welfare of Indianapolis . . . and vicinity."[5] The combination of the city's needs and the club's organizing principles attracted many businessmen. In two days, the club had eighty-seven members; within three months it boasted over a thousand. Not surprisingly, the Commercial Club and the COS had many members in common. Lilly served as Commercial Club president for five years; Fortune served as the club's secretary and later its president.

The Commercial Club's early initiatives tested the boundaries of the private and public sectors. It noted the inadequacy of existing municipal government, so it took matters into its own hands.[6] The club proposed model legislation for a new city charter, addressed "the street question" by inviting bids for resurfacing, lobbied for a city parks commission, vetted plans for a new jail, campaigned for public safety and public health measures, and lured conventions to town.[7]

The Commercial Club's first foray into social services came in 1893, when an economic panic struck the country after years of railroads' overbuilding. Almost one hundred railroads went bankrupt, triggering a run on banks. Over six hundred banks failed, and some cities saw as many as a quarter of their unskilled laborers without jobs.[8] The panic stretched into a protracted economic depression, the worst the country had yet seen. The Indianapolis National Bank closure in July 1893 created the greatest devastation locally.[9] Indianapolis, the Merchants National Bank history ominously recorded, would be swallowed by the "whirlpool of disaster."[10] Farm prices fell, factories closed, local railroads went bankrupt, and unemployment climbed.[11]

The economic downturn overtaxed existing charitable capacity in Indianapolis and prompted the COS and Commercial Club to work together for the first time. The COS had operated for fourteen years; developed and solidified its staff, volunteer, and donor base; and achieved status as a social welfare authority regionally and nationally. The COS, despite its prominence, expended its annual budget early in 1893 and would not be able to satisfy the usual increased demand for relief during the upcoming winter months. The men who led the COS and the Commercial Club developed the 1893 to 1894 poor relief scheme, which operated under the banner of the Commercial Club Relief Committee (CRC).[12]

Key members of the CRC's finance committee were seasoned COS members with charity fundraising experience who could apply their knowledge in the new public/private scheme.[13] Commercial Club leaders grafted the firmly established COS principles onto the CRC's model: registration, investigation, relief without creating dependence, a work test, and Indianapolis citizens given priority over transients. The CRC embedded these principles into its goals: to alleviate suffering with neither "pauperizing" influences nor "the humiliation of charity" and to protect Indianapolis against "imposition by an influx of dependents" from outside the city.[14]

The COS by 1893 possessed enough knowledge of the causes of poverty to see with absolute clarity that unemployment caused this crisis, not insobriety, illness, lack of ambition, lack of thrift, or any other personal lack of responsibility. The organization told the *Indianapolis Sun* that "everybody who calls upon us for aid nowadays would scorn an offer of money. They all want work—work." The COS, however, could not create the jobs for which the unemployed clamored. "We would be delighted in furnishing employment to seekers if it were possible to do so," the secretary stated, "but you know that we can't create positions."[15] True employment solutions could only come from government or businesses—which were reeling and laying off workers.

The Commercial Club Relief Committee held public meetings with the committee of the unemployed, the township trustee, and Mayor Thomas Sullivan to assess the situation and devise plans that would "not be confused with charity."[16] Both the COS and the workingmen's committee tried to keep up with the avalanche of aid requests as the CRC raised funds. By November, the workingmen channeled all applicants to the COS. At the end of the year, the CRC officially launched with the eight hundred families dependent on the COS receiving priority assistance.[17]

The COS registered applicants, as the CRC expected aid recipients to be able to work if at all possible. The society had trained case workers and put processes in place to conduct investigations. The CRC assumed the city would readily supply jobs. The Board of Public Works arranged for most unemployed men to clean streets, shovel snow, excavate a city sewer, and construct a dam and lake in the municipal Garfield Park. The COS arranged for women to wash clothes at the Friendly Inn, although it granted relief to most women without requiring them to work.[18]

With over a thousand members, the Commercial Club brought scale and capacity to the problem that the COS could never have marshaled on its own, although the COS operated as a full partner in the relief plan from its inception. Together the organizations raised over $18,000 from every business and most individuals in the city—more than triple the annual COS budget. Moreover, the COS's major donors gave at their customary levels.[19] As the COS's general operating funds were depleted, the CRC reimbursed the entire COS annual budget, plus surplus funds, coal, and shoes so that it could operate for the remainder of 1894. The township trustee, S. N. Gold, endorsed a city appropriation as the relief measures saved his office, and thus taxpayers, "many thousands of dollars" because he believed charity was more efficient than government.[20] Gold, while part of the municipal government himself, recognized that citizens clamored for government efficiency and oversight.[21]

When the 1893 panic struck, fewer than one hundred charity organization societies existed in the United States. Fewer than fifty had operated for more than ten years. Organized-charity historian Frank Dekker Watson credited established societies with a unique ability to address the unemployment crisis, even as the industrial depression "all but paralyzed industry." Cities without organized charity distributed relief "without machinery," therefore wastefully and overlooking the most urgent needs.[22] Watson singled out four cities that created temporary, multisector schemes as most effective: New York City, Chicago, Philadelphia, and Indianapolis. The efficient and cooperative Indianapolis plan, he noted, "clearly demonstrated the wisdom of the methods of charity organization."[23] No city supplied a comprehensive solution that addressed every case of need, but Indianapolis appears to have fared as well as possible, especially for a city of modest size.

The Indianapolis COS, as an early adopter, had originated as an organization to emulate. Now the COS's exceptional symbiosis with the business sector made it a model organization in a different way. The Commercial Club Relief Committee garnered national attention for the city as a model of scientific management.[24] A sociologist who studied relief efforts in American cities called Indianapolis the "most perfect arrangement for relief that has been devised."[25] Dr. Edward Devine, head of New York's COS, noted the executive leadership, control of the situation, and ingenuity of the scheme.[26] Inquiries came in from all over the country for advice and specifics of the plan. The 1893 panic thus solidified Indianapolis COS principles and the Commercial Club's centrality in matters of public welfare.

THE 1907 DEPRESSION

After its cooperation with the COS as leaders of the Relief Committee, business leaders of the Commercial Club felt empowered to remain at the intersection of business, philanthropy, and government. The next crisis to test the COS and the Commercial Club came in October 1907. The New York Stock Exchange lost approximately 50 percent of its value, setting off an economic panic, sometimes called the Bankers' Panic. The October crisis led to another economic depression, although far shorter than the 1893–1894 downturn. Indianapolis did not suffer the same bank collapses as in 1893 and demand for labor had exceeded supply for the preceding several years, so the 1907 depression paled in comparison. The COS wrote that it had evolved from its founding purposes to also be "an agency for the direction of emergency relief made necessary by fire, flood, or economic panic."[27]

By this time, the COS and the Commercial Club were well established and Indianapolis—and peer city—governments had evolved. City boards of health or welfare had begun to assert authority over charities in many parts of the United States, but the COS in Indianapolis still retained control over social welfare and endorsement of charities within its circle. The COS applied its relief-through-work strategy to combat the 1907 panic. During the 1893 depression, the COS had recognized that jobs were the solution that most people demanded, but the organization had neither the inclination nor the ability to create them. By 1907, the COS had been incubating the idea of building rent-free cottages for single mothers on the same grounds as the Summer Mission for Sick Children, a fresh-air mission on the grounds of Fairview Park (today's Butler University campus).[28] Unemployed men provided the labor for construction of small cottages at Fairview Park, allowing the COS to "kill two birds with one stone."[29] Men received food for their labor; the COS added cottages for a bargain price to launch its next project. Women received aid or did work at home in exchange for food. The COS conducted investigations consistent with its usual practice and gave priority treatment to the elderly and those not served by any other charities or churches.[30] The Commercial Club offered its assistance to the COS, not to colead the relief effort but to aid in fundraising. Together the organizations raised sufficient funds and material donations to keep up with applications, engaging churches, schools, and newspapers as fundraising organs.[31] Charity leaders around Indiana and the United States lauded the Indianapolis COS as an "inspiration," the ideal charity organization, as it had a sufficient critical mass of donors, staff, and effective charities to implement solutions that would someday eliminate the scourge of poverty from Indianapolis.[32]

But by the 1910s, a fault line began to develop between business and philanthropy. Growth in Indianapolis made the old "circle of charities," at one time fundamental to social welfare in the city, increasingly difficult for the COS to manage. In addition to the COS's own affiliates and social settlements, a plethora of other new specialized charitable agencies had formed. Increasing population, hospital development, national movements, and rising numbers of wealthy donors all contributed to their development. One local history lists five new organizations between 1879 and 1891 and thirty between 1891 and 1911.[33] The *Indianapolis Star* reported fifty-nine charities in the COS circle, not counting churches, at the end of 1909.[34]

The iterative shift from informal philanthropic self-regulation to external businesslike evaluation began in 1910. Hundreds of chambers of commerce launched in the United States in the 1910s with capacious scope, including social welfare. Communities gradually came to expect chamber leaders to comment on matters of social importance.[35] Chamber executives felt they were uniquely able to unite disparate interest groups because their members were from all walks of business life.[36] Chambers around the country gradually supplanted the charity organization societ-ies' charity evaluation, clearinghouse, and regulatory roles.

The Commercial Club president in 1910, Winfield Miller, re-minded members that the club had been founded for the "general welfare" of Indianapolis, such as elevated tracks, public health, child welfare, education, transportation, and public lighting.[37] Miller led an effort to correct perceived weaknesses in the mat-ter of charitable giving and evaluation based on models recently tested in Cleveland, Ohio.[38] The club recognized the "valuable service" of the COS, especially its investigative practices, but felt citizens remained vulnerable to beggars on the street and dishon-est charities.[39]

The Commercial Club in Indianapolis accordingly formed a Committee on Benevolent Associations to assert control over charitable evaluation and fundraising. The committee began to investigate individual charities, including the COS and IBS, based on mission, governance, solvency, revenue diversification, and fundraising methods.[40] The committee endorsed charities as either worthy or unworthy—reminiscent of how the COS ini-tially had handled individual applicants. It denied endorsement when charities did not provide complete information or came too close to proselytizing. By mid-1910, forty-four investigations were underway. Approved charities received a formal endorsement card that fundraisers were required to brandish when soliciting donations.

The Commercial Club believed this new venture "had more sincere and profound thought" than any of its other work that year. The Committee on Benevolent Associations paid particu-lar attention to matters heretofore the province of the COS— "the avoidance of much unnecessary duplication in charity work"—and looked forward to the "sympathetic cooperation of all the benevolent organizations of our city."[41] As 1911 began, the club resolved that it stood "aggressively" for organized-charity principles, including cooperation, nonduplication, efficiency, supervision, and clearinghouse methods. It recognized the COS for its "quiet but persistent advocacy" of those principles and its ability to affect change "on a limited scale."[42] The Commercial Club and COS, once full partners in poor relief and still with many members in common, had shifted in their positions of power over charity evaluation in Indianapolis.

WILLIAM FORTUNE AND THE INDIANAPOLIS CHAMBER OF COMMERCE

The Commercial Club and five other business organizations merged in 1912 to form the Indianapolis Chamber of Commerce.[43] The chamber thereafter remained active in bridging business, philanthropy, and government. It felt that management of the charitable sector was required to identify and eliminate scams purporting to be charities and refused to rely on local government to carry out this function.[44] The chamber justified its responsibilities on behalf of its membership as they represented the majority of charitable donors in Indianapolis.

The Commercial Club's Committee on Benevolent Associations became the Chamber's Committee on Relief and Charities and gained increasing authority over charities. The chamber's authority mirrored the rationale of corporate, not just individual, social responsibility to community across the country.[45] By 1915, chambers of commerce in most major cities formally endorsed charities.[46] The committee advised chamber members that it served as a form of insurance to assure high standards and insulate them from fraud. It surveyed and screened up to fifty charities annually and formally endorsed those it deemed reputable. Once endorsed, a charity's solicitors carried cards that stated, "The Committee believes it to be worthy the support of those who desire to further its aims."[47] The committee vetted charities against COS principles in its endorsement process: efficacy, ethics, and efficiency, meaning the elimination of duplication and waste. The committee acknowledged that the public now generally recognized organized-charity principles and credited the COS with having put the concepts into practice, albeit on a limited scale.[48]

The Committee on Relief and Charities simultaneously expanded on and undermined the COS's circle of charities. The committee wrote that charities were too numerous and complex to be coordinated, as the COS had done in the past. Organized principles remained sound, but the charitable environment had changed. By endorsing worthy charities and declining to assist those unworthy of public support, the committee promised to ensure—in Darwinian parlance—the "survival of the fittest" benevolent organizations in the city.[49] The committee brazenly required the COS, once the leader of Indianapolis social services, to apply for approval just like any other.

The Indianapolis COS increasingly looked to other cities and organizations for validation of its work, instead of acting as an advisor or model for others as it had done for decades. COS General Secretary Charles Grout solicited an external review from the Cleveland COS in 1915, which benignly validated that Indianapolis still followed traditional organized-charity principles.[50] Grout then consulted with the American Association for Organizing Charities and studied the structure of charity organization societies in six other cities. He reported that the COS could "bind all relieving agencies closely together" in its early decades, but the plethora of new public and private agencies made that function now impossible. "We have again numerous agencies," he stated, "and these often are working at cross purposes because their work touches and they are not in harmony." He noticed a decided trend toward "loose federations" of agencies, but he did not believe the COS could fill this role as currently configured.[51] The COS and Grout ground on without a clear agenda for another year before the board took action to rejuvenate the organization.

The COS board eventually concluded that change was in order and replaced Charles Grout with Eugene Foster, a social work executive from Cleveland. By the time the leadership transition stabilized, the Chamber's Relief and Charities Committee had co-opted former COS principles as entirely its own: "The said new [COS] reorganization will more nearly harmonize with the ideas and principles of the Relief & Charities Committee."[52] The COS operated for six more years, but it no longer held its central position as the hub of all charitable operations.

In 1917, the United States entered World War I, Red Cross fundraising began in earnest, and William Fortune became president of the Chamber of Commerce. These interrelated events ushered in William Fortune as the next generation's most influential civic and philanthropic leader and reflected the Chamber/COS struggle for control that was taking place around the United States. The war forged feelings of patriotism, civic unity, spirit of sacrifice, and commitment to the common weal. Civic obligation emerged as city populations burgeoned and thus became a middle-class, urban reinterpretation of noblesse oblige.[53] Chambers completely replaced charity organization societies as the ideal institutional vehicle to harness civic participation.

William Fortune combined his leadership positions at the Chamber of Commerce and the Red Cross in 1918 to manage the city's War Chest Board.[54] War Chests developed across the country to reduce overhead expense, harness individual giving, and allow corporations to deduct wartime charitable contributions from taxable income.[55] The Red Cross National Fund encompassed all War Chest giving into a single drive, raising over $100,000,000 in its first campaign. Nationally, lead million-dollar gifts from the Rockefeller Foundation, General Electric Company, and Anaconda Copper stimulated giving across the country and from all walks of life.[56] In Indiana, Fortune used his connections to organize the War Chest Board and raised an astounding sum: just under $3,000,000.[57] The War Chest aggregated more than the COS had collected during its entire forty-year existence, bringing questions of allocation, effectiveness, and evaluation to the foreground.[58] Fortune and his colleagues chose to allocate the funds to "provide for all war and benevolent needs in Indianapolis . . . according to the judgment of the War Chest Board as to their merits."[59] The board decided on a formal, businesslike approach to allocation that Fortune viewed as intertwined with charity evaluation.

THE BUREAU OF MUNICIPAL RESEARCH REPORT

Instead of relying on local expertise to advise it during the allocation process, the War Chest Board turned to a national firm. When the Commercial Club formed its first Committee on Benevolent Associations in 1909, it had considered forming an Indiana-based research organization. The club had invited a national expert, William Allen, then director of New York City's Bureau of Municipal Research (BMR), to address its members and evaluate whether Indianapolis should develop a similar bureau.[60] Allen and Frederick Cleveland, formerly of New York's Association for Improving the Condition of the Poor, founded the BMR in 1905 to apply scientific management à la Frederick Taylor, the founder of industrial engineering, to evaluate city governments. The founders' goal was to harness "the work of social betterment" by informing citizens how to encourage efficient and ethical local governments.[61] The city-reform movement erupted quickly with city clubs and municipal leagues that experimented with supervision of charities as part of a holistic view of cities' environments and recognition of the interdependence of poverty with living and working conditions. Cities' rapid growth and concomitant demand for services, however, far outpaced their management capacities.[62] The BMR developed in this reform context and thus focused its first decade of investigations around key themes: ousting corrupt officials, systematizing government processes with business models and scientific inquiry, and, above all, introducing budgeting and financial-management systems.[63] Men and women continued social welfare work in a range of ways, Camilla Stivers has found that such government reform, undertaken first locally and then nationally, "was almost entirely a male enterprise."[64]

The BMR, by 1917, had undergone its own reorganization, changing major donors, leadership, and staff in the process. The few women who had shaped the bureau's early years were no longer involved, and the broad "work of social betterment" agenda had narrowed to full-blown administrative surveys as its core business. Social welfare became peripheral to the BMR as the social survey developed as instruments of social settlement and foundation work.[65] The gender division grew gradually wider as women's wide-sweeping reform agendas included maternal and child welfare, workplace safety, and advocacy of social services for the poor.[66] What began as city-government reform shifted to research with "trained and experienced men" auditing municipal organization, finance, public safety, and public works.[67]

A number of cities created their own internal research bureaus, but the Chamber's Relief and Charities Committee retained the BMR to complete comprehensive studies of Indianapolis, *both* its government and charitable infrastructures. That the chamber retained the bureau to survey government administration is not remarkable in the least. That the bureau audited social welfare agencies leaves no doubt that men had wrestled control of the charitable agenda from their former female collaborators. It further explains the report's focus on organization, the scientific philanthropy language co-opted from the COS, and, above all, the emphasis on fundraising costs. The BMR applied the same method that had earned it prominence in rooting out government corruption to a far different set of agencies: social service nonprofits.

The BMR produced a survey report of city-government agencies in 1917 followed by a similar study of charitable organizations in Indianapolis in 1918. "Report on a Survey of the City" The War

Chest Board hoped the BMR would encourage charities to adopt three practices: sound philanthropic principles, responsible expenditures, and elimination of duplication and waste—harkening back to organized-charity goals of providing assistance to worthy recipients.[68] These practices were rather generic but couched one of the board's agendas: to lower fundraising expenses. The BMR's "Survey of Charitable Organizations" examined fifty-five social service agencies in Indianapolis. It did not consider other nonprofit fields, such as health, education, the arts, or wartime relief. Over two months, BMR staff toured facilities, read documents, and interviewed charity executives before reporting on the mission, operations, finances, and fundraising methods of each agency. For each charity, the BMR provided a summary of operations, recommendations for improvement, if needed, and commentary on the suitability and amount of War Chest funding.

The War Chest emphasized fundraising expenses with its own mantra: "The War Chest Board will serve the community as a matter of civic duty—without remuneration. . . . Not one cent of your contribution will be used for the expenses of the War Chest Campaign."[69] The BMR report accordingly consolidated the fifty-five agencies' revenues and expenses into one income statement to reveal what the city spent on social services vis-à-vis private donors. It totaled all "costs of services" into a single entry but isolated the cost of fund solicitation. To the relief, and possibly surprise, of the War Chest Board, agencies' engagement of solicitors turned out to be nominal. The BMR credited the Chamber's Relief and Charities Committee for discouraging professional fundraising and presumably assuring this result.[70]

The "Survey of Charitable Organizations" grouped the charities into seven categories: indoor relief, outdoor relief, health promotion, protective, social agency, boarding homes, and missionaries. The taxonomy reflected a shift in charitable reform from reforming individual morality, moving the charity applicant from undeserving to deserving and to improving the urban

environment. New charities had begun to consciously plan urban settings into "moral habitats," a departure from the COS's
first circle of charities.[71] The BMR found Indianapolis to be "no
wiser than other cities in preventing poverty" but noted wryly
that it could reduce relief payments with increased organizational effort.[72] The report's extensive discussion of the outdoor
relief agency group laid bare the overlapping work, inefficiencies,
and redundancies that had developed among the COS and its
subagencies—the very plurality of benevolence that the COS
had hoped to rein in when it formed in 1879. Considering the
COS and IBS as one and the same, the BMR complimented the
COS/IBS poor relief efforts: "The work done for the poor is .
. . of high character. The case work is good; the investigations
are not too formal; the relief is just sufficient and the contact
between the staff and the case humane."[73] Actual poor relief,
however, had never been any COS's raison d'être and revealed a
diminished function from the founding, "To see that all deserving cases of destitution are properly relieved."

The COS's management changes had created disruption, causing
the BMR to recognize that the charity faced "an up-hill fight . . . to
rehabilitate itself in the confidence of the public."[74] But organizations regularly undergo leadership changes that do not lead to the
end of their existence. Internal disarray was far from the COS's
fundamental business problem. The crux of the stagnation and
sense of futility that had crept into the COS was the wide array of
charitable work that had emerged all around as Indianapolis had
grown and diversified. Try as it might, the COS could not assimilate
the plethora of organizations that catered to increasingly narrowly
defined clientele within the circle of charities.

The BMR concluded that the COS had become a charity
clearinghouse, not for all cases of need in the city but "for cases
that no other organization wants to handle."[75] The COS was the
city's "best organized charity," but it had devolved to running
the Confidential Exchange and allowing other societies to "step

in and claim the supervision of this or that case."[76] In the past, the COS had delegated work to the circle of charities. Now, the COS handled intake, but the field of charities delegated to it was now the vestiges of the city's needy population that the rest of the field chose not to assist. Many charities, and the BMR, still touted organized-charity principles, but the very system that the COS had created allowed it to become the charity of last resort, handling only chronic cases of poverty that it once would have deemed unworthy. Commentary on evaluation methodology in the report was Spartan. Narratives on multiple charities emphasized the COS principles of work, self-sufficiency and self-respect, and the power of charitable intervention to transform individuals. The BMR occasionally commented that such results had been obtained by a particular charity, but the report does not reflect how the consultants arrived at that conclusion.

The "Survey of Charitable Organizations" complimented the Jewish Federation more than any other outdoor relief agency, reinforcing organized-charity principles on one hand and specialization on the other. The BMR readily gleaned that the Jewish Federation was a COS in miniature, exclusively operated by and for the Jewish population in the city. The report found that the system had been more successful than the citywide COS: "One cannot avoid seeing that the Jewish Federation cares for its poor in a more adequate and also in a wiser manner than do the other organizations in Indianapolis.... One cannot also help being impressed by the fact that their charities demand higher standards than is the case in other."[77]

The report went on to cite details from the federation's annual report, which were the cornerstones of organized charity. Charity organization societies in general were not under indictment. But the Indianapolis COS, in the BMR's view, was clearly at risk.[78]

William Fortune served as the Welfare Board's first president, making him the leading philanthropic power in Indianapolis.[79] Fortune held several national leadership positions with the Red

Cross and remained president of the Indianapolis branch until his death in 1942. He proposed a new Community Welfare Board to accept charitable gifts and bequests given to the city. An extension of the Chamber's Relief and Charities Committee, the Welfare Board carried on the charity evaluation function. When Fortune died, the *Indianapolis Star* recognized him for having raised "more money for public movements than any other citizen in the history of Indiana." The *Star* also credited him for creating the War Chest Board, the nucleus of what became the Indianapolis Community Fund.[80]

THE COMMUNITY FUND

The BMR reincorporated as the National Institute of Public Administration in 1921. By the early 1920s, urban planning was a profession in its own right. National publications such as Charles Fassett's *Handbook of Municipal Government* (1922) circulated among city managers. Chambers of commerce, therefore, began to appear like those of today, business leagues that advocate and lobby on behalf of their members. Their purview over charity evaluation had peaked, not to return.

Community funds would evolve to assume the evaluation role. Also known as Community Chests, funds stemmed from both World War I War Chests. Cleveland had piloted a community-wide fundraising campaign as an outgrowth of its interest in organized-charity work. Cleveland's chamber created a "federation" to make a coordinated appeal and allow donors to designate their gifts to particular charities. The chamber's board vetted both donors and charities, thereby increasing donations overall and directing funds to causes it deemed most important to the community. By 1918, fourteen cities adopted similar federated fundraising organizations.[81] Communities repurposed the federated concept to peacetime social welfare fundraising, and by the mid-1920s, over three hundred coordinated campaigns were active.[82] The "federation" and "federated giving" terms are still in use today, commonly known as the United Way.

Indianapolis organized its Community Chest later than its peer cities.[83] In 1920 the city created a "federation of agencies— of, by and for the agencies."[84] The Community Chest stated that it "unifies the soul of the community by breaking down selfishness, narrowness, prejudice and bigotry, and in awakening a general broad-minded heart interest in the things that affect the welfare of the city life as a whole."[85] The chest promised to induce cooperation and avoid duplication of effort, almost as though no entity had previously worked toward those aims.

One reason for the Indianapolis Community Chest's durability was its intimate connection to the Chamber of Commerce. For example, the 1920 Chamber of Commerce president, Charles F. Coffin, served as the chest's first campaign director. The chest headquarters, logically, was in the Chamber of Commerce building. This sort of linkage existed around the country. Since many cities' chambers were already acting as charity clearinghouses, or had welfare committees, raising money on a coordinated basis evolved quickly. If a chamber's welfare committee and federated-giving committee were different, the directorships were often interlocking so that the same men were intimately involved in community financing decisions.[86] Even businessmen who may have been reluctant to become involved in charity supervision were attracted to chest principles as they closely paralleled those valued in business, especially efficiency.[87]

In 1922 the Indianapolis Charity Organization Society, once the hub of social welfare fundraising and vetting, permanently ceded its evaluation role. The Chamber of Commerce had assumed the role of governing the charitable agenda in Indianapolis, signaling the shift from philanthropic self-regulation to external, businesslike evaluation. The evaluation function, tethered to fund allocation, evolved yet again as the Community Chest (later the Community Fund) gained traction.

Indiana citizens still debate questions of who qualifies to receive social service assistance and whether government or philanthropy are best equipped to aid the poor. The criteria we apply to determine a charity's worthiness or effectiveness will evolve into the future. Donors today often turn to independent evaluators for information on which they can rely. Regardless of form, trust, legitimacy, and evaluation have been and forever will be intertwined in philanthropy.

NOTES

1. Indianapolis COS records repeatedly claimed it was the fifth COS in the country. Indianapolis, New York City, Brooklyn, Philadelphia, and Cincinnati formed their COSs nearly simultaneously after the Buffalo COS was founded in 1877. Edward T. Devine, *The Principles of Relief* (New York: Macmillan Company, 1910), 343.

2. 1893 Annual Report, box 4, folder 7, The Family Service Association of Indianapolis records, 1879–1971, collection #M0102, Indiana Historical Society (hereafter: FSA records).

3. William Fortune (1863–1942) served in many business and philanthropic capacities in Indianapolis. After his brief career in journalism, he was president of several telephone companies, including the Indianapolis Telephone Company, president of Interstate Life Assurance Company, and director of Eli Lilly and Company. He founded and directed Indianapolis's Red Cross chapter and supervised its WWI war-relief fundraising campaign. He served as a COS member and belonged to the Indiana Press Club, Century Club, Country Club, Columbia Club, Contemporary Club, Woodstock, and the University Club. Paul Donald Brown, ed., *Indianapolis Men of Affairs 1923: A Volume in Which Appears a Compilation of Portraits and Biographies of Men of Achievement of the Great Indiana Capital* (Indianapolis: American Biographical Society, 1923), 207; Commercial Club of Indianapolis, "Reports of Officers, Sixteenth Year, 1906," Indianapolis Chamber of Commerce records, 1890–1959, collection #M0422, Indiana Historical Society (hereafter: Chamber records); "City Mourns William Fortune, Welfare and Civic Leader," *Indianapolis News*, January 29, 1942; "William Fortune, Veteran Red Cross Chairman, Dies," *Indianapolis Star*, January 29, 1942, ISL clipping file: biography.

4. E. J. Kahn Jr., *All in a Century: The First 100 Years of Eli Lilly and Company* (Indianapolis: Eli Lilly & Co., 1976), 28.

5. Commercial Club of Indianapolis, "Annual Report Fiscal Year Ending January 31, 1891," Chamber records.

6. The Commercial Club's public welfare activities were characteristic of urban leadership at the turn of the century.

7. George Geib and Miriam Geib, *Indianapolis First: A Commemorative History of the Indianapolis Chamber of Commerce and the Local Business Community* (Indianapolis: Indianapolis Chamber of Commerce, 1990), 21–37.

8. Otto N. Frenzel, Jr., *The City and the Bank, 1865–1965: The Story of Merchants National Bank & Trust Company of Indianapolis* (Indianapolis: Merchants National Bank & Trust Co., 1965), 46; Robert H. Wiebe, *The Search for Order, 1870–1920* (New York: Hill and Wang, 1967), 91.

9. Between 1872 and 1900, the two economic panics reduced Indianapolis-based banks from sixteen to three, leaving Fletchers', Indiana National, and Merchants National banks. Jacob Piatt Dunn, *Greater Indianapolis: The History, the Industries, the Institutions, and the People of a City of Homes*, vol. 1 (Chicago: Lewis Publishing Co., 1910), 351.

10. Frenzel, *The City and the Bank*, 46.

11. Clifton J. Phillips, *Indiana in Transition: The Emergence of an Industrial Commonwealth, 1880–1920* (Indianapolis: Indiana Historical Bureau and Indiana Historical Society, 1968), 38. Hoosiers referred to this panic as "the great depression," until the much more severe economic crisis of the 1930s.

12. Finance committee members who were also CRC members included John H. Holliday as chairman, C. C. Foster as secretary, and members Louis Hollweg, V. K. Hendricks, Frederick Fahnley, Thomas C. Day. Commercial Club of Indianapolis, *Relief for the Unemployed in Indianapolis: Report of the Commercial Club Relief Committee and its Auxiliary the Citizens' Finance Committee, 1893–1894* (Indianapolis: Carlon & Hollenbeck, 1894), 50; "Work of Home Charities," November 1889, BV 1170, FSA records.

13. Commercial Club, *Relief for the Unemployed in Indianapolis*, 3.

14. Commercial Club, "Annual Report Fiscal Year ending January 31, 1894," 9, Chamber records; Commercial Club, *Relief for the Unemployed in Indianapolis*, 10.

15. "Suffering in Our Midst," *Indianapolis Sun*, October 31, 1893, 1.

16. Commercial Club, *Relief for the Unemployed in Indianapolis*, 5.

17. "For the Poor," *Indianapolis Sun*, December 29, 1893, 1.

18. Charles Latham Jr., *William Fortune (1863–1942): A Hoosier Biography* (Indianapolis: Guild Press of Indiana, 1994), 59; Commercial Club, *Relief for the Unemployed in Indianapolis*, 4–40.

19. Treasurers Report and Contributors in Commercial Club, *Relief for the Unemployed in Indianapolis*, 51–64. Kingan & Co. made the single largest donation. COS annual revenues in subscription books, BV 1172, FSA records.

20. Commercial Club, *Relief for the Unemployed in Indianapolis*, 38.

21. Typical oversight was Indiana's Board of State Charities (1889), which supervised all of Indiana's public charitable and correctional facilities. Amos W. Butler, *A Century of Progress: A Study of the Development of Public Charities and Correction 1790–1915* (Indianapolis: Indiana State Board of Charities, 1916), 19.

22. Frank Dekker Watson, *The Charity Organization Movement in the United States: A Study in American Philanthropy* (New York: Macmillan Company, 1922), 249.

23. Ibid., 263.

24. Geib, *Indianapolis First*, 25.

25. Commercial Club, "Annual Report Fiscal Year ending January 31, 1894," 12, Chamber records.

26. Edward T. Devine, *The Principles of Relief* (New York: Macmillan Company, 1910), 413, 432. Indianapolis is mentioned favorably in Carlos C. Clossen, "The Unemployed in American Cities," *Quarterly Journal of Economics* 8, no. 4 (July 1894): 453–77.

27. Readers today recognize the mission of the American Red Cross in that statement. The Indianapolis Red Cross would not exist for another nine years, so in 1907 the COS managed the unemployment crisis on its own. Charity Organization Society of Indianapolis, *A Partial Report of Four Months' Work of the Unemployed by the Charity Organization Society of Indianapolis: December 1st, 1907 to April 1st, 1908* (Indianapolis: Hollenbeck, 1908), 1.

28. Mary Lewis Nash, "Recent Tendencies in Charity Organization Society Work" (Master's thesis, Indiana University, 1913), 23.

29. 1908 Annual Report, box 5, folder 1, FSA records.

30. Ibid.

31. Ernest P. Bicknell, "Benefits of Organized Charities to Business Men," *Indiana Bulletin: Proceedings of the Annual State Conference of Charities and Correction* (October 1901): 93; Franklin MacVeagh, "A Business Man's View of Organized Charity," *Indiana Bulletin: Proceedings of the Annual State Conference of Charities and Correction* (June 1903): 87, 89.

32. W. C. Ball, "Progress in Indiana in Organizing Charity," *Indiana Bulletin: Proceedings of the Annual State Conference of Charities and Correction* (June 1903): 123; Charles Meredith Hubbard, "Relation of Charity-Organization Societies to Relief Societies and Relief-Giving," *American Journal of Sociology* 6, no. 6 (May 1901): 789.

33. The author counted the COS and its programs as one charity although each are listed separately in the Seeley study. John R. Seeley, Buford H. Junker, R. Wallace Jones, Jr., N. C. Jenkins, M. T. Haugh, and I. Miller, *Community Chest: A Case Study in Philanthropy* (Toronto: University of Toronto Press, 1957), 102–3.

34. "Know Your City Better," *Indianapolis Star*, December 21, 1909, 8.

35. Kenneth Sturges, *American Chambers of Commerce* (New York: Moffat, Yard and Co., 1915), 215; and analysis of *American City* magazine for city planners and chamber executives, 1913 to 1930.

36. William C. Ewing, "The Town Meeting Idea and the Modern Chamber of Commerce," *American City*, August 1926, 129–30.

37. Miller was an executive with Connecticut Mutual Life Insurance Company. Winfield Miller, "The General Welfare," *Forward! The Magazine for Indianapolis* 2, no. 2 (March 1910): 47.

38. 1910 Annual Report, box 2, folder 3, Chamber records. The Cleveland Chamber of Commerce formed a Committee on Benevolent Associations to investigate fraudulent charities and complaints from established ones about their fundraising challenges. Peter Dobkin Hall, "The Community Foundation in America, 1914–1987," in *Philanthropic Giving: Studies in Varieties and Goals*, ed. Richard Magat (New York: Oxford University Press, 1989), 185–86.

39. Thomas C. Day, "The Cloak of Charity," *Forward! The Magazine for Indianapolis* 1, no. 1 (December 1909): 19–21.

40. Records do not indicate committee members' rationale for endorsement. Sample "Application for Endorsement, Commercial Club of Indianapolis Committee on Benevolent Associations," included in box 1, folder 8, FSA records.

41. 1911 Annual Report, box 2, folder 4, Chamber records.

42. Ibid.

43. The Commercial Club merged with these smaller associations: Adscript Club, Freight Bureau, Indianapolis Trade Association, Manufacturers Association, and Merchants Association. Geib and Geib, *Indianapolis First*, 29.

44. Ruth Hutchinson Crocker, "Making Charity Modern: Business and the Reform of Charities in Indianapolis, 1879–1930," *Business and Economic History*, 2nd series, 12 (1984): 165.

45. Morrell Heald, *The Social Responsibilities of Business: Company and Community, 1900–1960* (New Brunswick, NJ: Transaction Books, 1988), 19.

46. Watson, *The Charity Organization Movement*, 421.

47. Warren G. Bailey, "The Social Agencies of Indianapolis; A Study of Benevolent Social Agencies in Urban Life" (Master's thesis, Indiana University, 1917), 85.

48. 1911 Annual Report, box 2, folder 4, Chamber records.

49. Ibid.

50. Report of James F. Jackson, February 4, 1915, COS miscellaneous reports, ISL Pamphlet Collection.

51. Charles Grout did not expect that the April 8, 1916, board meeting would be his last. In May 1916, Indianapolis, for the second time, hosted the National Conference of Charities and Correction (NCCC) annual conference, the year in which Indianapolis's Monsignor Francis Gavisk served as NCCC president. Exactly one week later, COS general secretary Charles Grout resigned after twenty-three years in the position. Records do not reflect the specific circumstances of Grout's departure. General Secretary's Report, April 8, 1916, BV 1170, FSA records.

52. Subcommittee meeting minutes 1916, box 6, folder 141, Chamber records.

53. Boyer, *Urban Masses and Moral Order in America*, 252–57; Kathleen D. McCarthy, *Noblesse Oblige: Charity & Cultural Philanthropy in Chicago, 1849–1929* (Chicago: University of Chicago Press, 1982), ix–xiii.

54. Latham, *William Fortune*, 120. Prominent men comprised the War Chest Board: William Fortune, L. C. Huesmann, Stoughton A. Fletcher, Myron R. Green, J. K. Lilly, W. J. Mooney, Charles B. Sommers, Edgar A. Perkins, Charles W. Jewett, Frank D. Stalnaker, Aquilla Jones, and James W. Lilly. James W. Lilly also chaired the Chamber's Relief and Charities Committee. Subcommittee meeting minutes, box 6, folder 140, Chamber records; War Chest Board letterhead in COS minutes 1916–1920, BV 1171, FSA records.

55. Individuals were allowed tax deductions for charitable contributions in the war years, but corporations did not gain this permanent tax advantage until 1935. Seeley, *Community Chest*, 20, 89.

56. Scott M. Cutlip, *Fund Raising in the United States: Its Role in American Philanthropy* (New Brunswick, NJ: Rutgers University Press, 1965), 118–19.

57. Latham, *William Fortune*, 120–21.

58. In comparison, the COS's total earnings in 1917 were $22,844 and the largest individual gift was $500 (from Louis Hollweg). Partial Display

of Development (COS), box 1, folder 5; 1915 Annual Report, BV 1188; FSA records. Indiana's 1920 population of 2.9 million made it the eleventh largest state. The State of Indiana raised $4.7 million for the first and second war drives combined. The ten largest states raised more money, in direct proportion to state population: New York, Pennsylvania, Massachusetts, Connecticut, New Jersey, Illinois, Ohio, Missouri, Texas, and California. Cutlip, *Fund Raising in the United States*, 134–35.

59. Seeley, *Community Chest*, 89; US Census Bureau, www.census.gov.

60. 1910 Annual Report, box 2, folder 3, Chamber records.

61. Investigative journalism, especially Lincoln Steffens's *The Shame of the Cities* (1904), heightened the public's awareness of municipal government corruption, such as the fraud and abuse by Tammany Hall, which plagued New York City. Bruce D. McDonald, "The Bureau of Municipal Research and the Development of a Professional Public Service," *Administration & Society* 42, no. 7 (November 2010): 817–18.

62. John D. Buenker, *Urban Liberalism and Progressive Reform* (New York: Charles Scribner's Sons, 1973), chapter 2, 48–80; L. A. Halbert, "Boards of Public Welfare and Good City Government," *American City*, September 1913, 219–21; Robert H. Wiebe, *The Search for Order 1870–1920* (New York: Hill and Wang, 1967), chapter 7, 164–96.

63. Camilla Stivers, *Bureau Men, Settlement Women: Constructing Public Administration in the Progressive Era* (Lawrence: University Press of Kansas, 2000), 88.

64. Camilla Stivers, "Settlement Women and Bureau Men: Constructing a Usable Past for Public Administration," *Public Administration Review* 55, no. 6 (November–December 1995): 523.

65. The best-known studies, *Hull House Maps and Papers* (1895) and the *Pittsburgh Survey* (1907–1908), are considered landmarks of Progressive era sociological reform.

66. Such work is well-documented in LeRoy Ashby, *Saving the Waifs: Reformers and Dependent Children, 1890–1917* (Philadelphia: Temple University Press, 1984); Mary Ritter Beard, *Woman's Work in Municipalities* (New York: D. Appleton and Company, 1915); Linda Gordon, *Pitied but Not Entitled: Single Mothers and the History of Welfare, 1890–1935* (New York: Free Press, 1994); Michael B. Katz, *In the Shadow of the Poorhouse: A Social History of Welfare in America*, rev. ed. (New York: Basic Books, 1996); Robyn Muncy, *Creating a Female Dominion in American Reform 1890–1935* (New York: Oxford University Press, 1991); Theda Skocpol, *Protecting Mothers and Soldiers: The Political Origins of Social Policy in the United*

States (Cambridge, MA: Belknap Press of Harvard University Press, 1992); Susan Tiffin, *In Whose Best Interest?: Child Welfare Reform in the Progressive Era* (Westport, CT: Greenwood, 1982).

67. Barry Karl, *Executive Reorganization and Reform in the New Deal: The Genesis of Administrative Management, 1900–1939* (Cambridge, MA: Harvard University Press, 1963), 146; Stivers, *Bureau Men, Settlement Women*, 79.

68. Seeley, *Community Chest*, 90.

69. "How Can You Give to All the Worthy Appeals?," *Indianapolis Star*, May 20, 1918, 9.

70. Bureau of Municipal Research, *Report on a Survey of Charitable Organizations*, 3–4, 46.

71. Boyer, *Urban Masses and Moral Order in America*, 158–63, 179–87.

72. Bureau of Municipal Research (BMR), *Report on a Survey of Charitable Organizations*, 19.

73. Ibid., 128.

74. Ibid.

75. Ibid., 13.

76. Ibid., 129.

77. Ibid., 165–66.

78. In 1919, the COS fully subsumed the Indianapolis Benevolent Society (IBS) by integrating management and bookkeeping. As the BMR had observed, the COS and IBS had functioned essentially as one organization for many years, so this formal combination attracted little notice. Annual Meeting Report of General Secretary, November 20, 1919, BV 1192, FSA records.

79. Community Welfare Board became the Board of Public Welfare. Milton Gaither, "The Rise and Fall of a Pedagogical Empire: The Board of State Charities and the Indiana Philosophy of Giving," *Indiana Magazine of History* 96, no. 4 (December 2000): 343; Geib, *Indianapolis First*, 35; Latham, *William Fortune*, 122.

80. "William Fortune, Veteran Red Cross Chairman, Dies," *Indianapolis Star*, January 29, 1942, ISL clipping file: biography.

81. Eleanor L. Brilliant, *The United Way: Dilemmas of Organized Charity* (New York: Columbia University Press, 1990), 21; Hall, "The Community Foundation in America," 186; Heald, *The Social Responsibilities of Business*, 25; Watson, *The Charity Organization Movement*, 433.

82. Brilliant, *The United Way*, 23.

83. Brilliant, *The United Way*, 23; Watson, *The Charity Organization Movement*, 434.

84. Seeley, *Community Chest*, 90.

85. 1920 –1921 Community Chest pamphlet, COS miscellaneous reports, ISL Pamphlet Collection.

86. Heald, *The Social Responsibilities of Business*, 121; "The St. Paul Community Chest," *Survey* (August 16, 1920): 635; Seeley, *Community Chest*, 92.

87. Cutlip, *Fund Raising in the United States*, 73; "The St. Paul Community Chest," *Survey*, 635.

SOCIAL INNOVATION IN THE HEARTLAND

PETER WEBER AND CHEN JI

THE MISMATCH BETWEEN SCALE OF societal problems and the limits of both philanthropic and governmental resources has traditionally spurred philanthropic innovations. While the strategic use of philanthropic resources dates to at least the Progressive Era's scientific philanthropists, the trend accelerated in recent years. Social entrepreneurs created new legal structures as part of a search for financial sustainability and new models for social service delivery, while traditional grant makers experimented with investments that could maximize total value and total returns on investment.[1] Combining social and commercial goals blurred traditional boundaries between the public, private, and nonprofit sectors, thus sharing social responsibility across sectors and creating new spaces for innovation.[2]

The Indianapolis Foundation (IF) offers an example of a community foundation that leveraged societal forces to multiply the impact of its philanthropic funds. Founded in 1916, the IF is the state's oldest and largest community foundation. Strategically embedded in the Hoosier state's philanthropic network and host to multiple influential family philanthropies, the IF attracts both public and private resources to deliver social impact. In line with an approach typical of community foundations in this early period, bankers developed the IF and supported research endeavors aiming to identify community needs.[3] Playing—at different times—the role of philanthropic driver, partner, and catalyst, the IF developed innovative philanthropic approaches focused on supporting organizations and collaborative approaches seeking comprehensive solutions to cross-sectorial problems by playing a coordinating rather than grant-making role.[4]

This chapter analyzes two cases. First, the case of the foundation's decision to purchase a building and lease it to the Indianapolis Senior Citizen's Center for the nominal cost of $1 per year. This fits a pattern of real estate properties being held for charitable purposes and appearing on the IF's financial statements in the late 1950s. This historical case study exemplifies how a strategy, which would later be classified as program-related investments (PRIs), initially represented a financially safe approach to grant making rather than being part of a search for increased impact. Second, the chapter details the collaborative approach taken by the successor to the IF, the Central Indiana Community Foundation (CICF), when developing the Indianapolis Cultural Trail in the 2000s.[5] This section describes the civic leadership role of a community foundation. In the process of developing the Cultural Trail, the CICF served as aggregator, connecting and mobilizing philanthropists, private investors, and public agencies to address a complex task, namely the revitalization of downtown Indianapolis. Overall, this chapter details the dynamics, processes, and choices that lead philanthropic institutions to experiment with new philanthropic practices, tools, and approaches.

INNOVATION THROUGH INVESTMENT: ASSETS HELD FOR CHARITABLE PURPOSES

Starting in the late 1960s, program-related investments gained traction as a strategic way for foundations to support nonprofit organizations. The 1969 Tax Reform Act regulated the activities of philanthropic foundations in part out of concerns that holding a controlling interest in a business could lead to mission drift. At the same time, regulators created exceptions, including allowing foundations to make PRIs, which resemble grants and count toward the annual distribution requirements by meeting specific charitable goals.[6] PRIs typically take the form of loans and equity investments but may also include purchasing and maintaining property for charitable purposes. In so doing, they offer foundations a tool to maintain (if not increase) the level of assets available for grant-making activities that meet annual distribution requirements. While the use of PRIs has grown since the 1990s (peaking in 2004), the total number and dollar amount and the number of providers and recipients has declined since 2007.[7] Arguably, the limited use of PRIs—in spite of short-lived momentum in the 1990s—relates to foundations' lack in flexibility in making investments and the risk of the Internal Revenue Service (IRS) challenging the charitable purpose of the investments.

The IF began making regular investments in real estate with a charitable purpose in the late 1950s. While these activities blur the lines between investments and grant making, they also aimed to preserve and increase the value of IF assets. From 1959 to 1961, the IF held four properties with a stated charitable purpose (see tab. 1).

"Real estate held for charitable purposes" appears for the first time on the Form 990 for the calendar year 1959 under the line "Other assets."[8] Several of the properties listed in table 1 appear, however, in earlier financial statements as real estate purchased from the income of various trusts administered by the foundation.[9] These properties include the Emmerich Manual Training High School Delavan Smith Athletic Field and approximately 78.5 acres leased to the Boy Scout Farm (a third property of approximately 15.4 acres was sold in 1952), which were purchased out of income from the trust funds of two of the first donors to the IF, Delavan Smith and James E. Lilly.[10]

Real estate investments before 1959 are difficult to assess because of the erratic nature of the foundation's early grant-making

Table 1. Real estate held for charitable purposes by Indianapolis
Foundation (1959–1961)

Calendar Year	Leasing Agency
1959	Emmerich Manual Training High School, Totairn, Inc., Boy Scout Farm, and School of Practical Nursing property
1960	Emmerich Manual Training High School, Children's Bureau Foster Home, Boy Scout Farm, and School of Practical Nursing property
1961	Emmerich Manual Training High School, Children's Bureau Foster Home, Boy Scout Farm, and School of Practical Nursing property

Source: IF Financial Statements (1959–1961), in minutes, Board of Trustees, Indianapolis Foundation records, boxes 10 and 11, folders 1–7 and 1–4.

activities and reporting standards. It is unclear if purchasing was a strategy at all or simply several decisions made for specific donors or charitable institutions. In fact, in the 1920s, trustees rejected proposals from various agencies requesting the IF to build facilities and purchase property. In 1924 the board explicitly stated that "it was not the policy of the Foundation to purchase or own property."[11] Nonetheless, personal networks, interests, and publicity quickly trumped this clearly defined scope for the IF.[12] The IF presented the Delavan Smith Athletic Field, which in later financial records is listed as one of the highest valued properties with a charitable purpose, to the Emmerich Manual Training High School only four years later. Rather than exemplifying a new approach, the athletic field simply served as a memorial to Delavan Smith, whose trust was finally available to the foundation after multiple years of litigation.[13] Disentangling the rationale behind these investments is therefore complicated both because of a lack of documentation and the inconsistency of the foundation.

The available documents on the cases listed in table 1 suggest, however, the emerging of distinctive characteristics in the late 1950s and early 1960s. In 1958, the IF agreed to purchase a property to be leased for a nominal sum to the Totairn, Inc., a residential facility for the treatment of "women alcoholics," conditional to the organization's ability to provide satisfactory services.[14] When during the lease's first year, Jack Killen (executive director of the IF) expressed reservations about Totairn's financial sustainability, the board decided to continue the agreement only on a short-term basis and subject to review.[15] By the end of the year, these concerns led to the decision to end the agreement with Totairn and lease the same property to a different agency, the Children's Bureau of Indianapolis' Orphan Asylum.[16] In the same period, the Indianapolis School for Practical Nursing approached the IF with the suggestion to purchase a building able to accommodate the needs of the school, as the Indianapolis Public Schools lacked the funds for a new building.[17] The Board of Trustees authorized the purchase of a property on the condition that funds for remodeling the building come from other sources,[18] but they eventually agreed to cover these costs as well.[19] Interestingly, while the potential grantee approached the foundation with the suggestion to purchase a building, the IF attempted to leverage additional community support through this approach.

The best-documented investment in real estate with a charitable purpose by the IF is the one involving the Indianapolis Senior Citizen's Center (ISCC) in 1961. The available archival sources allow us to place this case within a broader approach to grant making, rather than categorize it into the separate and narrower notion of investment. At this time, a national survey of fifty-nine of the one hundred community foundations reporting active capital in 1959 showed that 38.5 percent of the total amount of grant money was distributed for capital needs, which typically included buildings and equipment.[20] At this point, community foundations were administering real estate trusts nationwide, and the IF had done so since the late 1920s, as Delavan Smith's bequest included real estate.[21] These cases thus blur today's distinction between grant making and investment. In fact, community foundations held the title of properties for the use of specific agencies because the original owners were often unwilling to donate the property unless assured that the lease could be canceled when the leasing agency did not need it anymore.[22] The case of the ISCC, discussed in detail in the following pages, therefore shows that investing in real estate should not be interpreted from the perspective of PRIs but rather as having emerged out of a broader understanding of grant-making activities, which included the buying, furnishing, and leasing of property.

The relationship between the IF and ISCC started before the founding of the latter. The establishment of the ISCC was the outcome of a multiyear study conducted by the Health and Welfare Council of Indianapolis and Marion County, Inc., which proposed the establishment of a downtown center for senior citizens.[23] The IF, in cooperation with Lilly Endowment Inc., helped establish and finance the research department of the Health and Welfare Council. From 1954 to 1956, the IF appropriated $22,500. In 1957 it granted an additional $12,500 as a sign of the IF Board of Trustees' confidence in the council, whose reports soon became a valuable source of information by helping to "make more intelligent decisions regarding expenditure of philanthropic funds."[24] The long-term relationship between the council and the IF made the latter an obvious contact partner for the ISCC.

Aware of the connections between the IF and the Health and Welfare Council, Allan H. Warne, president of the board of directors of the ISCC, contacted the IF requesting a grant of $86,600. The request included annual operating costs of $68,000 and an additional $18,600 for furnishings and program equipment.[25] In his letter, Warne pointed out that the total costs would "depend upon the Center site, the size, rental arrangements and the extent of equipment donated by community groups" and explicitly expressed an intent to complement support from public actors, including the City of Indianapolis and the AFL-CIO Central Labor Council of Marion County with support from private philanthropy.[26] The lack of response from the IF led the ISCC to submit a revised budget three months later. Reduced to $35,000 per year (over a three-year period), the budget would cover personnel costs, educational supplies, and contingencies.[27]

The new budget caught the interest of the IF Board of Trustees. The board discussed the request and concluded it would consider a grant covering 50 percent of annual costs for a three-year period on the condition that the "Center develops a workable, well planned program and budget."[28] While the IF was positively disposed toward the ISCC, it was concerned with the lack of a "suitable location" for the center, which made the development of a "realistic budget" problematic.[29] Worried about the ISCC's overall financial sustainability, the IF board also noted, "Thus far only [t]he Foundation has been approached for support" and wondered about "assum[ing] a substantial portion of the cost."[30] The minutes of the IF board meeting show the board, while interested in the ISCC, concerned with the organization's lack of other funding sources, in spite of the center's stated emphasis on attracting support from public agencies.

Subsequent interactions between Warne and Killen show how the IF decision to purchase a property to be leased to the ISCC evolved from a typical relationship with a potential grantee. In a letter to Wayne, Killen reported the decision of the IF Board of Trustees and argued that while the grant had not yet been authorized, the ISCC "may be in a better position to negotiate for other financing with this information," thus suggesting that Warne use the possible relationship with the IF to leverage additional resources.[31] Rather than follow Killen's suggestion, Warne provided additional information on the ISCC's progress in hiring an executive director, securing a location,[32] and further reducing the budget to keep it within $60,000—the limit set by the IF.[33] The ISCC attempted to win the grant by reducing the budget and showing how the reduction could be covered by the amount the foundation was willing to appropriate, no longer requiring additional funding sources. The breakthrough, however, occurred when Warne addressed an early concern of the IF by announcing that ISCC had found a suitable location: a three-story building owned by Local Union 1150 of the United Steel Workers. Warne suggested the foundation could further reduce the ISCC's budget by purchasing the building and leasing it for a nominal sum.[34] Perhaps sensing a breakthrough, Warne followed up, thirteen days later, sending Killen an appraisal of the building.[35]

The IF Board of Trustees discussed the new approach at its September 27, 1961, meeting. During that meeting, the board expressed its inclination to move forward with the ISCC and voiced its appreciation for the careful and conservative planning: "The group is measuring its steps carefully and merits confidence that they will select suitable personnel and carry out a workable, beneficial program in this area of need."[36] Nonetheless, while considering the purchase of the building, it still did not commit funds explaining, "In the event that the need for such a facility for senior citizens is not proven or later terminates, the Foundation will be protected."[37] Delays in funding forced the ISCC to request an extension of its purchasing option on the building.[38] Warne hoped to pressure the IF by immediately informing Killen of his correspondence with the United Steel Workers of America, relating the status of the option on the East New York Street property to no avail.[39] The cautionary approach was typical of the IF, which favored supporting "safe projects," both from a financial and public relations viewpoint.[40]

Two months later, on March 13, 1962, IF trustees decided to purchase the building for the ISCC. The turning point appeared to have occurred during a meeting—the day before—between Warne and Killen. During that meeting, Killen informed Warne that the ISCC secured a $50,000 grant from Lilly Endowment Inc., including $20,000 in unrestricted funds for the first year of operations and an additional $30,000 to be equally split between the second and third year of operations.[41] In addition to funds from Lilly Endowment Inc., the ISCC also received a pledge of $10,000 from the Steel Workers and United Auto Workers (UAW) for initial operations.[42] During the meeting of IF trustees on March 13, 1962, the ISCC's request was reviewed, and the trustees recommended to purchase the building because the center had provided "tangible evidence of its ability to start a program for senior citizens and has arranged for financing and management."[43] IF trustees also encouraged officers to consider a grant of $8,000 to the ISCC for the purchase of equipment.[44]

Retrospectively, Kenneth Chapman (IF executive director in the 1980s) identified the ISCC as a turning point for the foundation's PRI initiative. In an 1988 interview, Chapman viewed this case as epitomizing the positive characteristics commonly attributed to PRIs in that it allowed for preserving resources and reusing properties for other purposes once the original "need for which the real estate was purchased ceases to exist."[45] The case of the ISCC, however, seems in line with earlier investments in real estate rather than marking the emergence of a clear distinctive strategy, as the foundation supported local agencies in educational, health, and rehabilitative services through investments in real estate over this entire period.[46] Later cases do not differ in substance from those that preceded the ISCC example. For instance, in 1966, the IF Board of Trustees granted $5,000 to the Flynn Christian Fellowship Houses, Inc., of Indiana, an organization addressing homelessness and substance abuse, for the purchase of a building on 2042 North Alabama Street.[47] In 1968, the IF supported the Alpha Home—both a residential and comprehensive care facility for elderly citizens with marginal incomes—with a grant of $35,000 for the purchase of land and a $1,500 appropriation for the purchase of a property on 1920 North Senate Avenue in 1973.[48] In 1974, the board approved a new grant of $125,000 to support the purchase, remodeling, and furnishing of an office building located at 1405 Broad Ripple Avenue for use by the Indianapolis Speech and Hearing Center, Inc.[49]

While the records of the Indianapolis Foundation provide only limited details on these cases, a common pattern emerged: the IF purchased a building with the intention to lease it for a nominal sum to a specific agency. These agencies suggested the strategy as either an alternative or complement to a regular grant. In fact, the School for Practical Nursing, the ISCC, and the Indianapolis Speech and Hearing Center to the Indianapolis Foundation suggested this approach to the IF because they were unable to "afford to buy or shoulder the increase in rent and maintenance."[50] Interestingly, as IF executive director, Jack Killen was involved in all of the interactions resulting in investments in real estate for charitable purposes but never—at least in the available documents—suggested this approach to nonprofit organizations. Instead the grantee proposed this approach. This peculiar aspect also explains a second characteristic of these investments: The IF purchased a property with the intention to lease it to a specific organization. Only in the case of Totairn was the property leased to an organization other than the one for which it had been originally intended. The purchasing and leasing of property is therefore not yet clearly distinguished from regular grant making. Indeed, a guide to the organization, development, and operation of community foundations prepared by the National Council on Community Foundations and published in 1961 used the case of the ISCC to exemplify a typology of grants by community foundations aiming to meet the capital needs of local organizations.[51] Lastly, the IF typically sought to leverage additional resources by making the investment conditional to the organizations' abilities to secure funds from others to cover additional budgetary needs. In fact, the IF openly expressed reservations on the financial sustainability of almost all the organizations discussed here but eventually decided to support their capital needs, hoping that it would help organizations fulfilling a crucial role in the community to provide needed services.[52]

The IF decision to purchase the 61.9-acre Baker Farm in Putnam County in 1979 may suggest the beginning of a more mature phase in the foundation's PRI initiatives. The IF Board of Trustees approved a grant of $13,300 to improve and winterize the observatory at Baker Farm and lease it to the Indianapolis Public Schools for $1 per year after receiving a request from Dr. Magdalene A. Davis, director of Indianapolis Public Schools Education Center.[53] This case differed from previous PRIs because the IF did not purchase the land for this specific purpose. Rather, the IF responded to a need in the community by devoting a piece of real estate it already acquired to a charitable purpose. This case may indicate the emergence of a long-term investment plan in real estate that, if needed, could be used for charitable purposes, but the examples of this are sparse in the historical record.

The beginning of the Indianapolis Foundation's program-related investments thus diverges from traditional explanations of a philanthropic foundation's decision to use PRIs. IF investments in real estate held for charitable purposes predate similar initiatives by the Ford Foundation and the Taconic Foundation, which are commonly considered pioneers in the use of PRIs.[54] The IF's PRI initiative was not part of a conscious, strategic process but rather the outcome of a long process in which the purchasing and leasing of property was a financially safe alternative to regular grant making. The foundation recognized the financial benefits and starting in 1959 made an explicit link between the administration of real estate and its charitable purposes. Before the 1969 Tax Reform Act, the IF tried to apply for a partial tax exemption for its real estate investments by arguing the ownership of the property was "for a charitable purpose within the broad definitions of the word charity used in the Indiana cases."[55] By the late 1960s, therefore, the foundation seemed keenly aware of the potential tax benefits of investing in real estate with a charitable purpose. This case therefore contrasts typical explanations describing the emergence of PRIs as part of a conscious decision-making process driven by either external and societal factors or internal considerations.[56]

In addition to seeking new tools to support organizations, foundations engaged in cross- and multisector partnerships to better address issues affecting society. This approach is rooted in the realization that organizations are disconnected and in competition and "lack the capacity or will to act in coordination to solve multifaceted problems."[57] Rather than adopting a primarily grant-making role, foundations can play a coordinating role by leveraging resources from a variety of actors across sectorial divides for collective impact.[58] Public-private partnerships in particular received recent prominence with the Obama administration emphasizing collaborations with philanthropic foundations and the recession making partnerships more appealing in a time of scarce resources.[59]

Construction of the Indianapolis Cultural Trail: A Legacy of Gene & Marilyn Glick provides a Hoosier example of a public-private partnership aiming to revitalize downtown Indianapolis. The CICF, with Brian Payne as executive director, led the development of the Cultural Trail. This example shows how highly collaborative, cross-sector partnerships fit into the broader historical momentum of Indianapolis. The city's conscious efforts to use culture and arts to revitalize downtown provided a supportive context for Payne's project. Likewise, the Hoosier tradition of public-private partnership helped to find a measured balance between the many trades-offs of collaborative partnerships.

The Indianapolis Cultural Trail is a $63 million, eight-mile, urban pedestrian and bicycle trail project in downtown Indianapolis featuring over $4 million's worth of public art. Financed through a public-private partnership between the City of Indianapolis and the CICF, the trail aimed to connect Indianapolis's six cultural districts, enhance the city's art community, and revitalize the downtown area. While constructions started in 2007 and ended 2012, the trail was part of a long-term strategy of economic development for downtown Indianapolis, involving multiple actors across the political, corporate, and philanthropic spectrum.

Development of the Indianapolis Cultural Trail was embedded in the Hoosier tradition of collaborative approaches to economic development. Cross-sectorial partnerships were stimulated by Republican mayor Richard Lugar's 1970 decision to merge Indianapolis and Marion County, (the UniGov), with the goal of improving the city's image and rebuilding its downtown in the face of suburban growth.[60] In the words of former Indianapolis mayor William H. Hudnut, III, the merger created "a larger sense of 'family' and enabled business and civic leaders who resided in the suburbs to become more active in civic affairs."[61] In this new context, the region's elites worked with the Department of Metropolitan Development through the Greater Indianapolis Progress Committee (GIPC), a nonprofit organization bringing together representatives from all sectors to address challenges and opportunities for Indianapolis.[62]

With the help of strong mayors, both corporate and philanthropic leaders successfully transformed the face of Indianapolis. Following a conversation in 1972 between Mayor Lugar and Eli Lilly, Lilly Endowment Inc. (LEI) became heavily involved in the development of Indianapolis.[63] LEI supported GIPC through Juan Solomon, an executive of the Eli Lilly Company who was tasked with coordinating assistance to GIPC from both Eli Lilly and Co. and the endowment.[64] At the same time, with support from James Morris, a former aide to Mayor Lugar and a vice president of LEI, it contributed to the development in the late-1970s of the City Committee, a loose network of young professionals from business, law, and government that successfully transformed Indianapolis into the amateur sports capital of the country.[65] This broad-based cooperation across the business, philanthropic, and public sectors became a characterizing feature of the collective approach to issues relating to the progress of the city of Indianapolis, which was soon recognized nationally.[66]

The strategy to combine forces for shared interests proved highly successful. Of the more than fifty major development projects for the downtown area initiated between 1974 and 1999, seven related to building a sports identity for Indianapolis.[67] By the late 1980s, Indianapolis had hosted the World Indoor Track and Field Championships and the Pan American Games, and multiple national and international organizations moved their headquarters there. Later, in 1999, the National Collegiate Athletic Association (NCAA) also moved its headquarters to Indianapolis. Significantly, more than half of the $3 billion worth of capital development invested in downtown came from the private sector. The combined investment of the corporate and nonprofit sectors accounted for roughly two-thirds of all funds invested.[68] Indianapolis's success in leveraging funds for its redevelopment projects is a testament to the strength of public-private partnerships in the Hoosier state.

At the turn of the millennium, growing attention to the arts and cultural scene helped foster economic development, complementing the city's focus on sports. Two urban revitalization initiatives, the Cultural Districts and the Monon Trail, provided the initial framework for the development of the Indianapolis Cultural Trail, a strategic approach to using arts and culture to revitalize downtown Indianapolis.[69] The Monon Trail, a seventeen-mile pedestrian and bicycle path connected downtown Indianapolis to the nearby towns of Carmel and Westfield. The heavy traffic on the Monon helped inspire the concept of the Cultural Trail. Additionally, the six cultural districts, designed by the Indianapolis Cultural Development Commission with the goal of broadening the city's image beyond the established identity of a sports and convention center, provided the Cultural Trail with

a functional rationale, as it would be conceptualized as the con-
nector of these districts.

The leading role Brian Payne, executive director of the CICF,
had in the development of the Cultural Trail exemplified the role
community foundations sometimes play in mobilizing and connecting resources to support collective impact initiatives. Payne
argued that the "private" in Indianapolis's public-private partnerships had changed, with philanthropic actors progressively
replacing corporations.[70] In this context, Payne saw an opening
for CICF, as the foundation had connections and resources to
"impart information and expertise to its donors and fund-holders"
and "bring its donors' expertise to the community table as part
of a greater community solution."[71] Payne realized that the six
cultural districts in downtown Indianapolis "weren't getting any
traction because people thought they were too disconnected from
the heart of downtown."[72] Convinced of the possibility of developing an urban version of the Monon Trail to complement and
connect the city's cultural districts, Payne strategically leveraged
the connections of CICF to mobilize the city's multiple resources,
including philanthropists, the mayor's office, and construction
unions.[73]

CICF connections to local philanthropists proved to be crucial
in the project's early phase (2000–2004).[74] CICF board members
Lori Efroymson-Aguilera and Myrta Pulliam were among the
early supporters. Efroymson-Aguilera, chair of the Efroymson
Family Fund and a longtime supporter of the Indianapolis arts
scene, made a $1 million donation to the project. Myrta Pulliam,
daughter of *Indianapolis Star* publisher Eugene S. Pulliam, also
donated $1 million. Payne was then able to win the support of the
Nina Mason Pulliam Charitable Trust and the Lumina Foundation, which committed $500,000 each for the initial studies. The
Cultural Trail fit these early donors' long philanthropic tradition
of supporting arts and culture, as well as civic engagement in the
Indianapolis community.

Between 2000 and 2004, both Payne and CICF played the crucial role of catalyst, building community support for the Cultural Trail. Relying on CICF's connections with donors, fundholders, and other philanthropic foundations, Payne mobilized actors and resources for a project that promised to contribute to the development of downtown Indianapolis. Leveraging CICF's network of philanthropists and fundholders for early support proved vital because, as Payne later recalled, it gave the project "credibility," allowing him to approach Mayor Bart Peterson.[75] In 2004, the project obtained official approval from the mayor's office, and in that year's State of the City Address, Mayor Peterson went on record stating, "The Cultural Trail could be a national landmark that would further distinguish Indianapolis in a powerful way."[76]

CICF connections again proved crucial after the City of Indianapolis provided the right of way for the Cultural Trail in 2004 and 2005. At this point, Eugene and Marilyn Glick had given a major fundraising boost by committing $15 million as a lead gift. Like the Efroymson family, Gene and Marilyn Glick held a family fund at the community foundation so were important prospective donors for the Cultural Trail project. Originally, Payne approached the Glicks asking for a $6 million donation with the intention of naming a corridor of the trail after them. The Glicks' advisors, however, informed Payne that the couple was willing to donate $15 million on the condition that the trail include a Peace Walk.[77] Today, the Glick Peace Walk "celebrates the lives of individuals who made peaceful contributions to humanity."[78]

From a financial perspective, Payne and CICF played the primary roles of catalyst and resource mobilizer. The contribution of CICF and its affiliate was only $500,000 over seven years.[79] However, the contribution of CICF board members and fundholders was substantial, with Lori Efroymson-Aguilera, Myrta Pulliam, and the Glicks accounting for a total of $17 million in private donations. With its $15 million gift alone, Gene and Marilyn Glick accounted for over half of the $27.5 million coming from private donations. The remaining $35.5 million came from federal grants, including a $20.5 million grant from the US Department of Transportation through its Transportation Investment Generating Economic Recovery (TIGER) program. Although the total costs of the project increased to $63 million over the course of construction, the city did not contribute from its budget. The Cultural Trail relied exclusively on federal grants and philanthropic donations, thus following Indianapolis's history of philanthropic support for civic projects.

The Cultural Trail appears to have fulfilled its many promises. It stands out as a successful example of a public-private partnership in which CICF took a leading role in mobilizing, coordinating, and connecting multiple resources and actors across the city. Even before its completion, the Cultural Trail brought economic benefits as developers purchased and developed land adjacent to the trail. Between 2007 and 2010 "over 17.5 million of new commercial building permits and 36.4 million residential building permits were filed within one-half mile of the Cultural Trail."[80] An assessment by the Indiana University Public Policy Institute found that property values increased between 2008 and 2014 for a total value of $1,013,544,460, with twenty-five properties accounting for 68 percent of this increase.[81] The Cultural Trail had a major impact on real estate development also, as numerous businesses, including The Libertine, 500 Festival Headquarters, and Best Chocolate in Town, chose locations because of the trail.[82] Furthermore, according to one study, the Cultural Trail spurred investments and grants to expand transportation options downtown, provided for a more sustainable use of land along the trail, increased property values, and attracted more people to live in the downtown area.[83]

The Indianapolis Cultural Trail exemplifies a problem-solving philanthropy approach. Payne saw a role for CICF in the revitalization process of the downtown area, not simply by supporting individual nonprofit organizations but by taking a civic leadership role in public-private partnerships. This approach was rooted in the realization that most aspects of modern society transcend sectors and thus require collaboration. In this context, as head of the CICF, Payne was well positioned to mobilize human, financial, and reputational capital in the City of Indianapolis. Community foundations play a vital role in the community and—in the case of the Cultural Trail—CICF served as the backbone for local development by coordinating various actors and providing necessary resources.

CONCLUSION: A HOOSIER PATH TO INNOVATION?

Historically, philanthropists experiment with innovative practices to better leverage existing resources for increased effectiveness and social impact. Philanthropic innovations develop when philanthropists recognize the "adjacent possible" of either new (social, technological, or natural) phenomena or different combinations of existing practices.[84] Scientific philanthropy, venture philanthropy, and strategic philanthropy all center on the use of models and practices borrowed from other fields and adapted to the philanthropic world. Scientific philanthropy, developed with the recognition by wealthy donors (i.e., Andrew Carnegie and John D. Rockefeller) that the practices that made them successful in business could help them overcome the perceived naivete of charity to better address social problems.[85] Likewise, proponents of venture, strategic, and outcome-oriented philanthropy emphasized the benefits of using new tools and practices to leverage greater resources for complex social problems.[86]

The beginning of the IF's PRI initiative highlights how internal factors are rarely the exclusive drivers of strategic approaches to philanthropy. Rather, chance and context often determine the success of projects, whether they rely on experimentation with new philanthropic tools or new approaches to address specific socioeconomic issues. The IF started investing in real estate for

charitable purposes primarily as a financial strategy and not, like
the later cases of the Ford Foundation and the Taconic Foundation, as a strategy to maximize social impact. The cases examined in this chapter suggest that purchasing property became
a financially safe way of supporting local agencies when a traditional grant appeared risky because of concerns with the financial sustainability of the organization. Interestingly, in the few
documented cases, the School for Practical Nursing and ISCC
suggested this approach rather than IF executive director Jack
Killen, who had been involved in all the earlier cases. This pattern
may suggest that the IF was known within the network of local
agencies to support organizations through this type of investments. Investments in real estate for charitable purposes may
therefore not have been considered particularly innovative at the
time but rather a fallback option for cases in which regular grant
making seemed financially risky.

The example of the Indianapolis Cultural Trail shows how one
community foundation managed to leverage a broad range of
community resources.[87] Payne relied on the multiple relationships of the CICF with its donors, fundholders, local philanthropists, and other foundations to build a community of support
for the Cultural Trail. This broad network provided both moral
and financial support to a project that later developed along a
traditional pattern of public-private partnerships in Indianapolis.
While early investments in real estate had been driven by the
nonprofit organizations receiving grants—external to the IF—in
the case of the Cultural Trail, foundation leadership drove the
philanthropic strategy and investment. Part of this represents a
change in the ability of the community foundation to fund out
of its own budget and compel a strategy to leverage community
assets.

Philanthropic innovations played a central role in the philanthropic history of Indiana. The Indianapolis Foundation and,
later, the CICF were often at the center of new approaches and

tools to address complex social problems. The distinctiveness of these approaches in comparison to other regional trajectories, however, is difficult to assess. From a broad perspective, these cases show that the use of PRIs by the IF and the role of CICF in the development of the Cultural Trail do not substantially differ from earlier or later cases. At the same time, however, at least the case of the IF's investment in real estate for charitable purposes, it appears that these approaches were developed independently, in different times and for reasons particular to each case. In a sense, therefore, these cases suggest the fruitfulness of examining the multiple paths to philanthropic innovation and the need to historicize the notion of innovation itself, considering the continuous evolving of philanthropic practices, definitions, and overarching legal frameworks.

NOTES

1. Julie Battilana, Matthew Lee, John Walker, and Cheryl Dorsey, "In Search of the Hybrid Ideal," *Stanford Social Innovation Review* (2012): 52–53; Jed Emerson, "Where Money Meets Mission. Breaking Down the Firewall between Foundation Investments and Programming," *Stanford Social Innovation Review* (2003): 38–47; and Mark R. Kramer and Sarah E. Cooch, "The Power of Strategic Mission Investing," *Stanford Social Innovation Review* (Fall 2007): 43–51.

2. W. K. Kellogg Foundation, *Blurred Boundaries and Muddled Motives. A World of Shifting Social Responsibilities* (Battle Creek, MI: W.K. Kellogg Foundation, 2003).

3. Wilmer Shields Rich, *Community Foundations in the United States and Canada, 1914–1961: A Guide to Their Organization, Development, and Operation* (New York: National Council on Community Foundations, 1961), 10–12; David C. Hammack, "Community Foundations: The Delicate Question of Purpose," in *An Agile Servant: Community Leadership by Community Foundations*, ed. Richard Magat (New York: Foundation Center, 1989), 23–50. In a critical account of the IF, Mark Hardy stresses how commissioning surveys and supporting research were procrastinating tactics in the 1920s. In his interpretation, dominant factors in the distribution of grants were the trust's surviving family members, trustee familiarity

with grantees, personal and professional relationships between leaders of funded organizations, and the potential to create positive publicity and increase public esteem for the foundation. Mark Alan Hardy, *Defining Community Need through the Lens of the Elite: A History of the Indianapolis Foundation and Its Funding of the Indianapolis Symphony Orchestra, 1893–1984* (PhD diss., Indiana University, 2012).

4. On strategic philanthropy and the roles of foundations, see Paul Brest, "A Decade of Outcome-Oriented Philanthropy," *Stanford Social Innovation Review* (2012): 44–45 and Joel L. Fleishman, *The Foundation. A Great American Secret* (New York: Public Affairs, 2007), 3–9.

5. The Central Indiana Community Foundation (CICF) was formed in 1997 when The Indianapolis Foundation partnered with Legacy Fund, the community foundation of Hamilton County.

6. See David A. Levitt, "Investing in the Future: Mission-Related and Program-Related Investments for Private Foundations," *The Practical Tax Lawyer* (Spring 2011): 34–36. An investment qualifies as a PRI if it meets a three-part test: The investment must further the exempt purposes of the foundation, the return cannot be a significant purpose of the investment, and the investment cannot have a political purpose.

7. Indiana University Lilly Family School of Philanthropy, *Leveraging the Power of Foundations: An Analysis of Program-Related Investments* (Indianapolis: Author, 2013), 14 and Steven Lawrence, *Doing Good with Foundation Assets: An Updated Look at Program-Related Investments* (New York: Foundation Center, 2010).

8. For the previous years, "Schedule A—Balance Sheets" of the Form 990, where assets are typically listed, is left blank, thus not providing details on earlier cases. Indianapolis Foundation, financial records, Form 990, Indianapolis Foundation records, box 51, folders 40–41.

9. The Indianapolis Foundation was chartered by the Fletcher Trust Company, Indiana Trust Company, and Union Trust Company and only administered the income of the trust funds that remained under the control of the three financial institutions. Hardy, *Defining Community Need through the Lens of the Elite*, 60.

10. Financial records attached to the minutes of the Board of Trustees, Indianapolis Foundation Records, boxes 8–10.

11. Hardy, *Defining Community Need through the Lens of the Elite*, 164. This rejection referred to a request from Reverend Charles Linders of the Church Federation of Indianapolis to purchase the Cadle Tabernacle property. Earlier in the same year, the IF had rejected requests from both

the Little Theatre Society of Indiana and the Christamore Settlement House to contribute entirely or in part to the purchasing of buildings. Hardy, *Defining Community Need through the Lens of the Elite*, 154–55, 161–62.

12. Ibid., chapter 4.

13. Ibid., 212.

14. Jack Killen to William Cronin, January 24, 1958, Indianapolis Foundation records, box 10, folder 1.

15. Minutes of meeting of trustees of The Indianapolis Foundation, May 9, 1959, Indianapolis Foundation records, box 10, folder 5.

16. The Indianapolis Foundation, "Report on Examination of Combined Statement of Assets and Funds at December 31, 1960, and Related Combined Statement of Income (Cash Transactions) for the Year Then Ended," 3, Indianapolis Foundation records, box 10, folder 7.

17. Mary E. Huff to Robert A. Efroymson, February 23, 1959, May 9, 1959, Indianapolis Foundation records, box 10, folder 5.

18. Minutes of meeting the trustees of The Indianapolis Foundation, February 26, 1959, Indianapolis Foundation records, box 10, folder 2.

19. The Indianapolis Foundation, "Report on Examination of Combined Statement of Assets and Funds at December 31, 1960, and Related Combined Statement of Income (Cash Transactions) for the Year Then Ended," 3, Indianapolis Foundation records, box 10, folder 7.

20. Rich, "Community Foundations in the United States and Canada," 48.

21. Hardy, *Defining Community Need through the Lens of the Elite*, 139.

22. Rich, "Community Foundations in the United States and Canada," 44.

23. Health and Welfare Council of Indianapolis and Marion County, *Proposal for a Downtown Center for Older Persons*, Not Dated (approximately 1960–1961), Indianapolis Foundation records, box 64, folder 37.

24. The annual report of The Indianapolis Foundation for the year 1956, Indianapolis Foundation records, box 9, folder 3.

25. Allan H. Warne to Jack Killen, January 31, 1961, Indianapolis Foundation records, box 64, folder 8.

26. Ibid.

27. Allan H. Warne to Jack Killen, April 25, 1961, Indianapolis Foundation records, box 12, folder 5.

28. Minutes of meeting of the trustees of The Indianapolis Foundation, May 9, 1961, Indianapolis Foundation records, box 11, folder 7.

29. Ibid.

30. Ibid.

31. Jack Killen to Allan H. Warne, May 19, 1961, Indianapolis Foundation records, box 12, folder 6.

32. Allan H. Warne to Jack Killen, June 15, 1961, Indianapolis Foundation records, box 12, folder 6.

33. Allan H. Warne to Jack Killen, August 29, 1961, Indianapolis Foundation records, box 64, folder 10.

34. Ibid.

35. Ibid.

36. Minutes of meeting of the trustees of The Indianapolis Foundation, May 9, 1961, Indianapolis Foundation records, box 11, folder 7.

37. Ibid.

38. Charles E. Stimming to Richard Harvey, January 2, 1962, Indianapolis Foundation records, box 64, folder 12.

39. Allan H. Warne to Jack Killen, January 12, 1962, Indianapolis Foundation records, box 64, folder 19.

40. Hardy, *Defining Community Need through the Lens of the Elite*, 334.

41. Trustees of The Indianapolis Foundation, "Memorandum. Supplement to the Agenda for the Meeting of Trustees," March 19, 1962, Indianapolis Foundation records, box 64, folder 15.

42. Ibid.

43. Ibid.

44. Ibid.

45. Council on Foundations (1988), 15.

46. Years later, when the ISCC changed its location, the IF was able to resell the property, which was originally purchased for $85,000, for $250,000. However, the selling of property was not a complete novelty; in 1961 the IF sold a portion of the Boy Scout Farm. The Indianapolis Foundation, "Report on Examination of Combined Statement of Assets and Funds at December 31, 1961, and Related Combined Statement of Income (Cash Transactions) for the Year Then Ended," Indianapolis Foundation records, box 11, folder 4.

47. Jack Killen to Charles Cremer, August 11, 1966, Indianapolis Foundation records, box 58, folder 36.

48. R. H. People to Jack Killen, August 8, 1968, Indianapolis Foundation records, box 53, folder 26 and Emarita Pitts Murphy to Jack Killen, July 3, 1973, Indianapolis Foundation records, box 53, folder 26.

49. Jack Killen to Frank Price, September 30, 1974, Indianapolis Foundation records, box 64, folder 57.

50. Carl C. Rice to Jack Killen, May 5, 1970, Indianapolis Foundation records, box 64, folder 57.

51. Rich, "Community Foundations in the United States and Canada," 49.

52. Ibid., 45.

53. Kenneth Chapman to Magdalene Davis, February 27, 1979, Indianapolis Foundation records, box 54, folder 28.

54. PRIs were not an absolute novelty in the 1960s. Historically, Benjamin Franklin in the eighteenth century, the "Philanthropy at five" group in the nineteenth century, and the housing projects financed by some foundations (including the Russell Sage Foundation) in the early twentieth century all manifested forms of a social-investment approach. Ford Foundation, *Investing for Social Gain: Reflections on Two Decades of Program-Related Investments* (New York: Ford Foundation, 1991), 6.

55. Indianapolis Senior Citizen's Center, "*Exhibit A to Application for Property Tax Exemption of American Fletcher National Bank and Trust Company,* as Trustee for the Indianapolis Foundation and the Indianapolis Senior Citizens' Center, Inc.," Indianapolis Foundation records, box 64, folder 40.

56. For instance, in reflecting on its PRI program, the Ford Foundation described the beginning of its PRI initiative as a recognition that social needs emerging in the 1960s required extraordinary philanthropic responses. The Ford Foundation started its program in 1968 when Louis Winnick, former deputy vice president, proposed to use $10 million of the foundation's assets for PRIs. While Ford Foundation trustees had not considered favorable social investments before that date, the opportunity to stretch the foundation's assets proved persuasive. The Ford Foundation (1991), 6–7. See also Olivier Zunz, *Philanthropy in America. A History* (Princeton: Princeton University Press, 2012), 218–20 and David Hammack and Helmut Anheier, *A Versatile American Institution: The Changing Ideals and Realities of Philanthropic Foundations* (Washington, DC: Brookings Institution, 2013), 133. Moreover, recent analysis of PRI activities among foundations identified organizational size, age, type, leadership, and expertise as driving factors. Heng Qu and Una Osili, "Beyond Grantmaking: An Investigation of Program-Related Investments by US Foundations," *Nonprofit and Voluntary Sector Quarterly* 46, no. 2 (2017): 305–29.

57. Brest, "A Decade of Outcome-Oriented Philanthropy," 45.

58. John V. Kania and Mark Kramer, "Collective Impact," *Stanford Social Innovation Review* (2011): 36–41.

59. Alan Abramson, Benjamin Soskis, and Stefan Toepler, *Public-Philanthropic Partnerships: Trends, Innovations, and Challenges* (Arlington, VA: Council on Foundations, 2012), 3.

60. James A. Segedy and Thoma S. Lyons, "Planning the Indianapolis Region: Urban Resurgence, de Facto Regionalism and UniGov," *Planning Practice & Research* 16, nos. 3–4 (2001): 293–305 and Gamrat and Jake Haulk, *Merging Governments: Lessons from Louisville, Indianapolis, and Philadelphia*, Allegheny Institute report #05–04 (June 2005).

61. "The Civil City: An Interview with William H. Hudnut, III," *Indiana Magazine of History*, 102, no. 3 (2006): 261.

62. John W. Walls, *Onward and Upward—The Story of the Greater Indianapolis Progress Committee* (Indianapolis: Greater Indianapolis Progress Committee, 1999), 12–15.

63. S. M. Walcott, "The Indianapolis 'Fortune 500': Lilly and Regional Renaissance," *Environment and Planning* 30, no. 8 (1998): 1736 and Kimberly S. Schimmel, "Sport Matters: Urban Regime Theory and Urban Regeneration in the Late-Capitalist Era," in *Sport in the City: The Role of Sport in Economic and Social Regeneration*, eds. Chris Gratton and Ian Henry (New York: Routledge, 2001), 266.

64. Walls, *Onward and Upward*, 14–15.

65. Schimmel, "Sport Matters," 266–71 and Brian Payne, "Connecting to Community Themes, Changing Community Values," in *Here for Good. Community Foundations and the Challenges of the 21st Century*, eds. Terry Mazany and David C. Perry (Armonk, NY: M. E. Sharpe, 2014), 173.

66. Frederick C. Klein, "Star of Snow Belt: Indianapolis Thrives on Partnership of City, Business, and Philanthropy," *Wall Street Journal* 200, no. 9 (July 14, 1982).

67. Mark S. Rosentraub, "City-County Consolidation and the Rebuilding of Image: The Fiscal Lessons from Indianapolis's UniGov Program," *State & Local Government Review* 32, no. 3 (2000): 183 and Mark S. Rosentraub, David Swindell, Michael Przybylski, and Daniel R. Mullins, "Sport and Downtown Development Strategy: If You Build It, Will Jobs Come?," *Journal of Urban Affairs* 16, no. 3 (1994): 224.

68. Rosentraub, "City-County Consolidation and the Rebuilding of Image," 183 and Rosentraub et al., "Sport and Downtown Development Strategy," 225–27.

69. Owen Dwyer and Matthew McCourt, "Placing E Pluribus Unum on the Indianapolis Cultural Trail," *Indiana Magazine of History* 110, no. 1

(2014): 52–53. See also Partnership for Sustainable Communities, *Indianapolis Cultural Trail: Improving Livability in Central Indiana* (June 2013), 1.

70. Payne, "Connecting to Community Themes, Changing Community Values," 174–75.

71. Ibid., 177.

72. David Hoppe, "Cultural Trail Grand Opening: Interview with Brian Payne," *Nuvo* (May 8, 2013). See also Partnership for Sustainable Communities, *Indianapolis Cultural Trail: Improving Livability in Central Indiana* (June 2013), 1.

73. Lou Harry, "Defining the Indianapolis Cultural Trail," *Indianapolis Business Journal* (May 4, 2013).

74. Payne, "Connecting to Community Themes, Changing Community Values," 179.

75. Ibid., 178–79.

76. Bart Peterson, *2004 State of the City Address* (Indianapolis: City of Indianapolis, 2004).

77. Harry, "Defining the Indianapolis Cultural Trail."

78. "Glick Peace Walk," accessed on March 19, 2022, Indianapolis Cultural Trail, http://indyculturaltrail.org/ictart/glick-peace-walk/.

79. Payne, "Connecting to Community Themes, Changing Community Values," 184.

80. Partnership for Sustainable Communities, *Indianapolis Cultural Trail: Improving Livability in Central Indiana* (June 2013), 3.

81. Jessica Majors and Sue Burow, *Assessment of the Impact of the Indianapolis Cultural Trail: A Legacy of Gene and Marilyn Glick* (Indianapolis: IU Public Policy Institute, 2015).

82. Harry, "Defining the Indianapolis Cultural Trail."

83. Partnership for Sustainable Communities, *Indianapolis Cultural Trail: Improving Livability in Central Indiana* (June 2013).

84. This definition of philanthropic innovation is based on the discussion of social innovation in Katherine McGowan and Frances Westley, "At the Root of Change: The History of Social Innovation," in *New Frontiers in Social Innovation Research*, eds. Alex Nicholls, Julie Simon, and Madeleine Gabriel (New York: Palgrave Macmillan, 2015), 52–55.

85. See Judith Sealander, "Curing Evils at Their Source: The Arrival of Scientific Giving," in *Charity, Philanthropy, and Civility in American History*, eds. Lawrence Friedman and Mark D. McGarvie (Cambridge, UK: Cambridge University Press, 2003), 217–39 and Robert A. Gross, "Giving in America: From Charity to Philanthropy," in *Charity, Philanthropy, and Civility in American History*, eds. Lawrence J. Friedman and

Mark D. McGarvie (Cambridge, UK: Cambridge University Press, 2003), 29–48.

86.   See Michael E. Porter and Mark R. Kramer, "Philanthropy's New Agenda: Creating Value," *Harvard Business Review* 77, no. 6 (1999): 121–30; Christine W. Letts, William P. Ryan, and Allen S. Grossman, "Virtuous Capital: What Foundations Can Learn from Venture Capitalists," *Harvard Business Review* 72, no. 2 (1997): 36–44; and Emerson, "Where Money Meets Mission. Breaking Down the Firewall between Foundation Investments and Programming," 38–47.

87.   As David Hammack suggests, community foundations are, with few exceptions, unable to make large grants and therefore emphasize services to donors and their roles as catalysts for complex projects such as urban and rural development. David Hammack, "Community Foundations," in *Philanthropy in America. A Comprehensive Historical Encyclopedia*, vol. I, ed. Dwight F. Burlingame (Santa Barbara, CA: ABC-CLIO, 2004), 92.

PART II

TRENDS AND INNOVATIONS

SECTION III

ADJUSTING TO CHANGE AND MAINTAINING MISSION

SAME GOALS, DIFFERENT PATHS

*The Wheeler City Rescue
Mission and the Indianapolis
Community Fund in the
Mid-Twentieth Century*

AMANDA KOCH

LEONARD HUNT WAS FURIOUS. THE superintendent of the
Wheeler City Rescue Mission had grown impatient with the constant bickering with the Indianapolis Community Fund, an organization that conducted joint fundraising for local groups and
supported the mission's program for transient men. After years of
declining Community Fund appropriations and wrangling with
the businessmen in charge, Hunt finally reached his breaking
point in 1945. He wrote, "The Board of Directors of Wheeler Mission are coming to the opinion that the Fund does not want the
Mission's participation as an agency and their minds are being
made up slowly but surely to get out."[1] Why would Wheeler Mission consider withdrawing its membership after nearly twenty-
five years, which would mean giving up guaranteed income at a
time when donations were hard to secure? Exploring the conflict
between the Wheeler City Rescue Mission and the Indianapolis
Community Fund—precipitated by the financial strains of the
Great Depression and World War II—reveals how an evangelical

Protestant charity negotiated changes in philanthropy during the twentieth century.

The conflict, which lasted from the 1930s to the 1940s, stemmed from the two organizations' ideological divides over how best to achieve social change. Wheeler Mission's approach held that spiritual conversion was the only means of truly helping the poor, whose circumstances mission workers often blamed on individual sin. By contrast, the Indianapolis Community Fund (Community Fund) represented an emerging philanthropic sector that increasingly looked to science and business methods, rather than religion, to improve society. The new discipline of philanthropy employed more businesslike, empirical, and secular methods, based on data, measurable results, and professional expertise, and placed less emphasis on spiritual change. In this context, rescue missions, and their steadfast commitment to evangelism, began to look outdated. Even as the two camps diverged, they shared some common ground. Rescue missions embraced new practices such as keeping case records on clients and coordinating services with other community organizations. They also shared concerns about maintaining efficiency and professional business practices. Rescue mission religion was not necessarily anti-modern. In practice, it was flexible and often accommodated and absorbed twentieth-century social welfare innovations while retaining its historic theological beliefs. Philanthropic organizations worked with a variety of religious groups, especially in Indiana, where Protestant evangelicalism provided a set of shared values for many Hoosiers. Still, rescue missions and emerging philanthropic organizations, like community funds, experienced tensions as they tackled the problems of poverty and homelessness from different vantage points.

This chapter begins in the late nineteenth century with the creation of the rescue mission movement and Indianapolis's Wheeler Mission. It then charts how philanthropy developed from the late nineteenth through the early twentieth century, resulting in organizations like the Indianapolis Community Fund. The last section focuses on the conflict between Wheeler Mission and the Community Fund in the 1930s and 1940s and how the two groups eventually reconciled and continued their partnership.

WHEELER CITY RESCUE MISSION

Rescue missions began in the late nineteenth and early twentieth centuries by holding nightly evangelical gospel services. Soon many of these missions added free meals and beds for homeless men. Originating in large cities, such as New York and Chicago, and quickly spreading around the United States, rescue missions sought out the poorest urban residents in skid row or high-poverty areas. Rescue mission workers invited those considered beyond redemption—habitual drunkards, criminals, prostitutes, and the desperately poor—to attend nightly religious services. During those services, converts shared how Jesus saved them from similar circumstances; mission workers preached the gospel; congregations sang hymns like "He Lifted Me," "Amazing Grace," and "The Old Rugged Cross"; and, at the end of the service, penitents were invited to the front to pray for forgiveness and a new life.[2] Most rescue mission leaders were evangelicals of the fundamentalist stripe, people "professing complete confidence in the Bible and preoccupied with the message of God's salvation of sinners through the death of Jesus Christ."[3] Rescue mission preachers taught that all people suffered the same fundamental problem, "the sin nature of man," which led to bad choices, addictions, and other ills that put people on skid row—and for all, faith in "Jesus Christ is the answer."[4] They urged people to put their faith in Christ's sacrifice on the cross in the place of sinful humanity and accept his forgiveness. They believed that after a conversion experience, the Holy Spirit enabled converts to live reformed lives.

In Indianapolis, a branch of the Woman's Christian Temperance Union founded what would become the Wheeler City Rescue Mission in 1893. Originally, the mission housed prostitutes who wanted to reform and welcomed anyone to its evening gospel meetings. One of its most essential early volunteers was a hardware salesman and Methodist Episcopal layman William Vincent Wheeler, who ran the mission from 1895 until his death in 1908. The downtown mission, later named after Wheeler, reached out to impoverished men, women, and children by holding evangelistic gospel services three nights a week, distributing used clothing and furniture, and conducting a Sunday school for children.[5] Wheeler Mission eventually turned over its women's housing program to another organization and, like many rescue missions around the nation, focused on providing food and housing to homeless men and religious classes, food, clothing, and used furniture to families and children.[6]

From the start, William Wheeler insisted that the mission's goals were spiritual. His annual report for 1900 explained, "The purpose of the Rescue mission is to extend a helping hand and encouragement to the lowly by bringing them under the influences of the plain gospel truths as . . . exemplified in the . . . life of Jesus Christ. Believing as we do that the gospel . . . has lost none of its power to change hearts, natures and lives our experience in this work has proved conclusively to our minds that this remains true."[7] From its earliest years, Brother Wheeler's rescue mission was anchored in faith that the poor's deepest need was for spiritual salvation through Jesus Christ.

From 1923 through 1944, superintendent Rev. Herbert Eberhardt led Wheeler Mission. Eberhardt was an Indianapolis native and seminary-trained pastor in the Evangelical denomination (the precursor to today's United Methodists).[8] Eberhardt spearheaded a building campaign for Wheeler Mission in the late 1920s and dedicated a four-story, state-of-the-art building in 1929.[9] He

shared William Wheeler's commitment to evangelism. Rev. Eberhardt stated in 1939:

> Meals and lodgings will not change a man's life one iota—they might
> even damage him! . . . Surely these last years of government relief
> have vividly demonstrated that outward charity alone . . . may do
> real damage in the end. To be sure, every mission feeds, clothes,
> sleeps and ministers to the needy, wisely and gladly. But only to an
> end—that men and women might come to know the Giver of every
> good and perfect gift. . . . After 18 years in the work I honestly ques-
> tion any lasting visible results from physical relief alone, not however
> discounting its need. On the other hand, thank God, we can point
> out many examples of permanent transformation resulting from real
> conversions.[10]

In the same newsletter, Jessie Mueller, a mission staff member
hired to visit families, expressed similar sentiments when describing her work. She wrote, "We have discovered over and over
again after an interview with a mother, or a mother and father,
that the greatest need was not anything material but a greater
knowledge of their Lord and Saviour [sic] . . . *To know HIM in HIS
fullness, and to trust HIM for their every need was really their way
out.*"[11] From its founding and throughout the twentieth century,
Wheeler Mission, like other rescue missions around the nation,
held steadfast to its religious approach to helping people change
their behaviors and circumstances.

Even though rescue mission workers' primary goal was spiritual conversion of the poor, meeting people's physical needs also
concerned them. They argued that spiritual change would result
in material progress. Rescue mission staff and volunteers often
viewed the poor's financial struggles, unemployment, or addictions as stemming from sinful behavior. Conversion to evangelical Protestantism, they believed, would solve those problems
by making converts willing to work, more likely to save money,
more likely to reunite with and support families, and less likely

to drink or use drugs. If converts adopted such habits, mission workers assumed success in work and family life would necessarily follow. Mission workers, and most other evangelicals at the time, gave little attention to wider social structures that impeded upward mobility, such as a lack of job opportunities, poor education, or prejudice. They viewed poverty as an individual's fault, not society's, and the solution as resting solely with the individual.[12]

The conversion story of Dale MacKain, as told in a Wheeler Mission fundraising letter from the mid-1950s, illustrates the view that internal spiritual change manifests itself in steady employment and a stable family. MacKain came to Wheeler Mission as a confirmed alcoholic. After attending mission services for a time, he converted in 1947. Thereafter he lived at the mission, worked in the kitchen, drove the truck, and eventually became a building supervisor. He completed Bible school, received ordination, and became assistant superintendent at a rescue mission in Lincoln, Nebraska, and later a full-time pastor in a small Nebraska town. MacKain eventually became superintendent of the Home Sweet Home Rescue Mission in Bloomington, Illinois.[13] He married Ruby Davis, a Wheeler Mission Sunday school volunteer.[14] Wheeler Mission often cited MacKain's life as a flagship success story that showed how conversion at a rescue mission could enable an alcoholic to abandon old habits, hold important jobs, establish a happy family, and encourage other struggling men to do the same.[15]

The rescue mission claim that converts made good by getting jobs, supporting their families, and contributing to a stable society was a good public relations pitch for organizations dependent on private donations, mainly from middle-class Protestant churchgoers. Organizational funding sources, like community funds and local governments, could also embrace tangible results like helping people become sober and find jobs, even if they did not embrace sectarian goals of religious conversion.

THE EMERGENCE OF PHILANTHROPY

As Wheeler Mission expanded from the 1890s to the 1930s, innovations in business and science rather than the church increasingly influenced social welfare practices.[16] During these years, Indianapolis experienced rapid growth due to migration from rural areas and Europe, resulting in overcrowding and inadequate housing and sanitation.[17] Resistance to taxes and big government made Indianapolis slow to implement public city services, so there was great need for private efforts.[18] Consequently, reformers interested in the public welfare argued that a bigger city with larger-scale problems made earlier approaches of giving charity to individuals insufficient and counterproductive. The Indianapolis Benevolent Society, created in 1835, represented this older approach of giving assistance personally to the poor. The inability of society to address the problems of a modern industrial city became evident during the economic depression of the mid-1870s, which put the city on the edge of violence due to insufficient food and jobs.[19]

As an alternative to inefficient giving directly to individuals, people such as Indianapolis Congregationalist and social gospel minister Oscar McCulloch advocated "scientific charity," or "scientific philanthropy," the use of reason and knowledge to eliminate social problems at their root rather than simply giving "alms" to individuals.[20] McCulloch and others nationwide claimed giving money to individuals was not only inefficient and wasteful, because the poor could ask multiple donors to help with the same problem, but would also create paupers who were no longer capable of supporting themselves.[21] Proponents of scientific charity created Charity Organization Societies (COSs) throughout the nation in the late nineteenth century to coordinate aid among charitable organizations and prevent the duplication of services. COSs sent middle- and upper-class, volunteer "friendly visitors" to the homes of the poor to verify whether applicants' needs were genuine. They investigated applicants' situations to identify what reformers thought were their main problems, usually a lack of physical, mental, or moral ability. Visitors were supposed to refrain from merely giving money. Instead, they were to help elevate the character of the poor, which was considered the true root of poverty.[22] Oscar McCulloch spearheaded the reorganization of the Indianapolis Benevolent Society into the Charity Organization Society in 1880 to provide a more efficient solution to the city's social welfare problems.

COSs like McCulloch's relied on an idea that has been a fixture of American thinking since at least the eighteenth century: Some poor were worthy of help, and some were not. Those who were worthy were morally upright, hardworking individuals experiencing hardship through no fault of their own. COS organizers labeled as unworthy those who did not work or who seemed to have vices such as drunkenness.[23] Rescue mission workers often shared this belief and implemented a "work test" to distinguish between the worthy and unworthy poor. In the 1930s, Wheeler Mission required the men who stayed more than one night to work four hours a day in its woodyard, for example.[24] Nevertheless, it is notable that rescue missions, generally run by fundamentalist Protestants, often set out to help the least deserving of the poor: adult men who could presumably support themselves by working but who did not, sometimes because of alcoholism. Throughout the twentieth century, rescue missions consistently provided aid to this group, which was often underserved and received little sympathy from public or private social service workers.

COS supporters, along with rescue mission workers nationally, often found themselves questioning how best to help the homeless and what role, if any, religion should play in that work. New York COS director Josephine Lowell Shaw, criticized rescue missions' "sentimental, morality-laden, and indiscriminate relief" and defended COS policies of giving limited direct relief and prioritizing relief for the deserving poor.[25] For their part, rescue mission leaders in the late nineteenth century sometimes criticized what they viewed as the heartlessness of COSs' insistence on investigation and resistance to relieving immediate suffering. Late-nineteenth-century rescue mission workers, especially those from working-class backgrounds, often resisted distinguishing between worthy and unworthy poor and helped all in need, hoping that even the most unworthy would repent from their sins, accept Jesus as their savior, and live a new upright life.[26] In the early twentieth century, however, ideas from scientific charity filtered into many rescue mission circles, especially among middle-class workers, and some rescue missions introduced work tests, as Wheeler did.

In many cities, COSs failed due to a lack of funds, volunteers, and capacity, although the Indianapolis COS, in a moderately sized city with less poverty, was more successful than others.[27] Even as COSs fell out of favor in the early twentieth century, the trends they inaugurated of professionalization, bureaucratization, and, to a lesser extent, secularization grew. Volunteer "friendly visitors" paved the way for professional social workers by the 1910s. The social work profession soon offered its own advanced training and specialized skill of "casework"—a system of keeping records on clients in order to diagnose and relieve the root cause of their troubles.[28] Rather than being remedied by volunteers, social problems were increasingly the purview of educated experts in paid careers devoted to researching problems scientifically and proposing tested solutions.[29] Centralized organizations, such as COSs, contributed to the bureaucratization of social welfare as they grew in size and administrative complexity. The rise of social work also contributed to a more scientific and secular approach to social change. Scientific descriptions of clients or patients in need of treatment and casework replaced the religious language of sinners in need of redemption.[30] The twentieth century realized the growth of a nonprofit sector increasingly independent of religious organizations and religious institutions.

THE INDIANAPOLIS COMMUNITY FUND

During World War I, Indianapolis joined cities around the country in creating a War Chest to coordinate agencies to conduct one joint annual fundraising drive for the war effort, thus avoiding the costs of multiple campaigns and fatiguing donors with numerous appeals. After the war ended, the War Chest became the Community Chest to raise money for social agencies.[31] The Community Chest was renamed the Indianapolis Community Fund during World War II and eventually became today's United Way of Central Indiana.[32]

The Community Chest continued the COS quest for efficiency and rationalization of philanthropy. One of the Chest's earliest projects related to homelessness. Support to the Transient Committee in Indianapolis illustrates the Community Fund's approach to social problems, which continued to rely on many assumptions of scientific charity. The Transient Committee formed in 1923, after a steady uptick in housing demand for transients. The committee, which included businessmen and representatives of public and private social welfare offices, laid out a systematic approach to the problem, saying, "To meet this need effectively it was necessary to find out first just what the nature of the problem was, the sort of assistance that would be needed, the cost of maintaining a transient program and the extent to which different agencies could be expected to assume responsibility." The committee proposed a "centralized lodging plan," which assigned various organizations different classes of homeless people. Wheeler Mission took all White transient men to capacity until 9:30 p.m., after which they would be sent to the Salvation Army. Specific branches of the Young Men's and Young Women's Christian Associations accommodated African American homeless clients. Thus, both Wheeler Mission and the Community Fund acquiesced to the racial segregation common in Indianapolis at the time.[33] In its response to the need for housing for the transient population, the Community Fund valued efficiency, systematic research, and centralized planning.

The clergy who ran Wheeler Mission shared many of the Community Fund's goals of efficiency, coordination of services with other agencies, and prioritization of clients who were hardworking and deserving of assistance. But the differences Wheeler Mission had with the Community Fund stemmed, at least in large part, from the different strains of Protestantism they each embraced. Community Funds certainly had religious influences, but they were often different from the fundamentalist evangelicalism that shaped rescue missions.

Community Chests were some of the earliest organizations committed to overcoming religious differences among Protestants, Catholics, and Jews. In the late nineteenth century, liberal Protestants ventured into poor immigrant neighborhoods to offer services and encountered Jewish and Catholic agencies with similar goals. By the early twentieth century, liberal Protestant, Jewish, and Catholic groups tentatively worked together to avoid duplicating services, creating the momentum that would lead to the creation of Community Chests. This heritage of working across religious lines explains the Indianapolis Community Fund's commitment to nonsectarianism and only funding nonreligious activities. Notably, fundamentalist Protestants, especially in the 1920s, resisted interaction with Catholics and Jews beyond attempts to convert them to Protestantism.[34]

Although it did not fund religious activities, the Indianapolis Community Fund was not completely separate from or hostile to religion. It had personnel and member agencies with religious affiliations. The prominent businessmen—and their wives—who made up its board of directors in 1945 included many mainline Protestants, such as Eli Lilly, the pharmaceutical manufacturer known for his generous giving to religious causes.[35] In Indiana, Protestantism had long dominated the religious landscape in terms of both numbers and influence and continued to do so in the mid-twentieth century. But more theologically conservative evangelicals were also an important sector of Hoosier Protestantism, and they grew in numbers, influence, and wealth, especially in the second half of the twentieth century.[36] The significant presence of evangelicals in Indiana may have been one reason that Community Fund leaders felt they needed to continue to try to work with Wheeler Mission despite the tension.

The fund's member agencies in 1945 illustrate a concerted effort to expand beyond the Protestant mainstream to include minority traditions such as Roman Catholics and Jews, who also made important contributions to Indianapolis's religious philanthropy.[37] The fund's members included Catholic Charities, the General Protestant Orphan Home, the Jewish Federation, the Lutheran Child Welfare Association, the Salvation Army, the Volunteers of America, the Young Men's and Women's Christian Association, and Wheeler Mission.[38] The inclusion of Protestant, Catholic, and Jewish agencies shows the Community Fund's commitment to working across religious lines.

Community funds had historic ties to liberal Protestantism and were willing to support the nonsectarian social service programs of religious agencies but that did not prevent significant strain with the more conservative evangelical Wheeler Mission in the 1930s and 1940s. Fundamentalist-leaning mission workers were even slower to adjust to new social welfare methods than the liberal Protestants in other service organizations or community funds.[39] While their agreement on the values of efficiency and organization allowed Wheeler Mission and the Community Fund to work together, their differences over the place of religion in social welfare work ruptured their relationship in the 1930s and 1940s.

The Great Depression put tremendous pressure on United States' social welfare organizations. The need was so great and widespread that local and private charitable organizations were quickly overwhelmed, creating demands for federal-government action.[40] The Great Depression dramatically increased demand for Wheeler Mission's services to the homeless while at the same time reducing donations to both the mission and the Community Fund. In 1932, the mission faced a 53 percent increase in the number of transient men served, while reducing expenditures by 3.4 percent. It did this by eliminating services such as shoe repair, free laundry, and shaving.[41] Financial constraints forced the mission to lay off four employees in 1933.[42] At the same time, the Community Fund revenue declined and thus did its appropriations to member organizations.[43]

From the beginning of its involvement with the fund, the mission raised its own money to pay for religious programming for children and families, but the fund was supposed to provide funds for the transient program. Decreased Community Fund appropriations meant that the mission had to divert monies for its religious work to the transient program. The Depression forced a direct trade-off between religious work and relief work, causing Wheeler Mission to reverse its stated goal of putting religious work first. Instead, the mission used money that was designated for its religious programs to fund desperately needed housing and food for transient men, a necessity that troubled the mission's religious staff members. Superintendent Eberhardt, and his board, protested the situation to the Community Fund throughout the Depression and early World War II years, but he did not force the issue.[44] That approach changed in 1944, when the fiery Leonard Hunt took over as superintendent.[45]

A Presbyterian minister and graduate of solidly evangelical institutions, such as Wheaton College and the Moody Bible Institute, Leonard Hunt came to Wheeler after eleven years of working at rescue missions in Chicago.[46] Hunt was a charismatic man with a deep desire to evangelize the poor, but he was more temperamental than Eberhardt. He would not put up with frustrations with the Community Fund as patiently as his predecessor.

The relationship between Wheeler Mission and the Community Fund reached a boiling point by 1945, when the mission seriously considered withdrawing altogether. Tensions revolved around two main issues: money for the transient program and the amount of control the fund tried to wield over Wheeler's administration. On the first issue, Hunt wrote to the Community Fund in the spring of 1945 seeking approval of a potential solicitation letter for Wheeler's religious work: "When I was at your office you spoke about including a paragraph stating that the Community Fund supports Wheeler Mission's transient program as a community responsibility. However, I do not feel . . . that I can consistently enclose such a statement when . . . I do not believe the Community Fund is supporting the transient program totally, when money from our religious funds is going to support the transient."[47]

When the mission faced a deficit between $3,000 to $4,000 in 1945, Hunt informed the fund that "we do not intend to further penalize our spiritual existence by paying what has been raised in the city-wide drive to meet the needs of the transient men."[48] Hunt was particularly heated when recalling the Community Fund's 1942 decision to force Wheeler Mission to return $1,500 of its appropriation for that year. "This, to me, is as great an act of injustice as if they had put a gun to our heads and forced us to give over." In December 1945, the Community Fund informed the mission that due to a $200,000 shortfall in its annual campaign, Wheeler's portion was cut to $9,000 for the year, even though by Wheeler Mission's calculations it cost twice that to run the transient program. Additionally, the fund considered Wheeler's costs too high, especially because World War II greatly reduced the number of unemployed transient men.[49] This claim infuriated Wheeler's leadership, who argued the mission already operated on a shoestring budget with many fixed expenses.[50]

On a wider level, Wheeler Mission leadership believed its struggles stemmed from the Community Fund's lack of understanding of religious organizations. In correspondence with Community Fund administrators, Hunt wrote, "I need not tell you that we do not feel that you folk have understood our program or our budget needs."[51] On another occasion, he further insisted that "the spiritual program of the Wheeler Mission is not being run by the Fund or the Council of Social Agencies. The human instrument governing this program is the superintendent, his control the Board of Directors, his final authority the Lord Jesus Christ and the Bible. There is no substitution for this."[52] He later explained the heart of the issue in a letter to Wheeler's board of directors: Wheeler's insistence on the importance of its spiritual work. "This one thing I know, that there is no hope for the transient man apart from Christ. I would never want to see Wheeler Mission degenerate into merely a housing and feeding station for men and I am sure you agree with me that you never want to see this happen."[53] Squabbles over resources were symptoms of the mission's greater resentment of what they felt to be the fund's indifference toward religious programming. These circumstances resulted in the two groups nearly parting ways.

December 1945 marked a low point in relations between the two agencies, but things improved in the new year. The mission board conceded to following the Community Fund's rather burdensome accounting practices.[54] More importantly, the fund hired a new executive secretary in 1946, Paul Rake, who proved far more conciliatory in his dealings with the mission. In September 1946, the Community Fund paid Wheeler a settlement to eliminate the mission's 1945 deficit, and Hunt wrote to Rake, "May I express to you my personal appreciation of the part you had in bringing the Wheeler Mission and the Fund together again. I need not tell you that the relations between the two agencies were rather strained."[55] Wheeler's annual appropriation increased to about $12,000 for the next several years, and the mission continued supporting the fund's annual fundraising campaign.[56] Reconciliation between Wheeler Mission and the Community Fund came due to flexibility and compromise on both sides.

Wheeler Mission represented a broader national trend of tension between evangelical rescue missions and federated funding agencies. Missions in New York, Los Angeles, Washington, DC, and many other cities were not even members of their funds in the 1930s and 1940s. Hunt noted rescue missions' estrangements from local community funds when he wrote to Paul Rake asking for suggestions for a seminar on Community Chests to be held at the national rescue mission conference. Hunt exaggerated only a little when he wrote, "As I travel around the mission field I find that Indianapolis has the enviable position of being the only rescue mission that speaks well of the Chest."[57] As Paul Rake pointed out in his response, some missions were supported by Community Chests.[58] But on the balance, there was more tension than cooperation between missions and federated fundraising organizations, largely because missions perceived that such secular organizations did not fund religious institutions, or because community funds viewed rescue missions as unprofessional and poorly organized.

In Indianapolis, perhaps due to the city's general Protestant consensus, the local rescue mission and community fund managed to cooperate to a much larger degree than such organizations in other cities. In response to Hunt's letter, Rake noted that chests had a duty to treat all religious groups equally, but he made his own sympathy for Christian religious work clear: "I feel that a rescue mission can make an important contribution to the social service of the community . . . because of, its spiritual work . . . in many cases the spiritual approach to the individual is the most effective even when viewed from the standpoint of social service work. As you understand, there is a point in rescue mission work beyond which Community Chests cannot rightfully go in their financial support. This does not mean that Community Chests should or do frown on evangelism."[59]

Rake defended his organization's policy of only supporting temporal and not religious work. Rake reminded Hunt that rescue missions varied greatly in their degrees of professionalism and quality of services and thus some community funds rightly refused to admit poorly run organizations into their member-ship.[60] Rake's moderation and sympathy with Wheeler Mission's spiritual work were essential to bringing the mission and fund back into harmony. His attitudes show that the emerging phil-anthropic sector in Indiana was far from hostile toward religion and often partnered with religious agencies.

Wheeler Mission and the Community Fund would have subse-quent run-ins, particularly when the mission opened a girls' home in the 1950s without first securing Community Fund permission— even though the mission realized that it would not get Community Fund monies for this project and did not ask for them.[61] Neverthe-less, in the next few decades, relations did not deteriorate to the lows of the 1940s.

In addition to the personal cooperation between their lead-ers, Wheeler Mission and the Community Fund overcame their differences because the groups shared core values, such as inter-agency cooperation and careful business management. Rescue missions also incorporated many new aspects of philanthropy. Even fundamentalist institutions like rescue missions embraced new developments, such as casework, in a search for efficiency and better results. For example, Wheeler Mission, probably in the 1920s or 1930s, made a "Case Work Plan for Homeless Men," which mandated that staff personally interview every man com-ing to the mission and make a case record that included his name, age, residence, family, occupation, and some effort to understand his problem. All cases were cleared with the local Social Service Exchange to ensure that any man served had not already received help elsewhere.[62] Parolees and men with significant problems, including homelessness or alcoholism, often stayed longer to receive "the moral and spiritual care of the mission services."[63] Thus, the growth of a nonprofit sector increasingly independent of religious organizations or churches influenced how historically religious groups dispensed assistance.

The "moral and spiritual care" men received at rescue missions
became increasingly therapeutic as the twentieth century pro-
gressed and missions around the nation started rehabilitation
programs for men with drug and alcohol addictions. In the postwar years, those who worked with alcohol abusers increasingly
focused on rehabilitating them through therapy and structured
residential programs. For some, especially secular workers, this
was part of a larger move toward defining alcoholism as a disease,
rather than a sin, and providing alcoholics with more assistance
and less condemnation.[64]

Rescue missions embraced a more therapeutic, rehabilitative
approach to alcoholism while still holding that it was a sin and
spiritual salvation was essential.[65] Rescue missions' acceptance of
alcohol rehabilitation confirms historian Stephanie Muravchik's
argument that postwar Americans molded psychology to their
own ends and effectively blended it with their religious beliefs.
Psychology and therapy did not replace religion but often enhanced it.[66] Independent rescue missions and organizations such
as the Salvation Army established their own Christian versions of
alcoholism rehabilitation programs, which required men to live at
the mission for several months and complete a program of work,
spiritual training, and complete abstinence.[67] Rescue missions
also started therapeutic programs, like Alcoholics Anonymous
(AA). A Wheeler Mission program that functioned briefly in the
late 1940s was more explicitly Christian and probably modeled
on AA. It was called the Alcoholics Christian Club and involved
spiritually strong former alcoholics mentoring mission clients to
overcome addiction through faith in Christ.[68] Even still, Superintendent Hunt resisted focusing too much on rehabilitation to the
neglect of evangelism. In a report to his board, Hunt commented
that the mission was "not a place for psychological rehabilitation. Man is degenerating and in need of regeneration through
Christ."[69] On another occasion he commented to a journalist,
"We don't have a program, . . . We have a person. . . . We present

the one who can live in them and help them develop themselves
to their fullest capacity and then and only then will they be satis-
fied."[70] Hunt and Wheeler Mission staff embraced rehabilitation
and psychological therapy only insofar as they could harmonize
with Christian beliefs.

In addition to rehabilitation programs, rescue missions developed their own professional organization. Rescue missions
were easy to start and often run by individuals without denominational or church oversight or support. Consequently, leaders
of larger more established missions, like Wheeler, agreed with
many Community Fund leaders that some rescue missions were
not run as ethically or professionally as others. To address this
issue, mission leaders created the International Union of Gospel Missions (IUGM) in 1913. The organization was an association of missions "in good standing" with their local evangelical
churches and communities. The organization did not control or
regulate local missions' affairs but did expel missions that did
not meet ethical or business standards. The IUGM helped place
mission personnel where needed, helped start new missions and
assist existing ones with problems, facilitated mission networks
by publishing an annual directory and magazine, and hosted annual conventions where mission workers could worship, learn,
and network.[71]

By the mid-twentieth century, the IUGM produced books,
pamphlets, and courses for rescue mission superintendents and
staff that spelled out recommendations on business and legal
organization, supervision by a board of directors, fundraising
and accounting, education and training for workers (including
encouraging education in psychology or psychiatry and social
work, as well as in theology), providing quality shelter and food,
and carefully rehabilitating men.[72] Thus the IUGM was analo-
gous to other professional organizations created for medicine,
law, and social work because it tried to organize a group of workers who varied greatly in training and quality. Wheeler Mission

superintendents were involved in the IUGM leadership and felt
the organization was essential to building respect for mission
work. Reverend Hunt wrote to his mentor, saying that the IUGM
should have "some standards that would safeguard the work of
one mission as over against the fly-by-night type or promotional
type."[73] Hunt's comments show that he shared the Community
Fund's desire to see rescue missions become more professional
and businesslike and offer high-quality services.

CONCLUSION

Wheeler City Rescue Mission's conflict with the Indianapolis
Community Fund was more than just one organization griping
about insufficient funding. Wheeler insisted that its spiritual
work was fundamental to its efforts to rehabilitate homeless men,
while the fund insisted on maintaining religious neutrality and
relying on human ingenuity to eliminate need. As the twentieth
century went on, rescue missions came under increased criticism
because many social welfare workers had different assumptions
about how to address poverty, homelessness, and addiction. The
focus was increasingly on secular, scientific, and data-driven approaches conducted by educated professionals in bureaucratic
organizations.

While rescue missions like Wheeler did embrace new innovations, such as casework, and shared some long-held assumptions
about efficiency and the need to distinguish between worthy and
unworthy poor, missions continued to insist that spiritual conversion was the ultimate solution to clients' problems. As social welfare organizations like the Community Fund distanced themselves
from explicitly sectarian religious positions, Wheeler Mission perceived that its religious approach had fallen out of favor, setting
the stage for tension and conflict between the two organizations.

Examining how rescue missions such as Wheeler responded to
and were shaped by changes in social welfare tactics throughout

the twentieth century illuminates larger developments. It shows that religious organizations and religious ideas still shaped American social welfare significantly, despite the secularizing impulses of the twentieth century. Organizations with religious affiliations continued to provide a significant portion of social welfare services in the twentieth-century United States. The story of secularization, professionalization, and bureaucratization is thus incomplete. This is especially true in the historically Protestant state of Indiana, where religion was an important influence on the development of philanthropy. The Community Fund's willingness to compromise demonstrates philanthropy's openness to working with religious groups on nonsectarian goals, like providing food and housing.

Even as religious organizations like Wheeler Mission endured and maintained their religious message, they were in dialogue with philanthropic organizations that did not have religious affiliations. Wheeler Mission and the Community Fund reached an accord and worked together for decades after tensions threatened their relationship in 1945 because both groups proved to be flexible in their practices. The story of their encounter demonstrates the adaptability of American evangelicalism: It could accommodate changes in social welfare practices and yet continued to retain many of its historical doctrines and methods. Philanthropy, even with its more secular trends, maintained connections and developed significant partnerships with various religious groups. The emergence of philanthropy could be quite jarring to existing charities, but people with different views of social change coexisted and cooperated in Indiana throughout the twentieth century.

NOTES

1. Leonard Hunt to Mr. Osborn (Indianapolis Community Fund), December 18, 1945, box 3, folder 20, Wheeler Mission Ministries records, 1904–1992, Mss. 16, Ruth Lilly Special Collections and Archives,

University Library, Indiana University-Purdue University Indianapolis (hereafter WMM records).

2. Mr. S. P. Wright to Robert T. Brown, superintendent of Washington Street Mission (written from Bloomington, IL), October 10, 1939, box 5, folder 1, collection 193, Records of the Washington Street Mission, Archives of the Billy Graham Center, Wheaton, Illinois (hereafter WSM records); 80th Anniversary Banquet of Wheeler Rescue Mission at First Baptist Church (8600 N. College), April 23, 1973, box 3, folder 3, WMM records; "Organist to Highlight Union Rescue Services," *Los Angeles Times*, June 5, 1955, A15.

3. George M. Marsden, *Fundamentalism and American Culture: The Shaping of Twentieth-Century Evangelicalism: 1870–1925*, 2nd ed. (New York: Oxford University Press, 2006), 3.

4. "Union Rescue Group Marks Anniversary," *Los Angeles Times*, June 20, 1966, A3. See also "Plain Talk about Christ Held Needed," *Washington Post*, October 13, 1947, B1.

5. History of the Wheeler Rescue Mission, founded October 13, 1893 by Meridian W.C.T.U. n.d., box 9, folder 22, WMM records; "Rescue Mission Will Celebrate: Organization Started by M. [*sic*] V. Wheeler to Observe Twenty-Fourth Anniversary," *Indianapolis Star*, September 16, 1917, box 9, folder 22, WMM records; Martha L. Gipe, "The Origins and Founding of the Wheeler City Rescue Mission" [1920s–1940s], box 19, folder 16, WMM records; Joseph B. Snider, *A Door of Hope: A Century of Rescue at Wheeler Mission Ministries, 1893–1993* (Indianapolis: Wheeler Mission Ministries, 1993), 8–17.

6. Pamphlet on the Forty-Fourth Anniversary of the Wheeler City Rescue Mission, box 74, folder 32, Indianapolis Foundation Records, 1916–2000, Ruth Lilly Special Collections and Archives, University Library, Indiana University-Purdue University Indianapolis (hereafter IF records).

7. "Rescue Mission Work: Report of Superintendent W. V. Wheeler Submitted," *Indianapolis Journal*, October 21, 1900, box 9, folder 22, WMM records.

8. Mrs. Herbert Eberhardt, "The Lord Hath Done Great Things for Us Whereof We Are Glad Psalms 126:3" [1985], 2–10, box 19, folder 15, WMM records; Herbert Ernest Eberhardt, "35 Years Broadcasting the Word of God," Compiled by Mrs. Herbert Eberhardt, box 2, folder 25, WMM records.

9. Dedication Program for New Building, December 1 to 8, 1929, box 2, folder 3, WMM records; 39th Annual Report Wheeler City Rescue

Mission, 245 North Delaware St. (1931–1932), box 9, folder 29, WMM records.

10. Herbert Eberhardt, "A House of Miracles!," *Mission Life* 3, no. 1 (June 1939): box 18, folder 13 WMM records.

11. Mrs. Charles Mueller, "Family Work," *Mission Life* (June 1939): 3, no. 1, box 18, folder 13, WMM records. Italics in original.

12. Marsden, *Fundamentalism and American Culture*, 37.

13. Snider, *Door of Hope*, 89.

14. Fundraising Letter from Dale and Ruby MacKain on Behalf of Wheeler City Rescue Mission [mid-1950s], box 6, folder 2, WMM records.

15. Leonard Hunt to Robert E. Hizer (member of the missionary committee of Southport First Presbyterian Church in Greenwood, IN), February 25, 1975, box 6, folder 4, WMM records; Untitled document [stories of Wheeler Mission converts], n.d., box 9, folder 22, WMM records; *Fellowship News*, WCRM vol. IV, no. 6, October 25, 1953, box 18, folder 15, WMM records.

16. Olivier Zunz, *Philanthropy in America: A History* (Princeton, NJ: Princeton University Press, 2012), 8–11.

17. Ruth Hutchinson Crocker, *Social Work and Social Order: The Settlement Movement in Two Industrial Cities, 1889–1930* (Urbana: University of Illinois Press, 1992), 13–14.

18. Genevieve C. Weeks, *Oscar Carleton McCulloch, 1843–1891: Preacher and Practitioner of Applied Christianity* (Indianapolis: Indiana Historical Society, 1976), 57–58; John R. Seeley et al., *Community Chest: A Case Study in Philanthropy* (Toronto: University of Toronto Press, 1957), 52–53.

19. Patricia A. Dean, "Charity Organization Society," in *The Encyclopedia of Indianapolis*, eds. David J. Bodenhamer and Robert G. Barrows (Bloomington: Indiana University Press, 1994), 402–3; Seeley et al., *Community Chest*, 77–82; Nathaniel Deutsch, *Inventing America's "Worst" Family: Eugenics, Islam, and the Fall and Rise of the Tribe of Ishmael* (Berkeley: University of California Press, 2009), 21–22.

20. For distinctions between charity and philanthropy, see Robert A. Gross, "Giving in America: From Charity to Philanthropy," in *Charity, Philanthropy, and Civility in American History*, eds. Lawrence J. Friedman and Mark D. McGarvie (Cambridge, UK: Cambridge University Press, 2003), 31.

21. Walter I. Trattner, *From Poor Laws to Welfare State: A History of Social Welfare in America*, 6th ed. (New York: Free Press, 1999), 91–94;

Michael B. Katz, *In the Shadow of the Poorhouse: A Social History of Welfare in America* (New York: Basic Books, 1986), 58; Seeley et al., *Community Chest*, 82; Weeks, *Oscar Carleton McCulloch*, 49–53, 181–90. McCulloch was also an early leader of the eugenics movement, which connected people's character and class to their genetics. He argued that poverty and bad character were hereditary in *The Tribe of Ishmael: A Study in Social Degradation*, 4th ed. (Indianapolis: Charity Organization Society, 1891).

22. Robert H. Bremner, *American Philanthropy*, 2nd ed. (Chicago: University of Chicago Press, 1988), 86–96. Trattner, *From Poor Laws to Welfare State*, 93–99.

23. Katz, *In the Shadow of the* Poorhouse, 91–99; Michael B. Katz, *The Undeserving Poor: America's Enduring Confrontation with Poverty*, 2nd ed. (New York: Oxford University Press, 2013), 3–9, 84–85; Weeks, *Oscar Carleton McCulloch*, xvi–xvii, 49–53, 181–90.

24. Floyd Leary, "The Mission Woodyard," *Mission Life* 3, no. 1 (June 1939): box 18, folder 13, WMM records.

25. Priscilla Pope-Levison, *Building the Old Time Religion: Women Evangelists in the Progressive Era* (New York: New York University Press, 2014), 157.

26. Pope-Levison, *Building the Old Time Religion*, 157–58.

27. Katz, *In the Shadow of the Poorhouse*, 80–83.

28. Trattner, *From Poor Laws to Welfare State*, 102–3; Katz, *In the Shadow of the Poorhouse*, 164–67.

29. Katz, *In the Shadow of the Poorhouse*, 169–71.

30. Regina G. Kunzel, *Fallen Women, Problem Girls: Unmarried Mothers and the Professionalization of Social Work, 1890–1945* (New Haven, CT: Yale University Press, 1993), 1–3.

31. Katz, *In the Shadow of the Poorhouse*, 156–57; Bremner, *American Philanthropy*, 133–34; Seeley et al., *Community Chest*, 89–91.

32. Payton and Dean, "Philanthropy," in *The Encyclopedia of Indianapolis*, 156–57; Seeley et al., *Community Chest*, 95.

33. Ruth M. Deeds, "History of the Transient Committee," January 15, 1945; "Schedule for Handling Transients," February 20, 1936; and "Schedule for Handling Transients," Revised December 15, 1942, box 2, folder 32, WMM records; Snider, *Door of Hope*, 69.

34. Kevin M. Schultz, *Tri-Faith America: How Catholics and Jews Held Postwar America to Its Protestant Promise* (New York: Oxford University Press, 2011), 15–31.

35. James Madison, "Eli Lilly," in *The Encyclopedia of Indianapolis*, 910–11.

36. See chapter by David King in this volume.

37. Ibid.

38. Report of Examination, Officers' Club of Indianapolis, Inc.—Indianapolis, Indiana, December 31, 1945, folder 5, box 39, Clowes Family Collection, M1028, Indiana Historical Society, Indianapolis, Indiana, accessed March 22, 2022, https://images.indianahistory.org/digital /collection/dc058/id/924/rec/1.

39. Marsden, *Fundamentalism and American Culture*, 48–59.

40. Lizabeth Cohen, *Making a New Deal: Industrial Workers in Chicago, 1919–1939*, 2nd ed. (New York: Cambridge University Press, 2008), 253–90. Bremner, *American Philanthropy*, 136–47; Katz, *In the Shadow of the Poorhouse*, 207–10; Zunz, *Philanthropy in America*, 122–29.

41. H. W. Krause (president, Wheeler City Rescue Mission) to Indianapolis Community Fund, September 13, 1932, box 1, folder 46, WMM records.

42. Snider, *Door of Hope*, 55.

43. Seeley et al., *Community Chest*, 90–94.

44. Herbert Eberhardt to Raymond Clapp (manager, Indianapolis Community Fund), September 7, 1939, box 1, folder 44, WMM records.

45. Herbert Eberhardt to Wheeler City Rescue Mission Board of Directors, July 18, 1944, box 1, folder 13, WMM records.

46. Leonard Hunt to William Seath, September 22, 1951, box 8, folder 23, WMM records; Snider, *A Door of Hope*, 63–65.

47. Leonard Hunt to Kenneth Miller (Indianapolis Community Fund), April 2, 1945, box 7, folder 16, WMM records.

48. Leonard Hunt to Sidney B. Markey (tentative copy), October 11, 1945, box 7, folder 16, WMM records.

49. Fermor Cannon (chairman, Indianapolis Community Fund) to Harry W. Krause (president, Board of Directors, Wheeler City Rescue Mission), December 3, 1945, box 7, folder 16, WMM records.

50. Harry Krause to Fermor Cannon, December 12, 1945, box 7, folder 16, WMM records.

51. Leonard Hunt to Kenneth Miller (secretary, Indianapolis Community Fund), June 11, 1945, box 7, folder 16, WMM records.

52. Leonard Hunt to Mr. Osborn (Indianapolis Community Fund), December 18, 1945, box 3, folder 20, WMM records.

53. Leonard Hunt to Wheeler Mission Board of Directors, "Tentative letter," n.d., no signature, box 3, folder 20, WMM records.

54. Harry Krause to Fermor Cannon, January 26, 1946, box 7, folder 17, WMM records.

55. Leonard Hunt to Paul F. Rake, September 24, 1946; William H. Schmelzel (president, Board of Directors, Wheeler City Rescue Mission) to Paul Rake, September 23, 1946, box 7, folder 17, WMM records.

56. Warren T. Ruddell (chairman, Budget Committee of the Indianapolis Community Fund) to Leonard Hunt, December 22, 1948, box 7, folder 18, WMM records; Hunt to L. E. Ratcliff, October 15, 1952, box 9, folder 3, WMM records.

57. Leonard Hunt to Paul Rake, March 22, 1947, folder 16, box 7, WMM records.

58. Paul Rake to Leonard Hunt, March 27, 1947, folder 16, box 7, WMM records. Missions in Rock Island, Illinois, and Hartford, Connecticut, for example, received community chest support. G. O. Rodgers (superintendent, Rock Island Rescue Mission in Rock Island, Illinois) to Leonard Hunt, December 28, 1945, folder 16, box 7, WMM records; "Rescue Mission Leaders to Talk of Regenerations: May 6 Set Aside for Visitors Who Will Give Old-Time 'Experience' Talks," *Hartford Courant*, April 30, 1928, 3.

59. Paul Rake to Leonard Hunt, March 27, 1947, box 7, folder 16, WMM records.

60. Paul Rake to Leonard Hunt, March 27, 1947, box 7, folder 16, WMM records.

61. Michael F. McCaffrey (general manager, Indianapolis Community Chest) to Leonard Hunt, May 5, 1952; Leonard Hunt to Michael F. McCaffrey, May 7, 1952, box 7, folder 19, WMM records.

62. "Case Work Plan for Homeless Men Wheeler City Rescue Mission," n.d., box 9, folder 23, WMM records.

63. Ibid.

64. Ella Howard, *Homeless: Poverty and Place in Urban America* (Philadelphia: University of Pennsylvania Press, 2013), 114–15.

65. Eberhardt insisted that alcoholism was a sin, not a medical condition, in an address to the International Union of Gospel Missions convention. Eberhardt, "Alcoholics Victorious," *Our Missions*, January 1952, box 19, folder 15, WMM records.

66. Stephanie Muravchik, *American Protestantism in the Age of Psychology* (New York: Cambridge University Press, 2011), 1–4.

67. Muravchik, *American Protestantism in the Age of Psychology*, 162–68; Howard, *Homeless*, 101–5.

68. Wheeler City Rescue Mission Bulletin for January 16–23, 1949, box 18, folder 8, WMM records; Report to Mrs. Newman June 23, 1947, box 9, folder 22, WMM records.

69. Wheeler City Rescue Mission Board of Directors Meeting, May 17, 1972, box 9, folder 17, WMM records.

70. Russ Pulliam, "Hunt for New life: Indianapolis Mission Couple Offer Shelter and Bread," *Eternity*, April 1979, box 9, folder 20, WMM records.

71. William Seath, *Handbook of Rescue* (International Union of Gospel Missions, 1961), 96; "Mission Official Cites Central Union's Work," *Washington Post and Times Herald*, January 17, 1959, B7. On the IUGM convention, see Rev. Herbert E. Eberhardt, "A House of Miracles," *Our Missions* [July 1939], box 19, folder 15, WMM records and *Our Missions*, "convention issue," July 1961 (report on recent Omaha Convention), box 16, folder 34, WMM records. For examples of correspondence between IUGM executive committee members discussing how to help struggling missions and establish new ones, see Leonard Hunt to William Seath, January 3, 1950, box 8, folder 23, WMM records. There are many other examples of such letters in this folder.

72. Seath, *Handbook of Rescue*, chapters 3–9; Herbert E. Eberhardt, "A Challenge," *Our Missions* [January 1949], box 19, folder 15, WMM records; Leonard Hunt to Mr. Hardwick (United Fund of Greater Indianapolis), May 19, 1960, box 9, folder 6, WMM records.

73. Leonard Hunt to Rev. William Seath (superintendent, Chicago Christian Industrial League), April 23, 1953, box 5, folder 29, WMM records.

GARY NEIGHBORHOOD HOUSE

*Managing Mission and Uncertainty in
the Civil Rights Era*

RUTH K. HANSEN

NEIGHBORHOOD HOUSE, ESTABLISHED IN 1909, was the first social service organization in the young industrial city of Gary, Indiana, and one of four settlement houses that developed there.[1] As Gary matured into a major city, economically and politically driven by the steel industry and rife with racial segregation, crime, and labor struggles, Neighborhood House adapted to meet the changing needs and resources within its environment. Why, then, did the organization shut its doors in 1971? Three dynamics converged to destabilize the Neighborhood House's institutional environment. First, as a change-oriented organization, its multiple stakeholders and funders had contested visions of what it should be, with financial resources entangled in incompatible directions. Second, carefully cultivated political networks and citizen engagement helped overturn the local practice of racial residential segregation, changing the dynamics of its neighborhood clients and volunteers. Third, although Neighborhood House never received federal funds directly, volatility in government policy during the 1960s and 1970s further destabilized the environment and contributed to its closure. Nevertheless, the determination and creativity of its staff and volunteers, inspired by a vision of social justice as God's will, ensured that important projects survived beyond the organization itself.

After briefly addressing the development of Neighborhood House, this chapter focuses on the last ten years of the organization and its environment. This period was marked by the charismatic leadership of Reverend William Brooks, turbulent race relations locally and nationally, and a rapidly changing resource environment for policy, funding, and infrastructure. During these last ten years, its leadership reacted to a dynamic and challenging environment by grounding in the value of being a needed resource for the community.[2]

FOUNDING "GARY'S HULL HOUSE"

Gary began as a mill town for US Steel. In 1906, company directors opened a new facility by the shore of Lake Michigan and a planned city adjacent to the mill. As immigrants arrived to fill open positions, they found little affordable housing in the planned city. The boarding houses and tarpaper shacks of the "Patch" district, just to the south, were more accessible to new arrivals.[3]

Neighborhood House was the first social service provider responding to the dismal conditions in Gary's immigrant area. Kate and Jane Williams of Howe, Indiana, had planned to sponsor a kindergarten, a popular means for civic-minded women of the time to promote conditions for wholesome family life. Once they witnessed the tents, tarpaper shacks, and more than two hundred saloons of the Patch district, they realized that their intended kindergarten was only a start. With the support of the Synod of the Indiana Presbyterian Church, the Board of the National Missions of the Presbyterian Church, and the superintendent of schools, the new kindergarten at 14th and Washington hired workers who spoke several European languages and soon expanded to include older children and a summer program. The *Gary Daily Tribune* described Neighborhood House as "Gary's Hull House." By 1912, the Williams sisters, the Board of National

Missions, and the Synod of Indiana again collaborated to build a three-story brick building at 1700 Adams Street.[4]

Gary's population grew rapidly over the decades. Eastern European immigrants were followed by Black and Mexican migrants from the South in search of opportunity. Like other settlement houses, Neighborhood House adapted, rooting in the needs of the neighborhood and affiliating with the Community Chest (later, the United Fund). As migration into Gary continued through the 1950s, the Neighborhood House offered Gary's first health clinic, language school, citywide Christian education, and visiting nurse services. Both actual crime and Gary's reputation for lawlessness increased; by the mid-1950s, tabloids estimated that nearly half of workers' salaries were spent on underground industries, such as gambling, prostitution, and drugs. The city grew increasingly segregated, with African Americans concentrated in the area around Neighborhood House, now known as Midtown. The sponsoring Presbyterian Church was an early supporter of a racially integrated society, and Neighborhood House leaders showed distinctively progressive management in emphasizing professional training and racial balance for staff. Organizational programming emphasized the history of African Americans, world friendship, education, recreation, and, interestingly, community organizing. These choices showed an early professionalism and a commitment to engaging with community members rather than the more paternalistic relationship that developed in some other organizations dedicated to serving economically poor neighborhoods.[5]

REV. WILLIAM BROOKS: CIVIL RIGHTS AS A CHRISTIAN IMPERATIVE

The Reverend William M. Brooks was two months shy of his fifty-first birthday when he assumed the directorship of Neighborhood House in 1962. Brooks held a master of social work with a concentration in community organizing from Gammon Theological Seminary in Atlanta, Georgia. It was uncommon for social workers educated in the 1950s to specialize in community organizing; it was even less common for an individual with that education to work for a direct service organization. His presence at Neighborhood House speaks to his belief that working directly with the community in Gary would effectively improve the lives of urban African Americans. It is also noteworthy that the board of Neighborhood House embraced this newer approach to neighborhood-based service.[6]

In addition to his professional education, Brooks brought substantial life experience and personal motivation. During the Great Depression, he taught classes in labor legislation, workman's compensation, social security, and consumer education through the federal Works Progress Administration (WPA) program in Atlanta, Georgia. Brooks was a serviceman in World War II. For many African American soldiers, the experience of fighting a Nazi regime that praised American Jim Crow practices distilled a resolve to continue fighting racial discrimination when they returned home. After the war, he enrolled in college and worked as a mail carrier until he was charged with disloyalty to the United States and possible communist affiliation. The charges alleged that Brooks's prewar work with the WPA and his postwar affiliation with the United Negro and Allied Veterans of America (UNAVA) brought him in contact with communist sympathizers. UNAVA advocated for equal treatment for Black GIs but was denied accreditation by the Veterans Administration due to allegations of subversive activity; it subsequently closed. Brooks denied the charges and appealed the decision but was dismissed from the Post Office in 1950.[7]

Brooks kept the transcript of the hearings until his death, suggesting that the event was particularly meaningful, likely feeding his resolve to continue to seek justice. In 1956, he first delivered a sermon on the topic of "Conformity with Man or Transformity with God," a recurrent theme throughout his life. Linking civil rights with Christianity shaped Brooks's leadership and inspired others to engage in work toward the shared vision in which honoring love of God and neighbor translated into the active pursuit of social justice.[8]

MANAGING INSTITUTIONAL ARRANGEMENTS:
EXPANSION AND COLLABORATION

Reverend Brooks's leadership at Neighborhood House was marked by an expansion in programs, budgets, and people. Programs added a new focus on family-strengthening activities, community action, and local advocacy. While many settlement houses pursued federal advocacy through professional networks, Neighborhood House's choices were more locally focused and as an actively Presbyterian-sponsored organization, an example of church involvement in the growing civil rights movement.[9]

Operating budgets steadily increased during Brooks's tenure, with the entire budget typically spent each year. The United Fund, the precursor to the United Way, was the single largest source of income, underwriting about 60 percent of annual funding during his time. The second largest single source of funding was the Presbyterian Synod of Indiana, averaging about 25 percent of annual income. The Presbytery of Logansport was another significant supporter, although the amount given fluctuated.

A community organizer by training, Rev. Brooks valued cooperation and coordination, and so he developed and maintained professional and community networks. Campbell Friendship House, one of the other three settlement houses in Gary, was often a project collaborator. The governing board also increased, from twenty-five people in 1962 to thirty-nine in 1966. By cultivating relationships within the neighborhood, city, and region, Neighborhood House formed a network that allowed access to political and logistical mobilization.[10]

ESCALATING RACIAL TENSIONS

When Rev. Brooks took on the role of executive director in 1962, Gary was one of the most racially segregated cities in the north, with levels comparable to Birmingham, Alabama.[11] Overall, more than half of the population of Gary was African American, but the African American population was concentrated in the Midtown area near the Neighborhood House. Midtown was "known throughout the city for its high rate of crimes against persons, for prostitution, dope and gambling. Housing is crowded and in most instances is deteriorating. Most units are rented with a very few owner occupied. . . . The average income is about $1700 less than the average income throughout the city. The majority are employed as unskilled labor in the steel industries or in service jobs."[12]

That year, the city council debated an Open Housing Bill, introduced to reverse segregationist housing practices. Consistent with a 1917 US Supreme Court ruling against residential segregation—*Buchanan v. Warley*, 245 U.S. 60 (1917)—Gary zoning ordinances made no explicit mention of race but de facto segregation existed and was supported by council members and White voters. Private arrangements for racially exclusive real estate deals, which have been well documented in nearby Chicago, likely also existed in Gary. The 1962 Open Housing Bill failed to pass the Gary City Council. In 1964, Gary's new mayor, Martin Katz, supported a second attempt at fair housing legislation, this time in the form of an omnibus civil rights bill. Once again, the city council rejected it.[13]

Reverend Brooks and Neighborhood House sought to balance meeting the day-to-day needs of clients while encouraging systemic change. Racial disparities in employment were endemic in Gary, both in municipal jobs and large corporate jobs, and as the White residents of Gary moved to the suburbs, increasingly retail positions did, too. Steel jobs had declined, and US Steel, like others in the steel industry, systematically favored White employees over Black ones with similar education. The result was a mostly Black population in Gary for whom there were no local jobs that paid well.[14]

INTERACTING WITH THE RESOURCE ENVIRONMENT: SPONSORS AND GOVERNMENT, 1964–1967

Clarence Boebel, visiting from the Chicago Federation of Settlements and Neighborhood Centers, described Gary's Midtown as having "deplorable conditions . . . real poverty, and people like this need help in order to live in human dignity."[15] Reverend Brooks, the board, and staff intentionally cultivated both their professional and cultural competencies, acknowledging that "blind faith cannot stand with nothing else—the workers must have a knowledge of the neighborhood."[16] Neighborhood House continued to build a broad network of friends and colleagues. At the same time, Rev. Brooks increased the staff's work in community organizing, group work, and family counseling.[17]

As a sponsoring institution, the United Presbyterian Church of the USA was committed to social action as a religious imperative. At the national level, the General Assembly of the church elected Rev. Elder G. Hawkins as its moderator. Reverend Hawkins was a politically active minister who was once accused of ties to communism—an experience similar to that of Rev. Brooks. The synod, presbytery, and local churches sent money and people to support Neighborhood House. Neighborhood House, meanwhile, planned projects for its clients and church congregations, encouraging interaction and, where possible, mutuality.[18]

At the same time, the United Fund's significant funding of Neighborhood House gave it the power of the purse. The annual request process included de facto oversight of Neighborhood House programs and those of other similar agencies, giving the United Fund a voice in selecting which community priorities would be addressed, and how. Their preference was generally to work through established channels and try to avoid conflict.[19]

As a resource environment, the city of Gary also affected the well-being of its residents. The city administration was widely criticized for corruption, and in 1964, Neighborhood House denounced the city's systemic neglect of its citizens. Echoing the national civil rights movement, the Neighborhood House compared Gary to a patient unwilling to accept his diagnosis, and resolved to make the city aware of its people's needs. This local advocacy recognized the dependency of citizens and the organization itself on the larger political ecosystem and sought to improve the system in order to improve the well-being of its clients and community.[20]

One key strategy was collaboration among local organizations, using connections from its board and professional network. They held discussions with Campbell Friendship House to pursue a shared all-day nursery. They organized dialogues with a local progressive group, the Muigwithanians, about providing one-on-one mentoring for at-risk boys. And they sent a request to the United Fund that would allow them to hire an individual to coordinate between the four settlement houses. These discussions laid the groundwork for a future collaboration of the four Gary settlement houses: Gary Neighborhood Services (GNS). Further coordination with organizations such as Chicago's Erie Neighborhood House, the Visiting Nurse Association, and Gary city agencies resulted in expansion of referral networks to include Planned Parenthood and Meals on Wheels. In October, the Gary chapter of the NAACP presented Rev. Brooks with an award recognizing his "outstanding services rendered to the Community in the field of Human Relationships."[21]

From a policy standpoint, both federal and local decisions in 1964 shaped the environment for Neighborhood House actions. At the federal level, President Lyndon B. Johnson announced the War on Poverty, a centerpiece of the Great Society. Johnson was influenced by Whitney Young, president of the Urban League, who encouraged investing capital to rebuild urban ghettos. That plan included federal funding for Community Action Programs, VISTA volunteers, and Model Cities, all of which positively affected Neighborhood House. At the local level, Gary's "urban renewal" regimen of razing properties and relocating residents looked to the area served by Neighborhood House. The new federal programs pursued many of the same goals as Neighborhood House and acted to reinforce their efforts, but local urban renewal activities added tremendous pressure on residents, further straining organizational resources. Deciding to neither promote nor condemn urban renewal, Neighborhood House adopted a liaison role with the Gary Urban Renewal Office to act as "an instrument of information, education, and neighborhood participation in the plan of renewal."[22]

Uncertain whether the building at 1700 Adams would survive urban renewal, Neighborhood House continued regular maintenance but put off serious work. The dense network so carefully cultivated by organizational leaders yielded collaborative efforts with other nonprofits and government that benefited Neighborhood House clients, although it was impossible to plan for stability in an uncertain funding environment. Noting that its staff salaries were not competitive with those of similar public service jobs, the personnel committee approved modest increases and considered offering fringe benefits.[23]

Neighborhood House's engagement with the policy environment included political advocacy and demonstrations,—including those targeting the Lake County Economic Opportunity Center, which funded and cooperated with Neighborhood House on multiple programs. The organization's leadership considered their advocacy for adequate and open housing, civil rights, and low-income public housing to be confronting evil and sin by striving for justice, acting as "part of the prophetic church militant."[24] When Gary's city council finally passed the

Civil Rights Omnibus bill in 1965, opening the door to open housing, Neighborhood House helped area residents lodge complaints of housing discrimination.[25]

In a nationally watched race, African American lawyer Richard Gordon Hatcher ran for the office of mayor of Gary. The Lake County (Indiana) Democratic organization insinuated communist ties, resorting to the racist tactic used to smear other prominent African Americans. There was concern of possible election fraud and fear that if Hatcher was defeated, riots would engulf the city. There were, in fact, reports of defective voting machines and of poll workers being harassed, but Hatcher won the election with 96 percent of the Black vote and 12 percent of the White vote, becoming one of the first Black mayors of a major American city. Hatcher was a member of the Muigwuithanians, a group that collaborated with Neighborhood House; the investment in network building was poised to deliver a friendly reception in city government.[26]

During Mayor Hatcher's first term, the city of Gary was designated a Model City, an "urban laboratory" for the nation. With federal Great Society funding, the city supported anti-poverty programs and new jobs within the city government. Four VISTA volunteers, also federally funded, worked at Neighborhood House. Their assignments were actively political, promoting legislation for more liberal assistance grants and working to expand restrictive public housing eligibility. But as Hatcher's election and Neighborhood House alignment with federal priorities converged to provide much needed resources, locally the area around Neighborhood House was targeted for urban renewal. The board and staff began discussing mobile services and possible relocation.[27]

REACTING TO CHANGE: FOCUSED DISPERSION

Reverend Brooks was an advocate of the Social Gospel, applying the teachings of Christianity to the social and political issues of the day. "The church," he wrote, "must be the bulwark of basic human freedoms; freedom to learn, freedom to serve, freedom of fellowship, freedom from want, freedom from fear."[28] With this ambition, he responded to the federal Economic Opportunity Act, a centerpiece of Great Society legislation, by cofounding the Gary Metro Corps. The new agency would increase opportunities for economically disadvantaged individuals. Mayor Hatcher and Gary Neighborhood House volunteers Bernice Terry and Rev. Stanley Terry were among the other original trustees. Reverend Terry was both vice president at Neighborhood House and presided over the board of Gary Metro Corps. Reverend Brooks was a natural choice to direct the new community centers.[29]

Reverend Brooks transitioned to Metro Corps on November 1, recruiting longtime Gary civil rights activist H. Theo Tatum to codirect Neighborhood House, along with program director Helen Fields. The choice of Tatum for this role is important for two reasons: First, it shows a commitment to have leadership grounded within the community, and second, it indicates continued focus on social activism.

If the Brooks years represented expansion on all fronts— aggressive goals, new supporters, and integrated community action—the post-Brooks years at Neighborhood House show an undeniable contraction on paper but a determined push of action into the community. Staff shortages led to a dramatic cutback in professional capabilities, but three strategic choices helped broaden the organization's impact. First, Neighborhood House increased its reliance on people from the neighborhood in both paid and volunteer part-time positions to maintain programming. This was a change from a professionalization model to one of greater community engagement, at odds with the trend in other settlement houses but very much aligned with other popular models of social action. Second, Neighborhood House hired a dedicated community organizer who worked with VISTA volunteers and neighborhood residents on grassroots community-action programs and legislative lobbying. Finally, several collaborative projects were independently incorporated, ensuring a life for them beyond that of the Gary Neighborhood House as an organization.[30]

In his director's report at the end of 1968, Mr. Tatum noted "uncertain progress and achievement" for the year due to staff resignations and insufficient finances; in addition to Rev. Brooks, three other full-time staff resigned that year. While the situation was, as Mr. Tatum noted, one of instability, it also afforded the personnel committee an opportunity to evaluate needs and options. They decided to offer better salaries and benefits to fewer administrators, relying more on part-time and temporary positions that were filled by people from the neighborhood. Ms. Fields had the primary responsibility for hiring and training the part-time program staff.[31]

The board also hired a dedicated neighborhood developer, Jean Thurman. This position solidified a commitment to an activist church mindset and also helped address the dual destabilizing forces of urban renewal and open housing. The passage of open housing was a victory, helping area residents achieve greater quality of life and economic opportunity, but many of the more stable families that had anchored Neighborhood House programs moved, leaving the more vulnerable individuals and families behind. The need grew more concentrated, and the organization's human resources grew smaller. Neighborhood House responded with intensive development services for those residents staying in the neighborhood.[32]

Ms. Thurman started the Neighborhood Action Institute (NAI) to train leaders for civil rights and community organizations. Operating out of the Neighborhood House and funded through the New York–based Scholarship, Education and Defense Fund for Racial Equality, the NAI was chaired by Ms. Thurman and staffed with VISTA volunteers. The development of the NAI under the auspices of the Neighborhood House demonstrates Rev. Brooks's concept of church missions as risk-takers on behalf of the needy, actively inviting the participation of individuals "from the ghetto."[33] By focusing on indigenous leadership, NAI and Neighborhood House retained community legitimacy and consolidated civic action, taking a more active approach than many 1960s settlements.[34]

Reverend Stanley Terry assumed the presidency of the board and worked closely with interim directors Tatum and Fields. Board members would have been thinking about funding: in 1969, Nixon's administration changed the structure of federal grants, reducing the funding available to Gary's anti-poverty programs. This likely increased the need of Neighborhood House clients by shrinking other supportive programs. Facing program cuts, they prioritized welfare, education, and school programs, and staff assistance in political demonstrations. Reverend Terry noted that the break from more traditional settlement house activities upset "several who have some control over the purse-strings . . . They would give band-aid relief to cancerous growths without even giving the injured an examination."[35] Perhaps to appease the United Fund, which still supplied well over half of the organization's budget, the annual reports at this time chose United Fund imagery over that of the Presbyterian Church, although Neighborhood House remained a project of the synod.[36]

WHAT GARY NEEDS: CHOOSING
MISSION OVER STRUCTURE

By 1970, Gary was no longer being monitored for racially motivated violence by federal agencies, but turbulence continued. Mayor Hatcher led cooperative interracial efforts against US Steel's flagrant environmental pollution. At Neighborhood House, the years of turbulence had taken a toll, requiring decisions on how to effectively pursue its mission in the current reality. Continuing a focus on welfare rights, Jean Thurman represented the Gary Neighborhood House in planning Project Justice & Equality, a collaboration with Valparaiso's law school and other parties. The project recognized both the systemic need to reform existing laws and the immediate importance of effectively engaging poor and discriminated-against citizens in the legal process. The project was incorporated in 1971 and continued for more than thirty years.[37]

Another major decision led to the end of the Neighborhood House as a discrete organization. Building on the collaborative experience of the Gary Neighborhood Centers Association, the board agreed to a partnership with other Gary settlement houses to be known as Gary Neighborhood Services, which would focus on traditional social service programming. Unlike the association, GNS would formally incorporate, with each settlement house as a charter member. The final annual report for the Neighborhood House optimistically projected that individually governed boards would continue as branches of the umbrella organization. Neighborhood House recognized that its current spending levels were not sustainable in the face of projected funding reductions but had no expectation of disbanding: the report firmly commits to maintaining services and to increased community representation on the Neighborhood House board. However, by 1971, Neighborhood House was no longer an affiliate of the synod; at about that date, it was absorbed into GNS, as were the three other settlements.[38]

Such consolidations were common among agencies substantially funded by the United Fund. The last documented discussion of the Neighborhood House's decision to join GNS refers to shared resources and jointly submitting "a record-shattering budget to the United Fund." The United Fund / United Way continued to provide the core budget for the new organization. In fiscal year 1972, its allocation to GNS was nearly six times its allocation to Neighborhood House in 1970, and allocations grew substantially each year thereafter.[39]

Neighborhood House initially had significant influence in the new GNS. Joseph Kalousek, the president of Neighborhood House, was an incorporator, and the statement of purpose in its articles of incorporation was very detailed and reflects language used in Neighborhood House documents. Irwin Lewis, Jr., a social worker educated in Atlanta, relocated to Gary to serve as GNS executive director. Shortly thereafter, the statement of purpose was amended to reflect the less specific language more common in similar documents. Helen Fields transitioned to GNS as its assistant director; Jean Thurman stayed just through September 1972. GNS programming, likely reflecting the preferences of the United Fund, resembled the "traditional" programming that Helen Fields had overseen at Neighborhood House. The more system-focused advocacy work of Jean Thurman survived in the NAI and Project Justice & Equality.[40]

GNS was described as a merger, but incorporation paperwork lists no assets carried over from the other organizations. The building at 1700 Adams St., owned by the Presbyterian Synod of Lincoln Trails, did not carry over to GNS. Instead, the synod voted to sell it for $1 to Marona House, a recently founded organization that provided social services to drug addicts.[41]

As a formal organization, the Gary Neighborhood House ceased existence in 1971, but neither its mission nor its activities expired at that time. After its official records go silent, its voice was still heard condemning racial injustice locally and nationally during the high-profile trial of David Hilliard, a California member of the Black Panthers.[42] But the dispersion of ideas and action was the most compelling legacy of the Neighborhood House. As Helen Fields wrote, "The development of people has been our greatest contribution."[43]

The nonprofit sector in general grew during those years of expansion for the Gary Neighborhood House, while, at least by some measures, private giving declined, leading some to assert that more generous government welfare policies played an important role in the growth of nonprofits. The experience of the Gary Neighborhood House is certainly consistent with this hypothesis. But it is also interesting to consider the theory not supported by this case. Typically, we expect organizations to act in ways that ensure organizational existence by prioritizing access to stable resources, such as funding.[44] We see consistent choices at Neighborhood House during the years of expansion, looking to new board members and collaborators that opened resources of money, experience, networks, and infrastructure. And yet, in its final years, as government and nonprofits were on the cusp of a mixed economy and government contracting began to swell the budgets of many social service agencies, the Neighborhood House chose another path. It intentionally aligned its actions with its perceptions of justice to the detriment of expanding resources, upsetting "several who have some control over the purse-strings."[45]

Certainly reliance on one main source of funding carries risks. The 60 percent budget reliance on the United Fund during the early 1960s was high but not uncommon among other social service agencies. Other agencies with similar funding profiles in 1960 had, by 1980, significant government funding, leading to what Smith and Lipsky (1993) argue can be the danger of betraying their community impulses in favor of government funding and logics. The logic of government services is equity, and helping more people—similar to the controversy-averse United Fund; but Neighborhood House president Rev. Terry might respond that band-aids are hardly "fair" in the face of the cancerous growths of racism and discrimination that stifle opportunity and require systemic change; that it is not "fair" to make the wrong palatable, rather than to seek to right it.

Grounded in the Social Gospel, the leadership of Neighborhood House charted two paths. Part of their efforts aligned well with the United Fund interests and those of its funders; these relocated to the new GNS. But they were unwilling to relinquish

the more activist aspects of their outreach and took steps to protect the survival of those projects beyond the end of the organization itself. These steps resulted in the formation of the NAI,
Project Justice & Equality, and finally GNS. Contradicting more
conventional resource-driven options, they chose to be the risk-
takers on behalf of the needy, setting priorities that brought, as
Rev. Brooks described, "a lost [sic] of funds, people, and power"
and elevating the importance of community-based mission over
that of organizational survival.[46]

CONCLUSION

This chapter examines an organization in a distinct context: a
highly segregated northern city, negotiating the transition from
the Great Society through the civil rights movement and a turbulent environment locally, regionally, and nationally. Neighborhood House cultivated institutional arrangements to provide a
flexible net of services for its clients and position itself favorably
within the local political environment. Despite never receiving
government funds directly, changes in federal policies affected
the scope of need and the resources available to the organization to address those needs. Neighborhood House leadership responded with correspondingly distinctive choices that reflected
deep-seated values—to preserve mission-based activities rather
than extending the life of the organization itself. In their choices
we see an echo of the Williams sisters' impulse to be what Gary
needed, regardless of form.

Our nation's struggle with racism and urban poverty continues, raising again the importance of addressing structural issues.
In this, there are similarities to the situation faced by the Neighborhood House. After some improvement after the passage of the
Civil Rights Act, residential and school segregation has risen again.
Income inequality has escalated, and this rising gap also reflects
children's ability to access qualified teachers. Race relations, a

dynamic resource environment, transformational leadership, and the values and missions of organizations are themes that recur and intersect. Public policy decisions will continue to shape the environments within which organizations and their clients operate, more broadly than is measured by the direct financial grants and contracts recorded. Should the federal government reinvest in reducing poverty, inequality, and racial injustice, we may expect to see nonprofits funded for job training and placement, health care provision, teacher education, and youth development partnerships with community-based policing initiatives. We might expect this policy of social investment to lead to less inequality, lowering the scope of the need in the community. If federal policymakers choose otherwise, organizations will operate within the resulting environment. And those individuals directing service organizations will no doubt continue to discern their best responses within their own distinctive contexts.[47]

NOTES

1. I wish to acknowledge the helpful comments and expertise of several people, without whom this study would be poorer. Greg Witkowski, Kim Williams-Pulfer, Nancy Marie Robertson, Ruth Hutchinson Crocker, Karen Benjamin, Graham Peck, Dennis Baskin, and the anonymous reviewers who suggested many improvements. I thank them. Remaining errors are my own responsibility.

The other three settlement houses were Campbell Friendship House, sponsored by the United Methodist Church; Gary Alerding Settlement House, sponsored by the Gary Catholic Diocese; and Stewart Settlement House, sponsored by the African Methodist Episcopal Church. Neighborhood House was sponsored by the Presbyterian Church.

2. Throughout this chapter, the reader will note several terms referring to race. The author and editors have been thoughtful in word use, but preferred usage has changed over time (see, e.g., Paul Ortiz's discussion on historical terms of racial self-identity in *An African American and Latinx History of the United States* (Boston: Beacon Press, 2018). We generally follow preferred usage for the time, but over the time studied, preferred

usage included "Negro" and "Black," with African American as the current preferred term.

3. Edward Greer, *Big Steel: Black Politics and Corporate Power in Gary, Indiana* (New York: Monthly Review, 1979), 56–58; Ruth Hutchinson Crocker, *Social Work and Social Order: The Settlement Movement in Two Industrial Cities, 1889–1930* (Urbana: University of Illinois Press, 1992), 98–100, 134–35; James B. Lane, *City of the Century: A History of Gary, Indiana* (Bloomington: Indiana University Press, 1978), 28–37; GNH Annual Report, 1968, 1–2; "Gary Neighborhood House Director Is Minister, Writer, Social Worker," *Gary Post-Tribune*, February 21, 1962; Reverend William Brooks Papers, CRA 295, box 1, folder 1, Calumet Regional Archives, Indiana University Northwest. The "Patch" later became known as "the Central District," and eventually "Midtown."

4. GNH Annual Report, 1968, 1–2; Crocker, *Social Work and Social Order*, 134–41; Kathleen D. McCarthy, "Women and Political Culture," in *Charity, Philanthropy, and Civility in American History*, eds. Lawrence J. Friedman and Mark D. McGarvie (New York: Cambridge University Press, 2002), 179–97, esp. 193.

5. Raymond A. Mohl and Neil Betten, "Paternalism and Pluralism: Immigrants and Social Welfare in Gary, Indiana, 1906–1940," *American Studies* 15, no. 1 (Spring 1974): 5–30, esp. 7; Neil Betten and Raymond A. Mohl, "From Discrimination to Repatriation: Mexican Life in Gary, Indiana, during the Great Depression," *Pacific Historical Review* 42 (1973): 370–88, esp. 371; Judith Ann Trolander, "Social Change: Settlement Houses and Saul Alinsky, 1939–1965," *Social Service Review* 56, no. 3 (September 1982): 346–65, esp. 347–50; Eleanor Brilliant and Dennis R. Young, "The Changing Identity of Federated Community Service Organizations," *Administration in Social Work* 28, nos. 3–4 (2004): 23–46, esp. 29–30; GNH Annual Report, 1966, 1–5; Gary Neighborhood House Records, CRA 069, box 1, folder 18, Calumet Regional Archives, Indiana University Northwest; S. Paul O'Hara, "The Very Model of Modern Urban Decay: Outsiders' Narratives of Industry and Urban Decline in Gary, Indiana," *Journal of Urban History* 37, no. 2 (2011): 135–54; "Steel and Sex: Vice Dens Are Hotter Than Blast Furnaces!," *Quick* (May 1955): 52–57; Minutes, Gary Neighborhood House Executive Committee, July 2, 1945, Gary Neighborhood House Records, CRA 069, box 1, folder 13, Calumet Regional Archives, Indiana University Northwest; Andrew Hurley, "Challenging Corporate Polluters: Race, Class, and Environmental Politics in Gary, Indiana, Since 1945," *Indiana Magazine of History* 88, no.

4 (December 1992): 273–302, esp. 279, 289; Frederick J. Heuser, "Presbyterians and the Struggle for Civil Rights," *Journal of Presbyterian History*
(Spring/Summer 2012): 5–16, esp. 8, https://phs-app-media
.s3.amazonaws.com/s3fs-public/Heuser_Civil_Rights_optimized.pdf;
Minutes, Gary Neighborhood House Board, August 27, 1945; GNH Annual Report, 1946, Gary Neighborhood House, Gary Neighborhood
House Records, CRA 069, box 1, folder 13, Calumet Regional Archives, Indiana University Northwest; GNH Annual Report, 1962, 6, Gary Neighborhood House Records, CRA 069, box 1, folder 18, Calumet Regional
Archives, Indiana University Northwest.

6. "Gary Neighborhood House Director Is Minister, Writer, Social
Worker," *Gary Post-Tribune*; Trolander, "Social Change," 350.

7. Application for Employment, State Merit Service, Indiana State
Personnel Division, November 1967, Reverend William Brooks Papers,
CRA 295, box 1, folder 1, Calumet Regional Archives, Indiana University
Northwest; Transcript, Loyalty Hearing, 1950, Reverend William Brooks
Papers, CRA 295, box 1, folder 9, Calumet Regional Archives, Indiana Uni-
versity Northwest; Letter from United States Civil Service Commission
to Mr. Austin T. Walden, attorney-at-law, July 10, 1950, Reverend William
Brooks Papers, CRA 295, box 1, folder 9, Calumet Regional Archives, Indiana University Northwest; Howard Eugene Johnson and Wendy Johnson,
*A Dancer in the Revolution: Stretch Johnson, Harlem Communist at the Cot-
ton Club* (New York: Fordham University Press, 2014), 112–13. Johnson's
memoir describes the links between American communism and pre–civil
rights efforts for racial equity, including his own experience with UNAVA.
For more on the connection between fighting European fascism and domestic racism, see Matthew Delmont, "Why African American Soldiers
Saw World War II as a Two-Front Battle," *Smithsonian Magazine*, August
24, 2017, https://www.smithsonianmag.com/history/why-african
-american-soldiers-saw-world-war-ii-two-front-battle-180964616/. For
more on the discrimination against Black GIs after World War II, see Hil-
ary Herbold, "Never a Level Playing Field: Blacks and the GI Bill," *Journal
of Blacks in Higher Education* no. 6 (Winter 1994–1995): 104–8.

8. Transcript, Loyalty Hearing, 1950, United States Civil Service Com-
mission to Mr. Austin T. Walden, attorney-at-law, July 10, 1950, Order of
Service, Thirkield Memorial Chapel, Gammon Theological Seminary,
February 7, 1956, Reverend William Brooks Papers, CRA 295, box 1, folder
7, Calumet Regional Archives, Indiana University Northwest; William
Brooks, "Transform Region by Conformity with God," *Post-Tribune*,

October 13, 1973. Reverend William Brooks Papers, CRA 295, box 1, folder 1, Calumet Regional Archives, Indiana University Northwest.

9. GNH Annual Report, 1962. Trolander, "Social Change," 351–52. Richard I. McKinney, "The Black Church: Its Development and Present Impact," *Harvard Theological Review* 64, no. 4 (October 1971): 452–81, esp. 465–66.

10. GNH Annual Reports, 1962, 1964, 1966, and 1968, Gary Neighborhood House Records, CRA 069, box 1, folders 18–19, Calumet Regional Archives, Indiana University Northwest; Marcelo Bucheli and Jin Uk Kim, "The State as a Historical Construct in Organization Studies," in *Organizations in Time: History, Theory, Methods*, eds. Marcelo Bucheli and R. Daniel Wadhwani (Oxford: Oxford University Press, 2014), 241–62, esp. 241–45, 256.

11. Thornbrough, *Indiana Blacks in the Twentieth Century*, 175; Annemette Sørensen and Karl E. Taeuber, "Indexes of Racial Residential Segregation for 109 Cities in the United States, 1940 to 1970," *Sociological Focus* 8, no. 2 (April 1975): 125–42, esp. 128–30.

12. GNH Annual Report, 1962, 4.

13. Lane, *City of the Century*, 279; David E. Bernstein, "The Neglected Case of *Buchanan v. Warley*," *SCOTUSblog*, http://www.scotusblog.com /2010/02/the-neglected-case-of-buchanan-v-warley/; Municipal Code of the City of Gary, Indiana 1949; Municipal Code of the City of Gary, Indiana 1960; Letter, Paul Dudak, May 10, 1965, City of Gary Collection, CRA 010, box 9, folder 33, Calumet Regional Archives, Indiana University Northwest; Thornbrough, *Indiana Blacks*, 164; Heuser, "Presbyterians and the Struggle for Civil Rights," 13. On informal segregated housing practices, see Arnold Hirsch, *Making the Second Ghetto: Race & Housing in Chicago 1940–1960* (Chicago: The University of Chicago Press, 1998), 10, 254.

14. Greer, *Big Steel*, 36, 98–100, 102–4; Thornbrough, *Indiana Blacks*, 175, 181–82; Lane, *City of the Century*, 280, 285.

15. Clarence Boebel, executive director of the Chicago Federation of Settlements and Neighborhood Centers, speaking at the 55th Annual Meeting of the Gary Neighborhood House, October 23, 1964. Minutes, Annual Meeting, October 23, 1964, Gary Neighborhood House Records, CRA 069, box 1, folder 14, Calumet Regional Archives, Indiana University Northwest.

16. Clarence Boebel, address at 55th Annual Meeting, Minutes, Annual Meeting, October 23, 1964, Gary Neighborhood House Records, CRA 069, box 1, folder 14, Calumet Regional Archives, Indiana University Northwest.

17. Minutes, February 11, 1964; Highlights, meeting with Alfred Rath, February 14, 1964; Minutes, program committee, January 23, 1964, Gary Neighborhood House Records, CRA 069, box 1, folder 14, Calumet Regional Archives, Indiana University Northwest; GNH Annual Reports, 1964 and 1966, folder 18, Calumet Regional Archives, Indiana University Northwest.

18. Pamphlet, Ten Valid Reasons for Opposing Union with the United Presbyterian Church. Concerned Presbyterians, Inc. ca. 1973–74, https:// pcahistory.org/pca/concerned/TenValidReasons.pdf; Highlights, meeting with Alfred Rath, February 14, 1964, Gary Neighborhood House Records, CRA 069, box 1, folder 14, Calumet Regional Archives, Indiana University Northwest.

19. Brilliant and Young, "Changing Identity," 27–30.

20. "Guilty in Gary," *Time*, 80, no. 25 (December 21, 1962): 24. Kirsten A. Grønbjerg, David Street, and Gerald D. Suttles, *Poverty and Social Change* (Chicago: University of Chicago Press, 1978), 56; Annual Report, 1964, 8.

21. Minutes, program committee, January 23, 1964; Recommendations to Executive Board from Program Committee Meeting, January 3, 1964; Letter to Philip Lock, Louis Haller, and Dr. Brady from Reuben Olson and Rev. William Brooks, April 2, 1964, Gary Neighborhood House Records, CRA 069, box 1, folder 14, Calumet Regional Archives, Indiana University Northwest; GNH Annual Report, 1964, 9; Executive Committee Minutes, March 26, 1964, Gary Neighborhood House Records, CRA 069, box 1, folder 14, Calumet Regional Archives, Indiana University Northwest; Certificate of Merit, October 30, 1965, Reverend William Brooks Papers, CRA 295, box 1, folder 10, Calumet Regional Archives, Indiana University Northwest; GNH board member Jackie Shropshire was a Muigwithanian.

22. GNH Annual Report, 1964, 8–9; Agenda, Ad Hoc Housing Committee, October 20, 1964, Gary Neighborhood House Records, CRA 069, box 1, folder 14, Calumet Regional Archives, Indiana University Northwest; Grønbjerg, Street, and Suttles, *Poverty and Social Change*, 60; Bonnie Boswell, prod., *Powerbroker: Whitney Young's Fight for Civil Rights* (New York: Filmakers Library, 2012), accessed December 9, 2017.

23. GNH Annual Report, 1966, 6–18. The financial reports do not reflect direct government support, but program updates indicate external funding and a level of interdependence with other organizations that are not reflected in the financial statements.

24. Ibid., 9.

25. GNH Annual Report, 1966, 9, 17; Lane, *City of the Century*, 281–82.

26. Lane, *City of the Century*, 278, 289; GNH Annual Reports, 1964, 1966, 1968, Gary Neighborhood House Records, CRA 069, box 1, folders 18–19, Calumet Regional Archives, Indiana University Northwest; "Plea from Gary," *Time* 90, no. 11 (September 15, 1967): 28; Thornbrough, *Indiana Blacks*, 175; Federal Bureau of Investigation, memo, racial developments. Omitted. Issue Date: April 24, 1967, complete, 5 pages, reproduced in *Declassified Documents Reference System* (Farmington Hills, MI: Gale, 2014), Document Number: CK2349549245; O'Hara, "The Very Model of Modern Urban Decay," 142.

27. Thornbrough, *Indiana Blacks*, 177; Lane, *City of the Century*, 304. Minutes, January 23, 1967, and March 27, 1967, Gary Neighborhood House Records, CRA 069, box 1, folder 14, Calumet Regional Archives, Indiana University Northwest; Greer, *Big Steel*, 100.

28. Registration Supplement, submitted by Rev. William M. Brooks, no date, 1, Reverend William Brooks Papers, CRA 295, box 1, folder 1, Calumet Regional Archives, Indiana University Northwest; McKinney, *The Black Church*, 472.

29. Articles of Incorporation, Metro Corps of Gary, Inc., May 13, 1968, accessed April 6, 2022, https://inbiz.in.gov/BOS/Home/Index; "Farewell Dinner," *Post-Tribune*, October 30, 1968; Reverend William Brooks Papers, CRA 295, box 1, folder 3, Calumet Regional Archives, Indiana University Northwest; Certificate of appreciation, July 10, 1969, Reverend William Brooks Papers, CRA 295, box 1, folder 10, Calumet Regional Archives, Indiana University Northwest.

30. "Farewell Dinner," *Post-Tribune*; Lane, *City of the Century*, 270; Annual Report 1968, 9; Trolander, *Social Change*, 352–55.

31. GNH Annual Report, 1968.

32. Minutes, February 13, 1968, Gary Neighborhood House Records, CRA 069, box 1, folder 14, Calumet Regional Archives, Indiana University Northwest; GNH Annual Report, 1968.

33. Reverend William Brooks, commentary on Church, 1969, Reverend William Brooks Papers, CRA 295, box 1, folder 3, Calumet Regional Archives, Indiana University Northwest.

34. Certificate of incorporation, Neighborhood Action Institute, Gary Neighborhood House Records, CRA 069, box 1, folders 24, Calumet Regional Archives, Indiana University Northwest; GNH Annual Report, 1968, 16; Fact sheet, Neighborhood Action Institute, Gary Neighborhood

House Records, CRA 069, box 1, folder 25, Calumet Regional Archives, Indiana University Northwest; Reverend William Brooks, commentary on Church, 1969, Reverend William Brooks Papers, CRA 295, box 1, folder 3, Calumet Regional Archives, Indiana University Northwest; Trolander, *Social Change*, 352–55.

35. GNH Annual Report, 1969, 7–10.

36. GNH Annual Report, 1969; GNH Annual Report, 1970; Lane, *City of the Century*, 299, 302.

37. Thornbrough, *Indiana Blacks*, 188; Hurley, "Challenging Corporate Polluters," 273–75; GNH Annual Report, 1970, 10–14; "Business Services Online," Indiana Secretary of State, accessed April 6, 2022, https://inbiz.in .gov/BOS/Home/Index; Administrative Dissolution, Project Justice and Equality, May 19, 2004, https://secure.in.gov/sos/online_corps/.

38. GNH Annual Report, 1970, 4–6; GNS Annual Report, 1990, 2. City of Gary Collection, CRA 010, box 7, folder 11, Calumet Regional Archives, Indiana University Northwest; Personal e-mail correspondence, David Koch (Presbyterian Historical Society) to Judy Lucas (Synod of Lincoln Trails), March 17, 2014; Letter from J. Thurman to E. Monroe, in correspondence, 1968–1972, Gary Neighborhood House Records, CRA 069, box 1, folder 40, Calumet Regional Archives, Indiana University Northwest; GNS Annual Report, 1990, 2.

39. Kirsten Grønbjerg, Lori Harmon, Aida Olkkonen, and Asif Raza, "The United Way System at the Crossroads: Community Planning and Allocation," *Nonprofit and Voluntary Sector Quarterly* 25, no. 4 (December 1996): 428–52, esp. 441–42; GNH Annual Report, 1970, 5, 18; GNS Annual Report, 1990, 8–9.

40. "Opening the Doors to the Future," City of Gary Collection, CRA 010, box 7, folder 11, Calumet Regional Archives, Indiana University Northwest; GNS Annual Report, 1990; "Gary Picks Social Services Head," *Afro-American (1893–1988)*, October 23, 1971; Articles of Amendment, Gary Neighborhood Services, September 9, 1974, https://secure.in.gov/sos /online_corps/; GNS Annual Report, 1982; Letter from J. Thurman to E. Monroe; GNS Annual Reports, Summer 1975, 1982; Administrative Dissolution, Neighborhood Action Institute, January 1, 1978, https://secure.in .gov/sos/online_corps/ ; Administrative Dissolution, Project Justice and Equality, May 19, 2004, https://secure.in.gov/sos/online_corps/.

41. Articles of Incorporation, Gary Neighborhood Services, April 22, 1971, https://secure.in.gov/sos/online_corps/; Report of the Synod of Lincoln Trails, 1974, 35. Presbyterian Church (United States), Synod

of Lincoln Trails, Call Number: 04 112c, Presbyterian Historical Society, Philadelphia, PA; Marona flyer; Bankston bio, Various, Marona House (1970–1971); Gary Neighborhood House Records, CRA 069, box 2, folder 3, Calumet Regional Archives, Indiana University Northwest.

42. Press release, Regarding Death of Raymond Welch, May 12, 1971, Gary Neighborhood House Records, CRA 069, box 1, folder 57, Calumet Regional Archives, Indiana University Northwest; "Petition for Cross Section of Community on Juries and for Probation or Appeal Bail Bond for Brother David Hilliard," *Black Panther* 7, no. 2 (September 4, 1971): 7; Gary Neighborhood House Records, CRA 069, oversize, Calumet Regional Archives, Indiana University Northwest.

43. GNH Annual Report, 1970, 1.

44. Lester M. Salamon, *Partners in Public Service: Government-Nonprofit Relations in the Modern Welfare State* (Baltimore: Johns Hopkins University Press, 1995), 1, 192; Kirsten A. Grønbjerg, *Understanding Nonprofit Funding: Managing Revenues in Social Services and Community Development Organizations* (San Francisco: Jossey-Bass, 1993), 23; Karen A. Froelich, "Diversification of Revenue Strategies: Evolving Resource Dependence in Nonprofit Organizations," *Nonprofit and Voluntary Sector Quarterly* 28, no. 3 (1999): 246–68, esp. 247.

45. GNH Annual Report, 1969, 7.

46. Grønbjerg, Harmon, Olkkonen, and Raza, "United Way System," 429–30; Steven Rathgeb Smith and Michael Lipsky, *Nonprofits for Hire: The Welfare State in the Age of Contracting* (Cambridge, MA: Harvard University Press, 1993), 22–25, 122–24, 205, 234–37; Rev. William Brooks, "Commentary on Church," 1969.

47. Bucheli and Kim, "State as a Historical Construct," 241–45, esp. 256; Julian E. Zelizer, "Is America Repeating the Mistakes of 1968?," *Atlantic*, July 8, 2016, accessed July 12, 2020, http://www.theatlantic.com /politics/archive/2016/07/is-america-repeating-the-mistakes-of -1968/490568/; Fred Harris and Alan Curtis, "The Unmet Promise of Equality," *New York Times*, February 28, 2018, accessed July 12, 2020, https://www.nytimes.com/interactive/2018/02/28/opinion/the-unmet -promise-of-equality.html; Alan Curtis, "Healing Our Divided Society: Presentation to the United States Commission on Civil Rights," *Eisenhower Foundation*, July 13, 2018, accessed July 12, 2020, http://www .eisenhowerfoundation.org/link16.

PART II

TRENDS AND INNOVATIONS

SECTION IV

NETWORKS AND COLLABORATIONS

FOURTEEN

"THE PROBLEM OF EXPENSE"

Lay Religion, Hoosier Patrons, and Philanthropic Logics in Midcentury America

PHILIP D. BYERS

BY THE TIME D. ELTON TRUEBLOOD gathered a group of Earlham College students at his home in 1951, the philosopher had already fretted over the state of American religious life for more than a decade.[1] A modest midwesterner by birth, a committed Quaker by heritage, and a distinguished professor by concerted effort, Trueblood first began formulating his concerns in 1936. Over the fifteen years that followed, in books and speeches, his theme became clear: American religion was *tepid*. It required no sacrifice. "Many of the best people are not in the church," Trueblood concluded, "because they <u>are</u> the best people. They are looking for something that means business and often fail to find it."[2] Yet that night, in his den in Richmond, Indiana, Trueblood saw an ideal setting for the type of rigorous religious practice that promised to soothe anxious individuals and invigorate America's lethargic civil society. Introducing the students to his vision, Trueblood defined a "minimum discipline," which included five core practices that those gathered would pursue together: daily prayer, Bible reading, regular participation in organized worship, devoted religious study, and charitable giving.[3] Using language he had developed over several years, this small group would call themselves "Yokefellows."[4]

Few in attendance that evening could have imagined their gathering would help launch a lay religious renewal spanning several decades and thousands of miles, and in many ways that initial group bore little resemblance to what the Yokefellow movement became. But looking back, one founding participant stands out. Etsuko Hirooka was a Japanese foreign exchange student, and though she attended Earlham for only one year, she fully embraced the Yokefellow principles.[5] After her return to Japan, Etsuko married a young pastor named Tetsuo Kobayashi. Founding Sakuradai Church in Tokyo, the Kobayashis believed they could apply Yokefellow concepts to their congregational life, and a booklet published in 1956 revealed encouraging early results.[6] From their church-based kindergarten to the commitment cards they gave new members, the Kobayashis exemplified the movement's pursuit of rigorous spirituality in the context of daily life. However, by 1973, matters had changed. The Kobayashis' report for a booklet published that year evinced a plaintive tone. While the Yokefellow movement had seemingly stalled in Japan, the booklet described new branches in North Carolina, Pennsylvania, and Switzerland that pulsed with vitality.[7]

This contrast in the Kobayashis' status revealed a larger evolution in the Yokefellow movement that occurred in the decades following its inception. As materials from the founding years make clear, Trueblood conceived the Yokefellows as a project in lay Christian revitalization, a renewal within the "church universal" characterized by discipline in daily life with minimal centralized governance. Nevertheless, between the movement's founding and the mid-1960s, the prominent emphases in Yokefellow literature shifted noticeably. By the late 1960s, the Yokefellows prioritized establishing a network of regional retreat centers rather than facilitating religious practice in daily life. The early preference for informality had yielded to incorporation and a tax-exempt charter from the federal government, and a mailing list had replaced word-of-mouth membership.

What happened to initiate these shifts? What transpired in the seventeen years between the Kobayashis' testimonies? And what relevance might this tale possess for scholars of American philanthropy or students of Indiana history? Certainly, Trueblood's national religious, social, and political contexts demand consideration, but philanthropic histories often assume the predominance of universal themes. In contrast, the story of the Yokefellows reveals the pertinence of the local and immediate—in this case, a uniquely determined network of midcentury Hoosier philanthropists. The network involved a diverse range of actors, starting with institutions and individuals of humble means, expanding to wealthy patrons and a major philanthropic foundation. As funding began to increase in the early 1950s, substantial grants understandably came with substantial expectations for how recipients should apply those funds.

Unlike some accounts that frame philanthropy in conspiratorial or accusatory tones, this story does not impugn motives or endow philanthropists with unrivaled power.[8] Rather, it illustrates inherent limitations—opportunity costs—that accompany any potential promise of a philanthropic gift. As with other instances of foundation-funded social movements in the twentieth century, the case of the Yokefellows reveals a "channeling" effect. The very support that enabled the grassroots movement to build on its initial momentum simultaneously incentivized its leaders to adopt greater uniformity and centralization.[9] In other words, though increased sources of funding solidified the base upon which the Yokefellows functioned and allowed them to expand, that funding also appeared to limit the movement's potential to respond nimbly in different cultural contexts.

Likewise, this tale suggests two lesser, but still substantial, themes. First, it reveals a network of philanthropists rather than some heroic (or nefarious) lone actor.[10] As the Yokefellows transitioned from an ad hoc movement to a centralized organization, the individuals, institutions, and philanthropic foundations referenced above each provided the movement with unique types of aid. Second, the story raises questions about prevailing concepts of philanthropic effectiveness. While recent trends prioritize projects with the potential for global impact, the logic behind the contributions that funded the Yokefellows eschewed dreams of transformation in favor of local knowledge and moderation.[11]

CONTEXTUAL INFLUENCES AND
EARLY PRIORITIES

Though he was barely middle-aged when he first conceived the Yokefellow ideas in the mid-1940s, Elton Trueblood had already traveled widely across the terrain of American higher education. Born in 1900 to a family of multigenerational Quakers in south central Iowa, Trueblood left the family farm and spent time at humble liberal arts colleges, elite East Coast Ivies, and tony divinity schools before ultimately earning his PhD in philosophy at Johns Hopkins. After a nine-year stint as Stanford's university chaplain and instructor in philosophy of religion, in 1945 Trueblood made a momentous decision to relocate to Earlham College, a Quaker liberal arts institution in east central Indiana. His subsequent reflections on that move rooted this choice in the conviction that small colleges promote a "pattern of life which produces a high order of excellence."[12] Yet part of his decision surely hinged on Earlham's attractive offer. The college created a tailor-made position, what the outgoing president labeled a "roving professorship," which lightened Trueblood's teaching load and thereby freed him for a diverse array of speaking engagements.[13] The job offer proved just the first instance in which Earlham's institutional largesse—whether measured by the direct payment of monies or the indirect provision of time or facilities—provided transformative aid to Trueblood and the Yokefellows. Indeed, if his peripatetic academic career first introduced him to influential scholars and governmental elites, Earlham provided the means to expand his national profile and network of patrons.[14] Just as importantly, it served as a fine setting for inchoate ideas about religious renewal to swell into a full-fledged initiative.

While biographical details help explain Trueblood's identity as a midcentury religious leader and his decision to move to Earlham, the convictions he developed about the need for widespread religious revitalization originated in prevailing civic anxieties in Western society and broad traditions in Western Christianity. Since at least the 1880s, many American elites had grappled with what they perceived to be the enervating social and civic effects of widespread industrial capitalism. As cultural historian Jackson Lears recounts in his study of fin de siècle anti-modernism, observers feared that a "weightless culture of material comfort and spiritual blandness was breeding weightless persons who longed for intense experience to give some definition, some distinct outline and substance to their vaporous lives."[15] If the intervening decades provided numerous (and tragic) opportunities for "intense experience,"[16] early Cold War–era exigencies poured accelerant on these prior concerns. Historian George Marsden describes how 1950s-era best sellers, like David Riesman's *The Lonely Crowd* (1950), evinced a widespread fear of moral emptiness and civic pessimism, a concern that "'modern man' had become alienated, inauthentic, conformist, and phony."[17]

Trueblood published several books in the early Cold War years, and those texts reveal similar concerns.[18] In 1948's *Alternative to Futility*, for instance, he referenced the "sickness of Western man" in the opening sentence, clarifying that individuals "cannot live well in poverty or abundance unless they see some meaning and purpose in life."[19] At one level, the philosopher's concerns were theoretical, but he detected concrete dangers as well. "Two years after Hiroshima," as he signed the book's preface, Trueblood feared "millions will prefer war so long as they lack in their inner lives," so long as they sought a "glorious escape" from a mundane existence.[20] While numerous historians have demonstrated the link between Cold War business interests and the era's surge in religiosity, Trueblood doubted capitalism could soothe what ailed the American public.[21] Instead, he repurposed the words of Jesus to acknowledge that fealty to free markets could not provide sufficient purpose: "Man cannot live by economics alone."[22] For Trueblood, a reinvigorated religious culture provided the only tonic for this postwar existential despair.

While social and political trends certainly colored Trueblood's assessment of challenges facing Western society, he drew opinions about an appropriate solution from a variety of religious antecedents. Some examples were historical in nature, including allusions to St. Francis of Assisi or the development of the Jesuit order. Contemporary movements played an even greater role in forming his outlook, with no influence looming larger than George MacLeod's Iona Community.[23] Trueblood first discovered MacLeod's work in August 1948 when he visited Iona (one of the small islands west of Scotland that comprise the Inner Hebrides) after attending the London Yearly Meeting of Quakers.[24] A former soldier and minister in the Church of Scotland, MacLeod founded Iona in 1938 at the site of a centuries-old Benedictine abbey. Committing themselves to prayer, Bible study, fellowship, communitarian principles, and peace, community members also labored to restore the abbey's ruins.[25] In Iona's union of "physical work, meditation, study and discipline," Trueblood discerned an antidote to the lethargy besetting postwar Christianity, an apt remedy to "the general unreality of modern life, which separates brain and hand."[26] Trueblood biographer, James Newby, cites the philosopher recounting, "If it were not for Iona, I doubt there would have been a Yokefellow movement."[27]

Drawing on these sundry examples, Trueblood slowly clarified his vision through the late 1940s and early 1950s. Two themes merit special attention as they preview how philanthropy eventually influenced the movement: In Trueblood's earliest imaginings, the Yokefellows emphasized spiritual discipline in the context of daily life and decentralized governance as an aid to autonomy and creativity among the "church universal."

Given the social and political contexts, the necessity of rigor and discipline dominated Trueblood's vision for lay renewal. However, he recognized the esoteric allure (and danger) of a type of monastic withdrawal from society. Rather, the lay resurgence he envisioned would distinguish itself by observing "a strict voluntary discipline [while staying] in common life."[28] By "common life," Trueblood meant merely the warp and woof of American society, a position he unfolded in 1949's *The Common Ventures of Life*. There he contended that any vibrant modern religion "must be connected with the way we *eat*, the way we *work*, the way we *make love*, the way we *think*, the way we *dream*, and the way we *die*."[29] Fulfilling religion for the modern American could not exist as an irregular diversion or a sporadic practice; it needed to suffuse all of life.

Just as he yearned for Yokefellows to remain a vibrant presence in the quotidian functions of their communities, so did Trueblood aim for the movement to remain fully within the "church universal." Most practically, this emerged in his instinct to avoid burdening the Yokefellows with undue centralization, a preference he justified in two ways. First, he feared formal organization might imply that the Yokefellows viewed themselves as a breakaway movement. "The ideal," in his estimation, "would be a reformation *within* the Church, not a reformation *from* the Church.... Otherwise we merely become schismatic again and dissipate our power."[30] Informality, Trueblood hoped, would militate against separatism. Even more, he feared the potential for centralized governance to enervate an otherwise vigorous lay movement. Distracted or diluted effort posed one danger, as organization would demand that Yokefellows expend time, energy, and money on administration. Perhaps even more perniciously, at the subconscious level, formal organization implied achievement and sapped momentum in the process. Once any movement begins to elect board members or officers, it faces a "deadly" threat "because it gives the impression that something has been accomplished."[31] So even as an initial group of nine students met with Trueblood at Earlham and word of the "Yokefellows" spread in tandem with his growing national profile, the early 1950s found the philosopher inclined to keep the Yokefellows functioning on an informal, ad hoc basis.

NEW FUNDING YIELDS NEW COMMITMENTS

In no time at all, Trueblood faced a test to his preference for informality. By the end of 1951, the movement had begun to grow beyond his capacity to direct it. Fortunately, even as the professor first sensed this problem, he met a perceptive businessman who discerned the same. Cofounder of the American States Insurance Company, Edward Gallahue had enjoyed great business success and, consequently, a substantial public profile in Indianapolis; through the 1930s and 1940s, he frequently appeared in the *Indianapolis Star*'s society pages.[32] Perhaps more importantly, he also established his civic bona fides, working on the Methodist Hospital board and leading lay activities at his church.[33] In the leisure time not already occupied by business, social, or civic commitments, Gallahue applied himself to the study of philosophy and religion. This introduced him to Trueblood's work, and he subsequently invited the philosopher to deliver a sermon at North Methodist Church.

As Gallahue heard Trueblood opine on the merits of the Yokefellow movement, the entrepreneur reacted instinctively, encouraging Trueblood to incorporate. Not stopping at a mere recommendation, Gallahue offered the services of his personal attorney and provided Trueblood with a gift of $1,000 to support travel, postage, and administrative costs.[34] By 1952, Gallahue had also helped Trueblood form an early cabinet. The cabinet members agreed to guide the Yokefellows' vision and provide sustained funding that could replace the movement's prior reliance on infrequent gifts from well-meaning, but financially limited, individuals. Besides Gallahue, the early board included a Fort Wayne pediatrician, a Cleveland lawyer, and a New York businessman. They were denominationally diverse, counting Methodists, Presbyterians, Episcopalians, and Quakers among their ranks.[35]

Trueblood's recollections of this process—so seemingly inconsistent with his oft-avowed preference for informality—reveal an air of special pleading. In a newsletter marking the Yokefellow's first decade, he emphasized that the initial board had formed consistent with "the slightest organization possible compatible with effective work."[36] A decade later, in his autobiography, Trueblood insisted that early trustees had "continued to minimize organization" and "resolved consciously never to become administratively top-heavy."[37] By the time he penned a 1982 tribute to the late Gallahue, he reframed the episode entirely, avoiding the term *organization* altogether. Instead, he explained the movement's incorporation by noting that Gallahue was a man "always looking for new wineskins to contain the new wine."[38]

Surely the fruit of his instinctual aversion to formal organization, these accounts generally obscure the means by which Trueblood converted his informal social networks into a centralized governing body, but they reveal other important facets of the Yokefellows' story. First, they illuminate Trueblood's struggle to reconcile tensions that eventually face all grassroots social movements: how to handle the costs and benefits of top-down direction. In an essay on social movement philanthropy, sociologists J. Craig Jenkins and Abigail Halcli analyze this challenge according to a "channeling thesis." By incentivizing organization, they claim, "movement-based philanthropy [has] tended to professionalize indigenous-movement groups ... thus channeling movements into institutionalized actions." While their subject matter differs in many ways from the Yokefellows—designation as a "social movement" indicates a "previously unorganized or politically excluded group" seeking a "broader definition of citi-zenship rights"—in other ways, the phenomenon they identified applies quite well.[39] As the following pages demonstrate, the en-suing years would involve continuing negotiation between the Yokefellows' original grassroots priorities and an increasingly grasstops focus on uniformity and centralization.

If Trueblood's accounts obscure the means, however, they clar-ify the immediate catalyst of the movement's changing character: Edward Gallahue. Indeed, the cabinet Gallahue helped form, and then chaired, achieved the next step in formalization in Janu-ary 1954 by securing official charter. In February 1956, the group obtained official tax-exempt status from the US Treasury.[40] But, if Gallahue provided the Yokefellows with an initial surge of or-ganizational logic, the period between 1954 and 1956 introduced Trueblood and the Yokefellows to an even more powerful and sustainable source of support: Lilly Endowment Inc. (LEI).[41] Es-tablished in 1937, in the wake of the Revenue Act of 1935, LEI was notable both for the local focus of its beneficence and also for its interest in religion, an uncommon program area among the na-tion's largest foundations.[42]

Trueblood's concerns and intended solution dovetailed nicely with the philanthropic disposition of LEI's leaders, especially that of Eli Lilly himself. First, Mr. Lilly favored projects that pro-moted character development and inculcated a sense of moral values. These priorities stemmed from a conviction evocative of Trueblood's many books, namely that American "spiritual development has a hundred-year lag behind our material prog-ress."[43] Additionally, though his business expanded during his lifetime into a multinational behemoth, Lilly found his greatest pleasures close to home. His favorite getaway was a family cabin on northern Indiana's Lake Wawasee, and he devoted most of his leisure time to Indiana-focused hobbies, including local ar-chaeology. The same rang true for his philanthropic work. Bi-ographer James H. Madison quotes from a letter in which Lilly explained his outlook to his daughter. Faced with the challenge of determining "what objects . . . are worthwhile and what are not," Lilly responded by focusing on what Madison labels the "people and institutions he knew personally"; these preferences reflected Lilly's "wish to know more intimately the channels in which his philanthropy would flow."[44] These modest aspirations made Eli Lilly and the family foundation a good fit for Indiana's distinctive sociopolitical climate. In a separate survey of Indiana history, Madison notes that twentieth-century political changes in the state typically "occurred in ways that evidenced the tendency to seek moderation and to adjust the pace of change to traditions embedded in the Hoosier state."[45]

Even as Trueblood's project seemed a neat fit for LEI's mission and Indiana's culture, the philosopher could also rely on his personal network: By the mid-1950s, he had known Eli Lilly for nearly a decade. Meeting first at a 1946 benefit dinner, the two cooperated on a number of ventures in the interim. On a trip with the Friends Ambulance Unit later that year, Trueblood took Lilly-donated vitamin tablets to distribute among war-devastated Germans. In the late 1940s, Trueblood accompanied Earlham's president when he approached the philanthropist to request building funds.[46] Likewise, the pharmaceutical titan sometimes requested Trueblood's help. When Lilly initiated a program targeted at improving employee morale at his company, he invited the popular author to deliver a lecture highlighting many of the same themes that filled his best-selling books.[47] If these prior interactions inclined LEI leaders to look favorably on Trueblood's project, it surely helped that the foundation's secretary, G. Harold Duling, was a regular attendee at his local Quaker meeting and the husband of an Earlham alumna.[48] Duling attended the Yokefellows' first national conference in 1955, which was hosted at Earlham College in another demonstration of the institution's munificence, and he left impressed with the espoused mission. He and Trueblood began corresponding about what a partnership might look like, and by early 1956, the details were in place. LEI pledged $15,000 annually for a period of three years and contributed more than $75,000 to the Yokefellows between 1956 and 1961.

Trueblood's ideas for building on this newfound support often privileged the symbolic over the strategic. For example, he promoted the concept of a commitment card, small enough to fit in a wallet or handbag while including a list of the five core disciplines and a spot for the Yokefellow's signature. He believed the cards would facilitate group cohesion, reminding members of their commitment to discipleship.[49] Likewise, he wanted to disseminate bronze ox-yoke lapel pins in the hope that they would catch an observer's attention and prompt a discussion about the symbol's significance.[50] The project that most excited LEI, however, was what Trueblood summarized as the "first genuine laymen's seminary" in the United States.[51] In Richmond, this took concrete form in the 1956 establishment of the Yokefellow Institute, headquartered in Trueblood's former home on the Earlham campus. This initiative had a long genealogy in Trueblood's writing. The institute exemplified his "base/field" model of ministry, whereby Christian vitality emerged "not from being always in the field of service, and not from being always on retreat, but from alternating between the two."[52] In 1957, Samuel Emerick became the institute's first director, and the site quickly began hosting so much traffic that the board opted to construct a new facility to the south of Earlham's campus.[53] On the heels of this initial burst of success, providing space and resources for lay retreats became the centralized board's primary mission. Over the next twenty years, the board would facilitate similar efforts across the country, creating a network of like-purpose retreat centers in California (1956), Ohio (1960), North Carolina (c. 1960–63), Washington, DC (1963), Pennsylvania (1971), and Massachusetts (1972).

The evidence, then, suggests that philanthropy initiated some changes in the Yokefellow project. Acknowledging this influence does not require one to presume an intentional agenda among donors nor mindful capitulation in Trueblood and the early participants. Rather, it suggests that money carries with it a tacit but relentless logic, one with the capacity to redirect the missions of the nonprofits it supports. William McKersie's 1999 essay on local philanthropy elucidates this relationship. There, he notes that foundations rarely create programs from scratch but rather find existing nonprofits "able and willing to advance their grantmaking priorities." Rather than dictating from on high, foundations exist in "interdependence" with nonprofits and often need to "balance their own predilections with the interests and abilities of potential grantees."[54] In the case of the Yokefellows, willingness to balance interests flowed both ways, and pertinent changes from those interactions fell neatly within the two themes detailed above. First, increasing focus on "lay seminaries" and religious retreats, almost by definition, corresponded with a decrease in attention to the practice of minimum discipline within the domain of daily life. Second, as the movement's organization centralized and its brand became synonymous with the expanding network of retreat centers, the Yokefellows demonstrated less sensitivity to broad concerns within the "church universal" and less interest in divergent expressions of the Yokefellow ideal.

The list of retreat centers reveals how the Yokefellow Institute model spread to various municipalities across the United States, and close attention to material in Trueblood's private papers shows that this process began to dominate the movement's attention in the years after receiving LEI grants. For instance, information on retreats and the burgeoning retreat centers pervaded the June 1961 edition of the Yokefellows' biannual newsletter. Trueblood enclosed with each mailing a copy of "The Layman as an Evangelist," by Howard Butt, Jr. Son of a supermarket magnate and philanthropist, Butt's interests aligned perfectly with the Yokefellows' ascendant vision. That very month, in fact, Butt founded his own retreat center in Corpus Christi, Texas: the Laity Lodge.[55]

Along with that article insert, the newsletter included a summary of topics for the upcoming meeting of the Yokefellow board. Retreat center–focused items comprised the entire agenda, as directors considered: funding new physical plant work on the Earlham campus retreat facilities; the overall "role of a lay center"; the relationship between the institute in Richmond and other centers around the country; and "the relation of the National Board to all Yokefellow centers."[56] The June 1968 newsletter listed several "Yokefellow developments," and consistently this equated to "facility updates." North Carolinians had founded a "new kind of Yokefellow Center" in Forest City, and the Pennsylvania branch of the movement had finally established a base "after existing for several years without adequate facilities." The only attention to "ministry in common life" came in the form of a list of books that Trueblood recommended.[57] To be sure, he still cared deeply about religious vitality and the role of the lay Christian. However, where early materials highlighted the commitment card, the components of the "minimum discipline," and the ox-yoke lapel pin, materials published after several years of foundation funding revealed a notable reorientation toward the network of lay retreat centers. As the movement's vision effectively narrowed, the Yokefellows became less likely to promote expressions that deviated from this retreat-center norm, a shift consistent with Jenkins and Halcli's contention that by "provid[ing] alternative resources" social movement philanthropy inherently "encourage[s] the development of more centralized movements."[58]

For a case study of this process, consider the trajectories of the Yokefellow branches in Japan and Switzerland. Etsuko and Tetsuo Kobayashi believed that discipline in daily life comprised the core of the Yokefellow idea, an emphasis that neatly fit their cultural context in mid-1950s Japan. As Christians were only a small minority in Tokyo, "there seemed no need to mention unity or commitment to Christ"; cultural opposition meant that those qualities could be assumed and that "every Christian was then a fully committed person" by default. As such, the Kobayashis dispensed with the need for a separate movement and instead implemented Yokefellow ideas across Sakuradai Church. Members committed to Yokefellow principles at the point of their baptisms, receiving and signing a Japanese-language commitment card.[59] This also transformed the types of initiatives the Kobayashis pursued under the Yokefellow mantle. Work with Tokyo children became one major focus, as the Kobayashis launched what they called a "kindergarten" during the week, intending to establish Sakuradai as a church fully invested in the daily life of its local community.

Where the Kobayashis received consistent attention and even occasional funding from the Yokefellow board in the earliest years, their ministry model stood as an outlier after a decade of emphasis on retreat centers. The aforementioned 1973 booklet summarizing Yokefellow activity around the world illustrates this plainly. In their entry, the Kobayashis related sentiments that were more nostalgic than active. They remembered fondly how Etsuko brought Yokefellow principles back with her from Earlham, and they asserted that "read[ing] the discipline and wear[ing] the pin . . . filled [them] with new strength" ever since they first initiated their work in Tokyo. With these expressions of former indebtedness, however, the Kobayashis paired a litany of unrealized hopes. They "hope[d] to bring our people to the Yokefellow Conference in the States" someday soon; they hoped "to sow seed of Yokefellow [sic] in South East Asia"; they hoped "to translate pamphlets in Taiwan language [sic], Chinese, Thai, Malayan."[60] After twenty years of Yokefellow-inspired efforts, the Kobayashis lacked momentum, and they lacked funding from the parent movement.

In contrast, the booklet's entry regarding the Swiss House of Yokefellow brimmed with confidence and potential. Director Hans Schuppli recounted his first vision of a Swiss retreat house in 1969. While he eventually secured additional financial assistance from Swiss Quakers and other benefactors, Schuppli credited American Yokefellows with galvanizing the project. In Schuppli's summary, Yokefellow board chair H. Vaughn Scott (a Fort Wayne Presbyterian) had assured him "if financial limitations would hinder us to go forward, we could count on the support of the Yokefellows." With great detail, Schuppli's entry proceeded to describe the retreat house opening, its naming, and several of its earliest American visitors. To be fair, the "minimum discipline" aspect of Yokefellow life had not disappeared entirely in the Swiss iteration. Schuppli and his Swiss counterparts pared it down to three items: daily silence and devotional time, the "practice of the presence," and "group fellowship . . . in our day-to-day living."[61] Likewise, a group continued to meet monthly beyond any participation at the retreat house. But in total, the booklet left little doubt regarding the movement's direction. The tone of the various entries and the amount of space devoted to them revealed that retreats and retreat centers would be the primary Yokefellow outlet moving ahead. If the Kobayashis remained connected to the movement, the booklet made clear by implication that their model of church-based ministry in daily life no longer aligned well with central Yokefellow priorities.

CONCLUSION

The Yokefellow vision changed in the years after the movement incorporated and began receiving LEI grants. Current historical debates about the nature and efficacy of philanthropy offer contrasting ways to assess this transition. A long historiographical tradition might explain it as just another instance of well-meaning philanthropists failing to align their magnanimous impulses with the actual needs of those they sought to help.[62] And in many ways, this type of pitfall seems consistent with the relationship between the Yokefellows, the Kobayashis, and the changes wrought by foundation philanthropy. Once again, the 1973 booklet illuminates the issue. After recounting their struggles, the Kobayashis mentioned the prospect of a retreat center in Tokyo before quickly lamenting "the problem of expense ... we are all struggling hard to earn a living."[63] In that light, this scenario appears as one in which Trueblood and the Yokefellows failed to surmount a cultural barrier. In the United States, affluent but lethargic Christians needed a space for withdrawal and rejuvenation from the enervating aspects of modern life. But in the Kobayashis' Tokyo, retreats were a luxury only to be imagined.

Considering this data and the "channeling" thesis, then, one can reasonably conclude that substantial funding from Indiana philanthropists seems to have solidified the formerly grassroots movement's base—its organizational leadership, its physical plant, its communications—while simultaneously circumscribing its sphere of applicability. Moving forward, activities that would motivate the greatest financial outlays from the Yokefellow board and the heartiest application of its imprimatur focused on the very things that had excited the most support from outside philanthropists, namely facilities and spiritual retreats. Little in the documentary record indicates that this redirection stemmed from a calculated agenda. Instead, the evidence illuminates the power of invested money to reorient a movement by virtue of its mere presence. As matters stood in 1951, any number of possible initiatives lay before the Yokefellows. But as capital infusions generated results, those results developed a self-justifying momentum: Funding would go where funding had gone.

While these findings confirm that philanthropy generated substantial change, they nevertheless resist the popular "overbearing philanthropists" interpretation. Rather than some furtive group of self-interested puppet-masters, the relatively impersonal mechanics of social movement philanthropy drive this story. Lacking a familiar morality tale, then, what conclusions should students of philanthropy draw from the early history of the Yokefellows movement? One promising possibility involves reconsidering the presuppositions we bring to our analyses, especially regarding what constitutes philanthropic progress or "success." In this regard, the recent work of historians like Benjamin Soskis proves especially provocative. Soskis, and others, interrogate the "epistemic dominance" of the philanthropic model within the literature, asserting that most philanthropic history reflects an implicit but nonetheless normative framework that privileges stories of centralization, professionalization, and the global over the local.[64] Jeremy Beer's book *The Philanthropic Revolution* advances this line of criticism. Arguing that twentieth-century philanthropy often promoted a conception of "the good" that left no room for "geographic propinquity, loyalty, [or] kinship," Beer instead touts the idea of "philanthrolocalism." This approach to giving embodies "modesty about . . . human ability," favoring causes most likely to "increase opportunities for and strengthen the possibilities of authentic human communion." Community foundations receive special commendation in Beer's analysis, as they have generally remained "provincial enough to seek primarily to exercise leadership in their own communities."[65]

Such phrasing is especially notable in light of historical criticisms leveled against LEI. In 1985, for instance, commentator Waldemar A. Nielsen disparaged the foundation in his book *The Golden Donors*. Critical of its relationship with local government, Nielsen identified "parochialism" and lamented that LEI had forsaken the international causes it championed in the 1970s under Executive Vice President Landrum Bolling's leadership.[66] Without question, Nielsen's work epitomized the regnant epistemology of twentieth-century scientific philanthropy, so the nature of his criticisms should not surprise. Yet, through the lens of Beer's philanthrolocalism, Nielsen's quibbles appear incomplete at the very least; at most, entirely wrongheaded. For viewed with an eye toward local logics and traditions, the types of projects LEI liked to fund might instead reveal a measured philanthropic disposition, one fundamentally hesitant to tackle the types of "transformative" projects that commentators like Nielsen and subsequent scholars have so privileged.[67]

Indeed, one major benefit of studying LEI history might involve its ability to undermine epistemic assumptions and blur a periodization in philanthropic studies that analysts too often present as clean and stark. At least as early as Robert Bremner's celebrated survey of American philanthropy and continuing to the present, scholars have generally agreed that Gilded Age wealth and the Progressive belief in "experts" initiated a new era in American giving, a movement away from distributive charity and toward a "more scientific spirit and method in philanthropy."[68] The popularity of this assessment makes sense: Primary sources and extant scholarship provide ample support for the general trend. In contrast, LEI history suggests that twentieth-century American foundation philanthropy contained a bit more heterogeneity than the current record allows. Even at one of the nation's largest foundations and sixty years after the ascent of "scientific giving," some philanthropists continued to resist the push toward universal cures.

To be sure, LEI still reflected some of the characteristics that often mark American foundations engaging in social movement philanthropy. At the core of this essay lies the contention that mass infusions of outside funding will necessarily alter the nature of a grassroots movement. Despite all of Trueblood's anxieties about centralization and a loss of autonomy, the momentum of donated capital proved too strong to resist. Thus, observers reviewing this story can reasonably wonder if increasing centralization and its attendant imaginative limits led the Yokefellows to fail the Kobayashis. Stopping with that conclusion and pressing no further, however, leaves in place many of the literature's assumed value judgments—about professionalization, about globalization—regarding what constitutes effective philanthropy. Read with the values of philanthrolocalism in mind, the Yokefellows' increasing focus on one model of ministry might instead reflect philanthropic prudence. In this instance, that meant even if the Yokefellow retreat centers eventually expanded beyond state lines, their growing uniformity of purpose and practice makes sense in light of LEI's preference for known entities and Indiana's local traditions of incremental change. The Hoosier philanthropists who promoted a network of retreat centers stuck with a familiar problem—spiritual ennui in modern Western society—and a manageable solution—believing that local actors possess the greatest ability to affect lasting change.

These two conclusions need not be mutually exclusive; it is certainly conceivable that philanthropists could demonstrate modesty in the geographical scope of their ambitions even as they domineer and promote misguided projects. More than anything, then, this tale demonstrates the need for more research, regarding both the central role that LEI played in recent Indiana history and the broader influence of foundation philanthropy in shaping twentieth-century American religion. While overarching conclusions about these topics remain beyond the bounds of this essay, what emerges clearly is the formative part a network of Hoosier philanthropists played in directing and proliferating a vibrant expression of midcentury lay religiosity. First from Richmond and then from Indianapolis, Fort Wayne, and small municipalities, Indiana religious leaders, laypeople, and donors mobilized to initiate a movement that spread far beyond Hoosier state bounds.

NOTES

1. Along with my debts to editor Gregory Witkowski and the anonymous readers assigned by IU Press, I am grateful to the many colleagues and commenters who read prior iterations of this piece, including Darren Dochuk, Philip Goff, Danae Jacobson, David King, Rev. Paul V. Kollman, C. S. C., Suzanna Krivulskaya, Heather Lane, Andy Mach, Laurie Maffly-Kipp, John Nelson, Mark Noll, Todd Ream, Jonathan Riddle, James Strasburg, and Tom Tweed. Of course, all missteps remain my own.

2. D. Elton Trueblood, *Why I Originated the Yokefellow Movement,* unpublished manuscript, 1, emphasis original. Located in D. Elton Trueblood (DET) Papers, Friends Collection and Earlham College Archives, Richmond, Indiana.

3. D. Elton Trueblood, *While It Is Day: An Autobiography* (New York: Harper & Row, 1974), 110–11.

4. Trueblood stumbled upon the movement's name while reading the eleventh chapter in the gospel of Matthew, where Jesus implores his disciples to "take my yoke upon you." The yoke metaphor in the passage captured every growing conviction he had about Christianity: It represented "togetherness, for we are invited to wear Christ's yoke with Him" and "discipline, for the harnessed animal is set free from empty freedom and consequent meaninglessness." See Trueblood, *While It Is Day,* 108 and "Why I Originated the Yokefellow Movement," 4, DET Papers. The exact reference is Matthew 11:29.

5. To understand the broader postwar context of educational exchange programs, see Eisuke Sakakibara, *Structural Reforms in Japan: Breaking the Iron Triangle* (Washington, DC: Brookings Institution, 2003).

6. "Yokefellow International" booklet, n.p., DET Papers. See also, Trueblood, *While It Is Day,* 110 and D. Elton Trueblood, *Essays in Gratitude* (Nashville, TN: Broadman, 1982), 24.

7. Untitled, undated booklet, 9, DET Papers.

8. For an example of a text highly skeptical of foundation philanthropy's intentions and influence, see Inderjeet Parmar, *Foundations of the American Century: The Ford, Carnegie, and Rockefeller Foundations in the Rise of American Power* (New York: Columbia University Press, 2012).

9. On social movement philanthropy and the "channeling thesis," see J. Craig Jenkins and Abigail Halcli, "Grassrooting the System? The Development and Impact of Social Movement Philanthropy, 1953–1990," in *Philanthropic Foundations: New Scholarship, New Possibilities,* ed. Ellen Condliffe Lagemann (Bloomington: Indiana University Press, 1999), 229–56.

10. For example, see Lucy Bernholz, "The Future of Foundation History: Suggestions for Research and Practice" in *Philanthropic Foundations,* 359–76. Bernholz notes that "whether critical or positive," much philanthropic history has "overstate[d] vastly the role of foundations as influences on society and greatly underestimate[d] the degree to which they are responsive organizations" existing as one actor among many (360–61).

11. For examples of the literature on efficient philanthropy and effective altruism, see William MacAskill, *Doing Good Better: How Effective*

Altruism Can Help You Make a Difference (New York: Avery, 2015); Peter Singer, *The Most Good You Can Do: How Effective Altruism Is Changing Ideas about Living Ethically* (New Haven, CT: Yale University Press, 2015).

12. D. Elton Trueblood, "Why I Chose a Small College," *Reader's Digest* (September 1956): 39.

13. Thomas D. Hamm, *Earlham College: A History, 1847–1997* (Bloomington: Indiana University Press, 1997), 186–87.

14. Prior to arriving in Richmond, Trueblood's faculty appointments at Haverford, Harvard, and Stanford had introduced him to a diverse set of elites, including the Quaker spiritualist Rufus Jones, the realist theologian Reinhold Niebuhr, public intellectual Lewis Mumford, former secretary of the interior Ray Lyman Wilbur, and former president Herbert Hoover (also a Quaker).

15. T. J. Jackson Lears, *No Place of Grace: Antimodernism and the Transformation of American Culture, 1880–1920* (Chicago: University of Chicago Press, 1994), 32.

16. Historian Kristin L. Hoganson contends that one major source of the Spanish-American War involved the desire among American males to prove their masculinity in what they viewed as a feminized age. See *Fighting for American Manhood: How Gender Politics Provoked the Spanish-American and Philippine-American Wars* (New Haven, CT: Yale University Press, 1998). See also Gail Bederman, *Manliness and Civilization: A Cultural History of Gender and Race in the United States, 1880–1917* (Chicago: University of Chicago Press, 1995).

17. George R. Marsden, *The Twilight of the American Enlightenment: The 1950s and the Crisis of Liberal Belief* (New York: Basic Books, 2014), 25–32. Other illustrative best sellers include Arthur Miller's *Death of a Salesman* (1949), J. D. Salinger's *The Catcher in the Rye* (1951), Erich Fromm's *The Sane Society* (1955), Sloan Wilson's *The Man in the Gray Flannel Suit* (1955), and William Whyte's *The Organization Man* (1957).

18. Trueblood's affiliation with Harper & Brothers likely deserves much credit for solidifying his profile as a public intellectual and enlarging his social network. In his study of midcentury middlebrow religious publishing, historian Matthew Hedstrom recreates the book culture in which Trueblood flourished and explains that a title's selection by Harper's Religious Book Club "placed a new book, thinker, or idea before the most powerful people in American religious life." See Hedstrom, *The Rise of Liberal Religion: Book Culture and American Spirituality in the Twentieth Century* (New York: Oxford University Press, 2013), esp. 66–67. The books

Trueblood published under this mantle include *The Predicament of Modern Man* (1944), *Foundations for Reconstruction* (1946), *Alternative to Futility* (1948), and *The Life We Prize* (1951).

19. D. Elton Trueblood, *Alternative to Futility* (New York: Harper & Brothers, 1948), 13–15.

20. Trueblood, *Alternative to Futility*, 11, 17.

21. On the links between Cold War business interests and resurgent religiosity, see Jonathan P. Herzog, *The Spiritual-Industrial Complex: America's Religious Battle against Communism in the Early Cold War* (New York: Oxford University Press, 2011); Kevin M. Kruse, *One Nation Under God: How Corporate America Invented Christian America* (New York: Basic Books, 2015).

22. Trueblood, *Alternative to Futility*, 22, 27.

23. Another substantial modern inspiration was the Methodist ecumenist John R. Mott, from whom Trueblood borrowed the conviction that the future of Christianity depended upon the labors of laypeople; the professor called his endeavors an "adjunct" to what Mott had identified as the "liberation of the lay forces of Christianity." See D. Elton Trueblood, *The Retreat Movement*, unpublished manuscript, 8. DET Papers. In fact, Mott's work on lay involvement also depended on extensive support from a famous philanthropist—John D. Rockefeller, Jr. See Albert F. Schenkel, *The Rich Man and the Kingdom: John D. Rockefeller, Jr., and the Protestant Establishment* (Minneapolis: Fortress, 1995), esp. 155–64. For more on Mott and early twentieth-century interest in the laity, see Nicholas Apostola, ed., *A Letter from Christ to the World: An Exploration of the Role of the Laity in the Church Today* (Geneva, Switzerland: WCC, 1998); William Hutchison, *Errand to the World: American Protestant Thought and Foreign Missions* (Chicago: University of Chicago Press, 1987); Stephen Charles Neill and Hans-Reudi Weber, eds., *The Layman in Christian History: A Project of the Department on the Laity of the World Council of Churches* (Philadelphia: Westminster, 1963).

24. D. Elton Trueblood, *Iona in Scotland and in America*, unpublished manuscript, 1, DET Papers.

25. "Rev. Lord MacLeod, 96, Founder of Church Community in Scotland," *New York Times*, June 29, 1991.

26. Trueblood, *Alternative to Futility*, 53, 94.

27. James R. Newby, *Elton Trueblood* (New York: Harper & Row, 1990), 95.

28. D. Elton Trueblood, May 6, 1954 letter, 1, emphasis original, DET Papers.

29. Trueblood, *The Common Ventures of Life: Marriage, Birth, Work, and Death* (New York: Harper & Brothers, 1949), 18–20, emphasis original. See also D. Elton Trueblood, *The Yokefellow Movement*, unpublished manuscript, 3, DET Papers.

30. Trueblood, *Alternative to Futility*, 45, 51, emphasis original.

31. Ibid., 121.

32. For representative treatments of Gallahue's social life in the *Indianapolis Star*, see "Moods and Modes," October 28, 1935, 6; "Society to Witness 63d Kentucky Derby," May 4, 1937, 6; "Society and Personal," February 8, 1940, 6; "Lambs Club Frolic Tonight," April 7, 1945, 5.

33. "Methodist Nurse Plan Gets OK," *Indianapolis Star*, February 18, 1949, 11; "North Methodist Church Pastor Is Given New Auto By Members," *Indianapolis Star*, June 25, 1951, 5.

34. Trueblood, *Essays in Gratitude*, 53–55. See also "Why I Originated the Yokefellow Movement," 5–6 and Trueblood, *While It Is Day*, 111–12.

35. Trueblood, *Why I Originated the Yokefellow Movement*, 6.

36. Trueblood, *Quarterly Yoke Letter*, March 1960, DET Papers.

37. Trueblood, *While It Is Day*, 112–15.

38. Trueblood, *Essays in Gratitude*, 54.

39. Jenkins and Halcli, "Grassrooting the System?" 229–30, 241, 243.

40. "US Treasury Letter," February 8, 1956, DET Papers.

41. This was not the first or last time that Gallahue and LEI would lend financial support to the same project. Both provided substantial funding to a 1951 survey and report intended to overhaul Indianapolis's hospitals, and the two later united to construct and furnish a small library at Earlham College. See "Hospital Program," *Indianapolis Star*, April 26, 1951, 11; "New Library Dedicated at Earlham," *Indianapolis Star*, April 5, 1959, 1 (section 4).

42. For details regarding the Revenue Act, see Mark S. LeClair, *Philanthropy in Transition* (London: Palgrave Macmillan, 2014); Olivier Zunz, *Philanthropy in America: A History* (Princeton, NJ: Princeton University Press, 2011). Susan Wisely notes that the endowment's founding charter established the foundation's commitment to "religious, educational, or charitable purposes." See *A Foundation's Relationship to Its Public: Legacies and Lessons for the Lilly Endowment* (Indianapolis: Indiana University Center on Philanthropy, 1995), 2. This program focus remains rare among the country's largest foundations; according to one recent study by two sociologists, religious projects receive just 3 percent of all foundation grants. See Robert Wuthnow and D. Michael Lindsey, "The Role of Foundations

in American Religion," in *American Foundations: Roles and Contributions,* eds. Helmut K. Anheier and David C. Hammack (Washington, DC: Brookings Institution, 2010): 305–27, esp. 308–9.

43. James H. Madison, *Eli Lilly: A Life, 1885–1977* (Indianapolis: Indiana Historical Society, 1989), 191. In her essay on LEI history, former endowment administrator Wisely links the foundation's three programming branches—religion, education, and community development—through their relationship to Eli Lilly's overarching concern with virtue and character development, especially in relation to citizenship and classical republican theory. She identifies the foundation's initial vision as the development of "an American public educated in virtue through participation in religious and community life." See Wisely, *A Foundation's Relationship to Its Public: Legacies and Lessons for the Lilly Endowment,* 5.

44. Madison, *Eli Lilly,* 189–90, 267.

45. Madison, *Hoosiers: A New History of Indiana* (Bloomington: Indiana University Press, 2014). Susan Wisely elaborates a similar point regarding the importance of place: LEI, in her assessment, has been "heir to many legacies, familial and regional as well as professional," Wisely, *A Foundation's Relationship to Its Public: Legacies and Lessons for the Lilly Endowment,* 1, emphasis added.

46. Trueblood, *While It Is Day,* 54 and *Essays in Gratitude,* 44.

47. Madison, *Eli Lilly,* 115–16.

48. In LEI's governing structure, "secretary" was equivalent to "president" or "managing director"; though final funding decisions remained with the board, Duling assumed day-to-day responsibility for the foundation's functions when he succeeded J. K. Lilly III in this role beginning in 1954. See LEI Annual Report 1954. On Duling's involvement in Indianapolis's First Friends Church, see "Friends Church Begins Move to City's North Side," *Indianapolis Star,* January 3, 1953, 9; "Harold Duling Was Lilly Religion Head," *Indianapolis Star,* March 31, 1964, 5. On Kathryn Quigg Duling's youth in Richmond and attendance at Earlham College, see "Mrs. Kathryn Duling Dies in Richmond Home," *Indianapolis Star,* June 26, 1967, 29.

49. D. Elton Trueblood, *History of Yoke Movement,* unpublished manuscript, DET Papers. For a discussion of this practice's antecedents among Ohio Reformed churches, see Trueblood, *Alternative,* 96.

50. Trueblood, *Why I Originated the Yokefellow Movement,* 5 and "Quarterly Yoke Letter," 2, no. 1 (March 1960): DET Papers. Trueblood likely developed his interest in the lapel pins from his study of the Gideons; more

than once, he commended that organization in his books and unpublished papers, and Sarah Ruth Hammond notes how the Gideons employed lapel pins for purposes similar to those Trueblood envisioned. For an example of Trueblood's comments on the Gideons, see *Ventures*, 88; for Hammond's description of the practice, see Darren Dochuk, ed., *God's Businessmen: Entrepreneurial Evangelicals in Depression and War* (Chicago: University of Chicago Press, 2017), 78.

51. Trueblood, *History of Yokefellow Movement*, 6, DET Papers.

52. Trueblood, *Iona in Scotland and in America*, 1, DET Papers.

53. Trueblood, *While It Is Day*, 116–17.

54. William S. McKersie, "Local Philanthropy Matters: Pressing Issues for Research and Practice," in *Philanthropic Foundations*, ed. Lagemann, 329–58.

55. In fact, the Yokefellow centers and Laity Lodge emerged in a moment of surging interest in the concept of spiritual retreats, especially among those exploring Eastern religious traditions. Perhaps the most famous example of this is the Esalen Institute, founded by Stanford graduates in 1962 and a model for the retreat center in which Don Draper spends the series finale of AMC's *Mad Men*. Professor Philip Goff at IUPUI first noticed this link. For background on Esalen, see Jeffrey J. Kripal, *Esalen: America and the Religion of No Religion* (Chicago: University of Chicago Press, 2007).

56. Yokefellow Associates newsletter 3, no. 2 (June 1961): DET Papers.

57. Yokefellow Associates newsletter 10, no. 2 (June 1968): DET Papers.

58. Jenkins and Halcli, "Grassrooting the System?," 255.

59. "Yokefellow International" booklet, n.p., DET Papers. See also untitled, undated booklet, 9, DET Papers.

60. "Yokefellow International" booklet, n.p., DET Papers.

61. Ibid.

62. Judith Sealander, for example, details how early foundation philanthropists often betrayed a staggering ignorance of the situations they attempted to ameliorate. See *Private Wealth and Public Life: Foundation Philanthropy and the Reshaping of American Social Policy from the Progressive Era to the New Deal* (Baltimore: Johns Hopkins University Press, 1997), esp. 76, 126.

63. "Yokefellow International" booklet, n.p., DET Papers.

64. Jeremy Beer, *The Philanthropic Revolution: An Alternative History of American Charity* (Philadelphia: University of Pennsylvania Press, 2015), back cover. See also Benjamin Soskis, *Both More and No More: The*

Historical Split Between Charity and Philanthropy (New York: Hudson Society, 2014).

65. Beer, *The Philanthropic Revolution*, 86, 95, 99.

66. Waldemar A. Nielsen, *The Golden Donors: A New Anatomy of the Great Foundations* (New York: Truman Talley, 1985), 285–99. Interestingly, before his work with the endowment, Bolling served as president at Earlham College from 1958–1973; that position initiated his relationship with Eli Lilly. See Madison, *Lilly*, 178–79, 220–22.

67. Such a conclusion would dovetail nicely with current chairman and CEO Clay Robbins's recent observation that the endowment has generally evinced a predilection for "moderation and balance." See N. Clay Robbins, "Philanthropic Variety: Perspectives from an Indiana Practitioner," keynote lecture delivered at Hoosier Philanthropy conference, February 18, 2016.

68. For example, see Robert Bremner, *American Philanthropy*, 2nd ed. (Chicago: University of Chicago Press, 1988), 86. See also Sealander, *Private Wealth and Public Life: Foundation Philanthropy and the Reshaping of American Social Policy from the Progressive Era to the New Deal*, 16–21.

FIFTEEN

SEEDING COMMUNITY FOUNDATIONS IN INDIANA

A History of the GIFT Initiative

XIAOYUN WANG

FOR MORE THAN A CENTURY, American reformers believed in the power of community-based interventions to remedy social problems at the local level.[1] After World War II, the US government and private foundations devoted resources to support community-based organizations in an effort to combat poverty and advance social inclusion in cities, towns, and neighborhoods.[2] Community foundations constitute one type of community-based organization, which has garnered favor among some private foundations. Community foundations typically raise funds from local individuals and institutional donors and regrant those funds to local nonprofits. Since the 1980s, several private foundations like Mott, Kellogg, and Ford have nurtured community foundations both nationwide and around the globe.

Why did American foundations support community foundations? There are several possible answers. First, under President Ronald Reagan, federal funding for community social service agencies was cut. Private foundations expected community foundations to channel resources to nonprofit organizations within their respective communities.[3] Private foundations valued the staying power of community foundations, which allowed them to provide local funding even as government funding declined.[4] In addition, American funders perceived local knowledge and leadership as important criteria for addressing social problems. For instance, Russell G. Mawby, chairman of the Kellogg Foundation stated, "The most exciting solutions to today's problems are not those coming from Washington. . . . Local leaders are the ones who are closest to the problems, and are the ones best equipped to solve them."[5]

In Indiana, the Lilly Endowment Inc. (LEI) launched the GIFT Initiative in 1990, which supported nearly eighty new community foundations, or affiliates, and about fifteen existing ones throughout Indiana. Over the past twenty-seven years, LEI provided continuous support to Indiana community foundations. While the GIFT Initiative's strategy to develop community foundations with matching grants and technical assistance is not unique, it serves as one of the longest lasting programs to support community foundations and is a marker of community-foundation development in Indiana.

This article examines the history of the GIFT Initiative, focusing on how private foundations created awareness and encouraged local support for community foundations. This topic is important because community foundations, by definition, are intended to be locally supported. As such, the success in seeding community foundations would depend on whether private foundation funding was able to leverage local resources. To make such an assessment, I analyzed fourteen interviews from the GIFT Initiative's Oral History Project along with reports, grant guidelines, and publications of LEI and its supporting GIFT office. I found three factors played a role in the initiation and implementation of the project: LEI's enduring commitment and influence, the collaborative development of leadership networks across the nonprofit sector, and LEI's ability to conform its work to the culture and structure of local communities.

FORMATION OF A LEADERSHIP NETWORK

The evolution of Indiana community foundations was a gradual process before the GIFT Initiative was launched. While Indiana is composed primarily of large rural areas and a widely dispersed population, mainstream community foundations were developed in big cities with large populations and access to wealth. Since the model of most community foundations required building an endowment, population size and the number of people with enough wealth to contribute factored into assessments regarding sustainability in a particular location. Moreover, nonprofit leaders in the 1980s believed that, in order for a community foundation to "take-off," it would need to attract at least $5 million in assets, not an easy goal for a community with less than fifty-thousand people—the population size of most Indiana counties.[6] Indeed, in the 1980s, Indiana had only five active community foundations.[7] The Indianapolis Foundation, founded in 1916, was one of the oldest community foundations in the United States and the largest community foundation in Indiana, accounting for 70 percent of the total assets of then existing Indiana community foundations.[8]

Although community foundations were unfamiliar to most Hoosiers, Indiana nonprofit leaders started paying attention to them in the early 1980s. During that time, the Indiana Donors Alliance (IDA), now the Indiana Philanthropy Alliance (IPA), formed a coalition that gathered nonprofit leaders interested in community foundations. Initially, IDA did not plan to develop community foundations but rather strengthen connections among grant makers. The initiative began in 1983, when John Mutz, lieutenant governor of Indiana (who later became president of LEI), and Alan Shusterman, executive director of the Indiana Humanities Council (IHC), co-organized a conference for grant makers interested in discussing common concerns and raising local consciousness about philanthropy and the nonprofit sector. The success of that conference led to the establishment of a steering committee responsible for organizing annual conferences, the IDA.[9] Through the IDA, early pioneers of Indiana community foundations were well-connected. In fact, most members of the IDA steering committee were actively engaged in community philanthropy and community foundations. These individuals included Charles Johnson, then vice president of LEI, who later founded the GIFT Initiative; Douglas Bakken, executive director of the Ball Brothers Foundation, which supported the creation of a community foundation in Muncie; Edward Sullivan, executive Director of the Heritage Fund, a community foundation in Columbus; and Kenneth Chapman, executive director of the Indianapolis Foundation.[10] IDA meetings helped these foundation leaders find common cause that would lay an institutional foundation for LEI's GIFT Initiative. The IDA served as the starting point for the community-foundation efforts on a statewide level.

ROLE OF LEI

A significant player in the development of Indiana community foundations was LEI, the largest foundation in Indiana. LEI became deeply involved in establishing and sponsoring community foundations in the mid-1980s, a time during which the endowment encountered both internal and external pressures.

In the 1980s, the success of Eli Lilly and Company stock led to a tremendous increase in LEI revenues. Tax regulations meant that LEI needed to distribute 5 percent of the average market value of its assets in any fiscal year.[11] This meant that LEI had to increase the scale of its grant making significantly. At the same time, the endowment was preparing to expand the scope of its grant making throughout the state as it encountered criticism from within the philanthropic community for making grants only in central Indiana. Discussions regarding how to expand

LEI's grant making became a priority. At the time, Charles Johnson, then LEI's vice president, started learning about community
foundations. Before joining LEI, Johnson spent most of his life as
a fundraiser and development officer. He started working for the
endowment in 1978, using his expertise in fundraising to assist
Indiana nonprofits with capacity building. Responsible for the
institutional advancement of Indiana's nonprofit sector, Johnson
found community foundations to be an appropriate partner in
LEI's goal of expanding the scale and scope of grant making while
enhancing the capacity of local philanthropic communities.[12]
Moreover, the idea of partnering with community foundations
suited the philosophy of the endowment, which sought to maintain low administrative costs. LEI had a small team, relative to its
asset size, in the 1980s. For this reason, accepting and evaluating
grant applications from organizations throughout the state of
Indiana, let alone tracking the performance of every grantee, was
not a strategy LEI wanted to pursue given that it would require
an enormous investment in human resources.

Committed to the community philanthropy approach, LEI's
leaders believed that local citizens could best define and solve
local problems.[13] Instead of selecting grantees, the foundation
opted to nurture partners in different parts of Indiana who were
in a better position to judge the merits of an application and address needs in that community. Given that community foundations, in general, are designed to serve the needs of their respective communities, provide a neutral space to convene community
members, and cultivate local leaders, these partners fit nicely with
the goals of the endowment.

LEI's philosophy was different from many other foundations
promoting strategic philanthropy, which set clear goals for their
grantees, measured progress, and evaluated performance. Scholars David Hammack and Helmut Anheier point out that private
foundations often represented the central power that could
jeopardize the autonomy and integrity of local nonprofits and

suppress local solutions to social problems.[14] Different from these traditional approaches, LEI sought to encourage local efforts and empower local communities.

In 1982, the Council on Foundations and private foundations, including the Charles Stewart Mott Foundation and the Ford Foundation, launched a project to support the growth of community foundations nationwide. LEI was invited to join and Johnson encouraged the endowment to provide financial support as a way to get in touch with people and resources in the field. Around the same time, Douglas Bakken, executive director of the Ball Brothers Foundation, the second largest private foundation in Indiana, contacted the Council on Foundations to request support for its plan to launch a community foundation. Bakken was responding to a request from the Ball family to "broaden philanthropy"—the Ball Brothers Foundation was considered too influential and did not get the community involved in its work.[15] In 1984, Bakken visited Columbus, Indiana, and met Edward Sullivan, executive director of the Heritage Fund, a community foundation based in Bartholomew, Indiana. After a long conversation with Sullivan, Bakken recommended that the Council on Foundations push for a community foundation in Muncie.

Neither Johnson nor Bakken received positive feedback from the Council on Foundations about developing community foundations in Indiana. According to Johnson, the national movement preferred to support established municipal community foundations that had at least $1 million in assets and a population of at least two hundred and fifty thousand. Most communities in Indiana were too small to meet that threshold, and the Indianapolis Foundation was already too large to receive the council's support. Moreover, the big community foundations were nervous about small community foundations, suggesting that small foundations would be unsophisticated or might operate illegally, which could jeopardize the privileged legal environment enjoyed by the larger and more established ones.[16]

Both Johnson and Bakken recognized that there was little hope
the Council on Foundations would fund community foundations in Indiana. Skepticism from the national level frustrated
both Johnson and Bakken. However, they believed that with the
amount of resources and institutional capacities of their respective private foundations, it was still worth trying to support community foundations through local efforts.

THE EXPERIMENT OF THE INDIANA
COMMUNITY FOUNDATIONS

The Ball Brothers Foundation was the first Indiana private foundation to initiate a community foundation in Indiana. After researching the wealth potential in Muncie, Bakken believed the
city could develop a vibrant community foundation, despite
its small population (about eighty thousand). In 1984, the Ball
Brothers Foundation brought together resourceful people in
Muncie, including the president of a bank and several corporate
heads, as volunteers to push the project forward. "We tried to get
people on the band wagon," said Bakken. In 1985, the Muncie and
Delaware County Community Foundation was established. The
Ball Brothers Foundation provided $2 million in matching funds
to build the community foundation's endowment and a $100,000
operating grant for three years.[17] By 1988, the community foundation successfully raised a $5 million endowment and reached its
takeoff point.[18]

With the success of the Muncie and Delaware Community
Foundation, Johnson was more confident that support from a
private foundation could ensure the sustainability of a community foundation in small communities. In 1987, Johnson started
promoting the community-foundation project within LEI, sharing his optimism about community foundations with James Morris, president of the endowment, who offered his enthusiastic
support.[19]

The fundamental prerequisite for success of a community foundation was the local communities' interest in having one. Through IDA, Johnson and other pioneers of Indiana's community foundations, including Douglas Bakken, Edward Sullivan, and Kenneth Chapman, visited several Indiana counties to introduce them to the concept of community foundations.[20] Those first visits proved unsuccessful. Johnson said the failure was nobody's fault. "One of the things I learned from that [experience] was you can't just do a little bit and expect something to develop."[21] Yet, according to two other pioneers on the visit, the failure was partly due to a "cultural clash" between a fundraising expert participating in the visits and Indiana community members. The fundraising expert was a well-respected grassroots fundraiser. However, being liberal and progressive, with a strong sense of social justice, her approach was viewed as incompatible with the conservative culture dominating much of Indiana. According to the pioneers of Indiana's community foundations, the expert's emphasis on inclusiveness did not match the beliefs of leaders of Indiana's smaller communities. Instead, these leaders believed the community foundation should first engage the most powerful and resourceful people in a community.[22]

Although the initial attempt was unsuccessful, Johnson believed the Indiana communities he visited had both the necessary enthusiasm and potential to develop community foundations. John Mutz, who on retiring from his position as lieutenant governor succeeded Jim Morris as president of LEI in 1989, gave his wholehearted support to the community-foundation initiative. Support from Mutz gave Johnson confidence and courage, "Here is a man who knows all the byroads and highways of the state and thousands of people. He could see immediately that this would be a great thing to do. He encouraged me," said Johnson.[23] With support from Mutz, the community-foundation project was approved by the board of LEI.

STRATEGY AND INFRASTRUCTURE

In 1989 and 1990, Johnson started making a thorough plan for the community-foundation project. He considered hiring a senior consultant to assist with the design and implementation. His experience with the initial attempt to attract buy-in indicated a need to place greater importance on compatibility between Indiana community culture and the values of any hired consultant. The consultant needed to have knowledge and experience in community foundations but also an understanding of Indiana's communities and respect for existing social structure and norms.

In 1990, Johnson invited two nationally renowned community-foundation experts, Eugene Struckhoff and Helen Monroe, to LEI to discuss the design of the community-foundation project. Struckhoff had played a leading role in the creation of 140 community foundations across the United States. Monroe was born in Gary, Indiana, and was executive director of the San Diego Community Foundation. Her colleagues described her as candid, aggressive, and avant-garde. Both Struckhoff and Monroe were involved in creating the national agenda on the development of community foundations for the Council on Foundations. There was, however, one key difference between Struckhoff and Monroe's viewpoints. Struckhoff expressed concerns about Indiana community foundations since most would be founded in rural areas and small towns that may lack sufficient economic resources for the development of an endowment. On the contrary, Monroe believed LEI "should leave communities to decide whether they want a community foundation or not" regardless of a community's population size.[24] During a meeting with Johnson, Struckhoff said to Monroe, "You just don't want community foundations in all these little communities, because all they'll ever do with their money is painting the bandstand and that's not philanthropy." Monroe responded, "If a community wants to paint the bandstand and decide to do it, I think that's great."[25]

LEI chose Helen Monroe over Eugene Struckhoff as principal consultant. Compared to Struckhoff, Monroe was more compatible with the philosophy of LEI and the culture of Indiana. Community leaders, rather than an outside authority, would have autonomy to decide what program and geographic areas to serve, even if it meant that funding would be of immediate need more than long-term philanthropic goals. Monroe's values accorded with the conservative culture of Indiana, emphasizing autonomy of communities and the importance of local consensus and leadership.

Although Struckhoff did not become principal consultant, the project created by Johnson was based on suggestions from both Monroe and Struckhoff, which included four key elements: First, the endowment would commit $47 million in grants over fifteen years to support at least twenty communities interested in building and strengthening the network of community foundations in Indiana. The numbers were based on critical elements of building a community foundation that included: building endowed assets, making grants, and becoming engaged in communities. As Helen Monroe pointed out, an unsuccessful community foundation is worse than no community foundation because failure not only wastes philanthropic resources but also damages donor confidence.[26] Therefore, it was recommended that the endowment make a long-term commitment to ensure the community foundations could become self-sustaining.

The second key element was for LEI to provide three types of challenge grants: asset-building grants, operating grants, and project grants. One reason the endowment used matching grants was to avoid "tipping" public charities. The asset-building grants made a $1 for $2 match, ranging from $500,000 to $1.7 million. Community foundations determined how much they wanted. The purpose was to help community foundations quickly reach a $3–$5 million asset base. For most counties, $3–$5 million would make them the largest grant makers in their county. Operating grants were based on the notion that a community foundation needed at least one, half-time, paid staff member (executive director or an administrative role), an office (a shared space with other organizations or a donated office), and a telephone answered with the name of the foundation. These three expenses were deemed necessary and would be covered by the operating budget. The endowment would match up to one-third of the operating expenses, not to exceed $50,000 per year. Project grants gave community foundations an opportunity to make grants and experience all aspects of running a community foundation. Moreover, the project grant helped communities learn how to work with nonprofits. The project grant was a $1 for $2 match, ranging from $10,000 to $100,000. Community foundations had complete flexibility in deciding how to use their project grants.[27]

The third element of the plan was for LEI to provide free technical assistance to community foundations to help executives, board members, and other stakeholders understand the value and operations and assist them in attracting challenge grants. Technical assistance included on-site consultations and workshops that members could attend voluntarily. The endowment itself was not willing to house a technical-assistance team, preferring to be a grant maker rather than a program manager. Thus, it had to select an institution to operate the technical-assistance program. Ultimately, LEI chose IDA, the institution where the pioneers of Indiana's community foundations formed close relations. At that time, IDA was still unincorporated, but it displayed potential as an independent membership organization. The expectation of LEI was, fifteen or twenty years later, that IDA would serve as the voluntary association of Indiana community foundations to connect, manage, and promote the field without support from the endowment.[28]

The fourth and final element that both Struckhoff and Monroe recommended was to consider a county as the appropriate geographic unit for a community foundation and encourage

coalitions of community foundations—or community funds—
across several. Having several community foundations in one
county was deemed problematic, as individual community foundations may lack a sufficient population base and wealth to sustain them. However, so long as community foundations raised
enough funds to meet the challenge, LEI would make grants even
if there was more than one community foundation in a county.[29]

TAKEOFF

On June 24, 1990, LEI formally announced the GIFT initiative,
which stood for Giving Indiana Funds for Tomorrow, a name proposed by Helen Monroe's husband.[30] The announcement broke
an unwritten LEI rule of practice. The endowment's founder, Eli
Lilly, believed the best gifts were given anonymously, and all previous gifts were announced by grantees rather than LEI.[31]

In the news release, the endowment's chairman, Thomas Lake,
said, "We believe the best way to assist Indiana communities is
to help them generate local solutions to local problems." John
Mutz noted that LEI elected to fund community foundations
because they could place communities in a position to define
their own challenges and develop their leadership. Mutz also
emphasized that community foundations provide "neutral turf,"
where individuals with diverse viewpoints can meet to achieve a
consensus while offering a flexible vehicle for individual donors,
of either modest or vast means, to make contributions. Johnson
highlighted that there was no other comprehensive effort of this
magnitude to create a statewide network of community foundations, and there would be "vast reservoirs of wealth and good will
in Indiana that this effort will tap and mobilize."[32]

Besides the formal announcement, the endowment tried to
reach Indiana counties through person-to-person contact. As former lieutenant governor, Mutz was familiar with people and stories in every county and town in Indiana, so he helped to identify

and contact community leaders. Nancy DiLaura, who previously worked in the governor's office as deputy press secretary and primary speech writer, assisted with spreading the word to Indiana communities. Her expertise in communications and her familiarity with Indiana communities helped the GIFT Initiative reach local community leaders and key community organizations, targeting mayors and chambers of commerce in particular.

After the formal announcement, the response from local communities was overwhelming. DiLaura and Johnson got hundreds of calls from local communities during the first six months.[33] From 1990 to 1991, a resource group led by Helen Monroe that included the pioneers of Indiana's community foundations came to local communities to explain the idea and philosophy of them. For the most part, initial conversations between GIFT Initiative representatives and community leaders occurred in cafés. Monroe, Johnson, and other resource group members traveled around the state and talked to people expressing interest in establishing a community foundation. In addition, the technical-assistance team held workshops for local attorneys and CPAs. The purpose of these workshops was to increase awareness of community foundations among those who had a higher likelihood of success working with potential donors.[34]

In 1992 alone, thirty-five community foundations received grants from LEI and approximately twenty more requested funds within the next year. Of the $47 million committed to community foundations, nearly all of it was designated by the end of 1992. That same year, the endowment's board of directors decided to add an additional $13 million to its commitment, for a total of $60.1 million allocated to the GIFT Initiative in 1992.[35]

SEEDING

A key concern of LEI was how to help the community foundations work together with the existing philanthropic institutions and community mores. Kenneth Gladish, former president and CEO of Indianapolis Foundation, described the culture of Indiana communities as "conservative populism," which indicates local skepticism to central power, active civic involvement at the local level, the importance of community consensus, and the vitality of township life.[36]

In general, the GIFT Initiative was designed to be compatible with Indiana's culture. It conformed to Hoosiers' devotion to locality and their aversion to central power. In coping with local people's suspicion of monolithic power, LEI regarded community foundations as partners and colleagues instead of beneficiaries.[37] The technical-assistance team gave advice to local communities but did not intervene in the decision-making process of community foundations. Moreover, the GIFT Initiative gave community foundations autonomy and flexibility over how to use their project grants. In one case, a community foundation attempted to use the project grant to build a garage, which was considered a debatable project, but LEI approved the grant.[38] Johnson explained why the endowment supported this approach, "People out in X, Y, Z community know better what needs to be done then Lilly Endowment does." He believed that most community foundations made good use of the flexibility offered to them and benefited their communities in creative ways.[39]

Another challenge the endowment encountered was how to help community foundations build cooperative relationships with nonprofits in their respective communities. It was possible nonprofits might be concerned that community foundations would take away their funding sources rather than provide improved access. Given that such a mindset could threaten the viability of community foundations, LEI designed two strategies to address it. First, project grants that LEI matched sought to facilitate cooperative relationships between community foundations and other nonprofits. By making grants, community foundations would build partnerships with local nonprofits. Moreover, by creating their own funds in community foundations, local organizations could raise and manage funds through them to save administrative costs.

The second strategy LEI applied to assuage nonprofit concerns was through its technical-assistance program, which fostered a narrative that community foundations were partners rather than competitors to local nonprofits. LEI chose to stay out of these affairs; however, they engaged a technical-assistance team to allay possible concerns of local nonprofit organizations.

Bruce Maza, a program associate for the GIFT Initiative technical-assistance team, contributed to creating the desired narrative. Along with other community-foundation pioneers, Maza found a way to deal with the relationship between community foundations and the United Way. Using a simple analogy, he compared the relationship between United Way and community foundations to a checking account and a savings account. Although both were needed to serve communities, community foundations and United Ways have distinct focal areas and funding sources: Community foundations raise funds for perpetual endowment and United Way organizations raise funds for current and immediate needs.[40]

Regarding the relationship with other endowed charities, such as higher education institutions and museums, the technical-assistance team indicated that rather than being a competitor of endowment funds, community foundations would enhance the legitimacy of endowed philanthropy and justify the value of endowment giving. Using Bruce Maza's words, instead of giving for current and immediate needs "endowment gifts inevitably give a donor an opportunity to go against his or her mortality . . . it is a way for the donor to look into a future which they will not participate, but do in fact have some views on what the future ought to look like." Furthermore, Maza emphasized the difference between community foundations and other endowed charities. While other endowed charities persuaded donors to recognize and support their organizations' respective missions and programs, staff members of community foundations provided donors a vehicle to realize their own goals. In his words, community foundations built "a remarkable objective third party relationship that is based on the ability of representatives of community foundations to be sensitive and to honor the donors' devotions, hopes, and fears."[41]

Through carefully designed challenge grants and a technical-assistance program, the GIFT Initiative planted the seed and nurtured the concept of community foundations in local communities, helping them to build partnerships with local nonprofits. The endowment respected the autonomy of communities and gave flexibility to community foundations to determine the use of available grants. Using thoughtful narratives, the technical-assistance team shaped public perceptions of community foundations, which helped create a favorable environment for them to operate in local communities.

CONCLUSION

By 2014, Indiana had ninety-four community foundations and affiliates with assets totaling approximately $3 billion.[42] The GIFT Initiative not only helped create new community foundations, it also helped renovate existing ones. Influenced by the GIFT Initiative, the Indianapolis Foundation, which previously only accepted unrestricted gifts, proactively started fundraising to attract various types of funds, including donor-advised ones in the 1990s.

A historical analysis suggests three key factors contributed to the expansion and transformation of community foundations in the state of Indiana, each attributed—directly or indirectly—to LEI's GIFT Initiative. First, LEI made a long-term commitment to support the development of Indiana community foundations, providing challenge grants, technical assistance, and other support programs (internship programs, funding for strategic planning, evaluation, etc.) since the 1990s. Second, networks of nonprofit leaders, especially the network developed by IDA, provided technical assistance and facilitated a mutual aid network of community foundations. Through IDA, nonprofit leaders in private foundations, corporate foundations, and community foundations formed coalitions for collective action, effectively combining top-down and bottom-up efforts.

IDA developed a mutual aid group among Indiana community foundations. In 1992, neighboring community foundations started holding informal meetings to share and exchange ideas and experiences, which developed into five regional groups and a Community Foundation Technical Assistance Advisory Committee within IDA. Helen Monroe described the advisory committee as a determining element of the "self-sufficiency" of Indiana's community-foundation field.[43] She pointed out that technical assistance and challenge grants would not last forever—thus, the maturity of Indiana's community foundations would be defined by whether the field developed its own experts in multiple areas and could solve problems through mutual aid. The Indiana Community Foundation Advisory Committee facilitated mutual learning among community foundations, institutionalized the idea of community foundations, and spread the culture of endowed philanthropy at the state level. Having a collective voice to advocate for the field at the state and national level proved necessary for building a welcoming environment in local communities.

The third factor contributing to the growth of community foundations in Indiana is the cultural fit. LEI made a concerted effort to adapt to local conditions, which was reflected in its selection of a consultant and the autonomy it gave them regarding the use of their grants. By designing a program around local needs and conditions, community leaders proved more willing to establish community foundations.

Despite their impressive growth, the success of Indiana community foundations remains uncertain. Researchers and leaders are cautioned to consider two possible challenges. The first is the tension between empowerment and effectiveness. LEI gave autonomy and flexibility to community foundations and put trust in local wisdom. However, it remains unclear whether establishing community foundations in small communities are more effective than alternative approaches. One informed observer, Brian Payne, executive director of the Central Indiana Community Foundation, argued that a vibrant one should have at least $10 million in assets to be effective.[44] In 2016, nearly a third of Indiana community foundations had not met that goal.[45] However, the economy of small and rural communities has fundamentally shifted. Corporations moved from small towns to big cities, while the traditional economic base of rural communities is diminishing or becoming highly transitory.[46] It is uncertain whether community foundations in small rural communities can have sufficient resources to deal with the disruptive power of the internet and competition from national commercial financial institutions. Can issues, whose causes are not solely local, be addressed at the local level?[47] This remains an open and important question for further investigation.

A second challenge to consider relates to the identification and understanding of the term *community*. Most Indiana community foundations are county based. This is partly because LEI contacted community leaders, county-by-county, regarding the establishment of community foundations. Yet, with increasing mobility, a county may not necessarily reflect how people identify their communities. As pointed out by Emmett Carson, CEO of the Silicon Valley Community Foundation, people are now more mobile—often they were born, live, and work in different communities, which makes them less likely to feel a strong connection with one location.[48] Although traditionally Hoosiers have deep local roots and strong attachments to local communities and continue giving to community foundations even if they move to other states, this changing understanding of community challenges the concept of placed-based giving.[49]

Regardless of the abovementioned challenges, the GIFT Initiative was considered a huge success by LEI and other people involved.[50] According to Monroe and Johnson, before the GIFT Initiative, no one could offer an accurate estimation of the philanthropic potential of Hoosiers, and no one knew exactly how deep the pockets of Indiana communities were.[51] As it turned out, the response from local communities and the growth of Indiana community foundations exceeded expectations. Specifically, several Indiana communities that were considered to be the poorest in the state managed to develop rather sophisticated community foundations. Although the assets of individual Indiana community foundations are not comparable to big metropolitan ones, smaller amounts of money could produce positive changes in a rural community, and local people could feel and see the benefits of small grants more readily, which is a notable and distinguishing feature of community foundations in small communities.[52]

NOTES

1. I am grateful to Helen Monroe for many discussions and for reading the drafts of this paper and providing insightful advice; Gregory Witkowski for his helpful suggestions; and Charles Johnson, Kenneth Gladish, Ace Yakey, and Rosemary Dorsa for their time talking to me and providing me with important information about the GIFT Initiative. More than the usual thanks go to Dana Doan for editing this paper and improving its language. I also want to thank Brenda Burke for helping me access the data from the GIFT Initiative Oral History Project.

2. Alexander von Hoffman, "The Past, Present, and Future of Community Development in the United States," in *Investing in What Works for America's Communities*, eds. Nancy O. Andrews and David J. Erickson (Federal Reserve Bank of San Francisco, 2012).

3. Eleanor Sacks, "The Growth of Community Foundations around the World: An Examination of the Vitality of the Community Foundation Movement" (Washington, DC: Council on Foundations, 2000), https://cfinsights.issuelab.org/resource/the-growth-of-community-foundations-around-the-world-an-examination-of-the-vitality-of-the-community-foundation-movement.html.

4. "2012 Annual Report: Community Foundations: Rooted Locally. Growing Globally," C. S. Mott Foundation, 2013, https://www.mott.org/news/publications/2012-annual-report-community-foundations-rooted-locally-growing-globally/.

5. "Michigan Community Foundations' Youth Project: 20th Anniversary Report," Johnson Center for Philanthropy, 2013, https://www.michiganfoundations.org/sites/default/files/resources/MCFYP-Final-Report.pdf.

6. Eugene C. Struckhoff, *Ways to Grow: A Study of Community Foundations Serving Populations under 250,000* (Washington, DC: Council on Foundations, 1991); "Population and Population Change in the 1990s in Indiana," *STATSINDIANA: Indiana's Public Data Utility* (This file was produced from a US Census Bureau file posted in December 2001), accessed January 7, 2016, http://www.stats.indiana.edu/topic/population.asp.

7. Charles Johnson, interviewed by Sue Shepherd and Heather Weidman, July 10, 1995, transcript, GIFT Oral History Project, IUPUI University Library, Indianapolis, Indiana.

8. GIFT Office, *GIFT History* (Indianapolis, Indiana: GIFT Office, 2014).

9. Indiana Donors Alliance, *Indiana Donors Alliance, 1983–1998* (Indianapolis: Indiana Donors Alliance, 1998).

10. Ibid.

11. "Taxes on Failure to Distribute Income—Private Foundations," Internal Revenue Service, accessed March 24, 2022, https://www.irs.gov/charities-non-profits/private-foundations/taxes-on-failure-to-distribute-income-private-foundations.

12. Charles Johnson, interviewed by Sue Shepherd and Heather Weidman, July 10, 1995, transcript, GIFT Oral History Project, IUPUI University Library, Indianapolis, Indiana.

13. Charles Johnson, interviewed by Sue Shepherd and Heather Weidman, July 10, 1995; John Mutz, interviewed by Heather Weidman and John Lever, November 21, 1995, transcript, GIFT Oral History Project, IUPUI University Library, Indianapolis, Indiana.

14. David C. Hammack and Helmut K. Anheier. *A Versatile American Institution: The Changing Ideals and Realities of Philanthropic Foundations* (Washington, DC: Brookings Institution, 2013).

15. Charles Johnson, interviewed by Sue Shepherd and Heather Weidman, July 10, 1995, transcript, GIFT Oral History Project, IUPUI University Library, Indianapolis, Indiana.

16. Kenneth Gladish, interviewed by Heather Weidman and Sue Shepherd, July 7, 1995, tape 1, GIFT Oral History Project, IUPUI University Library, Indianapolis, Indiana.

17. Douglas Bakken, interviewed by Inger and Jonathan Lever, August 18, 1993, transcript, GIFT Oral History Project, IUPUI University Library, Indianapolis, Indiana.

18. Muncie and Delaware Community Foundation, "1988 Annual report of Muncie and Delaware Community Foundation," GIFT Oral History Project, IUPUI University Library, Indianapolis, Indiana.

19. Charles Johnson, interviewed by Sue Shepherd and Heather Weidman, July 10, 1995, transcript, GIFT Oral History Project, IUPUI University Library, Indianapolis, Indiana.

20. Ibid.

21. Charles Johnson, interviewed by Nancy DiLaura, April 13, 1994, Lilly Endowment, transcript.

22. Douglas Bakken, interviewed by Inger and Jonathan Lever, August 18, 1993, transcript; Kenneth Gladish, interviewed by Heather Weidman and Sue Shepherd, July 7, 1995, tape 1, GIFT Oral History Project, IUPUI University Library, Indianapolis, Indiana.

23. Charles Johnson, interviewed by Sue Shepherd and Heather Weidman, July 10, 1995, transcript, GIFT Oral History Project, IUPUI University Library, Indianapolis, Indiana.

24. Helen Monroe in discussion with the author, March 3, 2014.

25. Helen Monroe, interviewed by Heather Weidman, September 22, 1995, transcript, GIFT Oral History Project, IUPUI University Library, Indianapolis, Indiana.

26. Helen Monroe in discussion with the author, May 13, 2014.

27. Ibid.

28. Bruce Maza, interviewed by Heather Weidman and Sue Shepherd, July 3, 1995, tape 2, GIFT Oral History Project, IUPUI University Library, Indianapolis, Indiana.

29. "Community Foundation GIFT: A Major, New Philanthropic Program for Indiana Communities" (Indianapolis, Indiana: GIFT Office, 1992).

30. Rosemary Dorsa in discussion with the author, March 27, 2014.

31. Bruce Maza, interviewed by Heather Weidman and Sue Shepherd, July 3, 1995, tape 2, GIFT Oral History Project, IUPUI University Library, Indianapolis, Indiana. Charles Johnson, interviewed by Nancy DiLaura, April 13, 1994, transcript, Lilly Endowment Inc.

32. Lilly Endowment Inc., *Lilly Endowment Announces $47 million Effort to Help Indiana Communities* (Indianapolis, Indiana: Lilly Endowment Inc., June 24, 1990).

33. Nancy DiLaura, interviewed by Heather Weidman, July 18, 1995, transcript, GIFT Oral History Project, IUPUI University Library, Indianapolis, Indiana.

34. Indiana Donors Alliance, *1993 Interim Report to Lilly Endowment, Inc.* (Indianapolis, Indiana: Indiana Donors Alliance, 1993).

35. Lilly Endowment Inc., *Memorandum to Indiana Community Foundations and Organizing Committees: Additional Funds for the Community Foundation Program* (Indianapolis, Indiana: Lilly Endowment Inc., November 19, 1992).

36. Kenneth Gladish, interviewed by Heather Weidman and Sue Shepherd, July 7, 1995, tape 1, GIFT Oral History Project, IUPUI University Library, Indianapolis, Indiana.

37. Bruce Maza, interviewed by Heather Weidman and Sue Shepherd, July 3, 1995, tape 2, GIFT Oral History Project, IUPUI University Library, Indianapolis, Indiana.

38. Vincent Adele, interviewed by Sue Shepherd, July 5, 1995, tape 1, GIFT Oral History Project, IUPUI University Library, Indianapolis, Indiana.

39. Charles Johnson, interviewed by Sue Shepherd and Heather Weidman, July 10, 1995, transcript, GIFT Oral History Project, IUPUI University Library, Indianapolis, Indiana.

40. Helen Monroe, *The Primer* (Indianapolis, Indiana: GIFT Office, 1992).

41. Bruce Maza, interviewed by Heather Weidman and Sue Shepherd, July 3, 1995, tape 3, GIFT Oral History Project, IUPUI University Library, Indianapolis, Indiana.

42. GIFT Office, *GIFT Snapshot Report* (Indianapolis, Indiana: GIFT Office, 2015).

43. Indiana Donors Alliance, *Interim Report to Lilly Endowment: A Cumulative Summary of the Technical Assistance Component of the Community Foundation GIFT Initiative, July 1, 1994–December 31, 1994* (Indianapolis, Indiana: Indiana Donors Alliance, 1995).

44. Brian Payne, "21st Century Community Foundations," a speech at Indiana University Lilly Family School of Philanthropy, January 30, 2015.

45. GIFT Office, *GIFT Snapshot Report* (Indianapolis, Indiana: GIFT Office, 2015).

46. Paul Major, "Investing in Human Capital to Transform Rural Communities," in *Here for Good: Community Foundations and the Challenges of the 21st Century*, eds. Terry Mazany and David C. Perry (Armonk, NY: M. E. Sharpe, 2014).

47. Emmett Carson, "The Future of Community Foundations," in *Here for Good: Community Foundations and the Challenges of the 21st Century*, eds. Terry Mazany and David C. Perry (Armonk, NY: M. E. Sharpe, 2014), 43–58.

48. Emmett Carson, "The Future of Community Foundations," in *Here for Good: Community Foundations and the Challenges of the 21st Century*, eds. Terry Mazany and David C. Perry (Armonk, New York: M. E. Sharpe, 2014), 43–58.

49. James H. Madison, *Hoosiers: A New History of Indiana* (Bloomington: Indiana University Press; Indiana Historical Society Press, 2014).

50. Based on the interviews of the pioneers of the GIFT Initiative, GIFT Oral History Project, IUPUI University Library, Indianapolis, Indiana. See the foreword as well.

51. Helen Monroe, interviewed by Heather Weidman, September 22, 1995, transcript, GIFT Oral History Project, IUPUI University Library, Indianapolis, Indiana; Charles Johnson, interviewed by Sue Shepherd and Heather Weidman, July 10, 1995, transcript, GIFT Oral History Project, IUPUI University Library, Indianapolis, Indiana.

52. Edward Sullivan, interviewed by Heather Weidman and Sue Shepherd, July 5, 1995, transcript, GIFT Oral History Project, IUPUI University Library, Indianapolis, Indiana; Charles Johnson, interviewed by Sue Shepherd and Heather Weidman, July 10, 1995, transcript, GIFT Oral History Project, IUPUI University Library, Indianapolis, Indiana.

CONTRIBUTORS

KATHERINE BADERTSCHER is Director of Graduate Programs and Lecturer in Philanthropic Studies at IUPUI Lilly Family School of Philanthropy. She serves on the faculty of The Fundraising School.

PHILIP D. BYERS is Postdoctoral Research Associate with the Cushwa Center for the Study of American Catholicism.

JAMES J. CONNOLLY is George and Frances Ball Distinguished Professor of History and Director of the Center for Middletown Studies at Ball State University. He is author of *An Elusive Unity: Urban Democracy and Machine Politics in an Industrial Small City* and coauthor of *What Middletown Read: Print Culture in an American Small City.*

RUTH C. CROCKER is Professor of History Emerita at Auburn University. She is author of *Work and Social Order: The Settlement Movement in Two Industrial Cities, 1889–1930* and *Mrs. Russell Sage: Women's Activism and Philanthropy in Gilded Age and Progressive Era America.*

CAITLIN CROWLEY graduated from Augsburg University with a history major and is currently pursuing graduate school in social work.

NICOLE ETCHESON is Alexander M. Bracken Professor of History at Ball State University. She is author of *A Generation at War: The Civil War Era in a Northern Community* and *Bleeding Kansas: Contested Liberty in the Civil War Era.*

CHEN JI is a doctoral candidate in Philanthropic Studies at IUPUI Lilly Family School of Philanthropy.

TYRONE MCKINLEY FREEMAN is Associate Professor of Philanthropic Studies and Director of Undergraduate Programs at Lilly Family School of Philanthropy at IUPUI. He is author of *Madam CJ Walker's Gospel of Giving* and *Race, Gender, and Leadership in Nonprofit Organizations.*

RUTH K. HANSEN is Assistant Professor in the Department of Management at the University of Wisconsin-Whitewater and Research Affiliate in the Helen Bader Institute for Nonprofit Management at the University of Wisconsin-Milwaukee.

DAVID P. KING is Karen Lake Buttrey Director of the Lake Institute on Faith & Giving and Associate Professor of Philanthropic Studies at IUPUI Lilly Family School of Philanthropy

AMANDA KOCH is an independent scholar

JAMES H. MADISON is Thomas and Katherine Miller Professor Emeritus of History at Indiana University Bloomington. He is author of *Hoosiers: A New History, Eli Lilly: A Life, 1885–1977,* and *The Ku Klux Klan in the Heartland.*

PAUL C. PRIBBENOW is President of Augsburg University and editor of *Serving the Public Trust: Insights into Fundraising Research and Practice* (Volumes 1 and 2).

CLAY ROBBINS is Chairman and CEO of Lilly Endowment, Inc.

WILLIAM H. SCHNEIDER is Professor Emeritus of History, Medical Humanities, and Philanthropic Studies at IUPUI. He is author of *The History of Blood Transfusion in Sub-Saharan Africa* and editor of *Rockefeller Philanthropy and Modern Biomedicine: International Initiatives from World War I to the Cold War.*

ELIZABETH J. VAN ALLEN, PhD, is author of *James Whitcomb Riley: A Life* (1999) and managing editor of the *Encyclopedia of Indianapolis,* https://indyencyclopedia.org/.

XIAOYUN WANG is Assistant Professor at School of Public Administration and Policy, Renmin University of China.

PETER WEBER is Assistant Professor of Philanthropy and Nonprofit Studies, Auburn University.

INDEX

abolitionist movement, 35, 40, 56, 110, 190–91, 198–99

ACI (Associated Colleges of Indiana). *See* Independent Colleges of Indiana

Addams, Jane, 88, 229

African Americans: in civil rights movement, 68–69, 72, 122, 372, 384; collective consciousness of, 223; colonization movement and, 196, 198; education for, 232–33; fictive kin and, 223–24; Fletcher's charity toward, 194–97; Freedman's Aid Society for, 205; Freedman's Bureau and, 85; Great Migration of, 39, 59, 85, 248; hospitals for, 168; mutual aid for, 59, 67; philanthropy as viewed by, 223–24; in poverty, 123; religious philanthropy of, 67–69; settlement houses for, 39, 89, 90; social services for, 43, 230–31; World War II service of, 371; YMCA/YWCA for, 39, 68, 218–19, 233–35, 248–49. *See also* racism; segregation

agricultural societies, 199–200

agriculture, scientific, 199–200

alcoholism, 172, 316, 346, 348, 357–58, 366n65. *See also* temperance movement

Allen, Norman, 222

Allen, William, 297

Alpha Home, 220–21, 225, 320

Alternative to Futility (Trueblood), 399

amateur sports, 3, 18, 156, 324

American Cancer Society, 174

American Indians. *See* Native Americans

American Red Cross, 17, 256, 258, 296, 304n3, 306n27

American Settlement, 88, 90

Amish communities, 73

Anabaptists, 72, 74

Anheier, Helmut, 426–27

antibiotics, 174

antislavery movement. *See* abolitionist movement

apprentices, 82, 193

Asbury, Francis, 142

asset-building grants, 431

Associated Colleges of Indiana (ACI). *See* Independent Colleges of Indiana

Bacon, Albion Fellows, 11, 39

Badertscher, Katherine, 17, 19, 79, 283

Bakken, Douglas, 425, 427–29

Ball, Edmund Burke, 169

Ball Brothers Foundation, 13–14, 169, 425, 427, 428

Ball Memorial Hospital, 13, 169

Ball State University, 13, 141

Bankers' Panic (1907), 287–90

Baptists, 35, 36, 53, 55, 108

Beecher, Henry Ward, 54–55, 195

Beer, Jeremy, 412

Beito, David, 59, 115

beneficiaries: of educational philanthropy, 20–21; of health philanthropy, 21–22; middle-class, 19–24; of religious philanthropy, 20; upperclass, 19–20, 22. See also charity evaluation

benevolent associations: religious communities and, 35, 51; social service provision by, 83–84. See also specific organizations

Benjamin, Judson, 193

Bernholz, Lucy, 415n10

Bethel African Methodist Episcopal Church, 67–68, 216

Big Foundations, The (Nielsen), 254

Black Americans. See African Americans

Blake, James, 83

BMR. See Bureau of Municipal Research

Bobbs, John S. and Bobbs Free Clinic, 21, 166–67, 169

Boebel, Clarence, 374

Bolling, Landrum, 147, 256, 412, 421n66

bonding social capital, 106

Boon, Ratliff, 138

Breathalyzer, 175

Breedlove, Sarah. See Walker, Madam C. J.

Bremner, Robert H., 204, 205, 413

Bretton, Max, 119

bridging social capital, 106

Brokenburr, Robert and Alice, 234, 237n6

Brooks, William M., 369–75, 377–80

Brown, Andrew J., 69

Brown, Charlotte Hawkins, 220, 232, 233, 238n19

Broxmeyer, Hal, 180

Bryan, William Lowe, 250

Buchanan v. Warley (1917), 373

Buddhists, 75

Bureau of Municipal Research (BMR), 297–302

Butt, Howard, Jr., 407

Byers, Philip D., 15, 395

Cable, Mary, 217

Campbell Friendship House, 90, 372, 375

camp meetings, 55, 108

cancer, 175, 176, 179–80

Carlton-LaNey, Iris, 230

Carnegie, Andrew and Carnegie libraries, 13, 28n35, 37, 207, 229

Carson, Emmett, 224, 439

Catholics: community integration of institutions, 54, 64; interaction with Jews and Protestants, 351, 352; mutual aid for, 59, 63; percentage of Hoosiers identifying as, 52, 53; religious philanthropy of, 62–64; settlement houses for, 90–91; voluntary associations organized by, 40, 110, 113

Catholic Social Services (CSS), 63–64

Cavanaugh, Robert, 155

Cayton, Andrew, 109

Central Indiana Community Foundation (CICF), xxiii, 18, 313, 323–24, 326–31, 332n5. See also Indianapolis Foundation

cerebral palsy, 175

funding sources for, 402–10; in Japan, 396, 408–9, 411; LEI grants to, 15, 404–7, 410; lessons learned from, 411–12; origins of term, 415n4; philanthrolocalism and, 412–14; in Switzerland, 409–10; tax-exempt status for, 404. *See also* Trueblood, Elton D.

Young, Whitney, 376

Young Men's Christian Association (YMCA): African American chapters of, 39, 68, 218–19, 233–35, 248–49; Ball family support for, 13; civic engagement by, 112; Home for Friendless Women established by, 85; homeless clients at, 350; LEI as funding source for, 70; urban religious philanthropy, 58–59

Young Women's Christian Association (YWCA), 68, 350

Youth Philanthropy Initiative of Indiana, xxx